BULLETIN FOR BIBLICAL RESEARCH SUPPLEMENTS

Editor
Richard S. Hess, *Denver Seminary*

Associate Editor
Craig L. Blomberg, *Denver Seminary*

Advisory Board

Leslie C. Allen
Fuller Theological Seminary
Donald A. Carson
Trinity Evangelical Divinity School

Donald A. Hagner
Fuller Theological Seminary
Bruce K. Waltke
Knox Theological Seminary

EXPLORING THE COMPOSITION OF THE PENT

Exploring the Composition of the Pentateuch

EDITED BY L. S. BAKER JR., KENNETH BERGLAND, FELIPE A. MASOTTI, AND A. RAHEL WELLS

EISENBRAUNS | University Park, Pennsylvania

Library of Congress Cataloging-in-Publication Data

Names: Baker, Leslie Scott, Jr., editor. | Bergland, Kenneth, editor. | Masotti, Felipe A., editor. | Wells, A. Rahel (Abigail Rahel), editor.
Title: Exploring the composition of the Pentateuch / edited by L.S. Baker Jr., Kenneth Bergland, Felipe A. Masotti, and A. Rahel Wells.
Other titles: Bulletin for biblical research supplements.
Description: University Park, Pennsylvania : Eisenbrauns, [2020] | Series: Bulletin for biblical research supplement series | Includes bibliographical references and index.
Summary: "A collection of revised papers from a 2016 conference at Andrews University, exploring new ideas about the composition of the Pentateuch that arise from analysis of the biblical text"—Provided by publisher.
Identifiers: LCCN 2020020174 | ISBN 9781575069852 (hardback)
Subjects: LCSH: Bible. Pentateuch—Authorship—Congresses. | Bible. Pentateuch—Criticism, interpretation, etc.—Congresses.
Classification: LCC BS1225.52 .E97 2020 | DDC 222/.1066—dc23
LC record available at https://lccn.loc.gov/2020020174

Copyright © 2020 The Pennsylvania State University
All rights reserved
Printed in the United States of America
Published by The Pennsylvania State University Press,
University Park, PA 16802-1003

Eisenbrauns is an imprint of The Pennsylvania State University Press.

The Pennsylvania State University Press is a member of the Association of University Presses.

It is the policy of The Pennsylvania State University Press to use acid-free paper. Publications on uncoated stock satisfy the minimum requirements of American National Standard for Information Sciences—Permanence of Paper for Printed Library Material, ANSI Z39.48–1992.

Contents

Preface vii
Jiří Moskala
List of Abbreviations xi

Introduction 1
Roy E. Gane

PART I. HISTORY OF SCHOLARSHIP AND ALTERNATIVE APPROACHES

Chapter 1. A Critical Intellectual History of the Historical-Critical
Paradigm in Biblical Studies 7
Joshua A. Berman

Chapter 2. The Exodus, Debt Slavery, and the Composition
of the Pentateuch 26
Richard E. Averbeck

Chapter 3. Egyptian Language Practice:
A Model for Hebrew Poetic Use? 49
L. S. Baker Jr. and A. Rahel Wells

Chapter 4. Second-Millennium BC Cuneiform from the
Southern Levant and the Literature of the Pentateuch 66
Richard S. Hess

Chapter 5. The Hittite Treaty Prologue Tradition and the Literary
Structure of the Book of Deuteronomy. 73
Jiří Moskala and Felipe A. Masotti

vi   *Contents*

Chapter 6. Memorized Covenantal Instruction
and Legal Reuse in Torah. 95
Kenneth Bergland

Chapter 7. The Liturgical Function of Dates in the Pentateuch. 113
Michael LeFebvre

PART 2. EXEGETICAL STUDIES

Chapter 8. In the Tradition of Moses: The Conceptual and Stylistic
Imprint of Deuteronomy on the Patriarchal Narratives. 133
Daniel I. Block

Chapter 9. Was Moses the Last Prophet? An Analysis of a
Neo-Documentarian Interpretation of Document E 159
Duane A. Garrett

Chapter 10. Revisiting the Literary Structure(s) of Exodus. 173
Richard Davidson, Tiago Arrais, and Christian Vogel

Chapter 11. Was Leviticus Composed by Aaronide Priests
to Justify Their Cultic Monopoly? 195
Roy E. Gane

Chapter 12. The Reception of Priestly Laws in Deuteronomy and
Deuteronomy's Target Audience 213
Benjamin Kilchör

Chapter 13. The Relevance of Ezekiel and the Samaritans for
Pentateuchal Composition: Converging Lines of Evidence 226
John S. Bergsma

Bibliography 245
Ancient Source Index 273
Subject Index 291

Preface

Jiří Moskala
Dean, Seventh-Day Adventist Theological Seminary

The goal of the present publication, *Exploring the Composition of the Pentateuch*, is to present fresh evidence on a subject that has preoccupied scholars for more than two centuries. The composition of the Pentateuch has been one of the most hotly debated issues, as it lies at the center of the understanding and interpretation of the Pentateuch. The traditional view that Moses was the primary author or the principal contributor to the Pentateuch was challenged by nineteenth- and twentieth-century critical scholars, resulting in pentateuchal studies going through remarkable scrutiny. Different hypotheses of the composition of the Pentateuch and their rewriting were proposed (including the documentary theories with J, E, D, P sources). In recent years, new interest has been sparked among scholars of different persuasions, especially among evangelicals, regarding this particular field of study. This current attention has involved looking at the question of authorship with new eyes and new approaches, being boldly critical of the critical approaches, theories, and presuppositions as well as closely examining and analyzing the critical arguments and redoing comparative studies in relation to old material and new discoveries.

These new approaches to pentateuchal studies (literary and structural analysis, comparisons with ancient Near Eastern documents and the biblical text, ritual and rhetorical studies, form criticism, narrative analysis viewing the Pentateuch as a story, studies related to different literary genres within one document, and content comparison with archaeological data) led to the rejection not only of the classical distinction between J and E, but also to the redating of classical sources and to a dissatisfaction with the standard source criticism. This discontent leads one to ask of Mosaic authorship: innocent until proven guilty

viii   *Preface*

or guilty until proven innocent? In other words, should Moses be assumed as the author, as in text and tradition, or should methodological doubt override that assumption until demonstrated otherwise?

It is obvious that only a few things can be proven from extrabiblical evidence. As a matter of fact, material from certain periods is very sporadic or even nonexistent. Documents of ancient Near Eastern provenance cover only particular events from the second and first millennia BC. Unfortunately, few documents have survived or were even produced in ancient times, so scholars can only compare the biblical text with the historical documents that are available. It is good to remind ourselves that scholars build hypotheses and theories that may or may not fit the history as presented in the Pentateuch and may not be true to the reality of life from that time. The crucial thing is how we interpret historical evidence. This observation may be helpful for a reader who is not used to dealing critically with extrabiblical evidence. We should have realistic expectations of what can be demonstrated from evidence. As we know, historical research is dealing with the question of probability.

Faith does not stand on proofs but on the biblical testimony. However, evidence from extrabiblical documents, ancient history, cultural background, or comparative studies may enrich and confirm a faith position and/or the ancient tradition of believers. So we should not overestimate the value of extrabiblical evidence. It is significant but cannot overthrow the testimony found in the Scriptures. Ultimately the reader has to decide whether to believe reconstructed history built on extrabiblical evidence or the internal evidence of the biblical witnesses. It is best when they can be harmonized; thus, the analysis of the available documents is always crucial. Christians and Jews who take the biblical text at face value have no problem in assuming Moses's authorship of the Pentateuch (plus any updating and editorial remarks made when putting it together), even though it hardly can be proven or demonstrated on the basis of the extrabiblical evidence.

For these reasons, the Seventh-day Adventist Theological Seminary chose to sponsor a conference on the composition of the Pentateuch. On April 3–5, 2016, a group of outstanding scholars met at the SDA Theological Seminary, located on the campus of Andrews University in southwest Michigan, to tackle the problem of the composition of the Pentateuch from a synchronic perspective. These scholars (from a variety of denominational and faith backgrounds) are making contributions in terms of its historical development and effectively engaging the wider scholarly audience.

I would like to express my deep appreciation to all seventeen authors who submitted cutting-edge papers using their expertise on a variety of important aspects related to the synchronic reading of the Pentateuch. My wholehearted thank you goes to our sponsors, the North American Division of Seventh-day

Preface ix

Adventists, Andrews University School of Graduate Studies and Research, the Horn Archaeological Museum, and Ed Zinke. The four editors, under the skillful leadership of Kenneth Bergland, who, together with L. S. Baker Jr., Felipe A. Masotti, and A. Rahel Wells, sacrificed enormous time and dedicated countless hours to the production of this volume, deserve a million thanks. I hope this publication will stir fruitful discussion among biblical scholars in seeking fresh approaches to the old question of the authorship of the Pentateuch and even finding more convincing model(s) for the origin of the Pentateuch's composition.

Abbreviations

AB	Anchor Bible
ABD	Freedman, D. N., editor. *The Anchor Bible Dictionary*. 6 vols. Garden City, NY: Doubleday, 1992
ABR	*Australian Biblical Review*
ABS	Archaeology and Biblical Studies
AIL	*Ancient Israel and Its Literature*
AnBib	Analecta Biblica
ANES	*Ancient Near Eastern Studies*
ANET	J. B. Pritchard, editor. *Ancient Near Eastern Texts Relating to the Old Testament*. 3rd ed. Princeton: Princeton University Press, 1969
ANF	A. Roberts and J. Donaldson, editors. *The Ante-Nicene Fathers: Translations of the Writings of the Fathers down to A.D. 325*. 10 vols. Grand Rapids: Eerdmans, 1978–79
AOAT	*Alter Orient und Altes Testament*
AoF	*Altorientalische Forschungen*
ApOTC	Apollos Old Testament Commentary
ARM	Archives royales de Mari
ATS	Adventist Theological Society
AUSDS	Andrews University Seminary Doctoral Dissertation Series
AUSS	*Andrews University Seminary Studies*
AYBRL	Anchor Yale Bible Reference Library
BA	*Biblical Archaeologist*
BAR	*Biblical Archaeology Review*
BASOR	*Bulletin of the American Schools of Oriental Research*
BBB	Bonner biblische Beiträge
BBR	*Bulletin for Biblical Research*
BBRSup	Bulletin for Biblical Research Supplements

xii   *Abbreviations*

BETL	Bibliotheca Ephemeridum Theologicarum Lovaniensium
Bib	*Biblica*
BibInt	*Biblical Interpretation*
BibSem	Biblical Seminar
BKAT	Biblischer Kommentar Altes Testament
BN NF	*Biblische Notizen Neue Folge*
BSac	*Bibliotheca Sacra*
BZABR	Beihefte zur Zeitschrift für Altorientalische und Biblische Rechtsgeschichte
BZAW	Beihefte zur Zeitschrift für die alttestamentliche Wissenschaft
CBQ	*Catholic Biblical Quarterly*
COS	W. W. Hallo and K. L. Younger Jr., editors. *The Context of Scripture*. 3 vols. Leiden: Brill, 1997–2003
CTH	E. Laroche. *Catalogue des textes hittites*. 2nd ed. Paris: Klincksieck, 1971
CTJ	*Calvin Theological Journal*
CTS	*Chafer Theological Seminary Journal*
DBI	John H. Hayes, editor. *Dictionary of Biblical Interpretation*. Nashville: Abingdon, 1999
DOTP	M. J. Boda and J. G. McConville, editors. *Dictionary of the Old Testament: Prophets*. Grand Rapids: IVP Academic, 2013
EA	El-Amarna tablets
EBC	Expositor's Bible Commentary
ECC	Eerdmans Critical Commentary
ETL	*Ephemerides Theologicae Lovanienses*
ETS	Evangelical Theological Society
FAT	Forschungen zum Alten Testament
FRLANT	Forschungen zur Religion und Literatur des Alten und Neuen Testaments
GD	Gorgias Dissertations
HALOT	L. Koehler, W. Baumgartner, and J. J. Stamm. *The Hebrew and Aramaic Lexicon of the Old Testament*. Translated and edited under supervision of M. E. J. Richardson. 5 vols. Leiden: Brill, 1994–2000
HBS	Herders biblische Studien
HdO	Handbuch der Orientalistik
HDT	G. A. Beckman, *Hittite Diplomatic Texts*. Edited by H. A. Hoffner Jr. SBL Writings from the Ancient World 7. Atlanta: Scholars Press, 1996
HistTh	*History and Theory*
HSM	Harvard Semitic Monographs

HUCA	*Hebrew Union College Annual*
HvTSt	*Hervormde teologiese studies*
ICC	International Critical Commentary
IECOT	International Exegetical Commentary on the Old Testament
IEJ	*Israel Exploration Journal*
Imm	*Immanuel*
JAJ	*Journal of Ancient Judaism*
JANES	*Journal of the Ancient Near Eastern Society*
JANESCU	*Journal of the Ancient Near Eastern Society of Columbia University*
JAOS	*Journal of the American Oriental Society*
JATS	*Journal of the Adventist Theological Society*
JBL	*Journal of Biblical Literature*
JBS	Jerusalem Biblical Studies
JEA	*Journal of Egyptian Archaeology*
JETS	*Journal of the Evangelical Theological Society*
JHebS	*Journal of Hebrew Scriptures*
JHI	*Journal of the History of Ideas*
JHIL	*Journal of the History of International Law*
JSOT	*Journal for the Study of the Old Testament*
JSOTSup	Journal for the Study of the Old Testament Supplements
JSS	*Journal of Semitic Studies*
KBo	*Keilschrifttexte aus Boghazköy*
KUB	*Keilschrifturkunden aus Boghazköy*
LAI	Library of Ancient Israel
LHBOTS	Library of Hebrew Bible / Old Testament Studies
LTHS	Literature and Theology of the Hebrew Scriptures
NAC	New American Commentary
NICOT	New International Commentary on the Old Testament
NIVAC	New International Version Application Commentary
OBO	Orbis biblicus et orientalis
ÖBS	Österreichische biblische Studien
Or	*Orientalia* new series
OTE	*Old Testament Essays*
OTL	Old Testament Library
OtSt	*Oudtestamentische Studiën*
PIOL	Publications de l'Institut orientaliste de Louvain
PRSt	*Perspectives in Religious Studies*
PRU	*Le palais royal d'Ugarit*
PTMS	Pittsburgh Theological Monograph Series
QMHSS	Quantitative Methods in the Humanities and Social Sciences

xiv   *Abbreviations*

RB	*Revue Biblique*
RBS	Resources for Biblical Study
RelSRev	*Religious Studies Review*
ResQ	*Restoration Quarterly*
RS	*Ras Shamra*
RSR	*Recherches de science religieuse*
SAOC	Studies in Ancient Oriental Civilization
SBLDS	Society of Biblical Literature Dissertation Series
SBLSS	Society of Biblical Literature Symposium Series
SBS	Stuttgarter Bibelstudien
ScrHieros	*Scripta Hierosolymitana*
SFEG	Schriften der Finnischen Exegetischen Gesellschaft
SHBC	Smyth & Helwys Bible Commentary
SHS	Scripture and Hermeneutics Series
TDOT	Botterweck, G. J., and Ringgren, H., editors. *Theological Dictionary of the Old Testament.* Grand Rapids: Eerdmans, 1974–2006
THeth	Texte der Hethiter
TLC	K. A. Kitchen and P. J. N. Lawrence. *Treaty, Law and Covenant in the Ancient Near East.* Weisbaden: Harrassowitz, 2012
TynBul	*Tyndale Bulletin*
UF	*Ugarit-Forschungen*
UTB	Uni-Taschenbücher
VT	*Vetus Testamentum*
VTSup	Supplements to Vetus Testamentum
WBC	Word Biblical Commentary
WMANT	Wissenschaftliche Monographien zum Alten und Neuen Testament
ZAW	*Zeitschrift für die alttestamentliche Wissenschaft*
ZDPV	*Zeitschrift des deutschen Palästina-Vereins*

Introduction

Roy E. Gane
Andrews University

The Pentateuch (or "Torah") forms the foundation of canonical Scripture. As such, it holds a special place of authority over Jewish and Christian religion. The authority of this group of biblical books depends on the nature of its authorship. Therefore, understanding the composition of the Pentateuch matters. Exploring it is not an intellectual game. The stakes are high.

Identifying the authorship of the Pentateuch is challenging, due to factors such as (but not limited to) the following.

First, this authorship is mostly anonymous, although some passages indicate that Moses wrote several documents (Exod 17:14; Exod 24:4; 34:27; Num 33:2; Deut 31:9, 22, 24). At least some writing by one or more other authors or editors is apparent (e.g., obviously in the Deut 34 account of Moses's death), but the biblical text does not name them or clearly delineate the extent of their work.

Second, we do not possess the ancient autographs of the documents that were combined to comprise the Pentateuch. The language, scope, and script of such original documents would facilitate locating them in history, thereby enlightening us regarding their relationships to the events that they relate and to the edited and updated final canonical text.

Third, as yet there is no extant archaeological or extrabiblical textual evidence that directly and unambiguously confirms some of the most essential features in the pentateuchal narratives, such as the existence of the patriarchs and of Moses, the exodus from Egypt, and wilderness wandering of the Israelites. Most importantly, we lack empirical proof of the divine role in human history, including authoritative revelations to Moses, that the Pentateuch claims, and acceptance of which has made it normative Scripture for more than two millennia. Not only is such proof of unique divine activities not extant, it is irretrievable. The reader must choose to believe or disbelieve on the basis of other factors.

Fourth, the pentateuchal books are complex literary compilations in several genres and varying styles. They recount events and record speeches that occurred over a long period of time, with some parallel and even duplicating materials that can differ in perspective. These factors raise questions regarding authorial relationships between textual portions that differ in style and viewpoint. There is no question that the compositional development of the Pentateuch involved sources, redactions, forms, and traditions. The problem is how to connect the dots of available data with valid methodology in order to identify these factors without undue speculation.

During the last few centuries, scholars have largely abandoned acceptance of Mosaic authorship of the Torah on the basis of Jewish tradition and New Testament references. The historical-critical quest for an alternative reconstruction of the origin(s) and development of the Pentateuch or Hexateuch coalesced around the Documentary Hypothesis, which long dominated the field, albeit with a plethora of permutations. The heuristic power of this brilliant constellation of syntheses produced a consensus to the extent that an interpreter who did not operate within its framework was hardly regarded as a scholar. However, the relentless march of research has continued to bring new and refined analyses, data (including ancient Near Eastern [ANE] texts and the Dead Sea Scrolls), methodological tools, and criticisms of the older criticism, especially in terms of its assumptions.

Among the fundamental assumptions of the older criticism that are now challenged is the notion that absence of evidence is evidence of absence. This is patently false in the discipline of archaeology, but it is also false when it comes to deriving conclusions from the absence of direct evidence regarding the composition of the Pentateuch (see above). Rather than categorically ruling out possibilities of authorship and dating of texts because direct evidence for them is lacking at present, it is only logical and scientific to leave open the questions for which we do not have truly definitive answers.

Currently under scrutiny is another assumption that underlies the *modi operandi* of source and redaction criticism, namely the idea that textual features such as disjunctures, duplications, or shifts of perspective, including what could be regarded as contradictions, necessarily indicate changes of the authorial hand. Scholars who study ANE texts outside the Bible are beginning to recognize that such features could, at least in some cases, belong to original, unified compositions because ancient writers were not bound by modern conventions of consistency. It is true beyond doubt that biblical books utilize sources, some of which are named and most of which are not, but precisely identifying them and the ways in which they were incorporated into the larger compositions is problematic.

Nevertheless, critiques of documentarian and neodocumentarian studies should not be taken to indicate that such works lack value. Scholars who employ these approaches have uncovered a wealth of literary and linguistic nuances. While their presuppositions, motivation, and conclusions regarding reconstruction of sources can be challenged, their efforts have enriched our understanding of the biblical texts.

It is now generally recognized that the consensus around the once "assured results" of pentateuchal criticism has mostly dissipated. Scholars have been moving beyond previously dominant paradigms to analyze texts afresh in their search for more satisfying models. This situation and its rather chaotic result are described by Jan Christian Gertz et al. in their introduction to the massive recent volume titled *The Formation of the Pentateuch*:

Introduction 3

Over the past forty years, the source-critical method has come under unprecedented attack. In many quarters it has been rejected entirely: many scholars claim it no longer provides a secure starting point for investigating the history of Israelite religion or the literary formation of the Pentateuch. Recent decades have witnessed not simply a proliferation of intellectual models but, in many ways much more seriously, the fragmentation of discourse altogether as scholarly communities in the three main research centers of Israel, Europe, and North America increasingly talk past one another. Even when they employ the same terminology (for example, *redactor, author, source, exegesis*), scholars often mean quite different things. Concepts taken for granted by one group of scholars (such as the existence of the Elohist or the Yahwist sources) are dismissed out of hand by other scholarly communities.

. . . Yet, the lack of shared intellectual discourse hampers what might otherwise be a moment of opportunity in the creative development of the discipline. In the three major centers of research on the Pentateuch—North America, Israel, and Europe—scholars tend to operate from such different premises, employ such divergent methods, and reach such inconsistent results that meaningful progress has become impossible. The models continue to proliferate but the communication seems only to diminish.[1]

On the one hand, perhaps the present lack of scholarly unity could be viewed as "the worst of times" for pentateuchal scholarship. On the other hand, maybe the moment could be seized as a good time of opportunity for potential openness to new ideas, although it is not yet "the best of times" while discourse remains so dysfunctional.[2]

The present volume has developed from a thirst for interaction regarding new ideas that arise from careful analysis of the biblical text itself against its ANE background, in hope of continuing dialogue in the future. It consists of edited and in some cases expanded papers from a stimulating and enjoyable conference on "Exploring the Composition of the Pentateuch," which was held at Andrews University, April 3–5, 2016. Participants in the conference were scholars (including some PhD students) from several religious affiliations (Protestant, Catholic, Jewish) and five continents.

Paper topics covered a wide spectrum, relevant to the research foci of the individuals who presented. This variety is reflected in the chapters of the book,

---

1. Jan Christian Gertz, Bernard M. Levinson, Dalit Rom-Shiloni, and Konrad Schmid, "Convergence and Divergence in Pentateuchal Theory: The Genesis and Goals of This Volume," in *The Formation of the Pentateuch: Bridging the Academic Cultures of Europe, Israel, and North America*, ed. Jan Christian Gertz, Bernard M. Levinson, Dalit Rom-Shiloni, and Konrad Schmid, FAT iii (Tübingen: Mohr Siebeck, 2016), 2–3.

2. Borrowing language from the opening of *A Tale of Two Cities* by Charles Dickens (1859).

4   Roy E. Gane

which are grouped in two parts. The first part is primarily on methodology: the history of scholarship and alternative approaches regarding the development of the Pentateuch. The second part focuses on exegesis of particular texts relevant to the composition of the Torah.

These chapters represent the viewpoints of their authors, which vary in some respects from those of other authors or from those of the editors. This is healthy. Our project is to foster penetrating investigation and friendly dialogue in a spirit of humility, openness, and frankness, without imposing uniformity or pretending that all of our conclusions are definitive. Our exploration of the composition of the Pentateuch is a work in progress, so another conference was held on March 25–27, 2018, also at Andrews University.

The conference and resulting book arose from a project that began in a very small way with a conversation between myself and two doctoral students—Kenneth Bergland from Norway and Felipe Masotti from Brazil—during a break in my Ugaritic course at Andrews University in the summer of 2014. Kenneth recollects that "we were inspired by some of the phenomena we saw in the Ugaritic texts we were studying. Phenomena that are taken as signs of compositional layers in pentateuchal texts are observed also in other ANE texts." So we started talking about the possibility of opening a venue at our university to probe the composition of the Pentateuch in detail.

Our ideas progressed while the three of us were studying the Hittite Laws in my Hittite class in the fall of 2015. Meanwhile, in the fall of 2014 Kenneth and Felipe initiated "the Torah Group," an interdisciplinary group of doctoral students and one teacher (A. Rahel Wells, Department of Religion) at Andrews University. Others participated from distant locations via Skype. Meetings of the group included paper presentations and subsequent discussions between the members, who included biblicists, linguists, and archaeologists. After some time, the Torah Group developed the idea of organizing the "Exploring the Composition of the Pentateuch" conference. The central members of the planning committee for this event were Kenneth Bergland (chair), L. S. Baker Jr., Sarah Burton, Felipe Masotti, and A. Rahel Wells. The committee and participants are grateful to the sponsors of the conference (see preface) and to Richard S. Hess for his support and assistance in publishing this book in the Bulletin for Biblical Research Supplements series. We want to thank Barbara Weimer for preparing the indexes. We also want to thank the Penn State University Press team for their gracious and experienced hand in the completion of this volume: John Morris as the copyeditor, Amy Becker as the compositor, and Matthew Williams as the project manager.

Please note that throughout this volume verse references are those of the Hebrew Masoretic Text, with any differing English verse references following in brackets, e.g., Lev 6:20 [27].

PART I

History of Scholarship and Alternative Approaches

CHAPTER I

A Critical Intellectual History of the Historical-Critical Paradigm in Biblical Studies

Joshua A. Berman
Bar-Ilan University

Recently scholars have begun looking toward empirical models of textual growth to reconstruct the development of the Hebrew Scriptures.[1] Rather than focusing exclusively on irregularities within the received text, these scholars have sought out examples of documented textual growth from the epigraphic record of the ancient Near East. They have done so to probe how scribes amended and edited texts in the creation of new versions and of entirely new works. In light of the methodological impasse gripping the field, its extreme fragmentation and seemingly unbridgeable diversity, the pivot toward empirical models for textual development would seem a welcome and important development. In looking beyond the Hebrew Scriptures to the epigraphic corpus of the ancient Near East, we multiply the data from which to adduce theories of textual development. When biblicists hypothesize theories of textual development, they do so situated in a distinctly modern textual culture and are prone to project anachronistic attitudes and practices upon cultures at a great distance in time and place. Empirical models offer us methodological control as we observe how ancient scribes more closely contemporaneous with the scribes of Israel edited and expanded cherished texts across the centuries.

The pivot to empirical models would seem to be not only important, but overdue. The texts whose growth has been documented—the Gilgamesh epic, the Temple Scroll, the Atrahasis story, and the Etana epic—are texts that have

---

Author's note: This essay is an abridged version of my "Empirical Models of Textual Growth: A Challenge for the Historical Critical Tradition," *JHebS* 16 (2016): 1–25.

1. Karel van der Toorn, *Scribal Culture and the Making of the Hebrew Bible* (Cambridge, MA: Harvard University Press, 2007); David M. Carr, *The Formation of the Hebrew Bible: A New Reconstruction* (New York: Oxford University Press, 2011); Juha Pakkala, *God's Word Omitted: Omissions in the Transmission of the Hebrew Bible*, FRLANT 251 (Göttingen: Vandenhoeck & Ruprecht, 2013); Molly Zahn, "Reexamining Empirical Models: The Case of Exodus 13," in *Das Deuteronomium zwischen Pentateuch und deuteronomistischem Geschichtswerk*, ed. Eckart Otto and Reinhart Achenbach (Göttingen: Vandenhoeck & Ruprecht, 2004), 33–56; Seth L. Sanders, "Can Empirical Models Explain What Is Different About the Pentateuch?" in *Contextualizing Israel's Sacred Writing*, ed. Brian B. Schmidt (Atlanta: SBL, 2015), 281–304.

8   Joshua A. Berman

been the subject of scholarly attention for more than half a century.[2] Curiously, it is only recently that scholars have turned to the compositional history of these texts with an eye toward elucidating the textual growth of the Hebrew Scriptures.[3]

In May 2013, the Israel Institute for Advanced Study in Jerusalem sponsored a conference rightly billed as the largest meeting ever assembled to explore the mechanics of the textual growth of the Pentateuch.[4] Some of the speakers invoked empirical models based upon the textual growth witnessed in the neighboring cultures of the ancient Near East. In the discussion that ensued, opinion was split concerning the place that such approaches should take in developing theories for the growth of biblical texts. While some viewed these approaches as a welcome and even necessary corrective, other scholars—particularly those who work with more customary methods—were more circumspect. It may well be that in any field of inquiry, new methods will be viewed as a threat by those who have long practiced and published according to the older and accepted canons of convention. I maintain that the lateness of this pivot toward empirical models and its lukewarm reception in some quarters even now are not accidental. Rather, deeply rooted intellectual commitments within the history of the diachronic study of the Bible explain why this development is such a late one, and why it poses a challenge for many who study and write about the growth of biblical texts.

In this essay, I conduct a critical intellectual history of the historical-critical paradigm in biblical studies, with particular regard to theories of development of the biblical text. My interest is to understand the origins of the intellectual commitments that shape the discipline today and its disposition toward empirical models of textual growth. I shall examine how theorists over three centuries have entertained the most fundamental questions: What is the goal of the historical-critical study of the Hebrew Bible? What is the probative value of evidence internal within the text itself relative to evidence from external sources? What

2. On the Gilgamesh epic, see Andrew George, *The Babylonian Gilgamesh Epic: Introduction, Critical Edition, and Cuneiform Texts*, 2 vols. (Oxford: Oxford University Press, 2003). On the Temple Scroll, see Michael Owen Wise, *A Critical Study of the Temple Scroll from Qumran Cave II*, SAOC 49 (Chicago: Oriental Institute of the University of Chicago, 1990). On Atrahasis, see W. G. Lambert, A. R. Millard, and Miguel Civil, eds., *Atra-hasis: The Babylonian Story of the Flood* (Winona Lake, IN: Eisenbrauns, 1999). On the Etana epic, see James V. K. Wilson, *Studia Etanaica: New Texts and Discussions* (Münster: Ugarit-Verlag, 2007).

3. The notable exception to this lacuna is Jeffrey H. Tigay, *Empirical Models for Biblical Criticism* (Philadelphia: University of Pennsylvania Press, 1985).

4. "Convergence and Divergence in Pentateuchal Theory: Bridging the Academic Cultures of Israel, North America, and Europe," international conference convened at the Israel Institute for Advanced Studies, Jerusalem, May 12–13, 2013. Organizers: Bernard M. Levinson, Konrad Schmid, and Baruch J. Schwartz. Conference volume: Jan Christian Gertz, Bernard M. Levinson, Dalit Rom-Shiloni, and Konrad Schmid, eds., *The Formation of the Pentateuch: Bridging the Academic Cultures of Europe, Israel, and North America* (Tübingen: Mohr Siebeck, 2016).

is the role of intuition in the scholar's work? What is the role of methodological control? As we shall see, scholars in different ages offered very different answers to these questions, answers colored by the prevailing intellectual milieu of their respective times.

I proceed by surveying the intellectual currents during the formative period of the discipline, the two centuries between Spinoza and Wellhausen, with an emphasis on developments in nineteenth-century Germany. We shall see that the axioms that governed nineteenth-century German scholarship were at a great divide from those that governed earlier historical-critical scholarship. We shall see further that these axioms were based in intellectual currents that were particular to the nineteenth century, especially so in Germany. From there, I offer a brief summary of the claims of contemporary scholars who are looking toward empirical models to reconstruct the textual development of the Hebrew Scriptures. I conclude by demonstrating how this vein of scholarship undermines an array of nineteenth-century intellectual assumptions, but would have been quite at home in the earlier periods of the discipline's history. My hope is that this survey will stimulate a new self-awareness among scholars investigating these issues today.

Methodological Skepticism and the Beginnings of the Historical-Critical Paradigm in Biblical Studies

Spinoza's comments in the seventh chapter of his *Theological-Political Treatise* are rightly cited as a seminal point in the development of historical criticism of the Hebrew Bible. The questions he raises are those that scholars of the historical-critical school have grappled with ever since. However, later in that chapter, Spinoza sounds a note not often heard today among biblicists engaged in diachronic research:

> I must now therefore point out the limitations and difficulties in this method's capacity to guide us towards a full and certain knowledge of the sacred books. . . .
>
> . . . [This] requires a history of the vicissitudes of all the biblical books, and most of this is unknown to us. For either we have no knowledge whatever of the authors or (if you prefer) the compilers, of many of the books—or else we are uncertain about them. Also, we do not know under what circumstances these books whose compilers are unknown were composed or when. Nor do we know into whose hands all these books subsequently came, or in whose copies so many variant readings occur. . . . If we do not know its author or when and under what circumstances he wrote it, our efforts to get at its true sense will be fruitless. For if all this

is unknown, we cannot ascertain what the author intended or might have intended. I think these difficulties are so great that I do not hesitate to affirm that in numerous passages either we do not know the true sense of Scripture or can only guess at it without any assurance.[5]

Few diachronic scholars today would share in Spinoza's pessimism concerning our capacity to answer these fundamental questions. Scholarship today implicitly operates with two foundational assumptions putting itself at a distance from Spinoza. Scholars today have more confidence than did Spinoza that we can indeed trace the compositional history of the biblical texts. Second, in an earlier passage, Spinoza stated that when probing the history of the biblical text, "we must acknowledge exclusively what is certain and unquestionable."[6] However, scholars today are prepared to assign probative value to suggestive evidence, and do not insist upon admitting proposals that are "certain and unquestionable."

The skepticism that animates Spinoza's writings concerning the potential for historical-critical analysis of the Hebrew Bible is seen again a decade later in the work of the Frenchman Father Richard Simon, the most learned biblicist of his day. Like Spinoza, Simon points to fissures and discontinuities within the biblical text, and like Spinoza, Simon understands that human hands, historically situated, stand behind the creation of the sacred texts. And yet, commenting on the history of the received texts, he cautions:

What we have at present is but an abridgment of the ancient Records, which were much larger, and that those who made the abridgments had particular reasons which we cannot understand. It is better therefore to be silent in this subject and to keep to the general reasons we have related than to search farther into this matter, and condemn by a rash criticism what we do not understand.

. . . I believe it is unnecessary to inquire with too much niceness the particular Authours of each Book, because we can make but very uncertain conjectures.[7]

Spinoza and Simon established the basic questions that historical criticism asks of the texts today. Yet, at the same time, Spinoza and Simon are at a great remove from later proponents and supposed heirs of their method. Neither of

---

5. Benedict de Spinoza, *Theological-Political Treatise*, ed. Jonathan Israel, trans. Michael Silverthorne and Jonathan Israel, Cambridge Texts in the History of Philosophy (Cambridge: Cambridge University Press, 2012), 106–10.

6. Ibid., 101.

7. Richard Simon, *A Critical History of the Old Testament* (London: Walter Davis, 1682), 27, 29.

History of the Historical-Critical Paradigm in Biblical Studies   11

them attempts to decompose any existing text into its original component parts, be they sources or fragments. Neither attempts to explain the motives that might have contributed to any of these supposed components. Neither proposes a chronology of these components. We must recognize that they offer no solutions to these critical questions not because they thought them unimportant—indeed, they both claim that these questions are of the utmost importance to arrive at a true understanding of Scripture—but because they were convinced that we do not have the data to answer them with certainty, if the criterion for admissible solutions is, as Spinoza writes, "exclusively what is certain and unquestionable."

The Nineteenth-Century German Historicist Tradition

The field of critical biblical studies largely took shape in nineteenth-century Germany. To be sure, there were many important developments than transpired thereafter as well, but the main terms of reference that continue to dominate the compositional theory of the Hebrew Bible today—author, source, fragment, redactor, supplement, and editorial layer—were developed in this age. To appreciate the ways in which the field evolved at this time, it is crucial to examine it against the backdrop of nineteenth-century German historicism.

In earlier centuries, events of the past were retold for the purpose of illustrating morals and teachings, but the past had not been the subject of critical study in its own right. The end of the eighteenth and beginning of the nineteenth century witnessed a profound awareness of the need to critically assess the received traditions about past events. Frederick Beiser, a leading scholar of nineteenth-century German historicism, sums up the agenda of the historicist movement: "The agenda of historicism was simple but ambitious: to legitimate history as a science. Its aim was to show what makes history a science. All the thinkers in the historicist tradition . . . wanted to justify the scientific status of history. They used 'science' in a broad sense of that term corresponding to the German word 'Wissenschaft,' that is, some methodical means of acquiring knowledge."[8]

If history could become a science in its own right, then it would enjoy all the status and prestige of the natural sciences, such as biology, chemistry, and physics.[9] Historicism would prove phenomenally successful in its ambition: from the 1850s to the 1880s the movement would mark its golden years, when its prestige was deemed no less than that of the natural sciences. If the eighteenth century had been the age of reason, the nineteenth had become that of history.[10] If in the former period educated people turned to philosophy to unlock the

---

8. Frederick C. Beiser, *The German Historicist Tradition* (New York: Oxford University Press, 2012), 6.

9. Ibid., 7.

10. Ibid., 23.

12   Joshua A. Berman

mysteries of human life, during the late 1880s it was the scientific analysis of the past that would provide insight and inspiration in politics, law, economics, morals, and religion.[11] In this section I selectively survey three elements of this movement that shape the historical-critical study of the Bible to this day. As we shall see, these elements are axioms and attitudes that are challenged by the recent recourse to empirical models for textual development.

Individuation

Perhaps the most influential historicist writing of the early nineteenth century was an 1821 essay by Wilhelm von Humboldt, the founder of Berlin University, "On the Historian's Task."[12] In the essay, Humboldt places great stock in identifying the defining characteristic of a great person, an event, or a culture: "Every human individuality is an idea rooted in actuality, and this idea shines forth so brilliantly from some individuals that it seems to have assumed the form of an individual merely to use it as a vehicle for expressing itself. . . . The spiritual principle of individuality therefore remains active in the midst of the history of nations guided by needs, passions, and apparent accidents, and it is more powerful than those elements."[13]

The idea behind a person, nation, or epoch was nothing less than its individuating principle, what makes it this unique or distinctive person, nation, or epoch.[14] The expression in this passage assigns such individualization almost metaphysical status. This emphasis on the discrete and individuated nation/event/person is a hallmark of nineteenth-century German historicism.[15] In the analysis of historical phenomena, that which individuates is given place of pride over identifying that which is universal and common. This is a view of history infused with nineteenth-century Romanticism and its celebration of the greatness of the individual soul. A literary work is appreciated as a window into the soul of its creator, and hence the significance of the author comes to the forefront at this time.[16]

---

11. John H. Zammito, "Historicism," in *The Oxford Handbook of German Philosophy in the Nineteenth Century*, ed. Michael N. Forster and Kristin Gjesdal (Oxford: Oxford University Press, 2015), 792; Iain Provan, "Knowing and Believing: Faith in the Past," in *"Behind" the Text: History and Biblical Interpretation*, ed. Craig G. Bartholomew, C. Stephen Evans, Mary Healy, and Murray Rae, SHS 4 (Grand Rapids: Zondervan, 2003), 234.

12. Wilhelm von Humboldt, "On the Historian's Task," *HistTh* 6, no. 1 (1967): 57–71.

13. Ibid., 69.

14. Beiser, *The German Historicist Tradition*, 168.

15. Ibid., 5.

16. Manfred Oeming, *Contemporary Biblical Hermeneutics: An Introduction* (Surrey: Ashgate, 2006), 15.

Narratives of Causation

For these historians, it was insufficient to simply lay bare "the facts." The task of the historian was to connect these events through a historical narrative of cause and effect.[17] This aim paralleled the aims of scientists engaged in the natural sciences. Observed facts are transformed into a conjecture. Individual data must, upon closer inspection, reveal an interdependence.[18] Nineteenth-century German scholarship in all fields of inquiry sought out explanations that were all-encompassing. This was the age that spawned Freud's theories of the human psyche and Einstein's theories of relativity. Humboldt's essay cited earlier also stresses the importance for the historian of establishing the interdependence of events and their causation:

> The historian cannot be satisfied merely with the loose external relationships of the individual events . . . he has to proceed to the center of things from which their true nexus can be understood. . . . An understanding of them is the combined product of their constitution and the sensibility supplied by the beholder. . . . The historian must render strict account of their inner nexus, must establish for himself a picture of the active forces, must recognize their trends at a given moment, must inquire into the relationship of both forces and trends to the existing state of affairs and to the changes that have preceded it.[19]

The task of creating this narrative of coherence rested with the historian and his senses of empathetic intuition and interpretation. Inherent in this hermeneutic was the confidence that the observing historian could indeed recapture the causative relationship between events and the motivations of the actors responsible for them.[20]

Primary Sources

One of the hallmarks of nineteenth-century historicism was introduced by Barthold Georg Niebuhr and Leopold von Ranke, who asserted that history would earn its status as a science by basing its findings on original, authentic *sources*.[21]

---

17. Georg G. Iggers, "Historicism: The History and Meaning of the Term," *JHI* 56, no. 1 (1995): 131.

18. See Ernst Cassirer, *The Philosophy of the Enlightenment* (Princeton: Princeton University Press, 1951), 20, 32.

19. Humboldt, "On the Historian's Task," 64.

20. Beiser, *German Historicist Tradition*, 168, 213; Provan, "Knowing and Believing," 233.

21. Beiser, *German Historicist Tradition*, 16.

14   Joshua A. Berman

This, they believed, would provide the facts of what had really happened, the raw data. Tradition had passed down tales about the past, but only by returning to primary sources contemporaneous with the events under study could the historian attain a clear view of events past. Primary sources were viewed as bearing greater objectivity than secondary sources to the same account.[22] Niebuhr had pioneered this approach in the study of Roman history, and Ranke developed it as a methodology, sending his students to archives in search of documents contemporary with the age under study.

Presuppositions of the Historical-Critical Study of the Bible in Nineteenth-Century Germany

The premises outlined above permeated the critical study of the Bible in nineteenth-century Germany and remain central to the practice of historical-critical method in many circles of the discipline today. To illustrate the centrality of these premises in nineteenth-century scholarship, I take as an example the most celebrated study of the nineteenth century, Julius Wellhausen's *Prolegomena zur Geschichte Israels*. Note, in the first place, the genre of this classic work: it is not a commentary on a book or set of books from the Bible. Very few commentaries on the books of the Bible were written in the nineteenth century. What were composed were histories—histories of Israel and its religion.[23] In theory, the goal of the critical study of the Bible could have been to understand the text as the primary end, using all historical data available to elucidate it. However, in the nineteenth century the priorities were inverted: the Bible was studied in primary fashion to produce a religious history of the people and the culture that created it.

To arrive at a proper history of Israel, however, requires, as in all historical inquiry during this period, a return to the original sources. Of course, manuscripts of the biblical texts contemporaneous with the events they describe, or even from the biblical period, were and still are unavailable. But, imbued with the confidence of the scientific revolution, biblicists of the time believed that access to original sources was available through the careful literary mining of the received text. By identifying irregularities of all sorts within the text, they could reproduce its earlier precursors. Nineteenth-century biblicists were not of one opinion concerning source criticism, and already then some preferred a theory of assembled fragments, or supplements to a base text.[24] But in the end

---

22. Ibid., 276.

23. Jean-Louis Ska, *Introduction to Reading the Pentateuch*, trans. Pascale Dominique (Winona Lake, IN: Eisenbrauns, 2006), 109.

24. Thomas Albert Howard, *Religion and the Rise of Historicism: W. M. L. de Wette, Jacob Burckhardt, and the Theological Origins of Nineteenth-Century Historical Consciousness* (Cambridge: Cambridge University Press, 2006), 39–40.

History of the Historical-Critical Paradigm in Biblical Studies 15

the Graf-Wellhausen documentary hypothesis carried the day because its four sources offered a glimpse into the stages of Israelite religious development that preceded the redacted Pentateuch. Today, source criticism is thought of as one approach, or as a subfield within the broader field of biblical studies. In its original nineteenth-century German setting, however, just the reverse was true. Source criticism of the Bible was but a subset, or a mere iteration, of the general approach of source analysis (*Quellenkritik* or *Quellenforschung*), the standard scholarly tool for the investigation of all fields of human history and culture.[25]

As noted, nineteenth-century German historians believed that the master texts of a culture revealed their authors' particular distinctiveness and special genius. For biblicists, this meant that the texts of the Hebrew Scriptures needed to be viewed first and foremost in an Israelite context, and only thereafter in a broader ancient Near Eastern context. Biblicists therefore placed a premium on so-called internal evidence—seeming irregularities within the text—to parse the texts, before considering comparison with other extrabiblical materials.[26] Israelite and postexilic Jewish history had to begin by establishing the inner dynamic of development of Israelite culture as revealed by analysis of internal textual evidence, before expanding to see these texts in external cultural contexts that are only supplemental. To locate a biblical text primarily in its broader context would run the risk of flattening out the distinctiveness of Israelite culture in the search for universal phenomena.[27] The *Prolegomena* employs this hermeneutic, as virtually no external texts are invoked, and its argument rests on the internal evidence of the Hebrew texts themselves.

Wellhausen's hypothesis also shows us how a work structured by a historical-ideological narrative could capture the imagination of his age. More fully than anyone before him, Wellhausen had managed to correlate the discrete sources he identified with distinct, successive periods of the Israelite religious development: JE hearkened back to the period of the divided monarchy; D was composed in the period of Josianic reform in the seventh century; and P represented a more cultic emphasis of the postexilic period.[28] Wellhausen's hypothesis was greeted with immediate acclaim not because it was based on foolproof evidence—indeed, many aspects of his work have since been discarded by scholars working in the historical-critical paradigm—but because it produced a comprehensive *narrative* more fully than any earlier work. His narrative offered

---

25. Peter Machinist, "The Road Not Taken: Wellhausen and Assyriology," in *Homeland and Exile: Biblical and Ancient Near Eastern Studies in Honour of Bustenay Oded*, ed. Gershon Galil, Mark Geller, and Alan Millard (Leiden: Brill, 2009), 498.

26. Ibid., 501.

27. Ibid., 519.

28. John Rogerson, *Old Testament Criticism in the Nineteenth Century: England and Germany* (Philadelphia: Fortress, 1985), 266.

16   Joshua A. Berman

the clearest picture yet of how the identification and chronology of the putative sources reflected the romanticist notion of development.[29]

Today, of course, not all biblicists see the Pentateuch as dissolvable into constituent "sources," cobbled together by a redactor. Nonetheless, nineteenth-century German historicism bequeathed an agenda to diachronic biblical studies that is still at the core of the discipline today. Common to all contemporary theories of textual growth is the mandate to engage in four pursuits: (1) to identify fissures in the text as markers of diachronic development, on the basis of internal evidence; (2) if possible, to characterize the ideology that animates each of these component parts; (3) to adduce a theory of composition—sources, fragments, supplements, layers, and so on—that accounts for the shape of the final text; (4) to date the component parts and propose a chronology of textual growth.

Empirical Models and the Presuppositions of Contemporary Theories of Textual Growth

I turn now to canvass the claims of scholars who have invoked empirical models to reconstruct textual growth in ancient Israel. My aim is to explore the implications of these claims in light of the premises that for so long have guided much of the work on the textual growth of the Hebrew Bible.

The recent studies on empirical models of textual growth sound a consistent chord: the epigraphic evidence from the neighboring cultures of the ancient Near East suggests that many of the forms of editing routinely hypothesized concerning textual growth in ancient Israel are not attested in these comparative corpora. Contemporary theorists often assume that textual emendation in the ancient Near East can only be a process of supplementation but not of deletion.[30] Empirical models, however, demonstrate that revisions expanded but also suppressed earlier material.[31] Contemporary theorists often will assume that the entirety of an earlier source can be recovered through diachronic analysis. Empirical

---

29. David J. A. Clines, "Response to Rolf Rendtorff's 'What Happened to the Yahwist? Reflections After Thirty Years,'" SBL Forum Archive, http://www.sbl-site.org/publications/article .aspx?ArticleId=551. It is worth noting that Wellhausen had been promised no honorarium for his work. The book enjoyed such great sales, however, that the publisher shared its profits with him. See Suzanne Marchand, *German Orientalism in the Age of Empire: Religion, Race, and Scholarship* (Cambridge: Cambridge University Press, 2009), 183.

30. Cf. Ska, *Introduction*, 169–70; Christoph Levin, *The Old Testament: A Brief Introduction* (Princeton: Princeton University Press, 2005), 27; Uwe Becker, *Exegese des Alten Testaments*, UTB 2664 (Tübingen: Mohr Siebeck, 2005), 84. See discussion of these positions in Pakkala, *God's Word Omitted*, 16–25.

31. For discussion of the Gilgamesh epic, see Van der Toorn, *Scribal Culture*, 127. For a full-length discussion of a range of Israelite and Judean texts, see Pakkala, *God's Word Omitted*.

History of the Historical-Critical Paradigm in Biblical Studies   17

models, however, reveal that scribes rarely appropriate earlier compositions in their entirety.[32] Contemporary theorists, especially in pentateuchal studies, hypothesize the conflation of parallel sources. Empirical models, however, suggest that scribes did not preserve source documents unaltered and without gaps, and this is especially true in cases of conflation of parallel sources.[33] Some theorists envision multiple stages of revision and emendation. Empirical models reveal that even the most complex documented cases rarely feature more than two or three stages of major revision of a given text.[34] David Carr summarizes his findings: "The documented variety of readable sources that can be produced out of pentateuchal and other texts militates against the probability that such reconstructed sources ever existed in an earlier time. Instead, given what we know about partial preservation and modification of prior traditions by ancient scribes, it is more likely that most (semi-)readable texts produced by contemporary transmission historians are nothing but the inventions of their creators."[35]

These findings undermine several of the premises that have long guided much work on the textual growth of Hebrew Scriptures and beg a reassessment of their validity.

Internal Versus External Evidence: Which Is Primary?

German biblicists of the nineteenth century placed a premium on internal sources over against the elucidation to be garnered from external sources. No doubt this stemmed in part from the paucity of comparative materials available during that period. Nineteenth-century analysis of the Bible, its religion, and institutions predates the recovery of much of the data that we have today from the ancient Near East.[36] Instruction in Assyriology was hardly available at German institutions of this era. While French and British excavators began uncovering the riches of Mesopotamia in the 1840s and '50s, it was only in 1872 that George Smith offered his astonishing lecture that revealed an Akkadian precursor to the biblical flood story.[37] Significant efforts to analyze these epigraphic materials did not commence until the 1880s and '90s—more than a decade after the publication of Wellhausen's *Prolegomena*.[38]

---

32. Carr, *Formation of the Hebrew Bible*, 99–100.
33. Ibid., 112.
34. Ibid., 145.
35. Ibid., 114.
36. Machinist, "Road Not Taken," 469.
37. Ibid., 488.
38. Ibid., 505.

18   Joshua A. Berman

It could have been expected that with the advent of such analysis the study of the compositional history of the biblical texts would have undergone a paradigm change. It would have been hoped that scholars would have sought empirical evidence for how texts evolved and grew, based upon the epigraphic finds of the neighboring cultures. Indeed, some scholars took Wellhausen to task for failing to do just this. The eminent classicist Ulrich von Wilamowitz-Moellendorff wrote of Wellhausen, in his 1928 autobiography, "He remained just a theologian; this explains the entire orientation of his [*Prolegomena*]. He resisted, as he should not have done, working his way into Assyrian and Babylonian."[39] No less a figure than Hermann Gunkel wrote of the practice of source criticism in 1931, "[Wellhausen's] overall vision was sketched without reference to the history of the other areas of the Orient of the time and cannot in all parts be made to concur with the ancient oriental discoveries which have multiplied in such an unforeseen manner. The school . . . has buried itself in . . . increasingly fruitless literary criticism and has shown no serious comprehension of the literary history that has become more prominent in the last few years."[40]

The fact that the field generally failed to engage this line of inquiry until quite recently suggests that habits and ways of thought predisposed it from doing so. The romanticist proclivity of nineteenth-century German scholarship led scholars of that age to believe that the genius of individual cultures had to be first determined from within the inner dynamics of these master texts called the "sources." Today, most scholars would aver that Israel, like every culture of the ancient Near East, indeed displayed cultural and perhaps even literary practices that were *sui generis*. Yet, in large part—maybe even in major part—Israel's literary output is best seen as part of a scribal milieu of the ancient Near East. The insistence in some quarters of the field today that internal evidence trumps external evidence is a holdover from a bygone era. It is a claim that today requires legitimation. It cannot be assumed.

Moreover, empirical models threaten the very notion of so-called internal evidence. Internal evidence is deduced by noting irregularities within the text and decomposing the text into constituent parts. Meanwhile, scholars pointing to empirical models are concluding that the task of accurately separating the received texts into constituent parts is considerably more difficult than we may have thought. Time and again, we compare the earlier stage of an ancient text's development with a later stage, and see that there is no way that the later text could have yielded to analysis to produce the older, earlier text. Empirical

39. Ulrich von Wilamowitz-Moellendorff, *Erinnerungen 1848–1914* (Leipzig: K. F. Koehler, 1928), 189–90; translated and cited in Machinist, "Road Not Taken," 483n33.

40. Hermann Gunkel, "Wellhausen," in *Die Religion in Geschichte und Gegenwart*, ed. H. Gunkel and L. Zscharnack (Tübingen: Mohr Siebeck, 1931), 1821; translated in Marchand, *German Orientalism*, 262.

models demonstrate that writers often borrowed a range of elements in their compositions, from individual words to syntactic patterns to whole formulas. Later works are a bricolage of earlier works.[41] The romantic idea of the author as one who composes *ex nihilo* does not fit the empirical data of ancient Near Eastern epigraphic finds. There is no author in biblical Israel without the great train of mimetic transmissions that come before. This undermines the very attempt to ground theories of textual development on the basis of internal evidence alone.

For nineteenth-century scholars and for many today as well, the purpose of deconstructing the text was to recover windows into Israel's origins: to describe the major themes of those sources, their language, and, above all, their historical settings; and then to reconstruct the process by which they were compiled to create the received text. As Roland Barthes has written, the modernist notion of the author and literary criticism understood as historical criticism are notions that go hand in hand.[42] However, if empirical models are given pride of place in uncovering the literary practices of ancient Israel, then we must accept that we may not have clear access to these putative sources. Put differently, this means that we may not have trustworthy "windows" onto the world of earliest Israel, which is to say we may not be able to chart history itself in reliable fashion through recourse to so-called internal evidence.

The Problem of Experimental Method in Nineteenth-Century German Historicist Thought

To consider the place of empirical models in the reconstruction of the growth of the biblical text we need to consider the role of intuition versus the role of evidence and methodological control in scientific inquiry, and particularly how this issue evolved in nineteenth-century Germany.

At the dawn of the historicist era in the early nineteenth century, the natural sciences were viewed as an ally of the critical study of history. Humboldt was adamant in his affirmation of the close connection between natural science and the new science of history.[43] The physical world provided the analogies upon which the world of human activity could be comprehended and explained. Living nature presents the historian, the linguist, and the anthropologist the

41. The phenomenon is illustrated in full-length fashion in Victor Hurowitz, *Inu Anum Sirum: Literary Structures in the Non-juridical Sections of Codex Hammurabi* (Philadelphia: University of Pennsylvania Museum of Archaeology and Anthropology, 1994).

42. Roland Barthes, "The Death of the Author," Ubu Web Papers, http://www.ubu.com/aspen /aspen5and6/threeEssays.html#barthes.

43. See Peter Hanns Reill, "Science and the Construction of the Cultural Sciences in Late Enlightenment Germany: The Case of Wilhelm von Humboldt," *HistTh* 33, no. 3 (1994): 345–66.

20   Joshua A. Berman

analogies necessary for the establishment of these disciplines as sciences.[44] Inspired by the natural sciences, the scientific pursuit of history would be executed with a premium placed on induction, objectivity, and impartiality.

However, as the natural sciences progressed by leaps and bounds, the alliance of *Geisteswissenschaft* with *Naturwissenschaft* became a liability. The natural sciences were developing precise tools of measurement and experimentation. Statistical analysis of results ensured the solid base of the results. Practitioners of the human sciences had no hope of keeping up with the refined results achieved by natural "scientists"—a term that first appears in English in 1831. By comparison, the results of the human sciences seemed "soft" and unscientific. Champions of the human sciences were caught between a rock and a hard place. Since Newton, science had been considered the benchmark of rigorous method for critical inquiry. Yet it was this same "science"—the science of the natural world—which was demonstrating just how unscientific the *Geisteswissenschaften* really were. The solution was to cut loose and declare autonomy.[45] The human sciences, and with them history, were true sciences, their proponents claimed. But they operated under a different methodology. Only by recognizing the autonomy and legitimacy of the human sciences could advances be made. Chief in this effort was the man considered by many to be one of the fathers of the social sciences: Wilhelm Dilthey (1833–1911). For Dilthey, the positivist epistemology of the natural sciences, with its emphasis on statistics and experimentation, was claiming an undue hegemony over the human sciences.[46] The two realms, he claimed, pursued fundamentally different goals. The goal of natural science was *Erklären* (explaining), while the goal of the human sciences was *Verstehen* (understanding). For several decades, theorists would debate and clarify the differences between the two methods and the best ways to achieve each.[47] Critically, historians considered the methodology of their discipline *sui generis* and independent. This method of inquiry championed an epistemology that placed a high premium on the intuition and imagination of the investigating historian.[48]

German historians debated the issue: can the goals of the historian—to depict a coherent narrative of cause and effect of the past—be attained? What

44. Ibid., 356.

45. See Irmline Veit-Brause, "Science and the Cultural Politics of Academic Disciplines in Late 19th-Century Germany: Emil Du Bois-Reymond and the Controversy over the Role of the Cultural Sciences," *History of the Human Sciences* 14, no. 4 (2001): 31–56; Reill, "Science and the Construction," 346.

46. Zammito, "Historicism," 801.

47. See the essays contained in Uljana Feest, ed., *Historical Perspectives on Erklären and Verstehen* (Berlin: Springer, 2010).

48. Veit-Brause, "Science and the Cultural Politics," 37; Reill, "Science and the Construction," 361.

methodological control was necessary to ensure the accuracy of the conclusions? One of the preeminent thinkers of the age, Johann Gustav Droysen (1808–84), wrote that the critical school of Niebuhr and Ranke was fraught with naïve optimism in its uncritical confidence in what historical criticism can accomplish. Critical method is at its best with regard to the relatively recent past, where many original sources are available. The method is on far shakier ground with regard to ancient history, where there are often too few sources to work with.[49] Droysen writes that the naïve confidence of the critical school stems from the illusion that the process of sifting and sorting available evidence would allow the historian to distinguish the truth and discover, in von Ranke's words, "how things actually were."

Droysen's voice found little resonance within the field of biblical studies, and here, too, scholars were convinced that by carefully assessing the seeming irregularities in the text, the prized sources would become accessible. The results would be ensured by the investigator's intuition, which works on two levels within this hermeneutic. The biblicist's intuition allows him or her to correctly identify fissures within the text and identify them as markers of diachronic development. Second, intuition allows the biblicist to posit a theory of composition—sources, fragments, supplements, and so on.[50] The purpose of this sifting was to identify constituent sources that displayed the cherished trait of *consistency*. The cultural value of consistency at this time is reflected in the fact that the core of *Gymnasium* training at this time in Germany was the subjects of Greek and Roman grammar and mathematics, admired because they offered training in abstract, consistent forms of knowledge.[51]

The irony of this valuation of the scholar's own intuition is that it counters the very historicist ethos it seeks to embody. For all historicists of this period, literature is a product of a specific culture situated in a specific and individuated time and place. Conventions of coherence, of communication, and of literary production are all profoundly human constructs, and are themselves historically bound. We might have expected theorists—then and now—to sound a note of caution in adducing theories of textual composition. We might have expected investigators to take cognizance of their own situatedness, and to be wary that their own canons of coherence and of literary production could easily be

---

49. Johann Gustav Droysen, *Historik: Historisch-kritische Ausgabe*, ed. Peter Leyh and Horst Walter Blanke (Stuttgart-Bad Cannstatt: Frommann-Holzboog, 1977), 113; and discussion in Beiser, *German Historicist Tradition*, 309.

50. Provan, "Knowing and Believing," 233, 239.

51. Denise Phillips, "Epistemological Distinctions and Cultural Politics: Educational Reform and the *Naturwissenschaft/Geisteswissenschaft* Distinction in Nineteenth-Century Germany," in Feest, *Historical Perspectives on Erklären and Verstehen*, 19; cf. Marchand, *German Orientalism*, 79.

22   Joshua A. Berman

anachronistically superimposed upon the cultures of yore. And yet we see virtually no awareness of these pitfalls in the scholarship of compositional theory of
Hebrew Scriptures up until quite recently. This, I would suggest, is evidence of
the German historicist legacy of the nineteenth century. In the declaration of the
autonomy of the *Geisteswissenschaften*, and within those, the historical-critical
study of the Hebrew Bible, intuition and imagination assumed pride of place in
the governing epistemology. External control to check intuitive theories was an
element that was largely sacrificed—at least for biblical studies—in the great
divorce between *Geisteswissenschaft* and the *Naturwissenschaft*. The *Erklären/
Verstehen* debates, pitting knowledge about human beings and texts against
knowledge about the natural world, represented an epistemological distinction
peculiar to German-speaking Europe.[52] In his study of nineteenth-century biblical hermeneutics, John Rogerson notes that there was much greater creativity in biblical scholarship in Germany than in England. He attributes this to a
difference of philosophical disposition. English philosophy is grounded in an
empiricist tradition of evidence and experimentation. He concludes, "if I may
generalize from my own attitudes, English scholarship would prefer to say that
it does not know, rather than build elaborate theories upon slender premises."[53]

Here, then, we cut to the chase of the debate over the place of empirical
models for biblical composition: for the better part of two centuries, scholars
have not sought out external methodological control for their work, instead
relying upon intuition and the canons of coherence of their times to fit the data
of the biblical text into a procrustean bed of compositional theory. Those that
invoke empirical models are doing much more than introducing new evidence
to the field. Methodologically speaking, they are insisting on a mode of research
that the field has resisted for two centuries.

I would like to dramatize just how absent this way of thinking has been from
the field with reference to an experiment that could have been carried out even
by the earliest critics who originated the field of compositional theory of the
biblical text. An empirical experiment to test our capacity to develop accurate
theories of textual decomposition could have been conducted using the book of
Chronicles and the corresponding passages in the *Vorlage* of Samuel and Kings.
Imagine the following: a scholar takes the first book of Chronicles and carefully
notes all of the changes witnessed relative to the corresponding passages in
Samuel–Kings. On the basis of the evidence, the scholar then adduces a literary
algorithm that explains what the author of Chronicles does to the *Vorlage* of
Samuel–Kings to produce what we see in the later text. This literary algorithm
will tell us how the later text systematically adopts or adapts, supplements, or

---

52. Phillips, "Epistemological Distinctions," 15.
53. Rogerson, *Old Testament Criticism*, 292.

deletes material relative to the source texts—all on the basis of the collected evidence. The scholar now moves to the second book of Chronicles and tries to work back from that text, on the basis of the algorithm adduced from the work on 1 Chronicles and its *Vorlage*. To what degree would the scholar be able to accurately recreate the *Vorlage* of 2 Chronicles?

Such an experiment would give an indication of our capacity (or lack thereof) to recreate earlier texts on the basis of existing ones, in their final form. In fact, such an experiment would show us what the very best results are that we could hope for. This is because the work to recreate the *Vorlage* of 2 Chronicles would have been based on a wealth of evidence observed in the first half of the book and its sources. There is little theory or hypothesizing here. The beauty of this experiment is that it is totally empirical. It is remarkable that none of the early critics working in compositional theory of the Hebrew Bible thought to execute such an experiment. It is even more remarkable that to this very day this experiment has not been attempted. This oversight speaks volumes on the hallowed place of deduction and intuition in the discipline as opposed to the place of experimentation, control, and empirical models. In an oft-cited article, Steven A. Kaufman says that he began to try to do such an experiment with the Temple Scroll and its *Vorlage*, the Pentateuch, until he saw that it was "a consummately fruitless endeavor."[54]

Unwarranted Confidence

Finally, the invocation of empirical models undermines the presumed confidence with which scholars have produced theories of textual development since Astruc. Here, too, the threat of empirical models is not to biblical studies per se, but to a particular intellectual attitude that undergirds much of the discipline. David Carr's call for "methodological modesty" flies in the face of foundationalist thinking, which has guided the discipline for so long.[55] Foundationalists are motivated by a desire for certainty in their work, believing that if an elaborate system of analysis can be erected, such a secure foundation will be found. This motivation is what the philosopher Richard L. Bernstein refers to as Cartesian anxiety.[56] Descartes had insisted that we accept only knowledge that can be known with certainty. Researchers in all fields of study could do no less than to claim to have achieved this certainty, and scholars of the Bible were no exception. Witness the supreme confidence expressed in the writing of the

---

54. Stephen Kaufman, "The Temple Scroll and Higher Criticism," *HUCA* 53 (1982): 29.

55. Carr, *Formation of the Hebrew Bible*, 4.

56. See Richard L. Bernstein, *Beyond Objectivism and Relativism: Science, Hermeneutics, and Praxis* (Philadelphia: University of Pennsylvania Press, 1983).

24   Joshua A. Berman

nineteenth-century biblicist Charles Augustus Briggs, coauthor of the Brown-Driver-Briggs lexicon:

> The valleys of biblical truth have been filled up with the debris of human dogmas, ecclesiastical institutions, liturgical formulas, priestly ceremonies, and casuistic practices. Historical criticism is searching for the rock-bed of divine truth and the massive foundations of the Divine Word, in order to recover the real Bible. Historical criticism is sifting all this rubbish. It will gather out every precious stone. Nothing will escape its keen eye. . . . As surely as the temple of Herod and the city of the [H]asmoneans arose from the ruins of the former temples and cities, just so surely will the old Bible rise in the reconstructions of biblical criticism into a splendour and a glory greater than ever before.[57]

By contrast, we saw that the fathers of the historical-critical paradigm, Spinoza and Simon, were actually sanguine about our capacity to answer the historical-critical questions we ask of the biblical text. Scholars who are currently doing compositional work on the basis of empirical models are really reconnecting to the paradigm's earliest tradition of measured skepticism. Compositional theories that draw from nineteenth-century premises propagated by von Ranke perpetuate the belief that as historians of the ancient world, we have the types and quantity of social and economic data similar to scholars working in later historical periods where the documentation is more extensive. By drawing our attention to empirical models, these scholars provide a much-needed check and control for our work. But this control, perforce, must rob the discipline of the self-confidence that has been its hallmark since Astruc. Juha Pakkala has recently argued precisely this point. He notes the difficulty diachronic scholars will have with the empirical evidence, whereby later versions of a text frequently demonstrate suppression of earlier material: "The assumption that parts of the [earlier] text were omitted would leave the scholar with less tangible evidence about the past and with questions that the texts could not answer. The theories would become much less certain."[58] Although Spinoza and Simon represented only the dawn of the historical criticism of the Bible, their measured skepticism should be a guide to us as we go forward.

This essay has focused on the importance of empirical models as a control for the models we adduce for textual growth of the Hebrew Scriptures. Empirical models, however, are no less important as a control for determining literary unity

---

57. C. A. Briggs, *General Introduction to the Study of Holy Scripture* (New York: Scribner, 1899), 531–32.

58. Pakkala, *God's Word Omitted*, 14.

and disunity in a text. Indeed, many of the literary phenomena that diachronic scholars identify as fissures within the text have ancient Near Eastern literary precursors, where we can see that these phenomena were propagated by a single literary agent.[59] There is no intuitive way to determine "internal evidence"— what constitutes a fissure in a text from another period and another locale. These sensitivities must be learned, and acquired by careful study. When claims for revision rely on a perceived inconsistency or tension in the text and there is no external evidence to corroborate this perception, we may well be imposing modern canons of consistency on these ancient texts, effectively inventing the problem to which revision is the solution.[60] Source critics will need to become aware of the situatedness of their own aesthetic senses of literary unity.

There should be no delusion, however, that this critical reservoir of comparative data from the cognate literature will become fully available any time soon. The problem is particularly acute with regard to the genre of narrative. We have fine studies that survey the poetics of narrative in biblical literature.[61] To date, however, no comparable work has been written for any of the cognate narrative corpuses of the ancient Near East. There has been no survey of Egyptian narrative techniques, nor of the poetics of Mesopotamian narrative, that would allow us to test the bounds of literary unity in narrative for these ancient writers. Suffice it to say, there has also been no monograph produced that sets out to compare biblical narrative technique with that of the surrounding cultures. The work ahead is great. Lacking a thorough knowledge of the ancient notions of literary unity, modern scholars, perforce, perform their diachronic work in the dark, arriving at conclusions derived exclusively from their own notions of textual cohesion.

---

59. On this topic generally, see Joshua A. Berman, *Inconsistency in the Torah: Ancient Literary Convention and the Limits of Source Criticism* (Oxford: Oxford University Press, 2017).

60. See my study "The Biblical Criticism of Ibn Hazm the Andalusian: A Medieval Control for Modern Diachronic Method," *JBL* 138 (2019): 377-90. See also the discussion in Raymond F. Person Jr. and Robert Rezetko, "Introduction: The Importance of Empirical Models to Assess the Efficacy of Source and Redaction Criticism," in *Empirical Models Challenging Biblical Criticism*, ed. Raymond F. Person Jr. and Robert Rezetko (Atlanta: SBL, 2016), 1–23.

61. See, e.g., Robert Alter, *The Art of Biblical Narrative* (New York: Basic Books, 1981); Meir Sternberg, *The Poetics of Biblical Narrative: Ideological Literature and the Drama of Reading* (Bloomington: Indiana University Press, 1985).

CHAPTER 2

The Exodus, Debt Slavery, and the Composition of the Pentateuch

Richard E. Averbeck
Trinity Evangelical Divinity School

Torah scholarship as it is practiced in the academy today has a long and complicated history, and is an increasingly pluralistic affair. The historical-critical tradition goes back to the so-called Enlightenment, with even earlier precursors. As the tradition has continued to grow over the past few centuries, one method and its set of conclusions has led to the next, so that the buildup of the various competing or complementary methods and conclusions has yielded a complexity that is sometimes difficult to sort out. The goal of this essay is to propose and articulate some of the most important features of a revised, less intrusive, and more self-critical approach to the entire historical-critical enterprise. As a test case, we will then apply this approach to one of the key historical-critical issues for the composition of the Pentateuch: the debt-slave regulations in Exod 21:2–11; Lev 25:39–43; and Deut 15:12–18.

Toward a Revised Historical-Critical Approach to the Pentateuch

The Hebrew Bible has three primary dimensions—literary, historical, and theological.[1] First of all, what we actually have in our hands is a literary composition that needs to be treated as literature, no matter how one thinks it was composed. Second, according to this literary text, historical matters do indeed matter, both the history it recounts and its own history of composition.[2] Third, as a theological text, the Bible makes claims about God, people, the world, and the relationship between them. A holistic historical-critical approach to reading the text will pay careful attention to all three dimensions and the relationships between them. Moreover, there is perspective and variation in both the

---

1. See the brief discussion of these three dimensions in Richard E. Averbeck, "Factors in Reading the Patriarchal Narratives: Literary, Historical, and Theological Dimensions," in *Giving the Sense: Understanding and Using Old Testament Historical Texts (Essays in Honor of Eugene H. Merrill)*, ed. David M. Howard Jr. and Michael A. Grisanti (Grand Rapids: Kregel, 2003), 115–17.

2. See the approach represented, for example, in James K. Hoffmeier and Dennis R. Magary, eds., *Do Historical Matters Matter to Faith? A Critical Appraisal of Modern and Postmodern Approaches to the Bible* (Wheaton, IL: Crossway, 2012).

The Exodus, Debt Slavery, and the Composition of the Pentateuch 27

composition and reception of the Bible through the time of its composition amid various cultures and historical and theological developments.

To put it another way, there is a certain unity, but also diversity within that unity, in the Hebrew Bible as we now have it. According to the text, Moses did not live during the time of the patriarchs, for example, so the literary and historical perspective of Genesis is different from Exodus through Deuteronomy, where Moses is the main human character. Similarly, the perspective on the cult is different in the book of Leviticus from that in the book of Deuteronomy. From the point of view of the text as it now stands, one is written from a priestly perspective at the beginning of the forty years in the wilderness, and the other at the end of the forty years from a prophetic point of view, as Israel stands ready to enter the promised land. So, yes, there is a diversity of perspective in the Torah.

In the serious academic study of the Pentateuch this comes into play. It is the stuff of historical-critical investigation, where the study of the text itself in Hebrew, in its versions, and in its ANE context is primary, and where it is also important to be fully informed and able to interact in an intelligent and honest way with the scholarly study of it as practiced today in the academy. Given all of the above, in my view there are three principles of sound method that can help us sort out the academic scene and find a place to stand to do serious work that does not just add to the ongoing waves of pluralistic creativity.

Verifiable Data Versus Theories About the Data

The first and most helpful principle is the importance of clearly distinguishing between verifiable data, especially biblical, but also extrabiblical, as opposed to theories about the data. One of the major sources of confusion in this field is that theories are too often treated as if they are data. Scholars of all stripes and flavors sometimes confuse their theories with actual verifiable data, and proceed from there as if they are building on a solid foundation. This is a continuing problem.

Conversely, data can be used selectively in order to confirm a theory without giving due attention to other data that do not support it, or suggest other conclusions. This has led to a morass of multiple conflicting theories. In the midst of all this it is easy to lose sight of the distinction between verifiable data and the theories that have been propounded to explain the data. The result is a state of affairs where one theory built upon another simply cannot withstand the test of time and scrutiny, no matter how brilliant and convincing it may seem to some scholars at one time or another.

A good example of this phenomenon is the well-known and long-dominant "New Documentary Hypothesis" as articulated by Julius Wellhausen in his

28   Richard E. Averbeck

Prolegomena to the History of Israel, first written and published as his *History of Israel* in 1878.[3] The criticisms of it have been many, but it held sway in the field for most of the twentieth century, and for many it still does, at least in principle.[4] More recently, the so-called "Neo-Documentary Hypothesis" takes Wellhausen as its starting point but also represents a major shift in the perspective on the nature of the "documents" and what they represent in the history of Israel.[5] The unending shifts and competing theories are likely to continue in this brand of Torah scholarship due to the nature of what it presupposes, how it is carried on, and what it supposes to be its assured results.

I hasten to add, however, that much is helpful in this work even for those who do not find the "assured results" to be so assured. This is because it can help those of us who follow an approach like the one offered in this essay to be properly self-critical of our own more positive view of the composition of the Pentateuch. Reading Spinoza, Wellhausen, and von Rad, for example, as well as Carr, Levinson, Schwartz, Schmid, Nihan, Baden, Stackert, and many others, is essential and can be very helpful. They often make observations and arguments that might not have occurred to one who comes to the Hebrew text from a different point of view; for instance, not committed to the tradition of skepticism that is part and parcel of the historical-critical method as it is regularly practiced in the academy. Nevertheless, in my view, their approach leaves much to be desired, and undermines their reading of the text in a fair and methodologically sound manner. In particular, the negative bias of the method often causes them to unnecessarily fragment the text.

The Neo-Documentarian Joel Baden, for instance, shows this quite clearly in his recent book on the patriarchal narratives in Genesis.[6] On the one hand, when he reads the text according to his basic documentary method, he assigns the promise texts to different documents (J, E, and P), and refers to them as "confused" or "contradictory." On the other hand, when he comes back around to the same texts in his canonical reading, he labels them "tensions," "distinct emphases," or "divergent perspectives." The natural question is, why are they not the latter from the start? The answer is, because the source critical documentary approach to reading the text has a negative bias to begin with.

---

3. Julius Wellhausen, *Prolegomena to the History of Israel*, trans. J. S. Black and A. Menzies (Edinburgh: Black, 1885; repr., Atlanta: Scholars Press, 1994).

4. See, e.g., Richard Elliott Friedman, *The Bible with Sources Revealed: A New View into the Five Books of Moses* (New York: HarperCollins, 2003), 1–6.

5. See now, e.g., Jeffrey Stackert, *A Prophet Like Moses: Prophecy, Law, and Israelite Religion* (Oxford: Oxford University Press, 2014), especially his substantial criticism of Wellhausen's views. And see my review of this book: Richard E. Averbeck, review of *A Prophet Like Moses: Prophecy, Law, and Israelite Religion*, by Jeffrey Stackert, *Themelios* 42, no. 3 (2017): 520–22.

6. Joel S. Baden, *The Promise to the Patriarchs* (Oxford: Oxford University Press, 2013).

The Exodus, Debt Slavery, and the Composition of the Pentateuch

Baden argues, for example, that Abraham shows confidence in God's promises in Gen 12:1–3 (J) as we can see from his obedience, but this is contradictory to the patriarch's doubts in Gen 15:1–7 (E). The problem with this kind of argument, of course, is that a person of faith can sometimes struggle very deeply with their faith. Perhaps these passages are in tension, but if so, it would be a natural human tension. To tear them apart source critically is to rob them of their richness when they are read together in the first instance. And one always needs to pay attention to the changing circumstances of life, as in the contexts of these two passages. Examples could be multiplied.[7]

What We *Believe* to Be True Versus What We Can *Show* to Be True

The first principle, therefore, has to do with making a clear distinction between the data and theories about the data. We need to be able to sort out one from the other if we are going to understand what is happening in the discussion. It is important to be clear and self-critical about this principle in our own work from its inception.

The second principle that has become clear to me is our need to *make a clear distinction in our own minds between what we can show to be true as opposed to what we believe to be true*. It will become clear below that my concern here is *not* that we shed ourselves of our personal theological or religious beliefs, or compromise them, or even question them, in order to be more acceptable in the academy. Instead, the issue here is simply the need to stay focused on the task at hand, which is to build sound arguments upon verifiable data in order to develop reasonable and sustainable, even if theoretical, explanations for the data.

Some years ago Ronald Hendel lamented the effect the religiously committed were having on the kinds of things that were happening at the Society of Biblical Literature meetings.[8] More recently, Jeffrey Stackert has expressed the same frustration in the context of recounting Wellhausen's own personal struggles with the deleterious effect he anticipated his view of the Bible would have on the church.[9] I see their point. Certain venues are designed for serious academic work and others for open faith expression. We need to know the difference and respect it, whether we are people of faith or not.

This does not mean, however, that people of faith cannot function in the academy just as well as those who hold no faith, or a different kind. To do so

---

7. See Richard E. Averbeck, review of *The Promise to the Patriarchs*, by Joel S. Baden, *Themelios* 38, no. 3 (2013): 432–34.

8. Ronald S. Hendel, "Farewell to SBL: Faith and Reason in Biblical Studies," *BAR* 36, no. 4 (2010): 28, 74.

9. Stackert, *Prophet Like Moses*, 207–8.

30 Richard E. Averbeck

requires that we make the distinction highlighted here, and speak with scholarly finesse into the academy in a way that stands up under scrutiny even from those who do not hold to our faith commitments. Of course, opinions can vary on what might be a reasonable or sustainable explanation, and sometimes there is even uncertainty about whether the supposed data are verifiable, or whether they support the explanation given for it. That just naturally comes with the scholarly territory and should be recognized by all.

What the Text Plainly Tells Us About Its Own Composition

This brings me to the third principle. The first two are broad principles of approach to the data of the text and the world of the text; namely the need to clearly distinguish between actual data and theories about the data, and the importance of building reasonable and sustainable theories directly from the data, not from previous theories that themselves are questionable. One needs to distinguish between what they may believe to be true and what they can actually show to be true. The third principle focuses on *the need to start by turning the text of the Hebrew Bible back upon itself in order allow it to tell us about its own composition.* Of course, it is also important to consider other data as well; for example, literary compositional patterns and scribal practices in the ANE world. But we need to begin with what the Bible itself plainly indicates about its own compositional process.

This is not a new idea. Jean-Louis Ska, for example, begins his *Introduction to Reading the Pentateuch* this way.[10] He has a full three chapters early in the volume where he points to textual reasons that indicate, in his view, that we cannot read the Pentateuch as a unified composition. This was also one of the main burdens of the early chapters in Spinoza's *Theological-Political Treatise*, published originally back in 1670, at the headwaters of the historical-critical method.[11] Wellhausen himself made much of the importance of Spinoza's work for his own. Many of the basic principles of the historical-critical method go back to Spinoza, especially the "tradition of skepticism" about God, miracles, and the composition of the Bible, including the Pentateuch.

Spinoza was particularly concerned with the post-Mosaic features of the Pentateuch. He was right to point out that no one should argue that Moses wrote every word of the Pentateuch as we now have it. The Torah itself does not allow this. Aside from the report of Moses's death (Deut 34), Deut 2:12b tells us that the Edomites "destroyed the Horites from before them and settled in their place,

---

10. Jean-Louis Ska, *Introduction to Reading the Pentateuch*, trans. Pascale Dominique (Winona Lake, IN: Eisenbrauns, 2006).

11. Baruch Spinoza, *Theological-Political Treatise*, 2nd ed., trans. Samuel Shirley (Indianapolis: Hackett, 1991).

The Exodus, Debt Slavery, and the Composition of the Pentateuch   31

just as Israel did in the land the LORD gave them as their possession." This is clearly written from a postconquest point of view. Similarly, at one point the Esau genealogy in Gen 36 tells us that "these are the kings who ruled in the land of Edom before a king ruled over the Israelites" (v. 31). This verse is written from a historical point of view after there were kings over Israel; therefore, long after Moses. Apparently, a later writer added this section into the genealogy from some other source, whether it be the parallel passage in 1 Chr 1:43–50 (cf. Gen 36:31–39) or some other unknown source common to both. These are just a few examples.[12] On the one hand, therefore, we know from the text itself that Moses did not write every word of Pentateuch as we now have it. On the other hand, the text plainly tells us that Moses wrote down certain—sometimes major—portions of the Pentateuch (e.g., Exod 17:4; 24:4, 7 "the scroll of the covenant"; Deut 31:9 "Moses wrote this Torah," and vv. 19, 22, 30, which refer to him writing down הָאָזִינוּ, the magnificent poem recorded in Deut 32:1–43). In many other places the text tells us that God spoke to and through Moses. What should we make of this? Although many in the academy would deny that Moses ever existed, or that if he did, he had nothing or very little to do with the actual composition of the Pentateuch, many others take Moses seriously as a historical person and author of the Pentateuch. The point here is that the text itself no doubt claims there was a historical Moses, and that he had a good deal to do with the origin and composition of the Pentateuch.

We also know from the Pentateuch and other parts of the Hebrew Bible that preexisting sources were used in its composition, such as "the Scroll of the Wars of the LORD" (Num 21:14). There are also hints of such in, for example, "the Scroll of the generations of Adam" (Gen 5:1). Of course, this is very different from accepting the hypothetically reconstructed sources of source criticism (i.e., J, E, D, P). The text also plainly tells us that Moses was not alive at the time of the events of Genesis, and that there was a major temporal historical divide between the laws as given at Sinai and their exposition by Moses in Moab at the end of his life. The former took place circa forty years earlier and with the travel to the promised land in mind, whereas the latter occurred after the forty years, just before they were about to invade the promised land. With this shift, some of the laws shifted too, with a focus on the Israelites being spread out occupying the promised land, rather than dwelling around the tabernacle as an army camp.[13] This alone gives a diachronic perspective to the composition of the Pentateuch along with a careful synchronic reading.

---

12. See the further remarks Richard E. Averbeck, "Pentateuchal Criticism and the Priestly Torah," in Hoffmeier and Magary, *Do Historical Matters Matter?* 156–58 and literature cited there.

13. For more on this matter, see Richard E. Averbeck, "The Cult in Deuteronomy and Its Relationship to the Book of the Covenant and the Holiness Code," in *Sēpher Tôrat Mōšeh: Studies in the Interpretation of Deuteronomy*, ed. Daniel I. Block and Richard L. Schultz (Peabody, MA: Hendrickson, 2017), 232–60.

32   Richard E. Averbeck

Yes, we need to consider ANE scribal and compositional factors. Yes, there are post-Mosaic elements in the Pentateuch. Similarly, there are temporal, geographical, and situational shifts within history as it is presented in the Pentateuch. Allowing the text to speak into its own compositional history with these points in mind is important to both a fair reading of the text and unbiased approach to its composition. The question becomes, therefore, how well do these textual and historical realities account for the shape and content of the Pentateuch as it now stands? Of course, the proof of a method is in its actual application to biblical texts when we read them closely. So now we turn to applying the proposed method to debt-slave regulations in the three major units of the OT Law: the Covenant Code (Exod 21:2–11), the Holiness Code (Lev 25:39–43), and the Deuteronomic Code (Deut 15:12–18).

The Debt Slave Laws and Sequence of the Law Collections in the Pentateuch

As Bernard Levinson has noted, "Alongside the history of sacrifice and the festival calendar, the question of the sequence and relation of the laws concerning manumission of slaves has been essential to any larger attempt to construct a history of Israelite religion and a compositional history of the Pentateuch."[14] The standard historical-critical view followed by Levinson and many others has been that the debt slave law in Exod 21:2–11 came first (early preexilic). Deut 15:12–18 came next and revised the Exod 21 regulation in light of new conditions in the seventh century BC. The combined debt-slave regulations of Exod 21 and Deut 15, however, failed to carry the day in late preexilic Judah, according to the account in Jer 34. The later (exilic and/or postexilic) Holiness Code regulations in Lev 25, therefore, revised the failed Exodus and Deuteronomy debt-slave regulations, maintaining the institution but only in a substantially revised form in which the manumission would occur in the Jubilee Year, not in the seventh year after only six years of debt slavery.[15]

---

14. Bernard M. Levinson, "The Manumission of Hermeneutics: The Slave Laws of the Pentateuch as a Challenge to Contemporary Pentateuchal Theory," in *Congress Volume Leiden 2004*, ed. André Lemaire, VTSup 109 (Leiden: Brill, 2006), 281. For a very brief summary and interaction with Levinson's view, see Richard E. Averbeck, "The Egyptian Sojourn and Deliverance from Slavery in the Framing and Shaping of the Mosaic Law," in *"Did I Not Bring Israel Out of Egypt?" Biblical, Archaeological, and Egyptological Perspectives on the Exodus Narratives*, ed. James Hoffmeier, Alan Millard, and Gary Rendsburg, BBRSup 13 (Winona Lake, IN: Eisenbrauns, 2016), 169–75. The present discussion is a more complete treatment of the overall matter of debt slavery from a historical-critical point of view.

15. Levinson, "Manumission of Hermeneutics," 283, and also Levinson, "The Birth of a Lemma: The Restrictive Reinterpretation of the Covenant Code's Manumission Law by the Holiness

A substantial contingent of scholars from the Israeli school of biblical criticism generally turns the order of Deut 15 and Lev 25 around the other way. The Holiness Code comes before the Deuteronomic Code, so Deut 15 is dependent not only on Exod 21 but also Lev 25.[16] The major voices in favor of the latter alternative include Sara Japhet, Jacob Weingreen, and Jacob Milgrom.[17] More recently, Benjamin Kilchör has argued that this latter direction of dependence between the legal corpora is much more likely. He bases this, among other things, upon a carefully constructed and rather comprehensive literary analysis comparing the parallel debt-slave regulations in the three corpora, ending up with the sequence Exod 21 → Lev 25 → Deut 15.[18] His dissertation argues

---

Code (Leviticus 25:44–46)," *JBL* 124 (2005): 617–39. See also, e.g., Jeffrey Stackert, *Rewriting the Torah: Literary Revision in Deuteronomy and the Holiness Legislation*, FAT 52 (Tübingen: Mohr Siebeck, 2007), 141–64; Jean-François Lefebvre, *Le jubilé biblique: Lv 25—exégèse et théologie*, OBO 194 (Fribourg: Editions Universitaires; Göttingen: Vandenhoeck & Ruprecht, 2003), 266–98; Christophe Nihan, *From Priestly Torah to Pentateuch: A Study in the Composition of the Book of Leviticus*, FAT, 2nd ser., no. 25 (Tübingen: Mohr Siebeck, 2007), 523–35; and with some mediation between this and the earlier H view, also see Mark Leuchter, "The Manumission Laws in Leviticus and Deuteronomy: The Jeremiah Connection," *JBL* 127 (2008): 635–37 and 651–53.

16. See the helpful summary in Levinson, "Manumission of Hermeneutics," 285–88. Yehezkel Kaufmann was one of the first to argue for this historical order in the development of the three codes (Yehezkel Kaufmann, *The Religion of Israel: From Its Beginnings to the Babylonian Exile*, trans. and abridg. Moshe Greenberg [Chicago: University of Chicago Press, 1960], 166–211). But he also argued that there was no dependence of one upon the other in the historical development of their legal regulations and, therefore, no legal innovations between them. Consider the very helpful discussion of the history of this discussion with special emphasis on Kaufmann in Baruch J. Schwartz, "The Pentateuch as Scripture and the Challenge of Biblical Criticism: Responses Among Modern Jewish Thinkers and Scholars," in *Jewish Concepts of Scripture: A Comparative Approach*, ed. Benjamin D. Sommer (New York: NYU Press, 2012), 203–29. Also consider the careful analysis of the nature of the Holiness Code and strong arguments for its preexilic provenance in Jan Joosten, *People and Land in the Holiness Code*, VTSup 67 (Leiden: Brill, 1996).

17. Sara Japhet, "The Relationship Between the Legal Corpora in the Pentateuch in Light of Manumission Laws," in *Studies in Bible, 1986*, ed. Sara Japhet, ScrHier 31 (Jerusalem: Magnes VIII, 1986), 63–89; J. Weingreen, *From Bible to Mishna: The Continuity of Tradition* (New York: Holmes and Meier, 1976), 132–42; Jacob Milgrom, *Leviticus 23–27: A New Translation with Introduction and Commentary*, AB 3B (New York: Doubleday, 2001), 2251–57.

18. Benjamin Kilchör, "Frei aber arm? Soziale Sicherheit als Schlüssel zum Verhältnis der Sklavenfreilassungsgesetze im Pentateuch," *VT* 62 (2012): 381–97; Kilchör, "The Direction of Dependence Between the Laws of the Pentateuch: The Priority of a Literary Approach," *ETL* 89 (2013): 1–14; and now his full treatment in his published dissertation, Kilchör, *Mosetora und Jahwetora: Das Verhältnis von Deuteronomium 12–26 zu Exodus, Levitikus und Numeri*, BZABR 21 (Wiesbaden: Harrassowitz, 2015), 137–53.

I thank Joshua Berman for calling my attention to these works, and Benjamin Kilchör for supplying me with his dissertation soon after it came into print. See his very helpful review of the discussion of debt slavery in Kilchör, "Frei aber arm?" and Kilchör, *Mosetora und Jahwetora*, 137–53, esp. 141–47. His conclusions regarding Lev 25 (Kilchör, *Mosetora und Jahwetora*, 146–47) are quite similar to mine as argued below.

34   Richard E. Averbeck

persuasively for the Deuteronomic Code as the last composed after the Covenant Code and the Holiness Code, respectively.[19]

Exodus 21:2–11 Compared to Deuteronomy 15:12–18

There are important similarities between the regulations in Exod 21:2–11 and Deut 15:12–18. In both passages the debt slave works for six years and goes out from slavery in the seventh year (Exod 21:2; Deut 15:12). Similarly, in both cases the debt slave can elect to stay with the master as a perpetual slave because things are going well for the debt slave in the master's household (Exod 21:5–6; Deut 15:16–17). In Exod 21 this may be due not only to the good treatment of the slave by the master, in general, but the master has also given him a wife and she has born him children. He does not want to leave them behind (vv. 4–5; we will treat this matter further in the next section). This latter possibility is not considered in Deut 15, but the debt slave may nevertheless choose perpetual slavery with this master "because he loves you and your household, since things are good for him in your household (v. 16b, כִּי אֲהֵבְךָ וְאֶת־בֵּיתֶךָ כִּי־טוֹב לוֹ עִמָּךְ).

Another similarity has been the subject of some dispute. The introductory line in both passages refers to the debt slave as an עִבְרִי, usually rendered "Hebrew":

Exodus 21:2

כִּי תִקְנֶה עֶבֶד עִבְרִי שֵׁשׁ שָׁנִים יַעֲבֹד וּבַשְּׁבִעֹת יֵצֵא לַחָפְשִׁי חִנָּם:

If you acquire a Hebrew slave, six years he shall serve, but in the seventh he shall go out free, without payment.

Deuteronomy 15:12

כִּי־יִמָּכֵר לְךָ אָחִיךָ הָעִבְרִי אוֹ הָעִבְרִיָּה וַעֲבָדְךָ שֵׁשׁ שָׁנִים וּבַשָּׁנָה הַשְּׁבִיעִת תְּשַׁלְּחֶנּוּ חָפְשִׁי מֵעִמָּךְ:

---

19. For a relatively comprehensive treatment of the subject of debt slavery in Israel, see Gregory C. Chirichigno, *Debt-Slavery in Israel and the Ancient Near East*, JSOTSup 141 (Sheffield: Sheffield Academic Press, 1993); and Joe M. Sprinkle, *"The Book of the Covenant": A Literary Approach*, JSOTSup 174 (Sheffield University Press, 1994), 50–72. Raymond Westbrook, "The Female Slave," in *Cuneiform and Biblical Sources*, vol. 2 of *Law from the Tigris to the Tiber: The Writings of Raymond Westbrook*, ed. Bruce Wells and Rachel Magdalene (Winona Lake, IN: Eisenbrauns, 2009), 149–74, a reprint from *Gender and Law in the Bible and the Ancient Near East*, ed. V. H. Matthews et al., JSOTSup 262 (Sheffield: Sheffield Academic Press, 1998), 214–38, provides a very helpful analysis of Exod 21:7–11. For an earlier relatively brief treatment of the subject, see Richard E. Averbeck, "Law," in *Cracking Old Testament Codes: A Guide to Interpreting Old Testament Literary Forms*, ed. D. Brent Sandy and Ronald L. Giese Jr. (Nashville: Broadman & Holman, 1995), 131–34.

The Exodus, Debt Slavery, and the Composition of the Pentateuch 35

If your fellow Hebrew (lit. 'your Hebrew brother'), male or female, is sold to you, then he shall serve you six years, but in the seventh year you shall send him out free from you.

Some scholars regard עִבְרִי as cognate to Akkadian *ḥābiru/ḥāpiru*, in which case it would refer to displaced, foreign, and often indigent peoples known from other ANE texts, not *Israelite* debt slaves.[20] A major problem, among others, with this view is the juxtaposition of "your brother" with "male Hebrew or female Hebrew" in Deut 15:12, which strongly suggests that "Hebrew" there refers to a native Israelite as the debt slave.[21] This is likely the intended meaning in Exod 21 as well.[22]

This is not to deny that there is a plausible sociological relationship between Hebrew עִבְרִי and Akkadian *ḥābiru/ḥāpiru*, although a cognate linguistic connection is doubtful.[23] One could argue that the Israelites were in the category of *ḥābiru* generally, and that is why the term became used in reference to them in the first place. But in that case, here in Exod 21 it is referring specifically to Israelites who are עִבְרִי delivered out of slavery in Egypt by the Lord their God. In the Hebrew Bible the term גֵּר (resident alien) seems to cover the social (as opposed to ethnic) category of *ḥābiru*.

One of the major differences between the debt-slave regulations in Exod 21 and Deut 15 has to do with the female debt slave. The second part of the Exod 21 turns to the subject of the female debt slave, specifically, a family daughter whom the master has "appointed" (יעד) "for himself" (v. 8) or "for his son"

---

20. See the summary discussion in Sprinkle, *"Book of the Covenant,"* 62–64, and the full argument in favor of this interpretation in Christopher J. H. Wright, *God's People in God's Land: Family, Land, and Property in the Old Testament* (Grand Rapids: Eerdmans, 1990), 253–59; and more briefly, Wright, *Deuteronomy*, 192–93. See also John Sietze Bergsma, *The Jubilee from Leviticus to Qumran: A History of Interpretation*, VTSup 115 (Leiden: Brill, 2007), 134–35 and 144–45, for a favorable response to this theory.

21. Contra the arguments in Wright, *God's People in God's Land*, 254. See "your brother" versus "your foreigner" in Deut 15:3 and the remarks in Daniel I. Block, *Deuteronomy*, NIVAC (Grand Rapids: Zondervan, 2012), 370–71; and J. G. McConville, *Deuteronomy*, ApOTC 5 (Downers Grove, IL: InterVarsity, 2002), 256, 261–63.

22. See, e.g., Nahum M. Sarna, *Exodus*, JPS Torah Commentary (Philadelphia: Jewish Publication Society, 1991), 119, and the extensive discussion in William H. C. Propp, *Exodus 19–40*, AB (New York: Doubleday, 2006), 186–88. Consider also the substantial treatment of the issue in David P. Wright, *Inventing God's Law: How the Covenant Code of the Bible Used and Revised the Laws of Hammurabi* (Oxford: Oxford University Press, 2009), 125–29.

23. Richard S. Hess points out that any cognate relationship between Hebrew עִבְרִי and Akkadian *ḥābiru/ḥāpiru* is unlikely. Hebrew עִבְרִי lacks the *i* vowel between the last two consonants, and the consonantal spelling in Ugaritic has a *p*, not a *b* (personal communication). See also Richard S. Hess, "Alalakh Studies in the Bible: Obstacle or Contribution?" in *Scripture and Other Artifacts: Essays on the Bible and Archaeology in Honor of Philip J. King*, ed. Michael D. Coogan, J. Cheryl Exum, and Lawrence E. Stager (Louisville: Westminster John Knox, 1994), 205–8.

36   Richard E. Averbeck

(v. 9).[24] Raymond Westbrook insists that this refers to concubinage of the daughter, not marriage, since there is no clear indication of a marriage and the relationship is dissolved by the daughter being redeemed out of the relationship, not divorced (v. 8).[25] Others argue that it refers to legal marriage.[26] The latter seems more likely to me, since v. 10 refers to the master "taking" another woman/wife (אִם־אַחֶרֶת יִקַּח־לוֹ; lit., "if he takes another one for himself"). The verb "take" is the standard term for taking a woman in marriage. Also, it seems unlikely that if she was assigned to his son (v. 9), he would need to treat her "as a daughter" if she was not the son's wife.

In any case, the regulation makes it clear that there are protections for the daughter and her family. She does not go out in the seventh year because she is now under the legal protection of the master's household: she has been appointed to her master or his son. If he does not want her, then he must let her family redeem her out of his household. He cannot sell her away from her family to foreigners (v. 8). Thus, if he appoints her for his son he must treat her as one with the rights and privileges of a "daughter" of that household (כְּמִשְׁפַּט הַבָּנוֹת יַעֲשֶׂה־לָּה; lit. "according to the custom of daughters he shall do for her"). Even if neither the master nor his son accepts her as his wife, then he has to provide for her regular needs or else allow her to go out free, with no payment of money; that is, he does not get his money back from his purchase of the daughter.

Deuteronomy 15:12–17, on the other hand, makes it clear that if a woman debt slave was not slated to be a wife in the first place, then she would go out free in the seventh year just like any male debt slave. At least to some scholars, this would appear to be a good way to understand the relationship between Exod 21 and Deut 15. Jeffrey Tigay, for example, agrees that these two texts do not necessarily contradict each other.[27] Many scholars, however, have taken as a cardinal point in their analysis and comparison of these passages that the woman debt slave going free like the male debt slave is an innovation in Deut 15, intending

---

24. Contra Calum Carmichael, "The Three Laws on the Release of Slaves," *ZAW* 112, no. 4 (2000): 515–18, I take the *qere* reading in v. 8 ("for himself"; לוֹ), not the *ketiv* ("not"; לֹא). This seems to be the more natural reading, especially in light of the parallel in v. 9, where he designates her "for his son" (לִבְנוֹ) and the *lamed* preposition clearly means "to" or "for." See also the discussion in Wright, *Inventing God's Law*, 132–33.

25. Westbrook, "Female Slave," 150–56. See also Brevard S. Childs, *The Book of Exodus: A Critical, Theological Commentary*, OTL (Louisville: Westminster John Knox, 1974), 469. Propp suggests we should allow for both options, marriage or concubinage (*Exodus*, 196–200).

26. See, e.g., Sarna, *Exodus*, 120–21; and Douglas K. Stuart, *Exodus*, NAC 2 (Nashville: Broadman & Holman, 2006), 481–83; and now Wright, *Inventing God's Law*, 132 and n. 51.

27. See the helpful discussion in Tigay, *Deuteronomy*, 148–49, 466. He argues that "it is possible that the two laws refer to different cases," recognizing that Deut 15:12–17 is not taking into consideration the marital issues for the debt slave woman in Exod 21:7–11. See also Bergsma, *Jubilee from Leviticus to Qumran*, 136n118 and the literature cited there.

The Exodus, Debt Slavery, and the Composition of the Pentateuch   37

to revise or subvert Exod 21.[28] For instance, Jack Lundbom argues regarding Deut 15:12–18, "The present law reworks an earlier law in Exod 21:2–11, embellishing its legal provisions . . . , but also making substantive changes, e.g., in putting the Hebrew woman on an equal footing with the Hebrew man. . . . Also, under the old law, if a man sold his daughter into slavery, she would not go free as male slaves do (Exod 21:7). But here in Deuteronomy, both the Hebrew man and Hebrew woman—without qualification—go free in the seventh year."[29]

Similarly, Bernard Levinson notes the shift between Exod 21:2–6 and 7–11 and argues, "This insistence upon separate protocols based upon gender is pointedly rejected by Deuteronomy's manumission law: וְאַף לַאֲמָתְךָ תַּעֲשֶׂה־כֵּן, 'Even with respect to your female slave, you must do likewise' (Deut 15:17b). The formal exegetical analogy here responds to that of the Covenant Code. At issue is an innovation in the law that is only intelligible as a conscious revision of a legal *and textual* precedent. . . . Whereas the Covenant Code has two separate laws concerned with manumission, one for male slaves and another for female slaves, Deuteronomy folds both laws into a single law."[30]

For Lundbom and Levinson, and many others, there is no other way to read the relationship between the Exod 21 and Deut 15 debt-slave regulations. Levinson, in particular, points out that the Hebrew expression אָחִיךָ הָעִבְרִי אוֹ הָעִבְרִיָּה (lit. "your brother, the male Hebrew or the female Hebrew") in Deut 15:12 awkwardly uses both a male and female form of "Hebrew" for the male "brother." Moreover, he argues that verse 17b (וְאַף לַאֲמָתְךָ תַּעֲשֶׂה־כֵּן "Even with respect to your female slave, you must do likewise") "seems superfluous given the law's protasis" (cf. v. 12 just above), and v. 18 "reverts to the masculine focus" of the previous verses.[31]

In spite of our many disagreements, I have long appreciated the close reading of the Hebrew text evident in Levinson's work, and certainly respect his grasp of both the primary text and the secondary literature. Here we have come upon one of our major areas of disagreement. The only other occurrence of the singular "female Hebrew" (הָעִבְרִיָּה) in the Hebrew Bible is Jer 34:9,

לְשַׁלַּח אִישׁ אֶת־עַבְדּוֹ וְאִישׁ אֶת־שִׁפְחָתוֹ הָעִבְרִי וְהָעִבְרִיָּה חָפְשִׁים לְבִלְתִּי עֲבָד־בָּם בִּיהוּדִי אָחִיהוּ אִישׁ:

---

28. See, e.g., Gerhard von Rad, *Deuteronomy: A Commentary*, OTL (Philadelphia: Westminster, 1966), 107; Jack R. Lundbom, *Deuteronomy* (Grand Rapids: Eerdmans, 2013), 494; Levinson, "Manumission of Hermeneutics," 301–4.

29. Lundbom, *Deuteronomy*, 494.

30. Levinson, "Manumission of Hermeneutics," 301 (emphasis original).

31. See ibid., 302–3 and the literature cited there.

38 Richard E. Averbeck

Each man is to send out his male servant and his female servant, the male
Hebrew and the female Hebrew free, so that each man does not enslave
his Judean brother.

In verse 9b "his brother" is used in reference to both the male and the female
Hebrew debt slave in verse 9a, recalling Deut 15 in this and other ways throughout the passage. Deuteronomy 15:12 is more elliptical, but I am not convinced
that we should prefer the more redundant form in Jer 34:9a. Since this combination of male and female Hebrew is only called for twice in the entire Hebrew
Bible it seems questionable to make so much of the "asymmetry" of the text in
Deut 15:12, as Levinson puts it. Furthermore, it seems to me that the repetition
of the application of the same law to the female debt slave in Deut 15:17b only
reinforces what has been introduced in verse 12 in light of the rest of the law
being put into the masculine. In fact, it is quite a good structural device. The
next verse then comes back and reinforces the need to obey this regulation so
that the Lord's blessing would be upon them in the promised land, again in the
characteristic masculine grammar of the passage.

Levinson goes on to add that the centralization of the sanctuary required by
Deut 12 changes the venue of the ceremony for the debt slave who prefers to
remain with his (or her) master perpetually. Exodus 21:6 requires that the master
take the debt slave "before God" (אֶל־הָאֱלֹהִים)[32] and pierce his ear "into the door
or doorpost" (אֶל־הַדֶּלֶת אוֹ אֶל־הַמְּזוּזָה), whereas Deut 15:17 says simply "in(to) the
door" (וּבַדֶּלֶת). In Deut 15 this would be the door of a domestic home, since there
were no local sanctuaries allowed in Deut 12, but Exod 21:6 would require performing this rite before God at the local sanctuary (cf. Exod 20:24–26), according to Levinson.

In my view, yes, there is revision here. As noted above in the discussion of
method, according to the text there is a forty-year gap between the Law as it was
given at Sinai and that in Deuteronomy, and the situation has changed. Deuteronomy has Israel ready to enter into the promised land to conquer and occupy it.
This means they will be spread out in the land, as Levinson notes. Thus, certain
revisions in Deuteronomy allow for this change in the anticipated situation of
the people. Deuteronomy 15:17, therefore, calls for a change in the procedure
for piercing the ear, just as Deut 12:15–25 does for solitary slaughter.[33]

Furthermore, as Levinson notes, Deut 15:13–15 emphasizes "the dignity and
agency" of the debt slave.[34] The master is to provide him (or her) with plenty of

---

32. See the full discussion of whether this means "before God" or "before the judges/elders"
in Propp, *Exodus*, 192–95.

33. See the detailed discussion of Deut 12 and revision of the law in Averbeck, "Cult in
Deuteronomy."

34. Levinson, "Manumission of Hermeneutics," 304.

The Exodus, Debt Slavery, and the Composition of the Pentateuch   39

supplies to get started again when he (or she) leaves his household (vv. 13–14). The rationale is given as, "Remember that you were a slave in the land of Egypt, but the Lord your God redeemed you. For this reason I am commanding you with regard to this matter today" (v. 15).[35] This rationale for legal regulations based on the exodus from Egypt is characteristic of Deuteronomy. See, for instance, the rationale for the Sabbath in Deut 5:14–15 as compared to that in Exod 20:11, as well as other instances of exodus rationale in Deut 6:12, 20–25; 7:8, 18; 8:14; 9:12, 25–29; 10:19; 13:11; 16:1–3, 6, 12; 20:1; 24:17–22; 25:17; 26:5–10. The debt-slave regulations in Exod 21:2–11 do not include this concern for supply of the debt slave when the master releases him (or her), whether male or female. Deuteronomy has added it, but there is no contradiction between Exod 21 and Deut 15. One deals with it; one does not.

Recently, Joshua Berman has offered a careful and convincing explanation and evaluation of the two basic methodologies used in comparing the parallel legal regulations in the three major collections of law in the Torah.[36] On the one hand, he calls the method used by Levinson, Stackert, and Lundbom "supersessionist," meaning that when the authors of later law collections revised older ones they intended that the new law supersede the old one. On the other hand, he refers to the kind of approach I have offered here, comparing Exod 21:2–11 with Deut 15:12–18 as "complementary," meaning that the revising authors did not consider their revisions to be rejections of the standing of the earlier laws, but complementary to them, or reapplications of them. Scholars who follow this latter method include, for example, the lamented Raymond Westbrook, Barry L. Eichler, Eckart Otto, and Bruce Wells. Berman argues that the supersessionist approach relies upon modern views of "statutory law" rather than the "common law" practice of the ANE and, therefore, skews the intent of legal revision.

In my view, the distinction between statutory and common law must be taken into consideration in reading the Torah. Berman shows that the supersessionist approach to the reading of the comparisons between the law collections in the Torah is misleading. I do wonder, however, whether the distinction is absolute, or more on a continuum between the two ends of a line between them. One of the main features of ANE law is that the extant law collections (e.g., the laws of Urnammu, Lipit-Ishtar, and Hammurabi, etc.) do not make cross-references to each other and are not referred to in actual court cases and documents. They contain common law. In the Hebrew Bible, however, there are cases of

---

35. A good argument can be made that the exodus from Egypt provides the overall rationale of the Law in the Torah. See the full discussion of this feature of the Law in Averbeck, "Egyptian Sojourn and Deliverance," 143–75. See also the helpful remarks on this matter regarding Lev 25 and all of Lev 17–26 in Nihan, *From Priestly Torah to Pentateuch*, 533–35.

36. Joshua Berman, "Supersessionist or Complementary? Reassessing the Nature of Legal Revision in the Pentateuchal Law Collections," *JBL* 135, no. 2 (2016): 201–22.

40   Richard E. Averbeck

cross-reference of a sort, for example, when the text apparently refers to the Decalogue as given in Exod 20 or the legal regulations in Leviticus or Numbers with the expression "as I (or, 'the Lord God') have (has) commanded you" (Deut 5:12, 16; 12:21; 18:2; 24:8).[37] It seems that in the Hebrew Bible the laws fit somewhere on the continuum between the two extremes.

One major feature of the common law approach characteristic of the ANE is that the laws were not drafted "to cover every aspect of a given issue. Rather, each code selected only the facets necessary for its own discussion."[38] In my view, this is where Levinson and Lundbom, and others like them, fail in their comparative reading of the debt-slave regulations. The female regulations in Exod 21:7–11 do not stand opposed by the debt-slave regulations in Deut 15:12–18. They are dealing with different sets of concerns. In Exod 21 they are concerned with the situation in which "a man sells his daughter as a female slave" (וְכִי־יִמְכֹּר אִישׁ אֶת־בִּתּוֹ לְאָמָה). As noted above, the following verses make it clear that she is being sold not simply as a female slave, but as one who would become a wife (or concubine) of the master or his son. This is part of the data of the regulation. As a matter of fact, in Exod 21:2–11 both the male debt-slave (vv. 2–6) and the female debt-slave (vv. 7–11) regulations focus a good deal of their attention on issues of marital status (vv. 3–5 and 8–10), whereas Deut 15:12–18 says nothing of the matter. Fathers and daughters, husbands and wives, are not even contemplated. The latter text simply did not intend to contemplate the same issues as the former.

I find it distressing that this is virtually ignored, overlooked, or simply over-ridden by those who read Deut 15 as a subversive revision of female debt slav-ery in Exod 21. This is a rather cavalier way to treat such important primary textual data. It is an example of the theory overriding the verifiable data of the text as if the theory were data (see the remarks on method above). The two pas-sages are not referring to the same kind of female debt slavery in the first place. To read the text as if they do is to "level" the text to create a "flat" reading of it.

To take this one step further, the supplying of the debt slave upon release in Deut 15 should be seen as a revision of Exod 21, but not in such a way that it denies the ongoing validity of the older law. It simply adds a feature to the law that is in keeping with the theology of Deuteronomy. Yes, there is revision here, but not subversion. In other words, Deut 15 is not against the overall intentions and regulations as given in Exod 21. The latter simply highlights other kinds of protections for certain kinds of male and female debt slaves. This brings us to the relationship between the debt-slave regulations in Exod 21 and Deut 15 as compared to Lev 25.

---

37. See even the remarks on this in Berman, "Supersessionist or Complementary," 222.
38. Ibid., 210–11, summarizing the views of Westbrook and Eichler.

Exodus 21:2–11 and Deuteronomy 15:12–18 Compared to Leviticus 25:39–55

Leviticus 25 raises the issue of debt-slavery regulations to a whole different level. Even Tigay agrees that the debt-slavery and release regulations in Lev 25 most certainly subvert the regulations in Exod 21 and Deut 15.[39] One of the most obvious differences is that in Exod 21:2 and Deut 15:12 the debt slave serves for six years and goes out in the seventh, while Lev 25:40, 54 has him going out in the year of Jubilee. Thus, he could theoretically serve as a debt slave for as many as forty-nine years. The regular harmonistic approach is to argue that the debt slave serves six years (Exod 21:2; Deut 15:12) unless the Jubilee Year intervenes, in which case the slave goes free at the Jubilee (Lev 25:40). Moreover, even if he chooses to continue as a debt slave to his master after the six years (Exod 21:5–6; Deut 15:16–17), or is indebted to a resident alien or stranger and has not been redeemed by his family (Lev 25:47–53), he must still go free in the Jubilee (Lev 25:54–55). Tigay effectively refutes this explanation and argues that "Leviticus 25 represents a system for the relief of the poverty that is independent of the one in Exodus and Deuteronomy." He leaves open the question of whether Lev 25 derives from a different time and/or place than Exod 21 and Deut 15, or whether "it simply reflects the approach of another school of thought."[40]

Bernard Levinson, and following him Jeffrey Stackert, argue vehemently for the debt slave laws in Lev 25 as a text whose author(s) intended to subvert the regulations in Exod 21 and Deut 15.[41] More recently, Mark Leuchter has presented a rather elaborate argument for how a careful reading of Jer 34:9–16 will support the Levinson and Stackert rationale for reading the Lev 25 debt-slave regulation as a subversion of the Deut 15 regulation, as well as Exod 21.[42] To them it is not a matter of just another school of thought being expressed. Levinson makes much of the importance of rendering Lev 25:46a as follows:

וְהִתְנַחַלְתֶּם אֹתָם לִבְנֵיכֶם אַחֲרֵיכֶם לָרֶשֶׁת אֲחֻזָּה לְעֹלָם בָּהֶם תַּעֲבֹדוּ

---

39. Tigay, *Deuteronomy*, 466–67.

40. Ibid.

41. See esp. Levinson, "Manumission of Hermeneutics," 305–22; and Stackert, *Rewriting the Torah*, 141–64. As Berman notes, Stackert, unlike Levinson, does not think of this as a covert way of subverting the older text, but as a way to use its prestige to promote the legal innovation of the new revision (Berman, "Supersessionist or Complementary," 205–6 and 220–21).

42. Leuchter, "Manumission Laws," 635–53. See also the "reflections" on Levinson's understanding of legal revision in John Elwolde, "'Inner-Biblical Exegesis' and Bible Translation: Reflections on Bernard Levinson's *Legal Revision and Religious Renewal in Ancient Israel*," *Review of Rabbinic Judaism* 14 (2011): 223–34.

42 Richard E. Averbeck

You may give them [i.e., foreign slaves] as an inheritance to your sons after you to possess (them as) property. *You may enslave them perpetually.*[43]

After a good deal of helpful discussion, he concludes that we should read לְעֹלָם "perpetually" as the first word in the second clause, not the conclusion to the previous clause, as for example in the LXX "and they shall be your possession perpetually" (καὶ ἔσονται ὑμῖν κατόχιμοι εἰς τὸν αἰῶνα; the LXX leaves out the following "you may enslave them"). The ESV and NLT (perhaps the NRSV as well), for example, follow the LXX rendering, while the NIV and NASB reflect Levinson's analysis. I agree with this part of Levinson's treatment of the passage. The next step is the problem.

He goes on to argue that the text "cites the Covenant Code technical term for permanent indenture." Here he is referring back to the voluntary perpetual slavery in Exod 21:5–6, "But if the slave openly says, 'I love my master, my wife, and my children; I will not go out free,' then his master shall bring him to God and bring him to the door or door post and pierce his ear with an awl and he shall serve him perpetually (וַעֲבָדוֹ לְעֹלָם)." He concludes, "As a result, the older law has, for all practical purposes, been abrogated in terms of its original application to Israelites."[44] According to Levinson, Lev 25:46 abrogates the regulation in Exod 21:6, which allows for perpetual slavery of an Israelite, and applies it to foreign slaves instead. But there are serious problems with his argument.

Most significantly, Lev 25:46 does not actually use the Covenant Code's terminology for perpetual slavery. In Lev 25:46 the expression combines לְעֹלָם (perpetually) with the Qal verb עבד plus the preposition ב indicating the direct object, and the subject of the verb is the master(s), not the slave(s).[45] This combination of verb and preposition, with this syntax, means "to press into slavery; put to forced labor." It means this all ten times it occurs in the Hebrew Bible with reference to human slavery (Exod 1:14; Lev 25:39, 46; Jer 22:13; 25:14;

---

43. See Levinson, "Manumission of Hermeneutics," 305–16. This verse has been of special interest to me since I prepared the NET translation of Leviticus, which Levinson cites positively (Levinson, "Manumission of Hermeneutics," 313n87).

44. Levinson, "Manumission of Hermeneutics," 314. Stackert follows Levinson in this and other points of his argument; see Stackert, *Rewriting the Torah*, 154 and n. 94.

45. See *TDOT* 10:382. There is some question whether the ב here is instrumental or whether it indicates the direct object. In the discussion here it is treated as an indicator of the direct object. Levinson is fully aware of the distinctiveness of this verbal construction (Levinson, "Manumission of Hermeneutics," 305–6n69), but he does not recognize its real significance for the issue at hand. He writes, "H's rejection of the CC and D terminology of slavery with reference to the Israelite slave is underscored by its reapplication of this language to the foreigner, who alone may be enslaved. Both the initial protasis of the CC law and its formula for permanent indenture are reused in the second section of the Holiness Code's law (vv. 44–46)" (ibid., 306). The fact of the matter is that neither Exod 21 nor Deut 15 ever uses the Lev 25:39–46 terminology for permanent indenture.

27:7; 30:8; 34:9, 10; Ezek 34:27).[46] It occurs first in Exod 1:14, which refers to the Egyptians pressing the Israelites into slavery, "They made their lives bitter with harsh labor in mortar and brick, and in all field labor; all their labor they imposed on them (אֵת כָּל־עֲבֹדָתָם אֲשֶׁר־עָבְדוּ בָהֶם) with harshness (בְּפָרֶךְ)." We will come back to this verse in the discussion below.

Jeremiah 22:13 is part of a woe oracle against the one who "makes his own neighbor work for nothing (בְּרֵעֵהוּ יַעֲבֹד חִנָּם)." Jeremiah 25:14 refers to the Babylonians as those whom "many nations will enslave (עָבְדוּ־בָם גַּם־הֵמָּה גּוֹיִם רַבִּים)," and Jer 27:7 makes the same point with essentially the same terminology, but in reference to Nebuchadnezzar, "and many nations will subjugate him (וְעָבְדוּ בוֹ גּוֹיִם רַבִּים)." With regard to Israel, their restoration will include the fact that, in the coming day, "foreigners will enslave them no longer (וְלֹא־יַעַבְדוּ־בוֹ עוֹד זָרִים)" (Jer 30:8). Jeremiah 34:9–10 concerns the enslavement of fellow Israelites. In Judah "no one was to enslave his Judean brother (לְבִלְתִּי עֲבָד־בָּם בִּיהוּדִי אָחִיהוּ אִישׁ . . .)" (v. 9), so they made a covenant to the effect that they would release them and committed "not to enslave them again" (עוֹד (לְבִלְתִּי עֲבָד־בָּם עוֹד)" (v. 10). Unfortunately, they broke this covenant when they resubjugated (read the Qal form of כבשׁ "to subjugate" in the *qere*) the male and female slaves again (v. 11). The use of this verb here reinforces the understanding of עבד plus the preposition ב on the direct object as a reference not just to being a slave, but to forceful subjection to slavery. Finally, Ezek 34:27b looks forward to the time when the Israelites will know the Lord as the one who delivers them from the hand of "those who enslave them" (הָעֹבְדִים בָּהֶם).

The point is that the expression in Lev 25:46a means something quite different from the parallels in Exodus and Deuteronomy. Exodus 21:6 uses the Qal verb עבד, but without the preposition, and the subject of the verb is the one who is voluntarily entering into perpetual slavery, not the master (contrast Lev 25:46a, see above). The parallel passage in Deut 15:17 uses the noun, not the

---

46. See Abraham Even-Shoshan, *A New Concordance of the Hebrew Bible* (Jerusalem: "Kiryat Sefer," 1989), 817, meaning ד, and HALOT 773–74, meaning 5b (only nine occurrences listed here; they missed Jer 27:7). Meaning 5a also has six other occurrences of ב construed with the verb עבד, but as an indirect object (essentially a ב of price; i.e., one serves in order to obtain something or someone), not a direct object. See also the indirect object of location, for example, in Num 4:23, ". . . who come to serve (לַעֲבֹד) in the work at (בְּ) the tent of meeting." None of these occurrences match the syntax of the verb plus preposition in the passages we are concerned with here, where the subject of the verb is the one who is doing the enslaving and the object of the verb (indicated by the ב) is the one whom they are enslaving.

Note also the remarks on this construction in Jacob Milgrom, *Leviticus 23–27: A New Translation with Introduction and Commentary*, AB 3B (New York: Doubleday, 2001), 2220, where he also refers to J. G. McConville, *Law and Theology in Deuteronomy*, JSOTSup 33 (Sheffield: JSOT Press, 1984), 95–96. McConville takes note of the fact that the same syntactic combination appears, for example, in the regulation against working a firstborn ox (Deut 15:19) and in a few other places. These passages are not discussed here, since our subject is human slavery.

44   Richard E. Averbeck

verb at all, so again without the preposition. In terms of both their context and their lexical diction, the latter are expressions of voluntary perpetual slavery, which is very different from being pressed into slavery. Leviticus 25:46a in no way abrogates what is being legislated in Exod 21:6, or for that matter, Deut 15:17 either. Leviticus 25:46b, in fact, tells us that it was never intended that any Israelite would suffer this "harsh" (בְּפָרֶךְ) treatment (see also vv. 43 and 53; cf. Exod 1:14 above):

וּבְאַחֵיכֶם בְּנֵי־יִשְׂרָאֵל אִישׁ בְּאָחִיו לֹא־תִרְדֶּה בוֹ בְּפָרֶךְ

but among your brothers the sons of Israel, a man with his brother, you must not rule over him with harshness.

Actually, Levinson's argument is backwards. A careful reading of the text turns us around the opposite way so that we look at it from the other direction. As noted above, the same verbal expression (the Qal verb עבד with the preposition ב, meaning "to press into slavery") appears in Exod 1:14 for the Egyptians pressing the Israelites into slavery. So when the same terminology appears again at the beginning of the debt-slave regulations in Lev 25:39 (just a few verses earlier than v. 46), the point is that they must never press fellow Israelites into slavery like the Egyptians had done to them as a nation:

וְכִי־יָמוּךְ אָחִיךָ עִמָּךְ וְנִמְכַּר־לָךְ לֹא־תַעֲבֹד בּוֹ עֲבֹדַת עָבֶד:

And if your brother becomes destitute with regard to you and sells himself to you, you must not press him into service as a slave.

The Lord himself had delivered all of them from that (v. 38), so they cannot do it to one another. Instead, they should treat one another with all due respect, even when someone among them became destitute. This does not mean they could not be treated as "debt slaves" (as in Exod 21 and Deut 15). Yes, the destitute one could "sell himself" to them (v. 39), but the term "slave" is never used in the context in reference to him in order to make sure they are not treated as those who were "pressed into slavery" (as they were in Egypt). Only foreign slaves could be pressed into permanent and even generational slavery (vv. 44–46, discussed above). As Joshua Berman has put it: "The author of Lev 25 addressed the institution of the Jubilee, to take one example, and hence speaks of release during the Jubilee Year. We cannot know his opinion about release following the six-year term of work found in Exod 21 and Deut 15; these were not his subject matter. Within the statutory jurisprudence employed by supersessionists, textual silence in a code speaks with a full voice. Strict construction, however, should

The Exodus, Debt Slavery, and the Composition of the Pentateuch   45

not automatically guide the interpretation of a text whose culture has no knowledge of statutory law."[47] The question remains, however, how exactly does what Lev 25 prescribes relate to that which Exod 21 and Deut 15 prescribe? Why do we have such variations in Lev 25?

John Bergsma has also proposed that Lev 25 and Deut 15 simply "address two very different contexts." One does not contradict or subvert the other. The goal of the Jubilee debt-slave regulation is the agrarian concern to guard the landed Israelite—the *paterfamilias*—from being "reduced to slave status, rather only an indentured servanthood (Lev 25:39–40)," whereas the Deut 15 is focused on the urban context, where "the clan structure loses its significance and the nuclear family becomes more important." Thus, the "*shemittah* release (fallow) for the land every seven years . . . (Exod 23:11), becomes transformed into a *shemittah* that makes sense for an urban economy and benefits the urban poor: a *shemittah* of debts (Deut 15:1–11)."[48]

Therefore, the focus of debt slavery also shifts to "the many landless poor who may have congregated in the city to seek a living." It is for this reason that Bergsma follows Wright and Chirichigno in their proposal that עִבְרִי (and עִבְרִיָּה) in Exod 21:2 and Deut 15:12 refers to landless nonethnic Israelites who depended on landowning Israelites for their sustenance. He points out that the debt slave in Exod 21 and Deut 15 apparently does not have a landed inheritance to which he might return.[49]

On the one hand, there is much in Bergsma's discussion that has good potential for understanding the distinction between Lev 25 and Deut 15 (see also Exod 23:11), especially in regard to the shift from the agrarian to the urban focus of the *shemittah* (Deut 15:1–11). On the other hand, as noted above, I do not find his view of עִבְרִי compelling in the least.[50] Moreover, the fact of the matter is that six/seven-year ethnic Israelite debt slaves would not necessarily have the option of returning to their landed inheritance if it was not yet the year of Jubilee. Neither Exod 21 nor Deut 15 contemplates the Jubilee, of course. Ethnic Israelite debt slaves could well belong to a *paterfamilias* that has lost the family land through debt. This is one of the key differences between Exod 21 and Deut 15 as compared to Lev 25:39–41. The latter refers specifically to a *paterfamilias* (וְיָצָא מֵעִמָּךְ הוּא וּבָנָיו עִמּוֹ וְשָׁב אֶל־מִשְׁפַּחְתּוֹ וְאֶל־אֲחֻזַּת אֲבֹתָיו יָשׁוּב׃ "And he shall go out from you, he and his sons/children with him and shall return to his clan, and to the possession of his fathers he shall return"), while Exod 21 and Deut 15 assume the person may not even be married, much less with children, when he enters

---

47. Berman, "Supersessionist or Complementary," 211. See also the important review of arguments and objections to Levinson in Kilchör, *Mosetora und Jahwetora*, 145–46.

48. Bergsma, *Jubilee from Leviticus to Qumran*, 143.

49. See ibid., 144–45.

50. See the overall discussion above (at n. 20).

46   Richard E. Averbeck

into slavery, so he could not be a *paterfamilias* (see esp. Exod 21:3–5; and note that Deut 15:12–18 does not even bring up the issue).

It is important to keep in mind that the main subject in this part of Lev 25 is the year of Jubilee. This law, therefore, is written as part of the ongoing regulations for the fiftieth-year release. In my view, Adrian Schenker has a made a better argument for the position that the debt-slave laws in Lev 25 supplement and complement those in Exod 21 and Deut 15.[51] Like Levinson, Stackert, and others, he holds that the Holiness Code is later than Deuteronomy. Nevertheless, he writes in his first paragraph, "My purpose is to show that the jubilee of Lev 25 does not supersede the earlier biblical legislation on slaves, but implies and completes it."[52] In other words, the various slave laws are not contradictory, but complementary, no matter which Code depends on which.

Schenker contends that Exod 21 and Lev 25 are actually referring to two different categories of debt slaves: one who enters debt slavery single or married but without children in Exod 21:2–3, as opposed to one who enters debt slavery married and with children in Lev 25:39–43 (note esp. v. 41). The latter is the head of a family who enters slavery at a point of destitution. His circumstances have deteriorated to the point where he has even lost his landed inheritance due to debt. Thus, he enters "debt slavery," although he is not to be treated as a "slave" but "as a hired worker, as a temporary resident" (v. 40).[53] His purpose is not limited to paying off his debt, however. Part of the arrangement is that the master is responsible to provide for him and his whole family until the Jubilee. At that time his family land inheritance will revert back to him, so he can once again begin providing for his family from the produce of his own land. It would make no sense for such a person to go out of debt slavery before his land reverted back to him. That would leave him without the necessary resources with which to begin again.

On the master's part, there is a great deal of expense in providing for a whole family along with debt forgiveness. There would be little incentive to take on such a financial burden if the time period was limited to six years. So, in the case of a man who is the head of a family, the period of debt slavery needs to extend beyond the regular six-year period. Of course, if the period from the point of entering the debt-slavery agreement to the year of Jubilee is longer, there is

51. Adrian Schenker, "The Biblical Legislation on the Release of Slaves: The Road from Exodus to Leviticus," *JSOT* 78 (1998): 23–41, esp. 32–34; repr. in Schenker, *Recht und Kult im Alten Testament: Achtzehn Studien*, OBO 172 (Göttingen: Vandenhoeck & Ruprecht; Freiburg: Universitätsverlag Freiburg Schweiz, 2000), 134–49. See the earlier discussion of Schenker's proposal in Averbeck, "Egyptian Sojourn and Deliverance," 173–75, some of which is simply repeated here.

52. Schenker, "Biblical Legislation," 23. Levinson cites this sentence negatively in his last footnote in "Manumission of Hermeneutics," 323.

53. The term "temporary resident" (תּוֹשָׁב) can be paired with either "hired man" (שָׂכִיר; v. 40) or "resident alien" (גֵּר; v. 47). In the former it refers to an Israelite, and in the latter a non-Israelite.

The Exodus, Debt Slavery, and the Composition of the Pentateuch 47

more incentive for the master to do so, and if it is shorter there is less. This was a concern elsewhere in the ANE as well, as William Hallo has pointed out.[54] On the other hand, generosity toward one's fellow Israelite is part of the overall burden of Lev 25 to begin with.

In light of the complementary analysis of the relationship between the debt-slave regulations in the Torah as outlined above, the developmental scenario proposed here would go something like this. First, the debt-slave regulations in Exod 21:2–11 attend to certain considerations for poor Israelites who are not married, or at least do not have children that go into slavery with them. They might even enter slavery as part of a larger (landed) family's management of their debt. Second, Lev 25:39–43 adds special considerations for a *paterfamilias*, a father with his family (wife or wives and children), who has become so destitute that there is no option left but for the *paterfamilias* to "sell himself" (and his family) as an indentured servant until the year of Jubilee, when his landed estate will revert back to him.

Third, in the context of the seventh-year debt-relief regulations (Deut 15:1–11), the debt-slave regulations in Deut 15:12–18 follow the basic principles in Exod 21:2–11. However, the focus in Deut 15 is on individual independent male and female debt slaves without regard to marital status (contra Exod 21), and the need for the master to send them out with plenty of provisions to get a new start, in accordance with the ethos of regulations in Lev 25:39–43. Since Deut 15:12–18 is in the context of seventh-year debt relief and not the Jubilee, however, it does not consider the matter of going back to a landed inheritance.

Conclusion

The first part of this essay argues for a kind of approach to the scholarly historical-critical study of the Hebrew Bible that takes a "generous" approach to the text. We need to take historical-critical work seriously, but without the negative bias that it has toward the text as it stands. Both synchronic and diachronic analyses are important, but need to be pursued without falling into the pit of the diachronic fallacy or stepping into the trap of simplistic harmonizations. It is important to let the text have its own say about its own compositional processes, although it is not always explicit about such matters. There is a lot of open territory.

---

54. William W. Hallo, "Slave Release in the Biblical World in Light of a New Text," in *Solving Riddles and Untying Knots: Biblical, Epigraphic, and Semitic Studies in Honor of Jonas C. Greenfield*, ed. Ziony Zevit, Seymour Gitin, and Michael Sokoloff (Winona Lake, IN: Eisenbrauns, 1995), 88–93. See also Schenker, "Biblical Legislation," 33, 38–39; and Leuchter, "Manumission Laws," 638.

48   Richard E. Averbeck

This means we need to make a clear distinction between verifiable data (from the Bible itself and the ANE) and theories about that data, and not confuse the two, whether conservative or nonconservative. In turn, it is also essential to distinguish between what we believe to be true and what we can actually show to be true. It is true that an argument that is convincing to one scholar may not be to another. This will always be true because there is so much open territory. That is why we need to consider seriously the arguments presented by other scholars, engage with them squarely and fairly in an intellectually honest way, and present our own arguments with the same principles clearly in mind.

It will be for the reader to decide whether my application of these principles and procedures to the debt-slave regulations in the Torah has been up to the standards or not. In my view, these regulations are complementary, not contradictory. They come from different perspectives on various parts of the problem that debt slavery represents; namely the economic distress that led to it in the lives of real people and families in ancient Israel. There are both synchronic and diachronic exegetical issues at hand here, but there is no subversion or contradiction. Other proposals have been made, of course, and the discussion continues among scholars, but, as for me, I consider this to be the best way to read these texts in relation to one another. In my view, this is where the evidence takes us when we face it squarely and fairly, with neither negative bias toward the text as it stands nor simplistic harmonization.

CHAPTER 3

Egyptian Language Practice:
A Model for Hebrew Poetic Use?

L. S. Baker Jr. and A. Rahel Wells
Andrews University

Introduction

As happens with every language, Hebrew has developed through the ebbs and flows of time, adjusting to new dynamics and influences from the experiences of those who used it to communicate on a day-to-day basis, and also resisting change through the repetitions of oral readings of ancient texts written in it.[1] In pentateuchal studies, there is debate whether this development can be clearly seen or even exists at all.[2]

Some claim, for example, that the poetic portions of Exod 15 appear to be of an older language stage of Hebrew than the prose sections that surround it, while others maintain that it is of the same composition phase because the Hebrew used in both (poetry and prose) is of the same language stage. Is it possible for both to be right, or is there a third alternative?

This essay will review the arguments in the debate and then examine another partially Semitic language, Egyptian, to see if its language practices may shed light on an intriguing possibility that may explain what is happening in Exod 15.

Hebrew Language Practice

Hebrew poetry is generally considered harder to date than Hebrew prose. Most scholars divide the history of the Hebrew language into three main groups:

---

1. For discussions on this relationship, see Susan Niditch, *Oral World and Written Word: Ancient Israelite Literature* (Louisville: Westminster John Knox, 1996); and David M. Carr, *Writing on the Tablet of the Heart: Origins of Scripture and Literature* (Oxford: Oxford University Press, 2005). For a general overview of relevant ancient Near Eastern texts, see Kenton L. Sparks, *Ancient Texts for the Study of the Hebrew Bible: A Guide to the Background Literature* (Peabody, MA: Hendrickson, 2005).

2. For instance, Robyn C. Vern notes that "the variety of dating outcomes which linguistic evidence yields contradicts claims of objectivity and autonomy of linguistic evidence for dating purposes" (*Dating Archaic Biblical Hebrew Poetry: Critique of the Linguistic Arguments*, Perspectives on Hebrew Scriptures and Its Contexts 10 [Piscataway, NJ: Gorgias, 2011], 241).

49

50   L. S. Baker Jr. and A. Rahel Wells

Archaic Biblical Hebrew (ABH), Classical Biblical Hebrew (CBH, usually considered to be preexilic), and Late Biblical Hebrew (LBH, usually considered to be postexilic).[3] Poetic texts, on the other hand, are usually believed to be older than prose accounts of the same event, and are often assumed to be ABH (or concurrent with early CBH). For instance, Exod 15 is thought to be older than Exod 14, and Judg 5 older than Judg 4. There are several possible options for this appearance of age in poetry: (1) different language stages and different composition phases; (2) same language stage and same composition phase; or (3) different language stages but the same relative composition phase.

For the sake of simplicity, this essay will focus considerations of dating Hebrew poetry on the text of Exod 15. The Song of the Sea has been alternatively called a hymn, a thanksgiving psalm, an enthronement psalm, and a liturgy, but the characterization as a victory psalm seems the most likely based on connections to other victory songs.[4]

Although some have argued for Exod 15 having been written much later (e.g., late preexilic monarchy due to its cultic nature),[5] most scholars consider the older language and the "purely mythic character" of the poem to suggest an early date of composition, with a later composition phase for its integration into the narrative (different language stages and different composition phases).[6] Indeed, A. M. Butts recently noted that "over the past half century, it has become increasingly clear that Exod 15:1–18 is probably one of the oldest texts in the Hebrew Bible."[7] Archaic linguistic forms and obscure words, which have made

---

3. Among others, see Avi Hurvitz, "Can Biblical Texts Be Dated Linguistically? Chronological Perspectives in the Historical Study of Biblical Hebrew," in *Congress Volume Oslo*, ed. A. Lemaire and M. Saebo, VTSup 80 (Leiden: Brill, 2000), 123–42; Ian Young and Robert Rezetko, *Linguistic Dating of Biblical Texts*, vol. 1, *An Introduction to Approaches and Problems* (London: Equinox, 2008); Ian Young, Robert Rezetko, and Martin Ehrensvärd, *Linguistic Dating of Biblical Texts*, vol. 2, *A Survey of Scholarship, a New Synthesis, and a Comprehensive Bibliography* (London: Equinox, 2008); Jan Joosten, *The Verbal System of Biblical Hebrew: A New Synthesis Elaborated on the Basis of Classical Prose*, JBS 10 (Jerusalem: Simor, 2012), 8.

4. Richard D. Patterson, "Victory at Sea: Prose and Poetry in Exodus 14–15," *BSac* 181 (2004): 47–48.

5. F. M. Cross, *Canaanite Myth and Hebrew Epic* (Cambridge, MA: Harvard University Press, 1973), 120–23. A few even see this song as the product of the Persian period due to the connections with temple theology. For example, see Anja Klein, "Hymn and History in Ex 15: Observations on the Relationship Between Temple Theology and Exodus Narrative in the Song of the Sea," *ZAW* 124, no. 4 (2012): 516–27. Robyn C. Vern argues that supposed archaisms are not reliable to date Hebrew poetry, as they are stylistic, and Exod 15 was most likely written in the first millennium (Vern, *Dating Archaic Biblical Hebrew Poetry*, 241).

6. For example, see Mark Leuchter, "Eisodus as Exodus: The Song of the Sea (Exod 15) Reconsidered," *Bib* 92 (2011): 321–46. For a summary of scholarship, see Helmut Utzschneider and Wolfgang Oswald, *Exodus 1–15*, IECOT (Stuttgart: W. Kohlhammer, 2015), 321–30.

7. A. M. Butts, "A Note on *ne'darî* in Ex 15:6," *VT* 60 (2010): 170. Similar statements are made by Roland Hendel, "The Exodus as Cultural Memory: Egyptian Bondage and the Song of the Sea," in *Israel's Exodus in Transdisciplinary Perspective: Text, Archaeology, Culture, and Geoscience*,

Exod 15 very difficult to translate, also seem to indicate its early origins.[8] Some of these archaic forms include *zu* as a relative particle (vv. 13, 16); the pronominal suffixes in verse 2; the root consonant preservation in verse 5; the 3mp pronominal suffix written as -*mw* rather than -*m* in verses 5, 7, 9, 10, 12, 15, 17; and the feminine -*î* ending.[9] In addition, the active participle in a predicative state does not occur in any of the poems usually considered to be ABH, including Exod 15.[10] Other scholars see various linguistic features in Exod 15 to be borrowed from Canaanite literature, and consider that they survived only because they became part of religious texts that were passed down idiomatically and "petrified" in the text.[11] In addition, these and other features are present in Judg 5 and Deut 32, usually also considered to be very ancient poetry.[12]

The textualization of Exod 15 in other passages is another crucial piece of evidence for its archaic nature. References within Ps 74, 77, 78, 105, 106, 114, and Isa 11–12 confirm that Exod 15 was already considered liturgy when these later texts were written.[13] This is especially relevant since it is clear to most linguists that Exod 15 contains no later linguistic features, which is unusual within Hebrew poetry, suggesting that it was penned much earlier than other pieces.[14] Because of this, the argument goes, the poem is likely to have been composed at one time, or redaction would have changed some words to less archaic forms.[15]

---

ed. Thomas E. Levy, Thomas Schneider, and William H. C. Propp, QMHSS (Cham: Springer, 2015), 71; Michael Barré, "'My Strength and My Song' in Exodus 15:2," *CBQ* 54 (1992): 623.

8. Al Wolters, "Not Rescue but Destruction: Rereading Exodus 15:8," *CBQ* 52 (1990): 223–40.

9. Patterson, "Victory at Sea," 42–54; William Johnstone, *Exodus 1–19*, SHBC (Macon, GA: Smyth & Helwys, 2014), 299–300; Thomas B. Dozeman, *Exodus*, ECC (Grand Rapids: Eerdmans, 2009), 336. For further analysis of these features, see D. A. Robertson, *Linguistic Evidence in Dating Early Hebrew Poetry*, SBLDS 3 (Missoula, MT: SBL, 1972). Interestingly, most of these are found in other Semitic languages as well.

10. Tania Notarius, "The Active Predicative Participle in Archaic and Classical Biblical Poetry: A Typological and Historical Investigation," *ANES* 47 (2010): 241–69. Notarius also finds archaic language forms in the indicative forms of conversation and poetic narrative (Tania Notarius, "The Archaic System of Verbal Tenses in 'Archaic' Biblical Poetry," in *Diachrony in Biblical Hebrew*, ed. Cynthia Miller-Naudé and Ziony Zevit [Winona Lake, IN: Eisenbrauns, 2012], 193–207).

11. Simon B. Parker, "Exodus XV 2 Again," *VT* 21(1971): 379. See also Klein, "Hymn and History in Ex 15," 516–27. However, Klein does not consider the song to have been composed as a whole unit. In contrast, some have suggested that Exod 15 is premonarchy, due to the connections with Ugaritic literature and the use of certain phrases only found in Ugaritic texts. See Peter C. Craigie, "The Poetry of Ugarit and Israel," *TynBul* 22 (1970): 3–31.

12. Leuchter, "Eisodus as Exodus," 334–43; Michael A. Grisanti, "Old Testament Poetry as a Vehicle for Historiography," *BSac* 181 (2004): 163–78.

13. Although much later, Ms Neofiti 1 also makes additions to the text of Exod 15, but never deletions. See Étan Levine, "*Neofiti* 1: A Study of Exodus 15," *Bib* 34 (1973): 301–30; Patterson, "Victory at Sea," 42–54.

14. Mark Leuchter, "Eisodus as Exodus," 329. For instance, orthography, vocabulary, morphology, and syntax changes happen between the Pentateuch and the Samaritan Pentateuch, suggesting that the latter was composed at a later date than the former and was dependent upon the former.

15. Ibid., 330. However, he considers the time of its composition to be the early monarchy.

Other reasons to consider Exod 15 to have been written in a different language stage and composition phase from Exod 14 involve the differences in focus and theme from the narrative in Exod 14. For instance, Exod 14 includes the following elements not present in Exod 15: the fear of the Israelites, God's assurance to Moses, the actions of the angel, Moses's outstretched hand, the fear of the Egyptians, Israel's increased trust in God and Moses, and the people passing through on dry ground. Exodus 15 contains the following elements not found in Exod 14: the divine warrior, God's right hand, the anger of God, the perishing of the horse and rider and chariots, and God casting the sea on the Egyptians.[16] The poem is also full of imagery, seemingly exaggerated language, and various figures of speech, unlike Exod 14.

Despite all of these indications, there are those who consider the poetry of Exod 15 to be of the same composition phase as the prose of Exod 14 (although remnants of a previous language state may exist). Some of these scholars contend that the song was passed down in an oral fashion and was written down at a later time when the prose sections were written.[17] For instance, the poem seems to speak from a time of settlement in the promised land, including references to God's "holy abode" (15:13) and the sanctuary (15:17).[18]

In a different scenario, both Exod 14 and 15 could have been written in an archaic time (same composition phase and language stage), but the texts could have been transmitted through the centuries. Thus, the words/language of Exod 14 would have been updated to CBH, while many of the archaic forms would have been retained in the poetry of Exod 15 because of the nature of the genre, so as not to alter the rhythm, and so on.

Another possibility is that of archaizing, where a later author attempted to write in the style of earlier authors, but was not completely successful as more modern elements can be seen as well (same composition phase and language stage, but much later). For example, this sort of activity happened at Qumran, where the authors of the Temple Scroll tried to write in the style of the Pentateuch.[19] The adoption of foreign materials, such as Canaanite, Ugaritic,[20]

16. These differences are adapted from Patterson, "Victory at Sea," 42–54.

17. Craigie, "Poetry of Ugarit and Israel," 3–31. He argues this for Exod 15, that it was originally composed close in form to the canonical form, but was carried on in oral tradition until it was written down at a much later date.

18. W. Gunther Plaut, "Exodus," in *The Torah: A Modern Commentary* (New York: Union of American Hebrew Congregations, 1981), 491. However, Carol Meyers suggests that these terms can just as easily refer to God's celestial dwelling place, and may not reflect a connection to Jerusalem (Carol Meyers, *Exodus*, NCBC [Cambridge: Cambridge University Press, 2005], 120–23).

19. Hurvitz, "Can Biblical Texts Be Dated Linguistically?" 123–42.

20. Certain literary motifs, idioms, and mythologies are thought to have been imported into the song. See Craigie, "Poetry of Ugarit and Israel," 3–31. He gives many examples relating to conflict, temple, and kingship. However, we are not convinced that the borrowing could not have gone the other direction, or could not have been from a similar source or ideology, and conscripted to fit the need in both literatures.

Egyptian Language Practice   53

and Egyptian,[21] also seems to suggest that these texts were composed at a similar time, and not updated as much as previously assumed. In addition, Yigal Bloch argues that both poetry and prose were composed at a later date, and that most scholars have misunderstood the use of short prefix-conjugations of verbs (without a conjunction *w-*) to represent complete situations in the past, as representative of early Hebrew. He notes that there are some long prefix-conjugations in the supposedly early poems, and the short prefix pattern is seen in other poems that are usually dated much later, such as in Isa 41:1–5 and Ps 44.[22]

However, late linguistic features can mean several things: the text is late, a later addition was made to an earlier text, or the text was corrupted during transmission.[23] To identify late linguistic features, Hurvitz suggests an examination of the feature's distribution in the Hebrew Bible, its presence in extrabiblical sources, and linguistic opposition in other texts.[24] In light of this, a more recent proposal suggests that CBH and LBH may actually represent different stylistic forms, one more conservative, the other more free, and both can be considered postexilic, as they were being used at the same time.[25] A few scholars have even proposed that there is no single language type that can be called Biblical Hebrew poetry.[26]

For the third option, we suggest that in light of the prevailing scholarly opinions, Exod 15 exhibits an older language stage than Exod 14, but that this does not eliminate the possibility of the same composition phase.[27] In a more literary

21. Benjamin Noonan has confirmed that there is a preponderance of Egyptian loanwords in the Pentateuch, in comparison to the rest of the Hebrew Bible and other Northwest Semitic texts (Benjamin Noonan, "Egyptian Loanwords as Evidence for the Historicity and Authenticity of the Exodus and Wilderness Traditions," in *"Did I Not Bring Israel Out of Egypt?" Biblical, Archaeological, and Egyptological Perspectives on the Exodus Narratives*, ed. James K. Hoffmeier, Alan R. Millard, and Gary A. Rendsburg, BBRSup 13 [Winona Lake, IN: Eisenbrauns, 2016], 49–67). In addition, he notes that the preservation of an archaic Egyptian feminine ending indicates that these words were borrowed early, during the latter part of the second millennium BC.

22. Yigal Bloch, "The Prefixed Perfective and the Dating of Early Hebrew Poetry—A Reevaluation," *VT* 59 (2009): 34–70. However, he notes that the predominance of short prefixed forms in Exod 15 indicates that it must be at least slightly older than Isa 41 and Ps 44. Others suggest that the whole of the Hebrew Bible was written during the Persian period, at one point in time (e.g., Young, Rezetko, and Ehrensvärd, *Linguistic Dating of Biblical Texts*, vol. 2, 96–99). Hurvitz strongly refutes these minimalists (Hurvitz, "Can Biblical Texts Be Dated Linguistically?").

23. Joosten indicates that it is difficult to tell the difference between these, even with textual criticism and redaction criticism (Joosten, *Verbal System of Biblical Hebrew*, 8, 420–21).

24. Hurvitz, "Can Biblical Texts Be Dated Linguistically?" 123–42.

25. I. Young, ed., *Biblical Hebrew: Studies in Chronology and Typology* (London: T&T Clark International, 2003); Young and Rezetko, *Linguistic Dating of Biblical Texts*, vol. 2. There is a high level of diversity in the prose texts, but no consensus has developed.

26. Notarius, "Active Predicative Participle," 262. Some scholars characterize poetry in relation to chronological concerns, while others perform literary analysis to distinguish language types, so Notarius advocates for a more complex and unique approach to biblical historical linguistics.

27. Victor P. Hamilton seems to suggest something like this, but the time of composition is left vague and undefined (Victor P. Hamilton, *Exodus: An Exegetical Commentary* [Grand Rapids: Baker Academic, 2011], 228–33).

analysis, several others have recently suggested that Exod 14 and 15 were written together, because of the many connections between them. Both passages use similar words to describe the event, and there is a similar core of facts between the two. The song serves to accentuate the main focus on God's victory for Israel. Various shared themes and vocabulary include sea and waters, waters piled up by God's breath or wind, pursuit, waters congealed so Egyptians went in without fear.[28] The poem is part and parcel of the narrative, so much so that Janzen writes, "the liturgical celebration is so closely interwoven as part of the total event that it cannot be separated from it without changing the experienced character of the event."[29] In fact, this accentuates the difficulty in translating verbal forms in poetry, as the song and the narrative refer to the same situations, but the striking difference between the verbal forms continues to engender a variety of approaches to translation.[30] Although the poem and prose are closely interwoven, this does not mean that the language stages are indistinguishable, or that the composition phase was late (CBH or LBH).

Exodus 14 and 15 share several connections to Egyptian perspective that represent a similar time of composition, seemingly preexilic. Exodus 15 draws on the divine warrior motif from Egyptian and then Canaanite mythology, and "deliberately mimics Egyptian tropes" of the "invincibility of Pharaoh."[31] The motif of Yahweh's mighty arm derives from the Egyptian motif of Pharaoh's mighty arm.[32] The exodus and wilderness wandering narratives "contain significantly higher proportions of Egyptian terminology than the rest of the Hebrew Bible," and some, perhaps more, come from the Late Bronze Age.[33]

In addition, it is quite common for poetry to surround or supplement the main narrative, even though cuneiform texts do not usually mix the modes of presentation.[34] For instance, Egyptian texts often mix poetry and prose within a historical account.[35] Along these lines, Sailhamer argues that the Pentateuch is structured with poetic epilogues after major narratives.[36] A consideration of genre requires an evaluation of each chapter on its own merit, but together Exod

28. Patterson, "Victory at Sea," 42–54.

29. J. Gerald Janzen, "Song of Moses, Song of Miriam: Who Is Seconding Whom?" *CBQ* 54 (1992): 218.

30. Robert Shreckhise, "The Problem of Finite Verb Translation in Exodus 15.1–18," *JSOT* 32 (2008): 287–310. He examines three alternative translation schemes: prophetic perfect, preterite (Sinai provenance), and perfect-past, imperfect-present/modal/future (dual perspective model).

31. Hendel, "Exodus as Cultural Memory," 72.

32. James K. Hoffmeier, "The Arm of God Versus the Arm of Pharaoh in the Exodus Narratives," *Bib* 67 (1986): 378–87.

33. Benjamin J. Noonan, "Egyptian Loanwords as Evidence for the Authenticity of the Exodus and Wilderness Traditions," in Hoffmeier, Millard, and Rendsburg, *"Did I Not Bring Israel Out of Egypt?"* 49–67.

34. Patterson, "Victory at Sea," 42–54.

35. Ibid., 42–54.

36. John H. Sailhamer, *The Pentateuch as Narrative: A Biblical-Theological Commentary* (Grand Rapids: Zondervan, 1992), 35–36.

14 and 15 provide a "far richer portrait" of the Exodus than each would on its own.[37] Other scholars note that the poem actually adds historical details to the narrative, so was meant to be complementary to the prose, and not only to add emotion or rhetoric.[38]

Thus, it appears that Exod 14 and 15 exhibit different genres, purposes, and language stages. One advantage to an interdisciplinary approach is that insights sometimes arise from another partially related field of study that can shed light on a difficulty. This is useful here because if Exod 15 does appear older, there may be a need for an alternative proposal that could account for this different language stage with the possibility of a similar composition phase. Thus, we propose seeking guidance from another ancient language with ties to Hebrew.

Egyptian Language Practice

Considered "the oldest and longest continually attested" language in the world, Egyptian "belongs to the Hamito-Semitic family of languages."[39] Hebrew also comes from the Semitic phylum. James Allen, an Egyptian language expert, points out that Egyptian is "a distinct branch . . . with no close relatives of its own," making it "closer to the common ancestor of Hamito-Semitic than to either of the other two branches," with the relational ties to the Proto-Semitic branch being stronger than the Hamito based on "the value of some hieroglyphs."[40] As a result, Egyptian and Hebrew share a commonality and may share common language practices. However, before this can be suggested, it is important to review important features of the Egyptian language through time.

The Egyptian language went through five identifiable stages:[41] Old Egyptian, Middle Egyptian, New/Late Egyptian,[42] Demotic, and Coptic, with some of the

---

37. Patterson, "Victory at Sea," 52. Grisanti suggests that the poetry has a different purpose, so the divergences with the narrative are expected within that purpose (Grisanti, "Old Testament Poetry," 173). However, we are not certain that this answers the ultimate linguistic question concerning the dating of each passage.

38. Grisanti, "Old Testament Poetry," 172–73; K. Lawson Younger Jr., "Heads! Tails! Or the Whole Coin?! Contextual Method and Intertextual Analysis: Judges 4 and 5," in *The Biblical Canon in Comparative Perspective*, ed. K. Lawson Younger Jr., William W. Hallo, and Bernard F. Batto (Lewiston, NY: Edwin Mellen, 1991), 110–16.

39. James P. Allen, *The Ancient Egyptian Language: An Historical Study* (Cambridge: Cambridge University Press, 2013), 1.

40. Ibid., 2.

41. We are not dealing, on this level, with dialect changes between those who lived in the south (the Nile river valley, called "Upper Egypt") and those living in the north (the Delta region, called "Lower Egypt"). There is evidence that in ancient times there was a distinction (Allen, *Ancient Egyptian Language,* 4). This distinction can still be seen in the slight differences in dialect in Egyptian Arabic today between those from the north and those from the south (H. Palva, "Dialects: Classification," in *Encyclopedia of Arabic Language and Linguistics* 1:608).

42. Scholars are not unified on the term for this language stage.

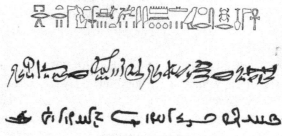

TOP: HIEROGLYPHIC
MIDDLE: HIERATIC
BOTTOM: DEMOTIC

FIGURE 3.1. Egyptian scripts. From top to bottom: hieroglyphic, hieratic, and demotic.

stages having been even further subdivided. The stages have been grouped into two general historical phases, based on significant grammar differences: Old and Middle in the first Egyptian phase and New/Late, Demotic, and Coptic in the last phase.[43] Scholars have spent a significant amount of time debating these differences.

Egyptian was expressed in written form using four scripts: hieroglyphic, hieratic, demotic, and coptic (see figure 3.1). Hieroglyphs, as the script of the gods (*mdw-ntr*, "god's words"),[44] were used primarily on monumental surfaces, while hieratic appears on papyri and ostraca. Both began about the same time, with the hieroglyphic script being attested slightly earlier[45] and being preserved in the archaeological record a bit later. Demotic and coptic were both rather late, with demotic appearing for the first time in the Third Intermediate Period and coptic first in use during the Ptolemaic Period. At least two of these scripts were always in use at any one time.[46] Thus, dating can be done in very broad, general terms based on the script, with more focused dating being identified in the language stage expressed by the script.

Phonologists note that words containing unusual spellings, where the depiction of a word in the script does not seem to reflect the language stage, are examples where the ancient scribes felt the tension between the desire to preserve the older etymology and the felt need to "reflect the contemporary

---

43. Allen, *Ancient Egyptian Language*, 4.
44. James P. Allen, *Middle Egyptian: An Introduction to the Language and Culture of Hieroglyphs* (Cambridge: Cambridge University Press, 2006), 42.
45. Ibid., 6.
46. Jan Assmann, *Stein und Zeit: Mensch und Gesellschaft im Alten Ägypten* (Munich: Wilhelm Fink, 1991).

pronunciation of words."[47] In the Old Egyptian language stage, most words had a consonant at the beginning and ending of a word (with a few exceptions). However, by the Middle Egyptian language stage, many words had changed so that there was a vowel at the beginning or ending. Thus, scribes could either choose to spell the word the old way or change the spelling to reflect the new colloquial use.[48] By the new grammatical stage of New/Late Egyptian, a curl -*w* was often used to reflect the new pronunciation.[49]

Foreign words were also written in two distinct ways. The Middle Egyptian stage used mostly an alphabetic system that grouped small Egyptian words to stand in place of the syllables in the foreign word, while the New/Late Egyptian stage used consonant-vowel syllables, written mostly with biliteral signs.[50] This served them well as they also used it for newly adopted Semitic loan words[51] that had come to them during the Hyksos rule of the Second Intermediate Period.

Another feature of ancient Egyptian (one that is also seen in biblical Hebrew) is its use of thought couplets, where the second line of thought parallels the first, so that elements match up. For example:

'ḥ' jb pw m ȝt sȝsȝ, "He is one steadfast of heart in the *moment of attack*;"
'nw pw nj rdj.n.f sȝ.f, "he is a *repeller* who does not show his back."[52]

This is seen most often in religious texts, where poetic hymns were "among the most carefully composed of all Egyptian literary forms,"[53] so that the compositions were "carefully arranged expositions of Egyptian thought about the nature and significance of the god being 'praised.'"[54]

Archaeologists and looters have recovered a significant amount of texts that upon analysis reveal another very interesting feature—that multiple language stages could be used concurrently.[55] This concept is not entirely unattested even today in modern English. Studies show that the first area of communication to change was colloquial speech.[56] This day-to-day language use appears in

---

47. Allen, *Middle Egyptian*, 218.

48. This also helps modern phonologists to determine the various registers (layers in a language). In Middle Egyptian, the definite and indefinite articles were not present, however they do appear in labels used to express speech in tomb scenes (ibid., 240). This is one of the ways it is possible to see the progression of a language from spoken to written.

49. Ibid., 219.

50. Ibid., 220.

51. Ibid., 221.

52. Ibid., 241.

53. Ibid., 341.

54. Ibid., 342.

55. See table 3.1.

56. F. Junge, "Sprache," in *Lexicon der Ägyptologie* 5:1176–1211.

FIGURE 3.2. Rosetta Stone, containing hieroglyphic, demotic, and Greek

laundry lists, grocery lists, graffiti, and other unofficial writing such as letters.[57] The next area to change was literature,[58] which follows more closely the slight changes of common language while still holding to a few older conventions. The most popular genre in literature appears to have been wisdom literature,[59] but stories were also cherished.[60] The third area to change was official communication, which can be seen in stele such as the famous Rosetta Stone.[61] The last to change was the religious texts,[62] seen most commonly in temples and tombs, both on monuments and on less grand surfaces. Thus, at any one moment of

57. Allen, *Middle Egyptian*, 386.
58. See Stephen Quirke, *Egyptian Literature, 1800 BC: Questions and Readings* (London: Golden House, 2004).
59. Allen, *Middle Egyptian*, 258.
60. Ibid., 280.
61. See figure 3.2.
62. Allen, *Middle Egyptian*, 315.

time, potentially four stages of language might appear, with potentially the same scribe writing all four.

Indeed, three periods in Egyptian history saw as many as three language stages in use concurrently: the eighteenth dynasty of the New Kingdom, the Third Intermediate Period, and the Ptolemaic Period. At some point early in the eighteenth dynasty (and possibly as early as the late Second Intermediate Period), spoken language began to change from Late Middle Egyptian to the much more grammatically complex New/Late Egyptian. However, in that same period Late Middle Egyptian was still used in both literature and official communications. Religious texts of that period still employed Classical Middle Egyptian. The same is true for the Third Intermediate Period, when Demotic was used for the first time as a spoken language, while New/Late Egyptian was used in literature and Neo-Middle Egyptian was used for both official communication and religious texts.

In the Ptolemaic Period, Greek was used alongside of Egyptian, so that Demotic was used both for day-to-day communication as well as in literature. Demotic was also used for official communication along with both Greek and Neo-Middle Egyptian. Neo-Middle Egyptian was also used for religious texts.

And while three historic periods saw three language stages in use, only one historic period saw only one language stage in use: the very first (early Old Kingdom, where there are not many texts available for study). In other words, two or more language stages were used concurrently in every period of Egyptian pharaonic history except the first. Thus, with the close grammatical ties that Egyptian has to Hebrew (as opposed to other languages), the question arises whether it is possible that Egyptian language practice might reflect a more general practice in the ancient Semitic world.

Discussion

Ideally a comparable parallel would be presented that could then be used to postulate language practice from one Semitic language to another. However, the Hebrew Pentateuch is a unique document in regards to the combinations of genre, purpose, and language. Complicating the matter further, the archaeological record is quite limited. Perhaps that is why this comparison has seemed to escape the attention of the scholarly world until now. On the other hand, there does appear to be precedent if the individual elements of Exod 14 and 15 are compared atomistically. The composite parts would include (1) historical narrative presented in mixed prose and poetry;[63] and (2) the use of multiple language

---

63. All of chapter 14 and at least vv. 1a, 19–20, 22–27 of chapter 15 are prose.

TABLE 3.1. Egyptian-Language Stages and Scripts

	OK	FIP	MK	SIP	18th Dyn	19th Dyn	20th Dyn	TIP	Late period	Ptolemaic	Roman
Theology	*Old Egyptian*			*Classical Middle Egyptian*		*Late Middle Egyptian*			*Neo Middle Egyptian*		
Official communication ("the state")											*Demotic and Greek*
Literature	...					*Late Egyptian*					
Day-to-day language	...								*Demotic*		

Hieroglyphic script

Hieratic script

Demotic script

Coptic

Adapted with permission from Richard Bussmann, University College London, and James P. Allen, Brown University.

stages in a single document with differing purposes composed at relatively the same phase.[64]

As for the use of mixed genre in a single composition, the temples at Luxor, the Ramesseum, and Abydos all contain a long version and a short version of the 2nd Ramses's battle at Kadesh.[65] The temple at Karnak also contains the long version, while the temple at Abu Simbel contains the shorter version of the same battle. A papyrus that is shared by the Louvre and the British Museum also contains an account of this event.[66] This is an epic historical account written in prose, but contains a poem as a song of triumph.[67] The tale of *Horus and Seth*, the Merenptah Stele, and the Piye Stele are three more examples of "Egyptian myths, mortuary autobiographies, and royal inscriptions [that] often switch from prose to hymnic poetry and back again."[68] Thus, there is a cultural precedent for the inclusion of poems in prose that were written to relate an event that was meant to be understood as historical.

As for the use of multiple language stages in a single document at approximately the same composition phase, Middle Egyptian tombs often contain offering formulas in Classical Middle Egyptian (see table 3.1) as well as occasional labels that contain features (such as the definite and indefinite article, which are not found in Middle Egyptian) of colloquial speech.[69] The walls of the tombs almost certainly have to be of the same composition phase. The purpose of the offering formulas was to present a perpetual offering to the gods on behalf of the deceased, whereas the labels almost certainly had the purpose of giving voice to the deceased. Thus, this provides an example of multiple language stages in a single composition phase, albeit for slightly varying purposes from that of the Pentateuch.

This essay is not attempting to prove that the Hebrew text has sections that are of an older language stage mixed in with sections that are of a younger language stage. It is presenting only the fact that Egyptians used multiple language stages in single composition phases and that if the Hebrew text is also of multiple language stages, this does not, of necessity, mean that the text is of multiple composition phases. Even if the Pentateuch was written later than the

---

64. The purpose of the prose is to teach the lesson that God can save in the recounting of a story, while the purpose of the poetry is to praise the God who brought about their salvation. These are related but slightly different purposes.

65. For a discussion on the relationship of the Kadesh inscriptions to Exod 14–15, see Joshua Berman, "The Kadesh Inscriptions of Ramesses II and the Exodus Sea Account (Exodus 13:17—15:19)," in Hoffmeier, Millard, and Rendsburg, *"Did I Not Bring Israel Out of Egypt?"* 93–112.

66. Alan Gardiner, *Egypt of the Pharaohs* (Oxford: Oxford University Press, 1978), 260.

67. "The Kadesh Battle Inscriptions of Ramses II," in Miriam Lichtheim, *Ancient Egyptian Literature* (Berkeley: University of California Press, 1976), 2:59.

68. James W. Watts, "Song and the Ancient Reader," *PRSt* 22, no. 2 (1995): 137.

69. Allen, *Middle Egyptian*, 240.

62 L. S. Baker Jr. and A. Rahel Wells

time of the Exodus event, the author(s) of the Pentateuch clearly had many connections with Egypt, and could still have been influenced by Egyptian language practice.

Egyptians used different language stages for various areas of communication simultaneously in the same composition phase. Theoretically, a single scribe could write in multiple language stages in the same day for various reasons. Thus, the evidence for multiple language stages in the Hebrew Bible is not of itself an indicator that the text is of multiple composition phases.

Reflection

Is there any indication in the content of the Hebrew text that multiple language stages were in play? Perhaps. In another portion of the Exodus account, there is a story that might suggest that the ancient writer(s) knew about language stages. This potential example is based on the ability to speak well.

Part of the reason the Egyptian language moved to become more complex in the New/Late Egyptian stage was the desired quality of speaking well.[70] A Middle Kingdom official is quoted as saying, "I am one who talks according to the style of officials, whose speech is free of $p\ni$'s,"[71] referring to the developing use in spoken language of substituting the demonstrative $p\ni$ for the definite article (something that become normative in the New/Late Egyptian language stage). Apparently, in this Middle Kingdom official's day, people of high standing did not use the common colloquialisms.

Turning a phrase, puns, and double meanings were all part of the new language stage. A good example of this is the classic phrase *wr wr wrw.f wr. (w)*, "Great is the great one whose great ones are great," which means, "A king whose high officials are great is truly great himself."[72]

Further, in regard to pronunciation of consonants, two major shifts in articulation occurred over time from Old Egyptian to Coptic. The first is called "fronting," in which the consonant moves "from the back of the mouth forward."[73] The second, "backing," is the opposite, where the consonant moves backwards in the mouth over time.[74]

Thus, the change was both in how words were used and in how they were pronounced. This resulted in the language stages. It is conceivable, then, that were someone to be removed from the process of change for a few decades, they

---

70. Ibid., 241.
71. Ibid., 54.
72. Ibid., 483.
73. Ibid., 54.
74. Ibid., 55.

Egyptian Language Practice   63

would consider themselves slow both in what words were to be spoken and in how the words were to be pronounced.

A common misconception of the Moses character is that the Exodus narrative portrays him as having had a speech impediment.[75] At the bush that did not burn up, Moses entered into a conversation with YHWH that ended with him being sent to Egypt to lead God's people out of bondage. Moses pushed back on this assignment with obvious reluctance in one final argument, which is recorded in Exod 4:10–13. He began this last phase of reticence by saying, "O my Lord, I am not eloquent, neither before nor since You have spoken to Your servant; but I am slow of speech and slow of tongue" (NKJV).

However, Ezek 3:5–6 uses the same phrase "slow of tongue" (כִּבְדֵי לָשׁוֹן) that Moses does to refer to foreign languages that are unintelligible (cf. Isa 33:19). "Heavy" (כְּבַד) usually refers to a medical condition, but here the use is extended to refer to linguistic difficulties.[76] Carol Myers makes the connection to an Egyptian ritual of "opening the mouth," and surmises that there was no medical condition in mind in Exod 4.[77] In addition, this "slowness" was not associated with a stuttering problem when this story was recounted by Stephen, one of the Christian church's first deacons, in Acts 7:22. Stephen is recorded as saying that Moses, during his life growing up as an Egyptian prince, "was learned in all the wisdom of the Egyptians, and was mighty in words and deeds" (NKJV). Being "mighty in words" obviously cannot reflect a speech impediment. Thus, those who held to the authenticity of the story by that late date seemed to understand Moses's slowness of speech to be something different than a problem with speaking.

Given the above, might the reason Moses claimed to be "slow of speech and slow of tongue" have been because of the growing complexities in the Egyptian language and in how the language was pronounced; a language that, according to the story, he would have been intimately familiar with some forty years earlier? We see the change in colloquial speech between the first and second

---

75. Jeffrey Tigay makes a case for Moses's speech difficulties being related to medical reasons (Jeffrey Tigay, "'Heavy of Mouth' and 'Heavy of Tongue': On Moses' Speech Difficulty," *BASOR* 231 [1978]: 57–67). In addition, Nyasha Junior and Jeremy Schipper state that Moses uses his disability as an excuse to avoid God's commands because of his varied and conflicting group identities (Nyasha Junior and Jeremy Schipper, "Mosaic Disability and Identity in Exodus 4:10; 6:12, 30," *BiblInt* 16 [2008]: 428–41).

76. Others who have proposed this see it as Moses forgetting his Egyptian, which would technically fit more closely with the theory we are proposing. For example, see Kaiser, "Exodus," 328; William H. C. Propp, *Exodus 1–18: A New Translation with Introduction and Commentary*, AB 2 (New York: Doubleday, 1999), 211. Johnstone sees this as an attitude of Moses, not an impediment (Johnstone, *Exodus 1–19*, 110).

77. Meyers, *Exodus*, 61. Similarly, Hamilton considers this to be simply Moses's lack of charisma, which God infuses with power (Hamilton, *Exodus*, 73).

phase[78] of Egyptian language at or near the beginning of the eighteenth dynasty in Egypt's New Kingdom.

When God responds to Moses's complaint, he states that he will "teach/instruct" (ירה) him what to say, not correct a speech impediment (4:12). In addition, in the account just prior to the Exodus event, when Moses later was joined by his brother Aaron (Exod 4:27) and they both returned to Egypt, it was Aaron who did the talking early on (Exod 4:30). It is not until the end of the second plague that the text states Moses spoke to Pharaoh (Exod 8:9). It seems conceivable that the rust could have shaken off by that point and that he would have been able to speak well once more.[79]

This understanding may provide another explanation for the potential Hebrew language stages if, indeed, Exod 15 turns out to actually be an older language stage than Exod 14. In the end, this does not prove that the Hebrew poetry of Exod 15 (or any other poem in the Pentateuch) is or is not of a different language stage of Hebrew than the prose around it. However, it does provide for another possibility for the indications of different language stages in the text, which could also be compatible with the content of the narrative of the story in Exodus (and Acts in the New Testament).

Conclusion

The Hebrew Pentateuch is a unique document that does not have an exact parallel in Egypt (or any other ancient culture, for that matter). Certain elements in Egyptian literature do parallel Exod 14 and 15, in that the ancient language practice was to use both prose and poetry for a narrative of an event meant to be viewed as historical (whether it is accurate to history or not). Additionally, multiple language stages do appear in single composition phases with the textual elements having different genres and purposes.

---

78. The first phase included both Old and Middle Egyptian, while the second phase included New/Late Egyptian, Demotic, and Coptic.

79. It is also conceivable that those living in Isaiah's and Ezekiel's era, as well as those living in the first century AD, being closer to the ancient cultures than we are, understood the language stages and uses, so that Stephen recounted the story of Moses from a perspective that modern scholars, who have only just grasped Egyptian language practices over the last half century or so, can begin to understand. Jewish commentators also see this possibility. For instance, Rashi's grandson Rabbi Shmuel Ben-Meir, who debunked the typical understanding of Moses having a speech impediment, suggested that he had been away from Egypt for so long that he no longer spoke the language well. Targum Onkelos interprets "slow of speech" as "weighty of speech" and "deep of tongue," turning it into a more positive framework. Indeed, throughout the Pentateuch, Moses has no trouble communicating with the people and leaders, so it seems his hesitation must have been linguistic and not a physical impediment. See Douglas K. Stuart, *Exodus*, NAC 2 (Nashville: Broadman & Holman, 2006), 134–35.

There may or may not be sufficient reason to consider the poetic portions of the Pentateuch (e.g., Exod 15) to be of an older stage of Hebrew than the prose sections (e.g. Exod 14). Whether actually older or not, an apparently older stage of language in a single document does not necessarily mean that the document was not written at the same composition phase.

Since at least one other ancient partially Semitic language, Egyptian, employed multiple stages of its language during the same composition phase, dating of a Hebrew document cannot be based solely on the establishment of the apparent presence of multiple linguistic stages.

CHAPTER 4

Second-Millennium BC Cuneiform from the Southern Levant and the Literature of the Pentateuch

Richard S. Hess
Denver Seminary

Introduction

The recent discoveries of cuneiform texts have not always been taken into consideration in the work that biblical scholars do. For example, a great deal has been written regarding oral tradition and its implications for the dating of biblical materials. The origins of texts within oral traditions can reasonably be related to some poetic materials within the Bible, insofar as poetry in many cultures is more often committed to memory than is prose. A text such as Exod 15 celebrates victory over Egypt in poetic form. Like other poetic narratives from the Mediterranean and ancient Near Eastern worlds, this could have originated in an oral form. Alongside the Ugaritic Baal cycle and the Homeric epics of the *Iliad* and the *Odyssey*, some poetic texts in the Pentateuch could be understood as having originated in an oral context.[1]

Oral Tradition in Prose

Scholars have extended this orality to wider areas of prose in the narratives. At the beginning of the twentieth century, Hermann Gunkel identified elements in the opening chapters of Genesis where he found oral traditions whose kernels began as myths.[2] Albrecht Alt developed theories about etiologies and other elements of sagas where legends emerged to explain names or customs whose

---

1. Cf. Frank M. Cross Jr., *Canaanite Myth and Hebrew Epic* (Cambridge, MA: Harvard University Press, 1973); Richard S. Hess, "Oral Tradition and the OT," in *Dictionary for Theological Interpretation of the Bible*, ed. C. G. Bartholomew, D. J. Treer, and N. T. Wright (Grand Rapids: Baker Academic; London: SPCK, 2005), 551–53.

2. Hermann Gunkel, *The Legends of Genesis*, trans. W. H. Carruth (New York: Schocken, 1901).

true origins were lost.[3] More recently, Susan Niditch developed criteria for the identification of oral traditions and Ron Hendel found a saga with oral origins in the Jacob stories of Genesis.[4] As a result, David Carr can affirm that the view of "most contemporary scholars" does not see written sources appearing before the first millennium BC. So while there probably were figures such as Abraham, Sarah, and Jacob, these have been thoroughly reshaped by the scribes of the later period.[5]

In fact, there are reasons for accepting an antiquity and authenticity to these traditions. Despite their well-known critique of parallels to Gen 12–37 from mid- and early second millennium BC archives from Alalakh, Mari, and Nuzi, John Van Seters and Thomas L. Thompson have not been proven correct in their claims that these accounts fit best in the culture of the mid-first millennium BC.[6] Numerous studies have critiqued the methods and analysis of the evidence used by these critics. For example, two collections of essays appeared, one in Britain and one in America, that addressed these claims.[7] In addition to these, and especially notable, is the work of Kenneth A. Kitchen. His original research has gathered a mass of data that connects Gen 12–37 with the second millennium BC.[8] More recently, Bill T. Arnold has reaffirmed close cultural connections with the second millennium BC. He has brought together the latest evidence, including that detailed by some of the work of Daniel E. Fleming on Mari texts. Such evidence was not available when Thompson and Van Seters first published their criticisms.[9]

---

3. Albrecht Alt, "The God of the Fathers," in *Essays on Old Testament History and Religion*, ed. Albrecht Alt, trans. R. A. Wilson (Sheffield: Sheffield Academic, 1989), 1–77. See the review of this earlier period in Douglas Knight, *Rediscovering the Traditions of Israel*, 2nd ed. (Atlanta: Scholars Press, 1975).

4. Susan Niditch, *Oral World and Written Word*, LAI (Philadelphia: Westminster John Knox, 1996); R. Hendel, *The Epic of the Patriarch*, HSM 42 (Atlanta: Scholars Press, 1987); Ron Hendel, *Remembering Abraham: Culture, Memory, and History in the Hebrew Bible* (New York: Oxford University Press, 2005). The latter work expands this method to other parts of Genesis.

5. David M. Carr, "Genesis," in *The Oxford Encyclopedia of the Books of the Bible*, ed. Michael D. Coogan (Oxford: Oxford University Press, 2011), 1:326–27.

6. Thomas L. Thompson, *The Historicity of the Patriarchal Narratives: The Quest for the Historical Israel*, BZAW 133 (Berlin: De Gruyter, 1974); John Van Seters, *Abraham in History and Tradition* (New Haven: Yale University Press, 1975); Van Seters, *In Search of History: Historiography in the Ancient World and the Origins of Biblical History* (New Haven: Yale University Press, 1983).

7. A. R. Millard and D. J. Wiseman, eds., *Essays on the Patriarchal Narratives* (Leicester: Inter-Varsity, 1980); A. R. Millard, James K. Hoffmeier, and David W. Baker, eds., *Faith, Tradition, and History: Old Testament Historiography in Its Near Eastern Context* (Winona Lake, IN: Eisenbrauns, 1994).

8. Kenneth A. Kitchen, *On the Reliability of the Old Testament* (Grand Rapids: Eerdmans, 1983), 313–43.

9. Bill T. Arnold, "The Genesis Narratives," in *Ancient Israel's History: An Introduction to Issues and Sources*, ed. Bill T. Arnold and Richard S. Hess (Grand Rapids: Baker Academic, 2014), 23–45. For Daniel E. Fleming, cf., e.g., "Genesis in History and Tradition: The Syrian Background of

68   Richard S. Hess

Assumptions for Oral Tradition in Genesis

Where does this leave us? Oral studies have not taken into consideration the presence of early written textual material. General criteria for the identification of oral tradition in the Bible include three assumptions: (1) earlier material in the Bible is oral; (2) literacy was virtually nonexistent in early Israel; and (3) the appearance of formulas and repetitions in written texts betrays their origins in oral traditions.[10] None of these arguments is airtight. Earlier material in the Bible, especially the prose of most of Genesis, does not prove oral origins. The site of Mari on the Euphrates River has yielded thousands of written cuneiform documents from the eighteenth century BC. Like earliest Israel, these people were Amorite or West Semitic. The culture was able to produce thousands of written texts, including many letters with sophisticated arguments and rhetorical flourishes. Yet the period of their writing lies within that purported by the writer of Gen 12–37 to be the period of the events described there. That period would be the Middle Bronze Age, approximately 2000–1550 BC.

The second argument, that literature was virtually nonexistent in early Israel, is demonstrated more in the absence of evidence than in the presence of any positive proof. I have continued a longstanding discussion with proponents of minimal literacy in ancient Israel and will not rehearse it here.[11] Recently, the

---

Israel's Ancestors, Reprise," in *The Future of Biblical Archaeology: Reassessing Methodologies and Assumptions*, ed. James K. Hoffmeier and Alan Millard (Grand Rapids: Eerdmans, 2004), 192–232.

10. For the first and third arguments, see especially the discussion of Niditch, *Oral World and Written Word*. For the second argument, see, e.g., Karel van der Toorn, *Scribal Culture and the Making of the Hebrew Bible* (Cambridge, MA: Harvard University Press, 2007), 9–16.

11. Ian M. Young, "Israelite Literacy: Interpreting the Evidence, Part I," *VT* 48 (1998): 239–53; Young, "Israelite Literacy: Interpreting the Evidence, Part II," *VT* 48 (1998): 408–22; William M. Schniedewind, "Orality and Literacy in Ancient Israel," *RSR* 26, no. 4 (2000): 327–32; William G. Dever, *What Did the Biblical Writers Know and When Did They Know It? What Archaeology Can Tell Us About the Reality of Ancient Israel* (Grand Rapids: Eerdmans, 2001), 202–21; Richard S. Hess, "Literacy in Iron Age Israel," in *Windows into Old Testament History: Evidence, Argument, and the Crisis of "Biblical Israel,"* ed. V. P. Long, D. W. Baker, and G. J. Wenham (Grand Rapids: Eerdmans, 2002), 82–102. The discussion also included Ian M. Young, "Israelite Literacy and Inscriptions: A Response to Richard Hess," *VT* 55 (2005): 565–67; William M. Schniedewind, *How the Bible Became a Book: The Textualization of Ancient Israel* (Cambridge: Cambridge University Press, 2004); Christopher A. Rollston, "Scribal Education in Ancient Israel: The Old Hebrew Epigraphic Evidence," *BASOR* 344 (2006): 47–74; Rollston, "The Phoenician Script of the Tel Zayit Abecedary and Putative Evidence for Israelite Literacy," in *Literature Culture and Tenth-Century Canaan: The Tel Zayit Abecedary in Context*, ed. Ron E. Tappy and P. Kyle McCarter (Winona Lake, IN: Eisenbrauns, 2008), 61–96; Rollston, *Writing and Literacy in the World of Ancient Israel: Epigraphic Evidence from the Iron Age*, ABS 8 (Atlanta: SBL, 2010), 127–35; Richard S. Hess, "Writing About Writing: Abecedaries and Evidence for Literacy in Ancient Israel," *VT* 56 (2006): 342–46; Hess, "Questions of Reading and Writing in Ancient Israel," *BBR* 19 (2009): 1–9; Hess, "Some Views on Literacy"; Hess, "The Bible and Interpretation," http://www.bibleinterp.com /opeds/views357905.shtml; Hess, review of *Writing and Literacy in the World of Ancient Israel: Epitraphic Evidence from the Bronze Age*, by Christopher A. Rollston, *BBR* 21 (2011): 394–96.

Second-Millennium BC Cuneiform   69

tone of this discussion has been raised to the odd pitch of alleging ideological protective strategies in my work.[12] I do not know what expertise enables someone to feel that they can ascribe otherwise unstated motives to another's work, especially in cases where my published and edited work contradicts those speculative criticisms.[13]

However, my concern here is to affirm that the case for no literacy, that is, no ability to read and write literate texts, among earliest Israel and its precursors remains unproven. The early archives of Mari and Alalakh, the early second millennium texts from Hazor and other sites in southern Canaan, and the abundance of literary material in neighboring Egypt—all from the time that the author of Gen 12–37 dates the figures described there—make it likely that people living in the midst of this milieu would have had access to scribes, especially if they had significant material resources.[14]

The appearance of formulas and repetitions in prose literature can occur as rhetorical forms. For example, the fourteenth-century BC Amarna letters, from princes of city-states in southern Canaan (such as Jerusalem) to the pharaoh, were written in the presence of the local leader and included a variety of sophisticated rhetorical devices. To name a few, these devices include specific formulas, threefold repetitions, chiastic structures, and two-line parallelisms (synonymous and antithetical).[15] Thus, from at least the middle of the second millennium BC in southern Canaan, scribes were present who could produce literary texts without the need for a significant period of oral tradition.

The Hebron Tablet

An additional piece of evidence should be mentioned regarding the accounts of Gen 12–37. According to these chapters, Abraham, Isaac, and Jacob and their wives and families lived and, in most cases, died in or nearby Hebron in

12. Stephen L. Young, "Maximizing Literacy as a Protective Strategy: Redescribing Evangelical Inerrantist Scholarship on Israelite Literacy," *BibInt* 23 (2015): 145–73.

13. Richard S. Hess, "Literacy and Postmodern Fallacies," in *Write That They May Read: Studies in Literacy and Textualization in the Ancient Near East and Hebrew Scriptures: Essays in Honour of Alan R. Millard*, ed. D. I. Block, D. C. Deuel, C. J. Collins, and P. J. N. Lawrence (Eugene, OR: Pickwick and Wipf & Stock, 2020), 384–91.

14. See also the broader sociological discussion of many levels of literacy from diverse cultures, occupations, and various socioeconomic levels in societies in Jack Goody, ed., *Literacy in Traditional Societies* (Cambridge: Cambridge University Press, 1968).

15. Richard S. Hess, "Rhetorical Forms in EA 162," *UF* 22 (1990): 137–48; Hess, "Smitten Ant Bites Back: Rhetorical Forms in the Amarna Correspondence from Shechem," in *Verse in Ancient Near Eastern Prose*, ed. J. C. de Moor and W. G. E. Watson, AOAT 42 (Kevelaer: Butzon & Bercker; Neukirchen-Vluyn: Neukirchener Verlag, 1993), 95–111; Hess, "Rhetorical Forms in the Amarna Correspondence from Jerusalem," *Maarav* 10 (2003): 221–44.

70 Richard S. Hess

southern Canaan.[16] Situated at the modern town of Hebron, Tell er-Rumeideh remains the best candidate for the site of ancient Hebron. According to analysis of the archaeology, people lived there in the Middle Bronze Age, that is, the first half of the second millennium BC. A single cuneiform tablet fragment was found in these strata in 1986 and published by Moshe Anbar and Nadav Na'aman.[17] The text was edited and published in the collection of Wayne Horowitz and Takayoshi Oshima.[18] Surprisingly, despite being the only text south of Jerusalem from this early date, it has received virtually no attention outside of occasional mention in a few specific studies of onomastics.[19]

The tablet includes eleven partially preserved lines on the obverse and seven on the reverse. The bottom of the tablet is missing, retaining only the first part of the text and the final concluding lines. The text is administrative in nature. This is clear on the obverse, where each line follows a repetitive style mentioning numbers of goats, lambs, and sheep, presumably offered by a Hili-El, who appears at the end of most lines. Along with some other West Semitic names that also appear, three of the last seven lines on the obverse refer to the king. On the reverse the list appears to continue. It then concludes with a note about female collectors (of taxes) and some seventy-seven mature, shorn sheep for offerings as well as another total of forty-six sheep or goats. These quantities indicate that a significant part of the tablet is missing, as the other numbers do not add up to this large a quantity.

Goats and lambs occur in the narratives of Gen 12–37 in the context of sacrifices and offerings (Gen 15:9; 22:7–8). Unlike the laws of the Pentateuch and much of the remainder of the Old Testament, cattle, oxen, and bulls are never mentioned in Genesis in the context of sacrifices. This is also true in the Hebron

---

16. Gen 13:18; 23:2, 19; 35:27; 37:14.

17. Moshe Anbar and Nadav Na'aman, "An Account Tablet of Sheep from Ancient Hebron," *Tel Aviv* 13–14 (1986–87): 3–12.

18. Wayne Horowitz and Takayoshi Oshima (with Seth Sanders addressing the alphabetic cuneiform texts), *Cuneiform in Canaan: Cuneiform Sources from the Land of Israel in Ancient Times* (Jerusalem: Israel Exploration Society and the Hebrew University of Jerusalem, 2006), 88–91. See also "Administrative Document from Hebron," trans. Richard S. Hess (*COS* 4.77:261).

19. See, however, Richard S. Hess, *Israelite Religions: An Archaeological and Biblical Survey* (Grand Rapids: Baker Academic, 2007), 136. For the onomastics, see, in addition to the publications already mentioned, Hess, "Personal Names in Cuneiform Texts from Middle Bronze Age Palestine," in *"He Unfurrowed His Brow and Laughed": Essays in Honour of Nicolas Wyatt*, ed. W. G. E. Watson, AOAT 299 (Münster: Ugarit-Verlag, 2007), 159; Nadav Na'aman, "The Hurrians and the End of the Middle Bronze Age in Palestine," *Levant* 26 (1994): 175–87, esp. 176, reprinted in Na'aman, *Canaan in the Second Millennium B.C.E.: Collected Essays*, vol. 2 (Winona Lake, IN: Eisenbrauns, 2005), 1–24, esp. 3; Ran Zadok, "A Prosopography and Ethno-Linguistic Characterization of Southern Canaan in the Second Millennium BCE," *Michmanim* 9 (1996): 97–145, esp. 104; Anson F. Rainey, "Taanach Letters," *Eretz-Israel* 26 (1999): 153*–62*, esp. 155* (Hebrew); Thomas Richter, *Bibliographisches Glossar des Hurritischen* (Wiesbaden: Harrassowitz, 2012), 89; and the mention by Karel van der Toorn, "Cuneiform Documents from Syria-Palestine: Texts, Scribes, and Schools," *ZDPV* 116 (2000): 97–113.

Second-Millennium BC Cuneiform   71

tablet. In both the Hebron tablet and these Genesis narratives, lambs and goats do occur for purposes of sacrifice.

Add to this the use of these animals for blood sacrifices, the appearance of kings over city-states and local regions (Gen 14:1, 8, 10, 18, 21, 22; 20:2; 26:1, 8), and the West Semitic nature of most of the names, similar to those found in Gen 12–37, and we have a remarkable set of cultural similarities between the Hebron tablet and Gen 12–37. These similarities are not found elsewhere in the Bible, nor do they all occur at any single time after the second millennium BC in southern Canaan.

Perhaps even more important is what this tablet indicates about the certainty of oral tradition. As an administrative tablet, it is unlikely to have been brought from outside the area of Hebron. Rather, a local scribe would have composed a text that records offerings and the collection of taxes. The formal and repetitive nature of the text does not reflect a high literary form, to be sure, but it does indicate that such parallelism and use of formulaic expressions did occur in writing in the Hebron area around the time of the ancestors of Genesis.

Conclusion

The three assumptions regarding oral tradition mentioned earlier are that (1) earlier material in the Bible is oral; (2) literacy was virtually nonexistent in early Israel; and (3) the appearance of formulas and repetitions in written texts betrays their origins in oral traditions. For (1), the Hebron tablet is not part of the Bible. However, the similarities in this written text to matters of location, culture, and religion in Genesis allow that the Genesis traditions could have been written down just like this cuneiform tablet.

Regarding (2), we have already seen the widespread presence of writing in nearby regions and closely related cultures with respect to the ancestors of Genesis. Now we have a written text (the Hebron tablet) from the precise location and the same period that Gen 12–37 assigns to Abraham, Isaac, Jacob, and their wives and families. It is no longer possible to regard Hebron as an illiterate backwater where writing could not occur. Nor does the administrative nature of the text mean that only settled people used written texts. There are no products of settled agriculture mentioned in this text. Only the products of pastoral and possibly tribal peoples appear. Geographically, sociologically, temporally, and culturally the Hebron tablet opens the door for written texts behind our Genesis accounts and that date back to the early or mid-second millennium BC in a manner that no other evidence demonstrates as clearly.

As for point (3), the question of the appearance of formulas and repetitions, we have seen how this administrative tablet has examples of these elements. Although not the sort of literature found in the book of Genesis, the Hebron tablet again opens the door to the use of rhetorical forms that may appear in texts close to the time of the occurrences they purport to describe.

The text recorded on the Hebron tablet does not demonstrate that the narratives of Genesis were written down in the early or mid-second millennium BC. It does, however, demonstrate that scribes were resident at Hebron at this time and that such records could have been written.

CHAPTER 5

The Hittite Treaty Prologue Tradition and the Literary Structure of the Book of Deuteronomy

Jiří Moskala and Felipe A. Masotti
Andrews University

Introduction

The first correlations between the biblical covenant and ancient Near Eastern (ANE) treaty traditions were made after the discovery and study of the Hittite treaty texts.[1] Based on Viktor Korošec's study on the literary form of the Hittite treaties,[2] George Mendenhall suggested an alternative perspective to the standard scholarly treatment of the Israelite covenant[3]—it was, by then, seen as a new perception/elaboration in the history of biblical Israel.[4] He proposed a

---

1. See an introduction to the discovery and decipherment of the Hittite language, as well as its importance in the comprehension of some biblical accounts, in Trevor Bryce, *Life and Society in the Hittite World* (Oxford: Oxford University Press, 2002), 1–7; cf. Billie Jean Collins, *The Hittites and Their World* (Atlanta: SBL, 2004).

2. Viktor Korošec, *Hethitische Staatsverträge: Ein Beitrag zu ihrer juristischen Wertung*, Leipziger rechtswissenschaftliche Studien 60 (Leipzig: T. Weicher, 1931).

3. George E. Mendenhall, "Ancient Orient and Biblical Law," *BA 17* (1954): 26–46; Mendenhall, "Covenant Forms in Israelite Tradition," *BA* 17, no. 3 (1954): 49–76; Mendenhall, "The Suzerainty Treaty Structure: Thirty Years Later," in *Religion and Law: Biblical-Judaic and Islamic Perspectives*, ed. Edwin B. Firmage, Bernard G. Weiss, and John W. Welch (Winona Lake, IN: Eisenbrauns, 1990), 85–100; cf. E. Bickerman, "Coupe une alliance," *Archives d'Historie du Droit Oriental* 5 (1950–1951): 133–56; Meik Gerhards, "Hethitische und biblische Historiographie," *BN*, n.s., 156 (2013): 107–30; Zsolt Simon, "Die angenommenen hethitisch-biblischen kulturellen Parallelen: Das Problem der Vermittlung," *BN*, n.s., 156 (2013): 17–38.

4. Ernest W. Nicholson divides the history of scholarship on the subject into four phases: "a generation of controversy, stimulated by Wellhausen's work, was followed by a period of widespread agreement on essentials. The third phase began in the mid-1950s and introduced into the discussion hitherto unexplored evidence from a study of ANE inter-state treaties, which, it is maintained, shed considerable light on the origin, nature and form of the covenant traditions and texts in the Old Testament. The fourth and current phase began in the 1960s and represents a sharp reaction to the two preceding ones. It argues that the covenant traditions were a late development in the Israelite religion and were as yet unknown to the prophets of the eighth century" (Ernest W. Nicholson, *God and His People: Covenant and Theology in the Old Testament* [Oxford: Clarendon, 2002], 56). See also Robert A. Oden, "The Place of Covenant in the Religion of Israel," in *Ancient Israelite Religion: Essays in Honor of Frank Moore Cross*, ed. Patrick D. Miller, Paul D. Hanson, and S. Dean McBride (Philadelphia: Fortress, 1987), 429–47.

74   Jiří Moskala and Felipe A. Masotti

parallelism between the reasonably stable literary form of the Hittite treaties and the structure of yhwh's covenant with Israel.[5] As a result, the study of the connection between ANE treaty traditions and biblical covenants became a standard approach to the topic of the origins of Deuteronomy.

The tendency in comparative studies, however, has shifted from Hittite to Neo-Assyrian treaties as the main source for the biblical concept of covenant[6]— becoming the dominant view among scholars.[7] The shift marks a partial return[8] to Wellhausen's stress on the absence of the covenant concept in Israel before the later prophets[9] and marks a sharp reaction to the preceding scholarly empha-

---

5. Mendenhall noticed the following parallels between the literary form of the biblical covenants and the Hittite treaty tradition: preamble, historical prologue, stipulations, provision for deposit in the temple and periodic public reading, the list of gods as witnesses, and the curses and blessings formula (Mendenhall, "Covenant Forms," 58–60). He also noticed a qualitative difference between the traditions, in that the biblical covenant is of a religious nature, whereas the Hittite tradition operates within a political framework (Mendenhall, "Covenant Forms," 64).

6. See, e.g., Rintje Frankena, "The Vassal-Treaties of Esarhaddon and the Dating of Deuteronomy," *OtSt* 14 (1965): 122–54; Delbert R. Hillers, *Covenant: The History of a Biblical Idea* (Baltimore: Johns Hopkins University Press, 1969); Moshe Weinfeld, "Covenant Terminology in the Ancient Near East and Its Influence on the West," *JAOS* 90 (1970): 190; Klaus Baltzer, *The Covenant Formulary: In Old Testament, Jewish and Early Christian Writings*, trans. David E. Green (Philadelphia: Fortress, 1971), 1–8; Moshe Weinfeld, *Deuteronomy and the Deuteronomic School* (Oxford: Clarendon, 1972), 59–60; Weinfeld, "Covenant Making in Anatolia and Mesopotamia," *JANESCU* 22 (1993): 135.

7. See particularly David Wright, "The Adaptation and Fusion of Near Eastern Treaty and Law in Law Collections of the Hebrew Bible"; Bernard Levinson, "Revisiting the 'and' in Law and Covenant in the Hebrew Bible"; and Bruce Wells, "Law and Covenant in the Neo-Babylonian Period" (papers presented at the Professor George E. Mendenhall Symposium: Law, Society and Religion. Ann Arbor, MI, October 7, 2016). Cf., e.g., M. Cogan, *Imperialism Religion: Assyria, Judah, and Israel in the Eighth and Seventh Centuries B.C.E.* (Missoula, MT: Scholars Press, 1974); Eckart Otto, *Das Deuteronomium: Politische Theologie und Rechtsreform in Juda und Assyrien*, BZAW 284 (New York: De Gruyter, 1999).

8. John Barton, "Biblical Scholarship on the European Continent, in the UK, and Ireland," in *Hebrew Bible, Old Testament: The History of Interpretation*, ed. Magne Soebø (Göttingen: Vandenhoeck & Ruprecht, 2015), vol. 3, pt. 2, 322–24; cf., eg., Stephen L. Cook, *The Social Roots of Biblical Yahwism* (Atlanta: SBL, 2004); Jeffrey Stackert, *A Prophet Like Moses: Prophecy, Law, and Israelite Religion* (Oxford: Oxford University Press, 2014), 194–209. See the interesting article by Peter Machinist on Wellhausen's use of Assyriology (Peter Machinist, "The Road Not Taken: Wellhausen and Assyriology," in *Homeland and Exile: Biblical and Near Eastern Studies in Honour of Bustenay Oded*, ed. Gershon Galil, Markham Geller, and Allan Millard, VTSup 130 [Leiden: Brill, 2009]: 469–532). Interestingly, Machinist points (492–93) and Stackert refers (Stackert, *Prophet Like Moses*, 13) to the fact that Wellhausen was especially attentive to Assyriology for relating Neo-Assyrian royal texts to the Israelite royal history (cf. Julius Wellhausen, "Ueber den bisherigen Gang und den gegenwärtigen Stand zer Keilentzifferung," *Rheinisches Museum für Philologie* 31 [1876]: 153–75).

9. "The relation of Yahweh to Israel was in its nature and origin a natural one; there was no interval between him and his people to call for thought or question. Only when the existence of Israel had come to be threatened by the Syrians and Assyrians, did such prophets as Elijah and Amos raise the Deity high above the people, sever the natural bond between them, and put in its place a relation depending on conditions, conditions of a moral character. . . . In this way arose . . . , as an

The Hittite Treaty Prologue Tradition   75

sis on Hittite treaties.[10] Such a perspective, however, has been counterpointed by some scholars,[11] who argue against a tendency to entirely discard any possibility for a Hittite connection with or influence over Deuteronomy—in spite of the strong form resemblances both traditions show.[12] Therefore, the ongoing debate about which tradition is the closest antecedent to the biblical covenants is connected to the dating of the Hebrew of Deuteronomy's text, as well as to doubts and/or certainties about its textual integrity.[13]

It is within the context of the debate on the textual integrity of Deuteronomy that the present essay revisits an aspect of its possible connection with the Hittite treaty tradition. The focus is on the suggestion that Deuteronomy and Hittite treaties have a common strategy for their historiography, adopting a legal perspective of history by combining a selective historical review with legal material. Accordingly, the conclusions suggest that this shared legal perspective of history—connected to the blending of literary genres—supports an intended synchronic reading of Deuteronomy's structure as a plausible possibility already

---

entirely new thing, the substance of the notion of covenant or treaty. The name Berith, however, does not occur in the old prophets, not even in Hosea. . . . After the solemn and far-reaching act by which Josiah introduced law, the notion of covenant-making between Yahweh and Israel appears to have occupied the central position in religious thought" (Julius Wellhausen, *Prolegomena to the History of Ancient Israel* [Edinburgh: Black, 1885; repr., Atlanta: Scholars Press, 1994], 417–19).

Bredenkamp observes that "Wellhausen . . . sees that if the idea of an historical covenant established with the people once for all time under Moses, with certain conditions, is of great antiquity and universal, then his historical structure has lost its foundation" (C. J. Bredenkamp, "The Covenant and the Early Prophets," *Old Testament Student* 4, no. 3 [1884]: 123).

10. See Nicholson, *God and His People*, 56–82.

11. See e.g., Meredith G. Kline, *Treaty of the Great King* (Grand Rapids: Eerdmans, 1963); Kline, *The Structure of Biblical Authority* (Eugene, OR: Wipf & Stock, 1997); Kenneth A. Kitchen, *On the Reliability of the Old Testament* (Grand Rapids: Eerdmans, 2003), 290; Joshua A. Berman, *Created Equal: How the Bible Broke with Ancient Political Thought* (Oxford: Oxford University Press, 2008); Kenneth A. Kitchen and Paul J. N. Lawrence, *Treaty, Law and Covenant in the Ancient Near East*, 3 vols. (Wiesbaden: Harrassowitz, 2012); Mark Steven François, "Something Old, Something Borrowed, or Something New? The Relationship Between the Succession Treaty of Esarhaddon and the Curses of Deuteronomy 28" (PhD diss., University of St. Michael's College, 2017).

12. René Lopez, "Israelite Covenants in the Light of Ancient Near Eastern Covenants: Part 1 of 2," *CTS Journal* 9 (2003): 92–111; Lopez, "Israelite Covenants in the Light of Ancient Near Eastern Covenants: Part 2 of 2," *CTS Journal* 10 (2004): 72–106. Cf. Baltzer, *Covenant Formulary*, 9–10; and Noel Weeks, *Admonition and Curse: The Ancient Near Eastern Treaty/Covenant Form as a Problem in Inter-cultural Relationships*, JSOTSup 407 (London: T&T Clark, 2004).

13. See Gordon Johnston, "What Biblicists Need to Know About Hittite Treaties" (paper presented at the Old Testament Backgrounds and Ancient Near East Study Group of the National Meeting of the Evangelical Theological Society, San Antonio, TX, November 16, 2016). Cf. John H. Walton, *Ancient Israelite Literature in Its Cultural Context: A Survey of Parallels Between Biblical and Ancient Near Eastern Texts* (Grand Rapids: Zondervan, 1989); Walton, *Ancient Near Eastern Thought and the Old Testament: Introducing the Conceptual World of the Hebrew Bible* (Grand Rapids: Baker Academic, 2006); Neal A. Huddleston, "Deuteronomy as *Mischgattung*: A Comparative and Contrastive Discourse Analysis of Deuteronomy and Ancient Near Eastern Traditions" (PhD diss., Trinity Evangelical Divinity School, 2015).

76   Jiří Moskala and Felipe A. Masotti

for a second-millennium BC literary milieu. Such a suggestion accordingly supports a synchronic reading of Deuteronomy's internal claims for authorship—acknowledging an early supplemental redactional activity in minor portions of the book, but in line with its unified literary covenantal form.

The Use of History in the Hittite Historical Prologue

The historical prologue is unique to the Hittite treaty tradition, being—in general—the second section of the standard Hittite treaty form—coming after the title/preamble section.[14] Unlike the Hittite treaties, Mesopotamian treaties consistently avoid this way of addressing a vassal,[15] which may indicate a different strategy in the suzerain's program for conservation of his empire's cohesion.[16] Despite the reasons for the absence of history in non-Hittite treaties, however, any possible analysis of ANE treaty historical prologues can be only

---

14. Mendenhall, "Covenant Forms," 56. Cf. William F. Albright, *From the Stone Age to Christianity* (Baltimore: Johns Hopkins University Press, 1940), 16; Herbert B. Huffmon, "Covenant Lawsuit in Prophets," *JBL* 78 (1959): 295; Kline, *Treaty of the Great King*; Kenneth A. Kitchen, *Ancient Orient and Old Testament* (Downers Grove, IL: InterVarsity, 1966), 91; Gordon J. Wenham, "The Structure and Date of Deuteronomy: A Consideration of Aspects of the History of Deuteronomy Criticism and Re-examination of the Question of Structure and Date in the Light of that History and of the Near Eastern Treaties" (PhD diss., University of London, 1969), 182–216; Kenneth A. Kitchen, *The Bible in Its World: The Bible and Archaeology Today* (Downers Grove, IL: InterVarsity, 1977), 79–85.

15. This situation may well be due to the partial lack of data for modern analysis. Additionally, the tablets are often too damaged at both their beginning and end, which especially affects the data comprising lost sections of possible historical prologues. It is important to take into account, however, a notable exception to the almost total absence of the prologue in Mesopotamian sources, the treaty between Ashurbanipal and the Arabian Qedar. The tablet presents three broken lines apparently containing a historical prologue in a first-millennium Neo-Assyrian treaty. It is questionable whether its fragmentary nature deposes against the presence of a full-fledged prologue or attests to a literary tradition of using history for the composition of a treaty. However, despite the interpretation one assumes, the consensus is that the tablet displays historical remarks in a non-Hittite treaty—perhaps of an exceptional nature. See K. Deller and S. Parpola, "Ein Vertrag Assurbanipals mit dem arabischen Stamm Qedar," *Or* 37 (1968): 464–66; A. F. Campbell, "An Historical Prologue in a Seventh-Century Treaty," *Bib* 50 (1969): 534–35.

16. Weeks writes, "In contrast [to Hittite treaties], the primary motivation for vassal fidelity in the Assyrian document was fear. Vassals were not promised blessings (although these may be implied), but they were warned instead that acts of infidelity would result in a curse from the gods and the wrath of the Assyrian army" (Weeks, *Admonition and Curse*, 8). Sparks argues for the importance of the curse in Mesopotamian treaties: "If the persuasive use of history is less prominent in Mesopotamia than amongst Hittites, what replaces it in Mesopotamia? That is, what induces loyalty to the relationship? The simple answer is found in the far greater emphasis on the curse in Mesopotamia" (Kenton L. Sparks, *Ancient Texts for the Study of the Hebrew Bible: A Guide to the Background Literature* [Peabody: Hendrickson, 2009], 442).

The two main theories comprising the reasons behind the existence of, and the literary practices in, the Hittite historical prologue are the "propaganda" and the "divine assembly/legal" theories. The "propaganda theory" is a trend in scholarship that had its outset with Korošec's work.[17] Under this proposal, the historical prologue basically shows the suzerain's intention of communicating the dangers that a vassal and his people would face in case of unfaithfulness to a treaty agreement—this being the core motivation upon which the entire treaty was based.[18]

and especially attained by the study of Hittite sources, a fact that makes such tradition a primary source for comparison with Deuteronomy's covenantal historiography.

Trevor Bryce points to an important aspect of the Hittite propaganda in the historical prologue: "On the basis of information from the archives, the preamble may be used to stress the loyalty of the vassal king's predecessors as a model for his own behavior. (Any past actions which contradict this can be conveniently ignored.) On the other hand if a vassal's predecessors have behaved contrary to their overlord's interests, a reminder of their fate and of the king's beneficence to the vassal throne's present incumbent may serve as a useful introduction to the treaty."[19] The propagandistic selection of history seems to have an important role in the suzerain's communication with the vassal, for history was carefully crafted to convey arguments promoting the vassal's faithfulness.[20]

An example of propagandistic selectivity is the available information about the Hittite king Suppiluliuma I's relations with the Ugaritic king Niqmaddu

---

17. Korošec, *Hethitische Staatsverträge*, 12–15, 31–33, 58–61. Cf., e.g., Gurney writing that "[the historical preamble] served to recall the past benefits conferred on the vassal and so to arouse his sense of duty and gratitude" (O. R. Gurney, *The Hittites: A Summary of the Art, Achievements, and Social Organization of a Great People of Asia Minor During the Second Millennium B.C. as Discovered by Modern Excavations* [Harmondsworth: Penguin, 1962], 173); cf. Dennis J. McCarthy, *Treaty and Covenant*, 2nd ed., AnBib 21 (Rome: Pontifical Biblical Institute, 1978), 53–54. See Raymond Cohen's interesting article on military intelligence during Amarna age. His conclusions support the existence of a highly developed international community nurturing the need for spies who sought concealed information probably for checking the "official" line represented by documents such as treaties and royal letters. This was potentially part of the background for the Hittite suzerain's propagandistic responses to crises, for a certain level of anxiety and uncertainty was inherent to the geopolitical game (Raymond Cohen, "Intelligence in the Amarna Letters," in *Amarna Diplomacy: The Beginnings of International Relations*, ed. Raymond Cohen and Raymond Westbrook [Baltimore: Johns Hopkins University Press, 2000], 85–98; cf. Kevin Avruch, "Reciprocity, Equality, and Status-Anxiety in the Amarna Letters," in Cohen and Westbrook, *Amarna Diplomacy*, 154–64).

18. See Daria Gromova's suggestion that the simple act of public reading is itself a propaganda device, for all the people of a given vassal were aware of the dangers his king would lead them in case of a revolt against their suzerain (Daria Gromova, "Idanda Archive and the Syrian Campaigns of Suppiluliuma I: New Pieces for the Puzzle," *Babel und Bibel* 6 [2012]: 478; cf. Gromova, "Hittite Role in Political History of Syria in the Amarna Age Reconsidered," *UF* 39 [2007]: 277–309).

19. Bryce, *Hittite World*, 68.

20. Cf. Hillers, *Covenant*, 30–31.

II, as expressed by two Akkadian treaty texts found at the Southern Palace at Ugarit. Both texts were written from the Hittite court in different moments. Both address the king of Ugarit and present different historical perspectives about what led Niqmaddu to surrender to Suppiluliuma:[21]

CTH 46

Thus says His Majesty, Suppiluliuma, Great King, King of Hatti, Hero:

When Itur-Addu, king of the land of Mukish: Addu-nirari, king of the land of Nuhashshi; and Aki-Teshshup, king of Niya were hostile to the authority of His Majesty, the Great King, their lord; assembled their troops: captured cities in the interior of the land of Ugarit; oppressed (?) the land of Ugarit; carried off subjects of Niqmaddu, king of the land of Ugarit-Verlag, as civilian captives; and devastated the land of Ugarit; Niqmaddu, king of the land of Ugarit-Verlag, turned to Suppiluliuma, Great King, writing: May Your Majesty, Great King, my lord, save me from the hand of my enemy! I am the subject of your Majesty, Great King, my lord. To my lord's enemy I am hostile, [and] with my lord's friend I am at peace. The kings are oppressing me. The Great King heard these words of Niqmaddu, and Suppiluliuma, Great King, dispatched princes and noblemen with infantry [and chariotry] to the land of Ugarit. And they chased the enemy troops [out of] the land of Ugarit [. . .] honored the princes and noblemen very much. He gave them silver, gold, bronze, [and . . .] He arrived [. . .] in the city of Alalah before His Majesty, Great King, his lord, and [spoke as follows] to His Majesty, Great King, his Lord: [. . .] with words of hostility [. . .] Niqmaddu is [not] involved [. . .] And [Suppiluliuma, Great King], witnessed [the loyalty] of Niqmaddu.

CTH 47

Thus says His Majesty, Suppiluliuma, Great King, King of Hatti, Hero:

When all the kings of the land of Nuhashshi and the king of the land of Mukish were hostile to His Majesty, Great King, their lord, Niqmaddu, king of the land of Ugarit-Verlag, was at peace with His Majesty, Great King, his lord, and not hostile. Then the king of the land of Nuhashshi and the kings of the land of Mukish oppressed (?) Niqmaddu, king of the land of Ugarit-Verlag, saying: "Why are you not hostile to His Majesty along with us? But Niqmaddu did not agree upon hostilities against His Majesty, Great King, his Lord, and His Majesty, Great King, witnessed the loyalty of Niqmaddu.

---

21. "Treaty Between Suppiluliuma I of Hatti and Niqmaddu II of Ugarit," trans. Gary Beckman (*HDT* 4:30–31 [= *TLC* 1.61:459–64; and *CTH* 46]); and "Edict Suppiluliuma I of Hatti Concerning the Tribute of Ugarit," trans. Gary Beckman (*HDT* 28A:151–52 [= *CTH* 47]). Cf. Sylvie Lackenbacher, *Textes akkadiens d'Ugarit: Textes provenant des vingt-cinq premières campagnes*, LAPO (Paris: Les Éditions du Cerf, 2002), 1–5. Both texts' dates are ca. 1344–22 BC. For the Akkadian text of *CTH* 46, see the tablet *RS* 17.340 in *PRU* 4:XLVIII–XLIX; and for its transliteration see *PRU* 4:48–52. For the Akkadian text of *CTH* 47, see the tablet *RS* 17.227 in *PRU* 4:XXIV–XXV; and for its transliteration, see *PRU* 4:40–44.

Joshua Berman has noticed that although both tablets converge in general lines, they present history from different angles.[22] Berman has observed that CTH 46 contains a detailed account with the names of the kings who invaded Ugarit, showing Niqmaddu's loyalty, even in face of his kingdom's destruction. The emphasis seems to be placed upon Ugarit's faithfulness and the Hittite king's respect for his vassal by acknowledging such a loyal attitude and avoiding entering Ugarit's territory for the ratification of a treaty. On the other hand, CTH 47 is much more concise in its description of Ugarit's invasion. In fact, if taken in isolation, the text does not even hint at military aggression from Nuhashshi and Mukish. It presents these countries as exercising mere political pressure over Ugarit, to which Hatti responds with war. In this case, the emphasis seems to be upon the Hittite king's right to keep Ugarit under a vassal treaty, for Suppiluliuma promptly delivered Niqmaddu from the hostile coalition.[23]

It is the phenomenon of historical selectivity that has led to the proposal that the historical prologue essentially serves as a tool for diplomatic propaganda. Rather than attesting to the multiplicity of sources, it was designed to inspire loyalty by exploring different aspects of a Hittite suzerain's self-projected image, depending on the particular historical setting to which a given treaty was answering. For example, in the case of Suppiluliuma I and Niqmaddu II's international relations, the first tablet shows the Hittite king as the merciful, respectful, and just deliverer of Ugarit, while the second document claims his rights as the suzerain and supreme lord of the vassal city. Both, however, are designed to inspire obedience according to their respective—at several instances unknown—historical momentum.

Although scholars hold a consensus regarding the final legal binding nature of ANE treaties, few defend this aspect as the driving force behind their composition.[24] In contrast, however, to this consensus stands an alternative view

---

22. Joshua A. Berman, "Histories Twice Told: Deuteronomy 1–3 and the Hittite Treaty Prologue Tradition," *JBL* 132, no. 2 (2013): 229–50. Cf. Berman, *Inconsistency in the Torah: Ancient Literary Convention and the Limits of Source Criticism* (Oxford: Oxford University Press, 2017), 63–80.

23. "Note that the words "I am a 'slave' of the Sun, the Great King, my lord!" by no means may be taken as suggesting that Niqmaddu was already subjugated. They rather present Niqmaddu's submission and express his readiness to become subordinate" (Amnon Altman, "The Role of the 'Historical Prologue' in the Hittite Vassal Treaties: An Early Experiment Securing Treaty Compliance," *JHIL* 6, no. 1 [2004]: 47–48). See also Itamar Singer, "A Political History of Ugarit," in *Handbook of Ugaritic Studies*, ed. Wilfred G. E. Watson and Nicolas Wyatt, HdO 1, Nahe und der Mittlere Osten 39 (Leiden: Brill, 1999), 635; and Gromova, "Hittite Role," 284. Cf. Amnon Altman, "The Submission of Sharrupshi of Nuhasse to Suppiluliuma I (CTH 53 A obv. 2–11)," *UF* 33 (2002): 27–48.

24. See, e.g., Amnon Altman, "The Kingdom of Amurru and the Land of Amurru, 1500–1200 BCE" (PhD diss., Bar-Ilan University, 1973); Guy Kestemont, *Diplomatique et droit international en Asie occidentale (1600–1200 av. J.C.)*, PIOL 9 (Louvain: Peeters, 1974).

80 Jiří Moskala and Felipe A. Masotti

to the "propaganda theory," which is "to think of vassal treaties in terms of negotiated settlements (in a political market that could favor buyers or sellers) than of imposed edicts. After all, all that a treaty added was the divine sanctions promised by the vassal's oath. If the overlord could impose his will by brute force, he would have no need of them."[25]

Westbrook observes that ANE treaties carefully seem to convey a politico-legal message, in which the rupture of an eventual deal could be punished mainly by the gods, for the human suzerain was naturally impotent to compre-hensibly do so at all times, in all his territory.[26] It is partially based on this aspect that Amnon Altman has proposed what can be labeled as "divine assembly/legal theory," meaning that the treaties were legal documents registering the divine project for the nations' relations and, as such, to be judged by the assembly of gods.[27] In light of such a possibility, the historical prologue rather conveyed the Hittite suzerain's legal presentation of his justification before the divine council for military incursions into and for imposition of overlordship onto other nations' territories.

The divine council or assembly of gods is a known motif of the ANE religion and culture. Several documents attest to the ANE belief that gods met together in assemblies for deciding human fate.[28] In some treaties, the list of gods serving as witnesses provides additional information indicating that at the moment of a treaty's ratification the divine council was believed to gather together and assume the role of judging future disputes regarding the treaty's stipulations. This can be seen, for example, in a treaty between the Hittite and the Hurrian nations: " [On account] of these [word]s of the treat[y], [may they take their stand, take note and be wi]tnessess. If yo[u, Shat]tiwaza, and (your) people of the [Hurri]-land, [do not observe the]se [w]ords of this treaty, . . . may these gods of the o[ath destroy you."[29] Even clearer is the treaty between Tudhaliya

25. Westbrook, "International Law in the Amarna Age," in Cohen and Westbrook, *Amarna Diplomacy*, 40.

26. Ibid., 40.

27. Amnon Altman, *The Historical Prologue of the Hittite Vassal Treaties: An Inquiry into the Concepts of Hittite Interstate Law*, Bar-Ilan Studies in Near Eastern Languages and Culture (Ramat-Gan: Bar-Ilan University Press, 2004), 34.

28. See, e.g., Patrick D. Miller Jr., "The Divine Council and the Prophetic Call to War," *VT* 18, no. 1 (1968): 100–107; E. Theodore Mullen Jr., *The Assembly of the Gods: The Divine Council in Canaanite and Early Hebrew Literature*, HSM 24 (Atlanta: Scholars Press, 1980); David Marron Fleming, "The Divine Council as Type Scene in the Hebrew Bible" (PhD diss., Southern Baptist Theological Seminary, 1989); Michael S. Heiser, "The Divine Council in Late Canonical and Non-Canonical Second Temple Jewish Literature" (PhD diss., University of Wisconsin–Madison, 2004); Daniel Porter, "God Among the Gods: An Analysis of the Function of Yahweh in the Divine Council of Deuteronomy 32 and Psalm 82" (PhD diss., Liberty Baptist Theological Seminary, 2010); Ari Mermelstein and Shalom E. Holtz, eds., *The Divine Courtroom in Comparative Perspective*, BibInt 132 (Leiden: Brill, 2015).

29. "Shattiwaza of Mitanni and Suppiluliuma I of Hatti," trans. Kenneth A. Kitchen and Paul J. N. Lawrence (*TLC* 1.56A:397 [= *CTH* 52.1; *HDT* 6B:47–48]). Cf. Mark S. Smith, *God in Translation:*

IV and Ulmi-Teshub (Kurunta) of Tarhuntassa: "Now regarding (the fact that) I have prepared this treaty-tablet for you, so now on this same occasion the Thousand gods into council are summoned. They shall see and hear, and be witnesses."[30]

Besides the express wording of the Hittite treaties, other documents indicate that treaties were stored in temples—and even ratified within them. This suggests that the gods were expected to divinely keep and enforce the order of circumstances described by these documents.[31] Altman adds that, within such a panorama, an eventual territorial expansion from the suzerain's part into a rival suzerain's country, or even a rebellious posture from a vassal's side, should be taken as a violation of the divinely assigned and earthly agreed order, unless expressly authorized by the gods.[32] This suggestion matches the Hittite practice of collecting the idols of conquered nations,[33] as well as the need to inform a god about an unknown fact, for gods were believed to be susceptible to captivity and human-like behavior.[34] This way, the Hittite historical prologue is also

---

Cross-Cultural Recognition of Deities in the Biblical World (Grand Rapids: Eerdmans, 2010), 57.

30. "Tudkhalia IV of Hatti and Kurunta of Tarhuntassa," trans. Kenneth A. Kitchen and Paul J. N. Lawrence (*TLC* 1.73:625 [= *CTH* 106.2]).

31. See EA 74 and ARM 26 24:10–13. Cf. Smith, *God in Translation*, 58.

32. Altman, *Historical Prologue*, 40–41. See also the interesting stipulation on the Ulmi-Tessub treaty: "If I, the sun-king, ask Ulmi-Tesub for any town or district then he shall give it to him willingly, without being forced. It shall be excluded from the oath of the gods. And if Ulmi-Tesub asks for anything from me, the Sun King, then I, the Sun King, shall give it to him. And this also shall be excluded from the oath of the gods. If he (= Sun-king) is unwilling to give any town or any district to Ulmi-Tesub, King of Tarhuntassa, but the latter forces him, and he takes by force,—then him shall these oath gods blot out utterly from upon the dark earth along with his descendants!" ("Tudkhalia IV (?) of Hatti and Ulmi-Tesub of Tarhuntassa," trans. Kenneth A. Kitchen and Paul J. N. Lawrence (*TLC* 1.74:641 [= *CTH* 106]).

33. See, e.g., the Annals of Hattusilis: "[Thereafter] I went to (the city of) Zalpa and destroyed it. I took its deities and three palanquins and carried them off for the sun-goddess of (the city of) Arinna. I carried off one golden ox and one golden rhyton in the shape of a fist to the temple of the storm-god. I carried off the deities that remained to the temple of (the goddess) Mezzulla. . . . I destroyed Ulma and sowed [cress] on its territory. And I carried off seven deities to the temple of the sun-goddess of Arinna, (including) one golden ox, the goddess Katiti, and Mt. Aranhapilanni. I carried off the deities that remained to the temple of Mezzulla" ("Annals of Hattušili I," trans. Gary M. Beckman, in *Historical Sources in Translation: The Ancient Near East*, ed. Mark W. Chavalas [Oxford: Blackwell, 2006], 219–20). It seems that the function of the captivity of such gods was to make them servants to the Hittite gods in their temples (Amnon Altman, *Tracing the Earliest Recorded Concepts of International Law: The Ancient Near East (2500–330 BCE)*, Legal History Library 8, Studies in the History of International Law 4 [Leiden: Martinus Nijhoff, 2012], 67–68).

34. The gods were apparently believed not to hold an omniscient perspective of the human world, having to carry inquiries whenever needed. See, e.g., *CTH* 70:ii.17 (*KUB* XIV 4) and *CTH* 71:ii.20–21 (*KBo* IV 8), in which the Hittite king Mursilli II asks for divine inquiry. See also the Anzu myth, in which the god Adad comes and goes from the battlefield as a messenger bringing news to the divine council ("The Myth of Zu," trans. James B. Pritchard [*ANET* 111–13]). Cf. the elaboration on these texts in Altman, *Historical Prologue*, 36f–37f. Cf. also Tugendhaft's suggestion that the "Baal's cycle" myth has been written with the brotherhood language proper to the interstate official correspondence of the period in mind. This Bronze Age Ugaritic myth represents the gods acting as

"designed to fulfill a legal function, and addressed not to the vassal king and his court but to the gods, the heavenly judges."[35]

The historical information attached to a given treaty represented the suzerain's selective perspective on the history that led the two represented nations to enter into a binding relationship. The document was carefully crafted to avoid claims of breach of the treaty before the divine assembly. Therefore, history in this section of the treaty was shaped into "legal arguments and claims pertaining to the question of the validity and legality of the suzerain's claim of overlordship over the second party's country."[36] This way, by entering into a treaty relationship with a Hittite king, the vassal was accepting the suzerain's version of history, which became the divine "real history" when ratified in a solemn ritual before the heavenly council, but which also was highly selective in its report and interpretation of the facts. This way, the Hittite prologue must be read as bearing as much legal force as the stipulation section, thus joining the other parts of the Hittite treaty in a document designed to be read as a unified work that had divine legal force in its overall form, message, and structure.

Deuteronomy: Historiography, Literary Integrity, and Authorship

Joshua Berman has shown the significance of the Hittite literary reworking of history for understanding Deuteronomy.[37] Berman reads the historical discrepancies of Deut 1–3 in regard to the history found in the Exodus–Numbers section of the Pentateuch in light of the principle of diplomatic signaling found in the Hittite historical prologue section and the Amarna letter correspondence.[38] Diplomatic signaling is the idea that changes in the diplomatic relationship between the Hittite suzerain and his vassals were communicated by correspondent changes in the suzerain's historical perspective as found in the historical prologue of a

---

suzerains and vassals of the human world, showing the intimate relation between royal and divine realms for the ANE mind:

Your vassal is Baal, O Yamm;

Your vassal is Baal, [O River,]

The son of Dagan, your captive

He will bring your tribute

As the gods, bring [your gift,]

As the holy ones, your offerings. (Aaron Tugendhaft, "How to Become a Brother in the Bronze Age: An Inquiry into the Representation of Politics in Ugaritic Myth," *Fragments* 2, no. 1 (2012): 89–104, http://hdl.handle.net/2027/spo.9772151.0002.008).

35. Altman, *Historical Prologue*, 34.

36. Altman, *Historical Prologue*, 41.

37. Berman, "Histories Twice Told," 229–50. Cf. Berman, *Inconsistency in the Torah*, 81–105.

38. Berman here borrows terminology from Christer Jönsson, "Diplomatic Signaling in the Amarna Letters," in Cohen and Westbrook, *Amarna Diplomacy*, 191–205.

new treaty tablet. Berman suggests that Deut 1–3 similarly approaches the past events of Israel for displaying the people's breach of YHWH's past covenant, and for communicating changes in the relationship between YHWH and Israel based on a distinctive historical perspective of past events. By telling history differently from the narratives in Exodus–Numbers, the text signals that the covenantal relationship has accordingly changed.

The propagandistic nature and diplomatic use of history supporting Berman's argumentation can be further nuanced by Altman's concept of history as presented to the divine assembly in the Hittite treaties. Both the propaganda and legal theories—originally proposed as alternative perspectives—can rather be taken as complementary. This way, the Hittite prologue tradition can be seen as both a propaganda tool and a human agreement on what was ultimately accepted as the divine version and the legal aspect of history. The section was primarily based on the suzerain's intention to display military power for enforcing the divinely assigned international order and communicate his divine decisions toward a needed diplomatic change (propaganda/diplomatic concept). However, this consequently validated the idea that the gods were on his side—that the divine council watches over the divinely assigned human dynamics (divine council/legal concept).

In parallel to Hittite prologues, Deuteronomy's historiography is mainly a historical review of Israel's past with specific emphasis on events that signal the need for the renewal of the covenant and highlight YHWH's salvific action in history. Unlike the Hittites, however, in Deuteronomy YHWH is alone both a supernatural suzerain acting in history and a divine lawgiver. The similarity and contrast between the traditions serve as a natural support for the communication of the commandments and their further legal expansion in Deuteronomy, since both history and law are presented as having divine origin and, as such, were designed to exert legal authority over the nation—reminding them of the supernatural power repeatedly witnessed in the process of getting into Canaan. The result is that the book of Deuteronomy can be seen as a natural culmination of the pentateuchal history, which can be summarized in seven parts/stages: (1) early history narrative (from creation to Abraham)—Gen 1–11; (2) patriarchal narrative (Abraham, Ishmael, Isaac, Esau, Jacob, and Joseph)—Gen 12–50; (3) Egypt narrative (from Joseph to the ten plagues on Egyptian gods and those who were associated with them)—Exod 1:1–12:30; (4) Exodus narrative (journey from Egypt to Sinai; three-month period)—Exod 12:30–18:27; (5) Sinai narrative (described one-year stay at the Mount of God)—Exod 19:1–Num 10:10; (6) wilderness narrative (forty years of wandering)—Num 10:11–21:35; and (7) Plains of Moab narrative (covers last months in the life of Moses)—Num 22–Deut 34.

History in Deuteronomy is connected to multiple genres. Rhetorical expressions of the three sermons (1:6–4:43; 4:43–28:68; 29–30) in the book are mixed

84   Jiří Moskala and Felipe A. Masotti

with historical narratives, and the covenant language is tied with song and poetry. The legislative material is put closely together with history and exhortations. Blessings are presented together with curses.[39] Such blending of literary genres, covenantal language, and history hints toward a parallel comprehension of history to the Hittite prologue, namely as holding legal force. In addition to its Hittite counterpart, however, Deuteronomy employs song and poetry for conveying its covenantal message, making the literary blend richer and more complex.

The blending of history, covenantal language, and diverse literary genres supports the plausibility of a synchronic reading of Deuteronomy's unified appeal for covenantal obedience,[40] for the literary diversity can be seen as a strategy for the communication of a unified legal perception of the book.[41] Nanette Stahl has noticed that the polyphonic nature of the pentateuchal discourse may have its roots in the several transitional points of Israel's history.[42] For Stahl, the liminal moments of Israel were marked by the communication of law, with a stress on the literary polyphonic discourse conveyed by its connection with narrative. She treats "biblical law as ambivalent, embedded communication. . . . In this view, law is defined functionally as an act in which words uttered communicate certain intentions to a community but the act is not complete until the listeners fulfill the instructions, injunctions, etc. that constitute those laws."[43] Stahl's

39. Lawrence writes: "Blessing formulae are normally used less than curses. For example, the Law Collection of Hammurabi (1792–1750 BC) only has two blessings, but has fifty curses. In the biblical material Exodus/Leviticus has 10 curses to 5 blessings, Deuteronomy has forty curses to eight blessings" (Paul Lawrence, *The Book of Moses Revisited* [Eugene, OR: Wipf & Stock, 2011], 76).

40. See Watts's observation about the blending of genres in ANE literature: "Ancient texts display their persuasive intentions overtly in the militaristic boasts and threats of kings or the promises and warnings of sages or, most obviously, by invoking blessings and curses from the gods on their readers and hearers. Persuasion was not limited to particular genres of discourse and literature but was frequently a stimulus leading authors to combine genres to create more persuasive forms. In this process, the rhetorical capacities of many different kinds of literature were harnessed for overtly persuasive purposes" (James W. Watts, "Story–List–Sanction: A Cross-Cultural Strategy of Ancient Persuasion," in *Rhetoric Before and Beyond the Greeks*, ed. Carol S. Lipson and Roberta A. Binkley [Albany: State University of New York Press, 2004], 197).

41. See Huddleston's suggestion that "the deuteronomic corpus comprises an intentional hybridization of discourse types incorporating a composite structure analogous to the Hittite subordination treaty in its interdiscourse relationships, and that Deuteronomy's synchronic form encapsulates this composite genre in parenetic and theologically significant language" (Huddleston, "Deuteronomy as *Mischgattung*," iv).

42. Nanette Stahl, *Law and Liminality in the Bible*, JSOTSup 202 (Sheffield: Sheffield Academic Press, 1995). Cf. T. W. Mann, *The Book of the Law* (Atlanta: John Knox, 1988); J. H. Sailhamer, *The Pentateuch as Narrative: A Biblical-Theological Commentary* (Grand Rapids: Zondervan, 1992); James W. Watts, *Reading Law: The Rhetorical Shaping of the Pentateuch*, BibSem 9 (Sheffield: Sheffield Academic Press, 1999).

43. Stahl, *Law and Liminality*, 21. Cf. J. R. Searle, *Speech Acts: An Essay in the Philosophy of Language* (Cambridge: Cambridge University Press, 1969), 50–53.

observation is especially pertinent in regard to Deuteronomy's blend of history and law in light of the Hittite treaty tradition. If one takes the concept of Hittite divine legal history into account, the boundaries between history and legal genres are to be taken as being intertwined into a unified literary appeal[44] for covenantal obedience (e.g., Deut 6:4–5; 7:7–8).[45] As Israel obeys, the promises of past covenants will be made true, and the renewal of the covenant will be as fruitful and effective as the witnessed divine activity in history that led the nation to this point (cf. Deut 30:1–10).[46]

As an appeal for covenantal fidelity, Deuteronomy's introduction states why the book was written: "Moses began to expound this law" (Deut 1:5b NIV).[47] The key Hebrew word is *ba'ar*, meaning "expound," "interpret," or "make

---

44. The book seems to use features of Egyptian literature in addition to the Hittite suzerain-vassal treaty traditional form for conveying such an appeal. See James K. Hoffmeier, *Ancient Israel in Sinai* (New York: Oxford University Press, 2011), 181–92. Cf. "The pentateuchal covenants, although essentially following the late Second Millennium treaty form, were not its slavish imitators" (Lawrence, *Book of Moses*, 62).

45. See, e.g., Averbeck's assertion: "In reality, therefore, there are a good number of instances seeded through the Law in which the call for good and fair treatment of resident aliens is based on Israel's past experience in Egypt. One could say that it is essential to the ethos of the whole Law, Exodus through Deuteronomy, from beginning to end, and in between. Whether laying foundations or coming to conclusions, the lawgiver gravitated toward the founding event and its implications for the good life in ancient Israel" (Richard E. Averbeck, "The Egyptian Sojourn and Deliverance from Slavery in the Framing and Shaping of the Mosaic Law," in *"Did I Not Bring Israel Out of Egypt?" Biblical, Archaeological, and Egyptological Perspectives on the Exodus Narratives*, ed. James K. Hoffmeier, Alan Millard, and Gary Rendsburg, BBRSup 13 [Winona Lake, IN: Eisenbrauns, 2016], 161). Cf. Lohfink's contention: "Der Pentateuch als ganzer präsentiert sich nicht als rhetorische Vermittlung von recht an seine Leser, und erst recht nicht als Rechtskodifizierung. Als ganzer ist er kein rechtsstiftender Sprechakt. Er ist eine Erzählung, Die Gestaltung als Erzählung ist auch keine Verkleidung einer Absicht, die sofort auf Rechtskodifizierung ginge" (Norbert Lohfink, "Prolegomena zu einer Rechtshermeneutik des Pentateuch," in *Das Deuteronomium*, ed. Georg Braulik, ÖBS 23 [Frankfurt am Main: Peter Lang, 2003], 42). We are indebted to Kenneth Bergland for these references.

46. See, e.g., Bernard S. Jackson's suggestion that the several covenant renewals found in the HB are embedded in narrative structures. For him, an author having the patriarchal narrative in mind composed the Deuteronomic law. Commenting on the Deuteronomic law of primogeniture (Deut. 21:15–17) and its probable association with Jacob's narrative, he argues that "even if it does have an independent, customary origin, the law, thus written, could hardly be read—or listened to—by anyone familiar with the patriarchal narratives without evoking such associations" (Bernard S. Jackson, *Studies in the Semiotics of Biblical Law*, JSOTSup 314 [Sheffield: Sheffield Academic Press, 2000] 229). Cf. Calum M. Carmichael, *The Laws of Deuteronomy* (Ithaca: Cornell University Press, 1974), 61–62; Carmichael, *Law and Narrative in the Bible: The Evidence of the Deuteronomic Laws and the Decalogue* (Ithaca: Cornell University Press, 1985), 142–5.

47. It is difficult to precisely determine the limits of the term "this law." However, "the fact that the phrase occurs randomly in narrative and legal contexts throughout the book (e.g., Deut 4:8; 17:18; 27:3; 31:9) strongly supports the conclusion that it refers to the large majority of the book rather than to any specific literary form within it" (M. J. Selman, "Law," in *Dictionary of the Old Testament: Pentateuch*, ed. T. Desmond Alexander and David W. Baker [Downers Grove, IL: InterVarsity Press, 2003], 500).

plain." The same term is used also in Hab 2:2. The plain summary of the purpose of the book is expressed several times. Moses speaks to the whole nation in order for them to learn how to fear God and maintain a proper relationship with the Lord their God in love and obedience to him. The best summary of the book's purpose is explained in Deut 31: "So they can listen and learn to fear the LORD your God and follow carefully all the words of this law" (Deut 31:12 NIV). It is reinforced in the following verse: "Their children, who do not know this law, must hear it and learn to fear the LORD your God as long as you live in the land you are crossing the Jordan to possess" (Deut 31:13 NIV).

The Deuteronomic law is connected in details to the Decalogue, depending and expanding on it, as Kaufman demonstrates. Kaufman aptly concluded his study with an emphatic note: "The efforts of a century of scholarship to propose elaborate redactional histories for DL [the Deuteronomic Law] must be deemed fruitless. DL did not grow in stages as these scholars would have us believe. It is rather a unified masterpiece of jurisprudential literature created by a single author . . . into a highly patterned whole—an expanded Decalogue."[48]

The notion of a synchronic-intended composition of Deuteronomy suggests that authorship is also to be read in accordance with the book's claims. In the book, Moses is presented in his speaking as well as writing capacities. Moses's writing ministry is well expressed and underlined in the book of Deuteronomy (see Deut 28:58; 29:20–21, 27; 30:10; 31:9–13, 19, 22, 24–26). Also, his writing activity is already explicitly mentioned in other places within the Pentateuch (Exod 17:14; 24:4; 34:27–28; Num 33:2).

This does not mean to exclude the work of an editor/narrator or editors/narrators who put all the material carefully together and added the account about Moses's death (34:5–12), updating notes (2:10–12, 20–23; 3:9, 11, 13b–14; 4:41–5:1a; 10:6–9; 27:1a, 9a, 11; 28:69–29:1a [29:1–2a]; 31:1–2a, 7a, 9–10a, 14a, 14c–16a, 22–23a, 24–25, 30; 32:44–46a, 48; 33:1–2a; 34:1–4a),[49] and con-

---

48. Stephen A. Kaufman, "The Structure of the Deuteronomic Law," *Maarav* 1, no. 2 (1978–79): 147. For the decalogic structure of Deut 12–26 see also Georg Braulik, *Die deuteronomischen Gesetze und der Dekalog: Studien zum Aufbau von Deuteronomium 12–26*, SBS 145 (Stuttgart: Katholisches Bibelwerk, 1991); Benjamin Kilchör, *Mosetora und Jahwetora: Das Verhältnis von Deuteronomium 12–16 zu Exodus, Levitikus und Numeri*, ed. Eckart Otto, BZABR 21 (Wiesbaden: Harrassowitz, 2015), 41–70.

49. For these possible editorial additions, see Daniel I. Block, *The Gospel According to Moses: Theological and Ethical Reflections on the Book of Deuteronomy* (Eugene, OR: Cascade, 2012), 30–33, who argues that "we hear the voice of the narrator in only sixty-four verses" (72). About Block's view on how the book of Deuteronomy was put together, see Daniel I. Block, "Recovering the Voice of Moses: The Genesis of Deuteronomy," *JETS* 44, no. 3 (2001): 385–408; repr. in Block, *Gospel According to Moses*, 21–51. See also his chapter "Will the Real Moses Please Rise? An Exploration into the Role and Ministry of Moses in the Book of Deuteronomy," in Block, *Gospel According to Moses*, 68–103. Cf. Jean-Pierre Sonnet, *The Book Within the Book: Writing in Deuteronomy*, ed. R. Alan Culpepper and Rolf Rendtorff, BibInt (Leiden: Brill, 1997).

The Hittite Treaty Prologue Tradition   87

ceivably even the introduction (1:1–5).[50] Moses could have written it himself
(Deut 31:9, 22, 24) or used a scribe for writing his speeches, song, and blessings.
In this case the best potential candidate for this scribal task was Joshua, as indicated by the fact that he was Moses's assistant during his life (Exod 24:13; Num
11:28; Deut 1:38; Josh 1:1) and successor (Num 27:18–23; Deut 31:7–8, 23; 34:9).
Paul Lawrence completes his study on the second and first millennia treaties
in comparison to the covenant structure reflected in the book of Deuteronomy
by stating that "there is no compelling reason to reject the traditional view,
that Moses was the 'author' of the Pentateuch or at least a very substantial part
of it, with Deuteronomy 34, the account of Moses's own death, being a clear
exception."[51]

The Literary Structure of Deuteronomy

As Moses's closing biography and testament, Deuteronomy stands as an integrated document intended to register and promote a wholehearted renewal of
the covenant between Israel and YHWH and to instruct the people on how to
live in the new conditions they would encounter in the promised land. This
renewal of the covenant is apparent from the whole structure of the book, which
is based upon the articulation of alternative historiographical perspectives,[52]
covenantal language/structure, and law. Three structures are combined: (1) the
rhetorical structure with the three speeches/discourses (1:6–4:43; 4:43–28:68;
29–30);[53] (2) the covenant structure with its six parts: introduction of parties

---

50. For example, the treaty preamble between the Egyptian king Ramses II and the Hittite
king Hattusili III from 1259 BC has basically the same structure as Deut 1:1 (see Lawrence, *Book of
Moses*, 67–68). Also, it is important to note that the Codex of Hammurabi (1792–50 B.C.) as well as
Lipit-Ishtar's (ca. 1930 B.C.) have historical prologues, as is the case with Deuteronomy.

51. Lawrence, *Book of Moses*, 123. Lawrence also strongly declares, "If our conclusions are
true it is time to leave behind the constraints that the JEDP Hypothesis places on our understanding
of the pentateuchal text. The evidence that we have considered clearly points to the Late Second
Millennium BC as the period when the first five books of the Bible were written. So I contend that
it is also time to reinstate Moses as the 'author'" (128). Cf. Kitchen's contention: "In other words,
somebody distressingly like that old 'hero' of biblical tradition, Moses, is badly needed at this point,
to make sense of the situation as we have it. Or somebody in his position of the same or another
name" (Kitchen, *On the Reliability*, 295).

52. It is important to notice, however, that unlike the Hittite prologue, the discrepancies
between the narrative in Exodus–Numbers section and Deuteronomy are not intended to convey
alternative versions of history, concealing factual history from the readers and/or hearers. They are
rather a selective retelling of history intended to emphasize the need for covenantal renewal. Cf.
Berman, "Histories Twice Told."

53. "Preliminary results from a consideration of the vocabulary of Deuteronomy show that
699 of the 1,285 individual words identifiable in the book can be found in non-Hebrew texts from
the third and second millennia (54.4 per cent of the whole), whereas only 97 words can be found

88   Jiří Moskala and Felipe A. Masotti

(1:1–6a), historical prologue (1:6b–4:43), stipulations (4:44–26:19), blessings and curses (27:1–30:20), witnesses (30:19; 31:19), and special provisions of the covenant (31:9–13);[54] (3) the exposition of each of the ten commandments of the Decalogue in the central part of the book, namely in the second sermon (first principles are clarified in chapters 5–11, and then each commandment is explained in chapters 12–26).[55] The result is the following:

The principal title of the book—choose life: love, obey, and fear the Lord
I. Introduction—the preamble of the covenant (1:1–6a): the background for the whole book and the first presentation of the Lord.
II. Moses's first speech/address—the historical prologue of the covenant (1:6b–4:43).
   A. Seven crucial reminders: seven characteristic stories from the time of the pilgrimage from Horeb/Sinai to the Jordan:
      a. God's promise and the appointment of leaders at Horeb (1:6b–18).
      b. Journey from Mount Horeb to Kadesh, sending spies and the rebellion against the Lord at Kadesh (1:19–45[46]).
      c. Wandering in the wilderness around the hill country of Seir and Transjordan—command not to fight with Edom, Moab, and Ammon (2:1–23).
      d. Victory over Sihon, king of Heshbon—the conquest of Transjordan (2:24–37).

---

exclusively in first millennium non-Hebrew texts (7.5 percent). Four hundred and fifty-four examples (35.4 per cent) of the vocabulary of Deuteronomy have no parallels outside of the Hebrew material, and 35 (2.7 percent) require further investigation" (Lawrence, *Book of Moses*, 12).

54. See Kitchen, *Ancient Orient and Old Testament*; Dennis J. McCarthy, *Old Testament Covenant: A Survey of Current Opinions* (Atlanta: John Knox, 1972); 90–102; McCarthy, *Treaty and Covenant*; Kline, *Treaty of the Great King*; Palmer O. Robertson, *The Christ of the Covenant* (Phillipsburg, NJ: Presbyterian & Reformed, 1980); John H. Walton, *Covenant: God's Purpose, God's Plan* (Grand Rapids: Zondervan, 1994); Lawrence, *Book of Moses*; Steven L. McKenzie, *Covenant* (St. Louis: Chalice, 2000); Mendenhall, "Covenant Forms"; and G. J. Wenham, *Exploring the Old Testament: The Pentateuch* (London: SPCK, 2003), 123–43; Skip MacCarty, *In Granite or Ingrained? What the Old and New Covenants Reveal About the Gospel, the Law, and the Sabbath* (Berrien Springs, MI: Andrews University Press, 2007); Kilchör, *Mosetora und Jahwetora*.

55. The elaborate Decalogue structure of the book of Deuteronomy was introduced by Friedrich W. Schultz, *Das Deuteronomium* (Berlin: G. Sklawitz, 1859), but improved by Kaufman, "Structure of the Deuteronomic Law," 105–58, and is now accepted and followed by many scholars: see, e.g., Walter C. Kaiser Jr., *Toward Old Testament Ethics* (Grand Rapids: Zondervan, 1983), 127–137; Eugene H. Merrill, *Deuteronomy: An Exegetical and Theological Exposition of the Holy Scripture NIV Text*, NAC 5 (Nashville: Broadman & Holman, 1994), 218; Denis T. Olson, *Deuteronomy and the Death of Moses: A Theological Reading* (Minneapolis: Fortress, 1994); Andrew E. Hill and John H. Walton, *A Survey of the Old Testament*, 2nd ed. (Grand Rapids: Zondervan, 2000), 131–43; Mark E. Biddle, *Deuteronomy*, SHBC (Macon, GA: Smyth & Helwys, 2003), 197–203; Edward J. Woods, *Deuteronomy*, Tyndale Old Testament Commentaries (Downers Grove, IL: IVP Academics, 2011), 49–55.

The Hittite Treaty Prologue Tradition 89

    e. Victory over Og, king of Bashan—the conquest of the Transjordan (3:1–11).

    f. Distribution of the land to the two and half Transjordan tribes and the command to them (3:12–20).

    g. Moses's encouragement to Joshua to conquer the land, and his plea with the Lord to enter the promised land (3:21–29).

B. Climax: "Hear, O Israel"—Exhortation to obedience and trusting the Lord with practical consequences for Israel (4:1–40)

C. Appendix: The three cities of refuge (4:41–43).

III. Moses's second speech/address—the exposition of the law, exhortations and warnings, blessings and curses of the covenant (4:44–28:68).

A. Covenant stipulations (4:44–26:19).

    a. The foundational principles and the spirit of the law (4:44–11:32).

        1. The proclamation of the Decalogue and exhortation to live it (4:44–5:30 [33]).

        2. The summary of the Decalogue and what it involves: "Love the Lord your God" (6:1–25).

        3. The possession of the land, separation from idolatry, and God's love for his people (7:1–26).

        4. "You shall remember the Lord your God"—encouragement and warning (8:1–20).

        5. Warning against self-righteousness and Israel's previous failures (9:1–10:11).

        6. "Fear the Lord your God" and keep his requirements (10:12–22).

        7. Israel's responsibility, stimulation to serve him, and the basic blessings and curses (11:1–32).

    b. The expansion of the Decalogue (12–26).[56]

        1. The first two commandments—worship[57] (12:1–31).

            a. True love and false worship (12:1–4).

            b. Right place and genuine authorized worship (12:5–14).

            c. Secular and sacrificial slaughter (12:15–28).

            d. Abhor pagan worship (12:29–31 [32]).

        2. The third commandment—name of God (13:1–14:29).

            a. Warning against false prophets and their punishment (13:1–8).

            b. Conduct of the holy people—making a difference between clean and unclean food (14:1–21).

            c. Tithe (14:22–29).

        3. The fourth commandment—Sabbath (15:1–16:17).

---

56. Kaufman, "Structure of the Deuteronomic Law," 147.

57. The summary of the Decalogue in ten key words follows Kaiser, *Toward Old Testament Ethics*, 129.

90   Jiří Moskala and Felipe A. Masotti

      a. The year of release, canceling debts, and the liberation of Hebrew slaves (15:1–18).

      b. Firstborn and the three main feasts (15:19–16:17).

   4. The fifth commandment—authority (16:18–18:22).

      a. Justice and the choice of a king (16:18–17:20)

      b. The rights of the priests and Levites, the true and the false prophet (18:1–22).

   5. The sixth commandment—homicide (19:1–22:8)

      a. Laws related to murder and cities of refuge (19:1–14).

      b. Laws related to witnesses (19:15–21).

      c. Concerning future wars (20:1–20).

      d. Atonement for an unsolved murder (21:1–9).

      e. Various instructions regarding defending or executing people and protecting life (21:10–22:8).

   6. The seventh commandment—adultery (22:9–23:18).

      a. Mixing the wrong together (22:9–12).

      b. Sanctity of marriage and sexual sins (22:13–29 [30]).

      c. The Lord's congregation: its constitution and holiness (23:1–18).

   7. The eighth commandment—theft (23:19–24:7).

      a. Concerning interest, keeping word, and sharing results of a harvest (23:19–26 [25]).

      b. Concerning protection of an accused woman, newly married, debtor and life (24:1–7).

   8. The ninth commandment—false charges (24:8–25:4).

      a. Various laws of protection of the community, the employee, and the innocent (24:8–16).

      b. Responsibility of protecting the weak, poor, offenders, and animals (24:17–25:4).

   9. The tenth commandment—coveting (25:5–26:15).

      a. Brother's wife, dishonesty, and the Amalekites (25:5–19).

      b. First fruits, tithe, and prayer (26:1–15).

   10. Appeal to renew the covenant (26:16–19).

B. The blessings and curses of the covenant (27:1–28:69 [68]).

IV. Moses's third speech/address—further exposition of blessings and curses, the ultimate appeal and enumeration of witnesses (29:1–30:20).

  A. Moses's final charge to Israel—the repetition of the covenant blessings and the restated curses (29:1–28 [29]).

  B. Return to the Lord your God and prosperity: the Lord is your life, so choose life (30:1–20).

    a. Witnesses (30:19; see also 31:19, 26, 28).

V. Preparation for the future: leadership transition and Moses's finalizing actions and words (31–33).

A. Leadership handover from Moses to Joshua and the Lord's Word to Moses (31:1–8).
B. Special provision of the covenant (31:9–13).
C. Israel's rebellion predicted (31:14–22).
D. The Lord's address to Joshua (31:23).
E. Moses's instructions about his Book of the Law (31:24–30 [29]).
F. The Last Song of Moses (32).
G. The Blessing of the Tribes of Israel by Moses (33).

VI. The death of Moses (34:1–8).
A. Moses's climb up Mount Nebo, and God's closing speech to Moses (34:1–4).
B. Death and burial of Moses (34:5–8).

VII. The epilogue (34:9–12).

The above-proposed structure displays the articulation of historiographical revision as a major element for the integration of Deuteronomy's literary structure. Seven characteristic stories from the nation's pilgrimage from Sinai to Jordan are retold (1:6–4:43), opening the book with a particular selection of events that stress YHWH's guidance (1:6b–18), rightful judgment (1:19–45, 2:1–23), supernatural protection (2:24–37, 3:1–11), and assigned order for Israel's division of the land (3:12–29). Of particular importance is the fact that in Moses's three discourses (1:6–4:43; 4:43–28:68; 29–30) "references to YHWH's deliverance of Israel from Egypt appear in some form throughout each major section of the book, permeating the Deuteronomic corpus"[58] (e.g., 4:20, 32–34, 35–38; 5:15; 6:21–23; 7:8, 18–19; 30:1–10, etc.). Huddleston suggests that this insistence on repeatedly reminding the reader about the origin and divine reasons behind the book's content mirrors closely the Middle Babylonian and Hittite paradigms for dealing with history, since both "make use of historiographical discourse on the mainline of the general paradigms as the foundation for a treaty participant's (continued) subjugation."[59]

History is also crucial for the book's usage of covenantal language in its sexpartite covenant-based form (historical prologue [1:1–6a], historical prologue [1:6b–4:43], stipulations [4:44–26:19], blessings and curses [27:1–30:20], witnesses [30:19; 31:19], and special provisions of the covenant [31:9–13]). All the sections of the covenant form are intermingled with explicit and implicit references to Israel's past history. As an example, the ultimate curse for an eventual covenantal unfaithful behavior is to return to Egypt (28:68, cf. Jer 43:7). In this verse, YHWH is presented as retributively undoing Israel's deliverance history, selling them as Joseph had been sold to the country he had promised they would

58. Huddleston, "Deuteronomy as *Mischgattung*," 465.
59. Ibid., 464.

92   Jiří Moskala and Felipe A. Masotti

not go back to (cf. 17:16). Therefore, as in the Hittite tradition, history is used as a legal paradigm for both divine blessing and judgment. In light of this parallel practice, it is important to observe that as any ANE covenantal document based on history, Deuteronomy shows that a biblical covenant could be renewed when needed, but not unofficially expanded/modified.[60] The awareness about a treaty's existence as a unified historical document and the protection of its integrity are part of what conveys its covenantal force for the involved parties. A document that did not exist as a fixed treaty at a given point in time, was not publicly acknowledged in a specific public ceremony, and was susceptible to secret revision as such would have no reason to use an ANE treaty form for its formulation. Consequently, an evolutionary "model of development is contrary to the very nature of the form itself."[61]

60. "To acknowledge the presence of the treaty formulary only in miniature in this or that passage of Deuteronomy but not in the overall structure of the book involves a decidedly selective type of perception. For those who do perceive that Deuteronomy as a whole exhibits the treaty pattern, one fact demands more serious attention than it has hitherto received. Such treaties were sealed legal witnesses not subject to scribal revision. When changes in the covenant arrangement were required, that was accomplished by preparing a new treaty, not by fictionally projecting the modified situation with its new terms within a bygone historical framework" (Kline, *Structure of Biblical Authority*, 14, 27–29). The fact that a treaty could be renewed and had to be so by the making of a new tablet has already been shown in the above discussion about the two tablets containing two different treaties between Suppiluliuma I and Niqmaddu II. In addition, it is important to notice that the intended perpetuity and unity of a treaty document can already be seen in the oldest known treaty, between Eannatum of Lagash and the Ruler of Umma (2500 BC). Besides the fact that this treaty was publicly registered in a stele, it has a curse against its destruction: "[if anyone damages this stela/inscription, etc., . . .] (and) it is brought to his (= a later ruler's) attention, (even) a king of Kish,—[(then) may his personal god never pass before Nigirsu, (and) may he never (so) pass, either! . . .]" ("Eannatum of Lagash and Ruler of Umma," trans. Kenneth A. Kitchen and Paul J. N. Lawrence [*TLC* 1.1: 15]). This curse was kept as a standard clause by the Hittite treaty tradition with an emphasis on the prohibition for the alteration of the treaty text: "whoever alters one word of this tablet—him and his descendants shall the storm-god, king of heaven, the sun-goddess of Arina, the mistress of the Hatti-lands, Sarruma, the son of the storm-god, Ishtar, and the Thousand gods of this tablet blot out from the Hatti-land!" ("Tudkhalia IV [?] of Hatti and Ulmi-Tesub of Tarhuntassa," trans. Kenneth A. Kitchen and Paul J. N. Lawrence [*TLC* 1.74:641]; cf. "Suppiluliuma I of Hatti and Niqmad II of Ugarit," trans. Kenneth A. Kitchen and Paul J. N. Lawrence [*TLC* 1.60:463]). This type of curse could occasionally appear in a more nuanced way. Notice the following prohibitions for hiding and altering the treaty tablet: "And whoever before the storm-god, Lord of the *kurinnu* of Kahat, alters this tablet, or hides it in a secret location, or if he smashes (it), or alters the words of the content on the tablet, on the basis of this treaty, we have invoked the gods of secret and the gods who (are) the lords of the oath. May they take their stand, take notice, and be witnesses" ("Suppiluliuma I of Hatti & Shattiwaza of Mittani," trans. Kenneth A. Kitchen and Paul J. N. Lawrence [*TLC* 1.55A:377]). Cf. Deut 4:2: "Do not add to what I command you and do not subtract from it, but keep the commands of the Lord your God that I give you" (NIV); and 12:32: "See that you do all I command you; do not add to it or take away from it" (NIV).

61. Weeks, *Admonition and Curse*, 169. Cf. Hillers's suggestion that such a scenario should foster more research on the presence of similar literary repetitions as those found in Deuteronomy—commonly taken as markers of textual conflation—in ANE treaty texts, not the other way around, for the overall unity of these documents suggests that repetition could be a major part of the overall

The Hittite Treaty Prologue Tradition   93

Finally, the exposition of the Decalogue (5–11) and its further expansion (12–26) start with a historical basis (5:1–6), and repeatedly alludes to it (e.g., 6:10; 7:18; 8:3, etc.), attesting to its intimate relation with Israel's history and inserting law in a liminal moment of the nation. As an example, this blend of history, covenant, and law is clearly seen in Deut 7:7–11, a text that is within the transitional section dedicated to explaining the foundational principles and the spirit of the law (4:44–11:32) and expresses the function of the section as a preparation for the expansion of the Decalogue:

> [Reference to history:] The Lord did not set his affection on you and choose you because you were more numerous than other peoples, for you were the fewest of all peoples. But it was because the Lord loved you and kept the oath he swore to your ancestors that he brought you out with a mighty hand and redeemed you from the land of slavery, from the power of Pharaoh king of Egypt. [Covenantal language:] Know therefore that the Lord your God is God; he is the faithful God, keeping his covenant of love to a thousand generations of those who love him and keep his commandments. But those who hate him he will repay to their face by destruction; he will not be slow to repay to their face those who hate him. [Reference to law:] Therefore, take care to follow the commands, decrees and laws I give you today. (NIV)

Conclusion

The articulation of history and its elaboration by means of covenantal language and structure, as well as its relation to legal material, seem to suggest that Deuteronomy follows a pattern close to second-millennium Hittite–vassal treaty prologue tradition.[62] Lawrence writes, "It is striking that Historical Prologues do not occur in the Aramaic and Neo-Assyrian treaties of the First Millennium" and that "there are no blessings in the First Millennium Assyrian treaties."[63] Scholars have shown that the second-millennium historical prologue served both as a tool for stressing the suzerain's propagandistic communication, and as the human settling on what was taken as the "divine version of history."

ANE literary practice for treaty making (D. R. Hillers, *Treaty Curses and the Old Testament Prophets*, BibOr 16 [Rome: Pontifical Biblical Institute, 1964], 32).

62. "So by way of a summary: It can be concluded that the form of the pentateuchal covenants has much more in common with the Second Millennium BC treaties than with their counterparts from the First Millennium BC. This suggests the pentateuchal covenants are Second Millennium BC in their origin" (Lawrence, *Book of Moses*, 64).

63. Ibid., 69, 76.

In a similar fashion, Deuteronomy's complex literary structure articulates history into a divine legal revision of Israel's past, using historical selectivity to signal the need for the renewal of the covenant with YHWH. The structure displays history as a legal statement on YHWH's redemptive activity and his consequent right for communicating the law. It also conveys a document intent on preparing Israel to transfer into Canaan and provides the crucial knowledge of how to settle, live, and prosper in the new territory.

Unlike the Hittite king in a treaty prologue, however, Deuteronomy presents YHWH as the God and suzerain who alone backs his law with historical activity/ narrative. Therefore, the structure of the book shows an intermingled approach in regard to genre, but a unified one in regard to its legal nature. It is law in its entirety, synchronically structured and intended to be synchronically read as such. Consequently, especially by analogy with the Hittite treaty historical prologue, the existence of such a complex literary arrangement as seen in Deuteronomy seems to indicate a unified literary document, which could viably be understood as addressing a mid-second-millennium BC audience.

CHAPTER 6

Memorized Covenantal Instruction and Legal Reuse in Torah

Kenneth Bergland
Andrews University

Introduction[1]

Dissimilarity between the different legal corpora has been and still is a major source of controversy in regard to the composition of the Torah.[2] A key question relevant to the present scholarly debate is the direction of dependence between the Book of the Covenant, Holiness Instruction, and Deuteronomy—especially the relation between the latter two.[3] A typical example would be the differences between the manumission instructions in Exod 21:2–11; Lev 25:39–46; and Deut 15:12–18. Critical scholars use the differences as arguments that the differing laws

---

1. This essay is based on and an abbreviation of chapters 2 and 3 in Kenneth Bergland, *Reading as a Disclosure of the Thoughts of the Heart: Proto-Halakhic Reuse and Appropriation Between Torah and the Prophets*, BZAR 23 (Wiesbaden: Harrassowitz, 2019).

2. In the following I will use "Torah" with particular reference to the instructive material in the Pentateuch, and "Pentateuch" as a reference to the books of Genesis–Deuteronomy. While it is common to speak of "legal discrepancy" or "apparent legal discrepancy" between the different instructions in Torah, the first postulates an actual discord between the legal corpora of Torah, while the second postulates that behind its appearance there is really an accord. In order to suspend such judgments of the textual material, acknowledging the limitations of our understanding, I rather prefer more neutral phenomenological descriptions like legal "dissimilarity," "dissimilitude," "differences," "diversity," "variation," and "tension."

3. I cannot, in this essay, give an adequate survey of the scholarly discussion on the direction of dependence between the legal corpora in Torah, but Bernard Levinson and Jeffrey Stackert can represent those who argue that the Holiness Instruction reused Deuteronomy (Bernard M. Levinson, *Deuteronomy and the Hermeneutics of Legal Innovation* [New York: Oxford University Press, 1997]; Levinson, *Legal Revision and Religious Renewal in Ancient Israel* [Cambridge: Cambridge University Press, 2008]; Jeffrey Stackert, *Rewriting the Torah: Literary Revision in Deuteronomy and the Holiness Legislation*, FAT 52 [Tübingen: Mohr Siebeck, 2007]), while Jacob Milgrom and Benjamin Kilchör represent those who argue for the reverse direction of dependence (Jacob Milgrom, *Leviticus 23–27: A New Translation with Introduction and Commentary*, AB 3B [New York: Doubleday, 2001], 2251–57; Benjamin Kilchör, *Mosetora und Jahwetora: Das Verhältnis von Deuteronomium 12–16 zu Exodus, Levitikus und Numeri*, BZAR 21 [Wiesbaden: Harrassowitz, 2015]). Yehezkel Kaufmann represents those who argue that there was no reuse between the legal corpora in Torah (Yehezkel Kaufmann, *The Religion of Israel: From Its Beginnings to the Babylonian Exile*, trans. and abridg. Moshe Greenberg [Chicago: University of Chicago Press, 1960], 153–211).

96   Kenneth Bergland

were composed by different authors, for more or less conflicting purposes, given the various needs at different stages of the history of ancient Israel. Scholars following the more traditional approach have tended to respond by attempting to harmonize the various laws, claiming they were written more or less as a unified and complementary document. In this essay, I want to focus on the phenomena of literary reuse between the legal corpora of Torah. More specifically, I will argue that the concepts of Torah as normative covenantal instruction and memorized reuse help us understand the phenomena of fluid and exact reuse between the legal corpora in the Torah. This model has promise to be a better approach to legal diversity in Torah than the critical or traditional approaches.

When dealing with legal reuse in Torah, the dual phenomenon of exact and creative reuse must be considered. First, why do we find that legal reuse is relatively fluid and innovative, with different instructions, at times standing in tension with each other? Second, why do we simultaneously find evidence of relative exact correspondence? Adequate explanations of both phenomena seem appropriate. The primary purpose of this essay is not to discuss specific cases of reuse, even if such studies evidently will be required. Rather, my intention is to outline a model for approaching legal reuse within Torah that will enable us to see better the compositional logic behind the simultaneous fluid and exact reuse as we find it in Torah. I will draw on scholars who have more recently questioned a legislative conceptualization of Torah, as well as scholars who have argued for a text-supported memorized reuse in ancient Israel. In my opinion, these two strands of scholarship merge into a helpful model for approaching legal reuse within Torah. Therefore, some of the following sections will be more like a survey, while I refer to some specific passages in Torah where particularly relevant.

The following discussion is not intended to resolve questions such as whether the pentateuchal texts should be approached from a source-critical perspective or by harmonization. However, theories regarding the composition of the Torah will be flawed if they do not adequately account for the dual phenomena of fluid and exact reuse that are testified in the textual material and that can be shown to operate with anachronistic characterizations of Torah. According to the proposed model in this essay, legal dissimilitude and innovations in Torah seem possible, even as the laws present themselves as loyal to earlier instructions. I have found Michael LeFebvre's discussion of the characterization of Torah in regard to the question of reuse particularly helpful,[4] together with David Carr's and Susan Niditch's discussion of oral and memorized reuse.[5] While many

---

4. Michael LeFebvre, *Collections, Codes, and Torah: The Re-characterization of Israel's Written Law*, LHBOTS 451 (New York: T&T Clark, 2006).

5. Susan Niditch, *Oral World and Written Word: Ancient Israelite Literature*, ed. Douglas A. Knight, LAI (Louisville: Westminister John Knox, 1996); David M. Carr, *Writing on the Tablet of the Heart: Origins of Scripture and Literature* (Oxford: Oxford University Press, 2005).

scholars in past years have argued against a legislative concept of Torah, the proposed positive characterizations of Torah often appear inadequate or flawed. Suggestions that Torah should rather be seen as "retrospective," "common law," or "descriptive" do not contain satisfactory precision. They either tend to reduce Torah to tradition and sociology,[6] thus compromising the Pentateuch's own claim of being revelation, or to neglect the normativity of the text even if it may be correct to reject seeing it as legislation. Further, as far as I have seen, there is a lack of studies combining the question of how to characterize Torah and memorized reuse into a model for how to approach variation in legal reuse in the Torah. It is to this area I hope this essay can make a contribution.

Torah as Covenantal Instruction

The Legislative Concept of Law and the ANE

Scholars assumed that the cuneiform law collections were legislation in the classical or modern sense when they were first found at the beginning of the twentieth century. The key question was whether they should be understood as codification or reform.[7] Later, several scholars questioned whether this really is a correct understanding of ANE law. The consensus today is that cuneiform law was written for purposes other than legislative ones.[8] According to this view, ANE legal practice functioned on the basis of custom rather than legal codes. This also raised the question of whether biblical law had a legislative function. Westbrook summarizes the differences between what he calls "legislation" and "academic treatise" as follows:

> Legislation is an authoritative source of law; the courts are bound to obey its precepts. That binding quality begins at a certain point in time, when the legislation is promulgated. And once promulgated, the text of the legislation takes on a life of its own—the text is the exclusive source of the law. For this reason, the courts must pay great attention to the wording

6. For a discussion of different sociological reductions of Torah, see Anne Fitzpatrick-McKinley, *The Transformation of Torah from Scribal Advice to Law* (Sheffield: Sheffield Academic Press, 1999), 23–53.

7. Raymond Westbrook, "Cuneiform Law Codes and the Origins of Legislation," in *The Shared Tradition*, vol. 1 of *Law from the Tigris to the Tiber: The Writings of Raymond Westbrook*, ed. Bruce Wells and Rachel Magdalene (Winona Lake, IN: Eisenbrauns, 2009), 73.

8. E.g., Bernard S. Jackson, *Studies in the Semiotics of Biblical Law*, JSOTSup 314 (Sheffield: Sheffield Academic Press, 2000); Raymond Westbrook, "The Character of Ancient Near Eastern Law," in *A History of Ancient Near Eastern Law*, ed. Raymond Westbrook and Gary M. Beckman (Leiden: Koninklijke Brill, 2003), 1–90; Westbrook, "Origins of Legislation"; LeFebvre, *Collections, Codes, and Torah*.

98   Kenneth Bergland

of the text, interpret its meaning, and cite it in their decisions. Even if the legislation does not change the existing law but merely codifies it, the effect is to exclude reliance on the earlier sources.

An academic treatise on the law may be good evidence of what the law is, but it is not an authoritative source. The treatise in describing the law in effect refers the court to the real authoritative sources thereof, whether they be statute, precedent, or custom. The date of the treatise is therefore of less significance; there is no particular point in time at which it comes into effect. And its text has no independent value. Courts need not cite it or pay attention to its wording, since they are essentially looking beyond it to the source that it reflects.[9]

These two concepts of law, the legislative and the academic, will therefore differ in how they reuse the legal texts. In a legislative concept of law, reuse is more likely to include exact wording and citation. On the other hand, in what Westbrook calls the "academic treatise," exact wording and citation is less likely in reuse. Therefore the question of reuse is dependent on what concept of law may be in use within the biblical material.

It may be that ANE law should be understood as "custom dressed up as precedent," as Westbrook suggested,[10] but I will skip the many questions and debates in recent scholarly literature on how best to characterize ANE law. For the present purpose, we can ask the following: does the Torah bear marks of being composed according to a legislative concept of law or not? If not, how should it be characterized? Is it simply reflecting custom, or is it also intervening and modifying custom? Is it simply descriptive of legal tradition, where tradition rather than the text is normative? Or is the text itself viewed as normative? As already argued by others, comparing the textual fluidity of ANE treaty relations helps us account for similar fluidity in the Torah literature.[11]

Characterization of Torah as Normative Covenantal Instruction

As mentioned, I will argue that Torah should be characterized as "covenantal instruction," and not seen as legislative in the classical or modern sense. The

---

9. Westbrook, "Origins of Legislation," 74. We could here also use the distinction between statutory and common-law, as Joshua Berman does (Joshua Berman, "The History of Legal Theory and the Study of Biblical Law," *CBQ* 76 [2014]: 21–22).

10. Westbrook, "Origins of Legislation," 91.

11. Cf. Amnon Altman, *The Historical Prologue of the Hittite Vassal Treaties: An Inquiry into the Concepts of Hittite Interstate Law*, Bar-Ilan Studies in Near Eastern Languages and Culture (Ramat Gan: Bar-Ilan University Press, 2004); Noel Weeks, *Admonition and Curse: The Ancient Near Eastern Treaty/Covenant Form as a Problem in Inter-cultural Relationships*, JSOTSup 407 (London: T&T Clark, 2004); Joshua A. Berman, "Histories Twice Told: Deuteronomy 1–3 and the Hittite Treaty Prologue Tradition," *JBL* 132, no. 2 (2013): 229–50.

reason why it is important to establish the concept of normative covenantal instruction in a discussion of reuse within Torah, is that it helps us to understand the presence of extensive parallels between the legal corpora. Former instructions were seen as normative, even if they were not seen as legislative, and were reused as authoritative texts. If only custom was seen as normative, it is less clear why we would find literary legal reuse within Torah. In other words, a nonlegislative characterization helps us understand why legal reuse within Torah might be more fluid, innovative, and contradictory than what we are used to in classical and modern legal thought. And the concept of covenantal instruction helps us understand why we nevertheless find significant literary parallels between the legal corpora within Torah.

The lexeme בְּרִית (covenant) is used in Exodus–Deuteronomy for a verbally explicated exclusive binding relation between YHWH and his people Israel, represented through their forefathers Abraham, Isaac, and Jacob, or the collective people at any given time.[12] The terminology used within Torah to describe its own genre seems well summed up as "covenantal instruction," even if it must be admitted that this phrase is somewhat an extratextual construct, singling out the terms תּוֹרָה and בְּרִית as representative for the rest. Even if they are not statistically the dominant terms used in Torah for its self-designation, conceptually they seem to summarize the rest. I will return to this point below.

In a legislative concept of law, the wording of the law is itself the final authority, and society should operate according to the "rule of law," where the lawbook is used as the "exclusive source of the law" in order to pass a verdict in court.[13] We will see that neither applies to Torah. In the debate whether ANE and biblical law was legislative, the litmus test seems to be whether or not it had a function in the court. To indicate why Torah should not be understood as legislative, we find some substantial indicators in the instructions given specifically to judges (Exod 18:21; 23:1–8; Lev 19:15–16; Deut 1:16–17; 16:19–20; 25:1). There Torah as such is nowhere explicitly said to be a source in ancient Israelite jurisprudence. In other words, it is not seen as an autonomous legal source with sufficiently comprehensive formulations to regulate and sanction the conduct of the people. As Patrick has already pointed out, it is a striking fact that none of the instructions to judges speak of consulting and judging according to Torah. Instead the judges are admonished to judge according to the more general standard of צֶדֶק (justice).[14]

---

12. The lexeme בְּרִית is attested in Exod 2:24; 6:4–5; 19:5; 23:32; 24:7–8; 31:16; 34:10, 12, 15, 27–28; Lev 2:13; 24:8; 26:9, 15, 25, 42, 44–45; Num 10:33; 14:44; 18:19; 25:12–13; Deut 4:13, 23, 31; 5:2–3; 7:2, 9, 12; 8:18; 9:9, 11, 15; 10:8; 17:2; 28:69; 29:8, 11, 13, 20, 24; 31:9, 16, 20, 25–26; 33:9.

13. Westbrook, "Origins of Legislation," 74.

14. Dale Patrick, *Old Testament Law* (Atlanta: John Knox, 1985), 191, 197–98.

100   Kenneth Bergland

I agree with Patrick that צֶדֶק cannot be limited to a literalistic reading of Torah. But he continues: "During the period in which the legal texts were being composed, the law of God was an unwritten law, that is, the principles and concepts constituting ancient Israel's understanding of justice and righteousness."[15] While Patrick sees the ultimate reference of law as "the sense of justice shared by the legal community" and "the fundamental norms of the social order,"[16] I would rather argue that the transcendent reference in Torah seems to be YHWH himself. In that sense, the reference of the court is "unwritten," as it refers to YHWH. But Torah is his instruction, the written formulation of his character.[17]

If we look at the instructions given for judges, the reference is not the "legal community" and "the fundamental norms of the social order"; it is YHWH, since the chosen judges are described as "fearers of God" (יִרְאֵי אֱלֹהִים, Exod 18:21). In Lev 19:16 the reference is again YHWH (אֲנִי יְהוָה). And Deut 1:17 could hardly make the ultimate reference of the court clearer, declaring that "the judgment belongs to God" (הַמִּשְׁפָּט לֵאלֹהִים הוּא).[18] Thus, the concept of "unwritten law" is not necessary and relieves us of the conjectural reasoning of trying to reconstruct what it might be. Rather, we have the written Torah and a transcendent reference beyond it, YHWH, who constitutes the final authority in all manners of life and justice. This also concurs with LeFebvre's point that the oracle, in the person of Moses the prophet (Exod 18:13–27), constituted the primary source for the judiciary in ancient Israel,[19] even if it cannot be assumed that the "high court" in Deut 17:8–13 would consult with an oracle.[20]

15. Ibid., 218.

16. Ibid., 192, 198.

17. Cf. Moshe Greenberg, "Some Postulates of Biblical Criminal Law," in *Yehezkel Kaufman Jubilee Volume: Studies in Bible and Jewish Religion Dedicated to Yehezkel Kaufmann on the Occasion of His Seventieth Birthday*, ed. Menahem Haran (Jerusalem: Magnes, 1960), 11–13. The closest analogy in genre within the biblical material itself might be the parent instructing his or her child through the wisdom literature. For a similar description of wisdom as here given of Torah, see Michael V. Fox, *Proverbs 1–9: A New Translation with Introduction and Commentary*, Anchor Yale Bible Commentaries 18 (New Haven: Yale University Press, 2008), 347.

18. The double reference to the land "which God is giving you" (אֲשֶׁר יְהוָה אֱלֹהֶיךָ נֹתֵן לָךְ) in Deut 16:18–20 is again a reminder that the judges judge on behalf of God in his land.

19. LeFebvre, *Collections, Codes, and Torah*, 40–47. In the following, I will argue that given that Torah was intended to be embodied by all the people, including the judges, it cannot be ruled out that Torah somehow influenced the ancient Israelite judiciary. Since all the people were supposed to memorize and embody Torah, something that would also apply to the judges, Torah would likely at least indirectly affect Israelite jurisprudence, even if it is not explicitly referred to in the instructions given specifically to judges (Exod 23:1–8; Exod 18:21; Lev 19:15–16; Deut 1:16–17; 16:19–20; 25:1). Still, I do concur with LeFebvre that the oracle stood at the center of jurisprudence in ancient Israel. In all four legal cases mentioned in the instructive material of Torah (Lev 24:10–23; Num 9:1–14; 15:32–36; 27:1–11) we simultaneously find the centrality of the oracle. This fits with seeing YHWH as the transcendent reference of Torah.

20. Alexander Rofé, "The Organization of the Judiciary in Deuteronomy (Deut. 16.18–20; 17.8–13; 19.15; 21.22–23; 24.16; 25.1–3)," in *The World of the Aramaeans: Biblical Studies in Honour*

The conclusion of the above, even if just briefly discussed, is that Torah does not fit a legislative concept of law. Literalistic reuse is therefore not needed, as in a classic or modern court, where the lawbook is quoted verbatim as the "exclusive source of the law."[21] This accounts for the fluidity we find in legal reuse both within Torah itself and in other passages of the Hebrew Bible (HB).

On the other hand, we still find a second and simultaneous phenomenon in the passages with legal reuse in Torah that also needs to be accounted for, namely a significant amount of literal legal reuse in Torah, in the form of identical or similar lexemes, phrases, and concepts in the very same passages with more fluid reuse. I will suggest that characterizing Torah as normative covenantal instruction can account for this phenomenon.[22] I will here briefly summarize eight reasons why I believe Torah is best characterized as "covenantal instruction."

1. Torah intervenes and modifies custom; it does not simply reflect and describe it.[23] An example pointed out by Greenberg is the separation in Torah between human life and monetary compensation, in contrast to ANE custom of monetary compensation for the loss of human life.[24] The internal evidence, at least as explicitly formulated, tells us that YHWH, not custom, was the primary source for Torah (see the discussion above of YHWH as the transcendent reference).

2. Whether Torah was written on a tablet (לוּחַ), scroll (סֵפֶר), pillar (מַצֵּבָה), or stone (אֶבֶן), or whether it was read publicly or spoken privately, the didactic function seems predominant.[25]

---

of Paul-Eugène Dion, ed. P. M. Michèle Daviau, John W. Wevers, and Michael Weigl, JSOTSup 324 (Sheffield: Sheffield Academic Press, 2001), 99.

21. Westbrook, "Origins of Legislation," 74.

22. Daniel Block's observation concerning Deuteronomy probably could apply just as well to the entire Torah: "Recognizing the fundamentally covenantal character of Deuteronomy has extremely significant implications for the message we hear in the book" (Daniel I. Block, *The Gospel According to Moses: Theological and Ethical Reflections on the Book of Deuteronomy* [Eugene, OR: Cascade, 2012], 8). Cf. how he writes on the same page: "Contrary to prevailing popular opinion Deuteronomy does not present itself as legislation, that is, a book of laws. This is prophetic preaching at its finest."

23. Cf. Umberto Cassuto, *A Commentary on the Book of Exodus*, trans. Israel Abrahams (Jerusalem: Magnes, 1997), 262–64.

24. Greenberg, "Some Postulates," 5–28.

25. Cf. Deut 4:36; 5:1, 31; 6:1; 11:2. In my opinion, Jackson's division into the monumental, archival, didactic, and ritual uses of Torah is imprecise. First of all, the monumental and archival uses do not say so much about function as location of Torah. Second, the ritual use of Torah could easily be seen as a subcategory of the didactic. One of the passages quoted by Jackson, Deut 31:9–13, makes this adequately clear (Jackson, *Studies in the Semiotics*, 139). Twice in this passage the explicitly stated purpose of the ritual reading of Torah is that the people should learn (using the root למד). It therefore seems difficult to sustain a strict separation between the ritual reading and the didactic function of Torah. The reading of Torah is not "fulfilled by the act of public reading itself" (ibid.). In my opinion, the inscription of Torah upon a monument, tablet, or סֵפֶר as media can be summarized

102   Kenneth Bergland

3. The terminology used within Torah to describe its own genre (מִשְׁפָּט, דָּבָר, חֹק, תּוֹרָה, חֻקָּה, מִצְוָה, and בְּרִית) seems well summed up as "covenantal instruction." If we limit the textual parameters to the legal sections (Exod 18:1–23:33; Lev 1:1–27:34; Num 5:1–6:27; 15:1–41; 19:1–22; 27:1–30:17; 33:50–36:13; Deut 4:1–28:69), we can give the self-designation in Torah a statistical presentation. Key terminology here is דָּבָר (100, of which 35 can be said to refer to Torah as genre), מִשְׁפָּט (65), מִצְוָה (54), חֻקָּה (39), תּוֹרָה (37), חֹק (35), בְּרִית (28).[26]

4. The legal sections of Torah share formal features and content with ANE treaty, law, and covenant.[27]

5. The relatively frequent use of the first and second person in the legal material of Torah, in contrast to the dominant—if not exclusive—use of the third person in other ANE law, creates an immediate discursive and dialogical setting for the instructions.[28] This agrees with the fact that in Exod 18:20 we read וְהִזְהַרְתָּה אֶתְהֶם אֶת־הַחֻקִּים וְאֶת־הַתּוֹרֹת וְהוֹדַעְתָּ לָהֶם אֶת־הַדֶּרֶךְ יֵלְכוּ בָהּ וְאֶת־הַמַּעֲשֶׂה אֲשֶׁר יַעֲשׂוּן ("and enjoin upon them the laws and the teachings, and make known to them the way they are to go and the practices they are to follow" [NJPS]). Jethro here states that Moses should continue to enjoin (וְהִזְהַרְתָּה) the laws and instructions upon the people. Even though Moses would be the Torah expert, all the people were to be instructed in them.[29] This also accords with the observations that Torah's

---

as having an instructional function, with the judicial implications involved in this instruction also serving as a witness against the people.

26. Among words used in the instructive sections of Torah to refer to its own genre, דָּבָר and מִשְׁפָּט are the most frequently used. We would of course expect a high frequency of the word דָּבָר in a discourse setting such as this one, and many of the references are not to Torah as such. In 35 cases דָּבָר can be said to describe the genre or parts of Torah (Exod 20:1; [34:28]; Lev 8:5, 36; 9:6; 10:7; 17:2; Num 15:31; 30:2–3; 36:6; Deut 4:2, 10, 12–13; 5:5, 22; 6:6; 9:10; 10:2, 4; 11:18; 12:28; 13:1; 15:2, 15; 17:19; 19:4; 24:18, 22; 27:3, 8, 26; 28:14, 58, 69). For the use of דָּת in the *qere* in Deut 33:2 as LBH see Jan Joosten, "Diachronic Linguistics and the Date of the Pentateuch," in *The Formation of the Pentateuch: Bridging the Academic Cultures of Europe, Israel, and North America*, ed. Jan Christian Gertz, Bernard M. Levinson, Dalit Rom-Shiloni, and Konrad Schmid, FAT III (Tübingen: Mohr Siebeck, 2016), 343.

27. Cf. Kenneth A. Kitchen and Paul J. N. Lawrence, *Treaty, Law and Covenant in the Ancient Near East Part 2: Text, Notes and Chromograms* (Wiesbaden: Harrassowitz, 2012), 259–65, who have recently argued for the form-critical proximity between the legal sections of Torah and ANE legal texts, particularly Hittite treaties. Among critical scholars it is common to see the closest parallels between Torah and the vassal treaties of Esarhaddon (e.g., Moshe Weinfeld, *Deuteronomy and the Deuteronomic School* [Winona Lake, IN: Eisenbrauns, 1992]).

28. If we define Exod 18:1–23:33; Lev 1:1–27:34; Num 5:1–6:27; 15:1–41; 19:1–22; 27:1–30:17; 33:50–36:11; Deut 4:1–28:69 as the instructive material in Torah, we get the following statistics: The PNG (person, number, gender) distribution of verbs would be 1cs 5.06 percent, 2ms 18.16 percent, 2fs 0.08 percent, 3ms 47.49 percent, 3fs 9.78 percent, 1cpl 0.49 percent, 2mpl 11.97 percent, 2fpl 0 percent, 3mpl 6.19 percent, and 3fpl 0.79 percent. The PNG distribution of suffixes would be 1cs 5.46 percent, 2ms 20.84 percent, 2fs 0.75 percent, 3ms 33.24 percent, 3fs 11.54 percent, 1cpl 1.22 percent, 2mpl 12.36 percent, 2fpl 0 percent, 3mpl 13.62 percent, 3fpl 0.98 percent.

29. Shalom M. Paul, *Studies in the Book of the Covenant in the Light of Cuneiform and Biblical Law* (Eugene, OR: Wipf & Stock, 2006), 34, 46–47. According to Greenberg, the publication of Torah is interlinked with the call of Israel "to live in dedication to God after the manner of priests"

Memorized Covenantal Instruction and Legal Reuse in Torah 103

imperatives regarding specific mental states do not fit a legislative concept of law. Having surveyed the general tendency in Deuteronomy to command attitudes and feelings, Carasik writes that "the psychological commands in general do not fit into our notion of an objective system of law."[30] Weeks finds the use of terminology like "good," "love," "know," and "son" to be likely covenantal language.[31] Uncoerced willingness is expressed by terms like "love" and "joy," both found in Israelite and ANE legal traditions.[32]

6. The sanctions, including covenant curses (Lev 26; Deut 28) and the need to expiate sins in case of failure or breach of the covenantal relationship (e.g. Lev 4–5), indicate normativity.[33] In all four legal cases mentioned in the instructive material of Torah (Lev 24:10–23; Num 9:1–14; 15:32–36; 27:1–11) we simultaneously find the proximity of instruction and practice, again showing an assumed normativity of the instructions.[34]

7. It seems difficult to separate the instructive material from the narrative covenantal setting. Averbeck has made a convincing argument that the deliverance narrative permeates the entire instructive material of the Book of the Covenant: "Virtually at every turn, the rationale for the Law depends on the people's deliverance from slavery in Egypt and its implications for the way that they must treat the poor and disadvantaged in Israel, including the resident alien."[35] It thus becomes understandable why the manumission instructions introduce the Book of the Covenant. But Averbeck points out how manumission instructions also conclude the Sinai Instructions in Lev 25:39–55.[36] He sums it up succinctly as follows: "there would be no Law without the exodus."[37]

(e.g., Exod 22:30; Lev 20:26, and Deut 14:2), implying that Torah "is to function as a pedagogue, a trainer in a course of life" (Moshe Greenberg, "Three Conceptions of the Torah in Hebrew Scriptures [1990]," in *Studies in the Bible and Jewish Thought*, JPS Scholar Distinction Series [Jerusalem: Jewish Publication Society, 1995], 14–15). On the individual Israelite as the analogy to the subordinate king in suzerainty treaties, see Joshua A. Berman, *Created Equal: How the Bible Broke with Ancient Political Thought* (Oxford: Oxford University Press, 2008), 41–42, 115.

30. Michael Carasik, *Theologies of the Mind in Biblical Israel*, StBibLit 85 (New York: Peter Lang, 2005), 202.

31. Weeks, *Admonition and Curse*, 160.

32. Yochanan Muffs, *Love and Joy: Law, Language and Religion in Israel* (New York: Jewish Theological Seminary of America, 1992), 124, 127, 148, 187.

33. For the sanction of כרת ("to cut off") see Donald J. Wold, "The Meaning of the Biblical Penalty Kareth" (PhD diss., University of California, Berkeley, 1978).

34. Cf. Fitzpatrick-McKinley, *Transformation of Torah*, 110–11.

35. Richard E. Averbeck, "The Egyptian Sojourn and Deliverance from Slavery in the Framing and Shaping of the Mosaic Law," in *"Did I Not Bring Israel Out of Egypt?" Biblical, Archaeological, and Egyptological Perspectives on the Exodus Narratives*, ed. James K. Hoffmeier, Alan Millard, and Gary Rendsburg, BBRSup 13 (Winona Lake, IN: Eisenbrauns, 2016), 157–58.

36. Averbeck, "Egyptian Sojourn and Deliverance," 158–59, 161, 163.

37. Ibid., 166. Cf. Norbert Lohfink, "Prolegomena zu einer Rechtshermeneutik des Pentateuch," in *Das Deuteronomium*, ed. Georg Braulik, ÖBS 23 (Frankfurt am Main: Peter Lang, 2003), 42; Lohfink, "The Priestly Narrative and History," in *Theology of the Pentateuch: Themes of the Priestly Narrative and Deuteronomy* (Edinburgh: T&T Clark, 1994), 136–72.

104   Kenneth Bergland

According to Joosten, "the theme of the Exodus underpins the entire discourse of H. . . . There is not one single subject treated in H that is not directly connected in some way with that momentous event from the past."[38] Nihan has recently argued for the narrative coherence of the Exodus–Numbers account, simultaneously seeing the divisions into separate books as following the logic of the pentateuchal narrative.[39] He observes that the so-called formula of self-presentation (אֲנִי יְהוָה אֱלֹהֵיכֶם / אֲנִי יְהוָה) within the exhortations and laws themselves, found especially in Lev 17–26 but also in the other legal corpora, points to a close and inseparable relation between the instructive material and the narrative covenantal setting.[40]

8. Material outside the instructive material of Torah seems to corroborate a concept of Torah as normative covenantal instruction, like the normativity of covenants in the patriarchal cycles (e.g., Gen 21:22–33; 26:26–31, 44–54) and the prophetic indictment of the people on the basis of Torah (e.g., Isa 58; Jer 34:8–22).[41]

These are some arguments for why it is preferable to see Torah as normative covenantal instruction. This concept also seems best to account for the dual phenomena—often seen in the same passages—of creative and exact reuse. The rejection of a legislative model for Torah helps us understand why cases of reuse of Torah in the HB do not seem to belong to the literalistic type of reuse we are used to in modern law. In Torah's covenantal character, YHWH becomes the ultimate reference, not the literary formulations themselves. The Torah instructions

---

38. Jan Joosten, *People and Land in the Holiness Code: An Exegetical Study of the Ideational Framework of the Law in Leviticus 17–26* (Leiden: Brill, 1996), 101. Cf. his discussion of this point at 93–101.

39. Christophe Nihan, *From Priestly Torah to Pentateuch: A Study in the Composition of the Book of Leviticus*, FAT, 2nd ser., no. 25 (Tübingen: Mohr Siebeck, 2007), 69–95.

40. Ibid., 400. Cf. p. 399. See also Joosten, *People and Land in the Holiness Code*, 94 for a cautious, but similar point. The following passages in Exodus–Deuteronomy include the phrase אֲנִי יְהוָה אֱלֹהֵיכֶם/ אֲנִי יְהוָה: Exod 6:2, 6–8, 29; 7:5, 17; 8:18; 10:2; 12:12; 14:4, 18; 15:26; 16:12; 29:46; 31:13; Lev 11:44–45; 18:2, 4–6, 21, 30; 19:2–4, 10, 12, 14, 16, 18, 25, 28, 30–32, 34, 36–37; 20:7–8, 24, 26; 21:8, 12, 15, 23; 22:2–3, 8–9, 16, 30–33; 23:22, 43; 24:22; 25:17, 38; 25:55–26:2; 26:13, 44–45; Num 3:13, 41, 45; 10:10; 14:35; 15:41; 35:34; Deut 29:5. As will be easily seen from this distribution, within instructive material, the phrase is found predominantly in Leviticus.

41. Cf. B. Gemser, "The *Rib*- or Controversy-Pattern in Hebrew Mentality," in *Wisdom in Israel and in the Ancient Near East*, ed. Martin Noth and D. Winton Thomas (Leiden: Brill, 1960). For further studies on the concept of covenantal lawsuit see Noel Weeks, *Admonition and Curse*, 159; Richard M. Davidson, "The Divine Covenant Lawsuit Motif in Canonical Perspective," *JATS* 21, nos. 1–2 (2010): 45–84; Shalom E. Holtz, "The Prophet as Summoner," in *A Common Cultural Heritage: Studies on Mesopotamia and the Biblical World in Honor of Barry L. Eichler*, ed. Grant Frame (Bethesda, MD: CDL, 2011), 19–34; Job Y. Jindo, "The Divine Courtroom Motif in the Hebrew Bible: A Holistic Approach," in *The Divine Courtroom in Comparative Perspective*, ed. Ari Mermelstein and Shalom E. Holtz, BibInt 132 (Leiden: Brill, 2015), 76–93. For how prophets are part of the divine courtroom, and how the divine courtroom appoints human rulers and judges for the maintenance of cosmic order, see ibid., 81–82.

Memorized Covenantal Instruction and Legal Reuse in Torah 105

therefore do not introduce a "rule of law," but find their origin and possible revisions with YHWH, and are thus contingent. Since the primary relation is between YHWH and his people, where the instructions become an aid in this covenantal relationship, the final reference is not the instructions but YHWH. On the other hand, as the words of YHWH, the normativity of the instructions invites a close reading and, at points, exact reuse of the Torah instructions.[42] The goal is a covenantal relationship between YHWH and his people, where the instructions function didactically to facilitate a holy and righteous way of life together with a holy and righteous God. They set the stage for the covenantal relationship, defining and indicating how it is to be lived out. And as the Torah instructions are concerned not only with regulating external conduct but with instructing the people in how to live covenantal forms of lives with YHWH,[43] they invoke love, joy, and gratitude as motivations for covenantal obedience. As Torah addresses the heart, the form of life lived after reading or listening to the Torah instructions thus also becomes a disclosure of the thoughts of the heart. Since the dynamics of this covenantal life cannot be reduced to words and instructions, Torah takes the form of pointers and examples to this covenantal life. For example, Torah is thus not "fulfilled by the act of public reading itself."[44] Rather, Torah is only fulfilled through covenantal forms of lives. Torah sets the frame of such a covenantal life, but does not exhaust it. And it is within this frame that room is found for literary originality and innovation, where implications of previous Torah instructions or additional revelation fill in or paint for the first time a part of the picture not yet seen.

As poets and authors have known for a long time, words and instructions can never exhaust the dynamics of a personal relationship, or specifically a covenantal life for that matter. As healthy relations have a stable root in the known and familiar, creating a basis for adventuring into the unknown, legal reuse finds its "home" in exact correspondence of lexemes, phrases, or concepts, but also opens for exploring the covenantal relation through literary creativity,

---

42. Stackert helpfully distinguishes between two modes of conceptualizing textual authority. He writes that "it is important to contrast redaction/canonization with divine revelation as claims to textual authority. Specifically, the locus of authority differs between these two modes of legitimation. In the case of divine revelation, the claim of authority is internal to the text itself: the very words of the deity are contained in that text. By contrast, the authority of canon is external to the texts canonized: it is not the text's own claim but rather a secondary authorization that legitimizes such a text" (Jeffrey Stackert, *Rewriting the Torah: Literary Revision in Deuteronomy and the Holiness Legislation*, FAT 52 [Tübingen: Mohr Siebeck, 2007], 215). In my opinion, it seems clear that both in Torah and the prophets the claim to textual authority resides in the claim to contain divine revelation, not a claim of canonicity. This problematizes a canonical approach to intrabiblical reuse. For further discussions of this question see Christine Hayes, *What's Divine About Divine Law? Early Perspectives* (Princeton: Princeton University Press, 2015).

43. For the phrase "forms of life" see the reflections on this in Ludwig Wittgenstein, *Philosophical Investigations*, trans. G. E. M. Anscombe (Oxford: Blackwell, 1968).

44. Jackson, *Semiotics of Biblical Law*, 139.

106   Kenneth Bergland

invention, and even revision where needed. Maybe we dare even claim that later literary compositions about covenantal forms of life have a creative imperative. A mere repetition of Torah would be a poor expression of covenantal instructions. But rooted in the previous Torah instructions, reuse needs to go beyond, by once more directing the readers and listeners to forms of lives in covenant with YHWH. Instead of seeing legal dissimilitude as a problem that needs a source-critical solution or harmonization, I want to propose that, given Torah as covenantal instruction and memorized reuse, such legal variation is rather something we should expect. The potential for falsification of this model is therefore seen if we can find textual cases within the HB where legal material is reused *in toto* literalistically,[45] as we are used to in a legislative concept of law.[46] Legal innovation and revision itself will not falsify the model. I therefore argue that the typical pattern is pointillistic exact reuse, where this pointillism parallels the form of specific locutions or concepts borrowed from previous instructions, combined with a certain free and creative reuse of Torah. I suggest that this may better account for legal variation in Torah than the typical source-critical or traditional harmonizations do.[47]

Scribal Enculturation and Memorized Torah

> Why should I memorize something I can so easily get from a book?
> —attributed to Albert Einstein

Scribal Enculturation in the ANE

Above I argued that seeing Torah as normative covenantal instruction better accounts for the dual phenomena of exact correspondence and creativity seen in legal reuse within Torah than the options proposed by source-critical theories or

45. Here we can recall Karl Popper's theory of testability, or falsifiability. The strength of a theory is found in its potential to be falsified, not verified (Karl R. Popper, *Conjectures and Refutations: The Growth of Scientific Knowledge* [London: Routledge, 2002], 45–48, 51–52, 294, 345; Popper, *The Logic of Scientific Discovery* [New York: Harper Torchbooks, 1968], 112–45, 265–81).

46. Even in cases of extensive verbatim citation in the HB, like the Decalogues (Exod 20; Deut 5) and the parallels between Kings and Chronicles, we find alterations. These examples tend to confirm the claim that biblical scribes did not feel constrained to reproduce their source unchanged. Rather, the norm seems to have been alteration of the source where the scribe saw this was needed. It therefore seems reasonable to take modification as the norm in reuse in the HB, and when we do find extensive exact reuse we should be surprised and then ask what special reasons the scribe might have had reusing exactly—the reverse of our expectation according to the modern literary standard.

47. For indicators of reuse and direction of dependence see Michael A. Lyons, *From Law to Prophecy: Ezekiel's Use of the Holiness Code*, ed. Claudia V. Camp and Andrew Mein, LHBOTS 507 (London: T&T Clark, 2009), 59–75; William A. Tooman, *Gog of Magog: Reuse of Scripture and Compositional Technique in Ezekiel 38–39* (Tübingen: Mohr Siebeck, 2011), 26–34.

traditional harmonizations. The following section will continue the exploration of the dual phenomena of creative and exact reuse. But instead of asking the question of how Torah should be characterized, as in the previous section, here I instead want to approach the dual phenomenon from the question of the literary culture in ancient Israel. Relevant is the question of how scribes in the ANE worked with revered texts, and how their audience would have perceived and received their productions. We will see how revered texts were to be memorized and embodied. It is easy to see how memorized and embodied reuse has the potential for simultaneous exact reproduction and more literary creativity than a reuse dependent on a visual consultation of the sources. Locutions and concepts from memorized texts become part of the "language-game" of the scribe, to use Ludwig Wittgenstein's phrase,[48] becoming a stock of lexemes, phrases, and concepts to think by. I believe this complements the discussion of the dual phenomenon of reuse in the previous section.

David Carr has argued convincingly that the ANE scribal culture both in Mesopotamia and Egypt was to use written texts as an aid to preserve, memorize, and become initiated into the culture represented by the ancient revered texts.[49] In Mesopotamian culture there seems to have been an ideal of learning revered texts thoroughly, even knowing them by heart. For example, in "Erra and Ishum" we read, "The scribe who learns it [i.e., the present text] will survive even in enemy country, and will be honored in his own, In the shrine of craftsmen where they ever proclaim my name, I shall make them wise [lit. "I shall make them open their ears"]."[50] The same ideal is found in tablet VII of "Enūma Elish": "The wise and knowledgeable should ponder (them [i.e., the fifty names of Marduk]) together, The Master should repeat, and make the pupil understand."[51] This corroborates the idea of repetition and reflection of compositions, whether written or oral. In Assurbanipal's hymn for Shamash the ideal of memorizing—or learning by heart—the revered texts is even clearer: "Whoever learns this text by heart and honors the judge of the gods, Shamash may he bring into esteem his [words], make good his command over the people."[52]

The following passages from Egypt show an even clearer idea of memorization and embodiment of revered texts. Carr writes, "Prospective members of the ruling class were inducted into that class through having these cultural texts 'in their heart.' Doing so made one, for the first time, into a full human being."[53] He finds differences between Egypt and Mesopotamia: in Egypt "we

---

48. Wittgenstein, *Philosophical Investigations*.

49. Carr, *Writing on the Tablet*. Many of the following references are already given by Carr.

50. "Erra and Ishum," trans. Stephanie Dalley (*COS* 1.113:416). Cf. Eduard Nielsen, *Oral Tradition: A Modern Problem in Old Testament Introduction* (London: SCM, 1954), 19.

51. "Epic of Creation (*Enūma Elish*)," trans. Benjamin R. Foster (*COS* 1.111:402).

52. "An Assurbanipal Hymn for Shamash," trans. Alasdair Livingstone (*COS* 1.143:474).

53. Carr, *Writing on the Tablet*, 64.

108   Kenneth Bergland

find a culture that is, if anything, even more textually oriented than the cultures of ancient Mesopotamia. . . . Indeed, writing had immense prestige in Egypt. It was seen as a means of overcoming the faults of memory and as a tool from the gods."[54] He continues, "There is no Egyptian critique of writing, such as that found in Chinese or Greek philosophical systems. Indeed, other cultures, like Greece, saw Egypt as the prototypical written culture, occasionally lampooning Egyptian claims to textually based wisdom."[55]

In the Egyptian "Satirical Letter," describing an educated scribe, it is written, "You are, of course, a skilled scribe at the head of his fellows, and the teaching of every book is incised on your heart."[56] Even if the description is here given in satirical terms, it illustrates how a scribal ideal was to have books written on one's heart. In the Egyptian *Instruction of Any* we find that Any asked his son to memorize written wisdom, to "study the writings, put them on your heart" (20.4–5). At the same time the instruction ends with a reflection by Any's son, Khonsuhotep, where he points out how memorization without understanding and embracing the words is deficient:

The son, he understands little
When he recites the words in the books.
But when your words please the heart,
The heart tends to accept them with joy.
Don't make your virtues too numerous,
That one may raise one's thoughts to you;
A boy does not follow the moral instructions,
Though the writings are on his tongue![57]

A scribe's task therefore consisted of inscribing a text not only on clay tablets, skin, papyrus, or other material, but also on one's own lips and heart.[58] At the same time memorization was only a means for embodying the texts in lived life. Orality and writing functioned together so the scribe could embody and perform the treasured tradition.[59]

54. Ibid., 63. In contrast to Plato, *Phaedrus*, in *Complete Works*, ed. John M. Cooper (Indianapolis: Hackett, 1997), 551–52 (274c–75b), 553 (276c–77a), where writing was seen as a reminder, not an aid to memory as such.

55. Carr, *Writing on the Tablet*, 64.

56. As translated by Carr, ibid., 8. Hans-Werner Fischer-Elfert renders it "Du bist doch der erfahrene Schreiber an der Spitze seiner Kollegen. Die Lehre aller Bücher ist eingraviert in dein Herz" (Hans-Werner Fischer-Elfert, *Die satirische Streitschrift des Papyrus Anastasi I: Übersetzung und Kommentar* [Wiesbaden: Harrassowitz, 1986], 1:94).

57. "Instruction of Any," trans. Miriam Lichtheim (*COS* 1.46:114).

58. Nielsen, *Oral Tradition*, 28.

59. Carr, *Writing on the Tablet*, 7, 18. Cf. 53, 74. For more on the Egyptian scribal culture see Alan H. Gardiner, "The Mansion of Life and the Master of the King's Largess," *JEA* 24, no. 1 (1938):

Orality, Writing, and Memory in Torah

For the question of legal reuse, it is important to understand to what extent the biblical texts, as we have them, were composed by drawing from other sources committed to memory. The question of memorized reuse is linked to the question of oral scribal cultures. This does not imply that we need to follow scholars who have argued for an original oral stage of composition prior to the biblical texts being committed to writing. Rather, we are interested in indicators of oral aspects and performance of the written sources, in order to detect whether they belong to a scribal culture reusing revered texts from memory or not.[60] Of course, the topic is vast, and my aim here needs to be limited. So I have chosen to focus on the most significant book in the Pentateuch for the question of orality, memory, and writing, namely Deuteronomy.[61]

Deuteronomy itself can be divided into Moses's three speeches (1:1–43; 4:44–26:19; 29:2–31:13), with some intermediate material (27:1–29:1), the Song of YHWH (31:14–32:47), and Moses's benediction (32:48–34:12). In other words, Deuteronomy itself is presented as an oral speech, transmitted to us in written form. In this book we find the mention of the Ten Words written on tablets that are archived inside the ark (4:13; 5:22; 10:1–5), "this Torah" having been written down in "this book" (הַתּוֹרָה הַזֹּאת הַכְּתוּבִים בַּסֵּפֶר הַזֶּה, 28:58, cf. v. 61), a monumental instruction of "this Torah" (הַתּוֹרָה הַזֹּאת, 27:1–4, 8–10), curses of the covenant written (אָלוֹת הַבְּרִית הַכְּתוּבָה) in this book of Torah (בְּסֵפֶר הַתּוֹרָה הַזֶּה, 29:19–20, 26), YHWH's commandments and decrees written in this book of Torah (מִצְוֹתָיו וְחֻקֹּתָיו הַכְּתוּבָה בְּסֵפֶר הַתּוֹרָה הַזֶּה, 30:10), the writing down of "this Torah" (הַתּוֹרָה הַזֹּאת) to be read every seventh year to all the people at the Feast of Booths (31:9–13), the writing down by Moses of the Song of YHWH as he also taught them the song itself (31:19, 22, 30), and the complete work of "this Torah" (הַתּוֹרָה־הַזֹּאת) archived beside the ark (31:24–26; cf. 6:9; 11:20; 17:18).

As we saw in the case of Exod 18:20, the focus upon the people knowing the instructions is again found in Deut 5:1: וַיִּקְרָא מֹשֶׁה אֶל־כָּל־יִשְׂרָאֵל וַיֹּאמֶר אֲלֵהֶם

83–91; Christopher Eyre, *The Use of Documents in Pharaonic Egypt* (Oxford: Oxford University Press, 2013), 9–10, 21. For further studies on ANE scribal culture and how it relates to the question of the composition of the Pentateuch, see Karel van der Toorn, *Scribal Culture and the Making of the Hebrew Bible* (Cambridge, MA: Harvard University Press, 2007).

60. Cf. Niditch, *Oral World and Written Word*, 6.

61. Carasik distinguishes between books where writing is prominent, while memory plays a minor role (book of Kings, Ezra, Esther, and Daniel), books where reference to memory is common, but to writing is sparse (Genesis, Isaiah, Psalms, Job, Ecclesiastes), and those where both writing and memory play a prominent role (Exodus, Deuteronomy, Jeremiah, and Nehemiah) (Carasik, *Theologies of the Mind*, 57–72). For more detailed discussions on orality, writing, and memory in Deuteronomy see Nielsen, *Oral Tradition*, 41–42, 45, 57–58; Jean-Pierre Sonnet, *The Book Within the Book: Writing in Deuteronomy*, ed. R. Alan Culpepper and Rolf Rendtorff, BibInt (Leiden: Brill, 1997); Carasik, *Theologies of the Mind*, 66–68, 72–73, 81–82, 181–215.

שְׁמַע יִשְׂרָאֵל אֶת־הַחֻקִּים וְאֶת־הַמִּשְׁפָּטִים אֲשֶׁר אָנֹכִי דֹּבֵר בְּאָזְנֵיכֶם הַיּוֹם וּלְמַדְתֶּם אֹתָם וּשְׁמַרְתֶּם לַעֲשֹׂתָם (And Moses called all Israel and said to them: Hear, Israel, the laws and rules which I speak in your ear today! Learn them and observe them so as to do them!). As McConville states, "The aim of Torah is to create a righteous community."[62] Deuteronomy breaks with scribal elitism,[63] holding intimate knowledge of the revered texts as a prerogative of a social elite. It lays the foundation of a common knowledge of Torah among the individual members of society.

In all of the instructive corpora of Torah we see an emphasis upon embodiment of its instructions so it is enacted in life. While the injunction to know Torah in the instructive material is addressed to the individual Israelite and might have implied memorization and the responsibility of parents to educate their children in Torah, this injunction is explicitly stated in Deut 6 and 11. Both Deut 6:6–9 and 11:18–21 testify that the goal is an inscription on the heart of and in the actions of each individual member of the community.

While Deut 6 and 11 speak of having the words upon one's heart (. . . וְהָיוּ עַל־לְבָבֶךָ הַדְּבָרִים הָאֵלֶּה, 6:6), placing them upon one's heart and person (וְשַׂמְתֶּם אֶת־דְּבָרַי אֵלֶּה עַל־לְבַבְכֶם וְעַל־נַפְשְׁכֶם, 11:18), and repeating them to one's children (וְשִׁנַּנְתָּם לְבָנֶיךָ, 6:7), what we would locate as inner dimensions, there is also a strong focus upon more "external" acts, such as speaking about them (וְדִבַּרְתָּ בָּם, 6:7 / לְדַבֵּר בָּם, 11:19), teaching one's children to speak them (וְלִמַּדְתֶּם אֹתָם אֶת־בְּנֵיכֶם לְדַבֵּר בָּם, 11:19), binding as a sign (וּקְשַׁרְתָּם, 6:8 / וּקְשַׁרְתֶּם, 11:18), having them as a symbol (וְהָיוּ לְטֹטָפֹת, 6:8; 11:18), and writing (וּכְתַבְתָּם, 6:9; 11:20) upon more "external" objects. It therefore seems more precise to speak of memorization of texts in order to appropriate, embody, and enact them in life. It is not merely an internalization, but also a simultaneous externalization of the words of Torah. In these passages, we see an interplay between the oral and written aspects of Torah, the spoken and the written.[64] The goal is a memorized Torah, becoming an embodied Torah, resulting in a living Torah, using both Torah in written and oral form didactically.[65]

Having spoken of the delight that YHWH will take in blessing the people with what is good, Moses in Deut 30:10–14 turns to a focus upon Torah, speaking

62. J. G. McConville, *Deuteronomy*, ApOTC 5 (Downers Grove, IL: InterVarsity, 2002), 43.

63. For the scribal elitism in the ANE in contrast to ancient Israel, see Carr, *Writing on the Tablet*, 13; Berman, *Created Equal*, 111. Frank Polak, however, has criticized Carr for looking too narrowly at the educational centers, arguing that ancient texts had a cultural and religious role that went beyond the scribal elite (Frank H. Polak, "Book, Scribe, and Bard: Oral Discourse and Written Text in Recent Biblical Scholarship," *Prooftexts* 31, nos. 1–2 [2011]: 131).

64. Cf. Carasik, *Theologies of the Mind*, 66–67. Just one caveat here. Even if some have taken Deut 6:6–9 as a basis for arguing for a general literacy in the Israelite population, the text, of course, only states what the goal is, not what the actual practice became.

65. Cf. Niditch, *Oral World and Written Word*, 100; Block, *Gospel According to Moses*, 6. For how Jesus is portrayed as the perfect embodiment of Torah, see ibid., 11–12; Craig S. Keener, *The Gospel of John: A Commentary*, 2 vols. (Grand Rapids: Baker Academic, 2003), 1:339–63.

of how the written word should be heard, and how "the word is very close to you [כִּי־קָרוֹב אֵלֶיךָ הַדָּבָר מְאֹד], in your mouth and in your heart [בְּפִיךָ וּבִלְבָבְךָ], to observe it." A similar focus upon embodiment of Torah is found in Jer 31:31–34. In 31:33 YHWH promises to place his Torah in their midst and write it upon their hearts (נָתַתִּי אֶת־תּוֹרָתִי בְּקִרְבָּם וְעַל־לִבָּם אֶכְתֲּבֶנָּה). While Deuteronomy places the responsibility for the embodiment of Torah upon the individual Israelites (Deut 6:6–9, 20–25; 11:18–21), Jeremiah's emphasis upon divine agency in this embodiment counters human agency and takes the member of the covenant community beyond the mental processes of memorization. Carasik comments, "Writing upon the heart—that is, into the mind—eliminates the impermanence of memory without reducing it to a text which can be folded up and stored away, lost or forgotten. Instead, a Torah that is written on the heart marries the permanence of writing to the awareness of the mind."[66]

Implications of the Model of Memorized Covenantal Instruction for Legal Reuse and Discrepancies

Above I have proposed a model for how to best account for the dual phenomena of pointillistic exact correspondence of lexemes, phrases, and concepts coupled with a certain fluidity and creativity in legal reuse in Torah. I have suggested that seeing Torah as normative covenantal instruction and being reused from memory might better account for this dual phenomenon than source-critical solutions or traditional harmonizations. That we find legal dissimilarity and variation between the different legal corpora of Torah seems to be where we need to take our departure when reflecting on this dual phenomenon. While both critical and traditional scholarship tend to insist on a concept of literary coherence,[67] either in the Pentateuch as a whole or subdocuments or fragments such as J, E, P, and D, the proposed model here rather suggests that we should expect a certain legal dissimilitude and variation, even revision, given Torah as covenantal instruction and memorized reuse. Of course, the concept of "embodied covenantal instruction" may not be adequate to explain all aspects of cases

---

66. Carasik, *Theologies of the Mind*, 72. For the idea of remembering and forgetting in Jeremiah, see ibid., 79, 85–86. Cf. Greenberg, "Three Conceptions of the Torah," 19–20. For indicators of oral register and memorized reuse, see Nielsen, *Oral Tradition*, 36; Niditch, *Oral World and Written Word*, 6, 10–11, 13–17, 38, 78–107, 120, 125; Carr, *Writing on the Tablet*, 4–5, 98, 105, 159; Frank H. Polak, "The Oral and the Written: Syntax, Stylistics and the Development of Biblical Prose Narrative," *JANES* 26 (1998): 59; Raymond F. Person, *From Conversation to Oral Tradition: A Simplest Systematics for Oral Tradition* (New York: Routledge, 2016), 142–43, 158–64.

67. Eckart Otto, "A Hidden Truth Behind the Text or the Truth of the Text: At a Turning Point of Biblical Scholarship Two Hundred Years After De Wette's *Dissertatio critico exegetica*," in *Die Tora Studien Zum Pentateuch: Gesammelte Aufsätze*, BZABR 9 (Wiesbaden: Harrassowitz, 2009), 3–6, 8.

of legal reuse in Torah. In several cases there is simply not enough evidence, at present, to give strong conclusions, so our readings cannot avoid a certain tentativeness. Nevertheless, I do propose that "embodied covenantal instruction" and "memorized reuse" provide a more adequate way of approaching the dual phenomenon of exact legal reuse coupled with innovation than is often seen in the present and dominant approaches to legal dissimilitude in Torah.

CHAPTER 7

The Liturgical Function of Dates in the Pentateuch

Michael LeFebvre

Pastor, Christ Church Reformed Presbyterian

Specific dates are rare in the Pentateuch. In fact, there are only twenty-one dates in the pentateuchal narratives (see table 7.1). Considering the vast sweep of history covered between Genesis and Deuteronomy, this fact might seem remarkable. However, ancient history writers did not use dates the way modern historians use them. Sacha Stern explains, "Ethnographers have found that in many—if not *all*—'primitive' or non-modern societies, the concept of time as a[n] entity in itself simply does not exist. Reality is explained in terms of events, changes, and processes, but in these world-views, the notion of 'pure time' or an overarching 'time-dimension' is completely absent and unknown."[1]

Like other primitive histories, the biblical histories present events in sequences connected by concrete processes rather than connecting events to an abstract timeline. This being so, it is not the rarity of dates in the Pentateuch that should surprise us; rather, we should be curious why dates are used at all in those points where they do appear.

The most recent comprehensive review of dates throughout the Pentateuch was completed more than sixty years ago (1959) by Jan van Goudoever.[2] He concluded that there exists a pervasive interest in Passover in the Pentateuch's use of dates: "Three Passovers are mentioned. . . . The first Passover, kept in Egypt, in the first year of the Deliverance [Exod 12]. The second Passover, kept in the wilderness, in the second year [Num 9]. The third Passover, kept in the Promised Land, after forty years [Josh 5]."[3] Van Goudoever believed that this interest in Passover dates was significant; however, other dates in the Pentateuch

---

Author's note: This material appears in expanded and more developed form in chaps. 4 and 5 of my book *The Liturgy of Creation: Understanding Calendars in Old Testament Context* (Downers Grove, IL: InterVarsity, 2019). Used by permission of InterVarsity Press.

1. Sacha Stern, *Time and Process in Ancient Judaism* (Oxford: Littman Library of Jewish Civilization, 2007), 12.

2. Jan van Goudoever, *Biblical Calendars* (Leiden: Brill, 1961), esp. 54–61. Cf. Mark Smith, *The Pilgrimage Pattern in Exodus*, JSOTSup 239 (Sheffield: Sheffield Academic Press, 1997), 290–98.

3. Van Goudoever, *Biblical Calendars*, 54. Cf. Smith, *Pilgrimage Pattern*, 290–98.

114   Michael LeFebvre

TABLE 7.1. Catalogue of Dates in the Pentateuch

	Reference	Date (Y | M | D)			Event
1	Gen 7:11	600*	02	17	Flooding of the world begins (*years refer to Noah's age)
2	Gen 8:4	[600]	07	17	Ark comes to rest
3	Gen 8:5	[600]	10	01	Mountaintops become visible
4	Gen 8:13	601	01	01	Waters finish receding
5	Gen 8:14	601	02	27	The ground is dry
6	Exod 12:2		01		Month of exodus appointed as start of Israel's year
7	Exod 12:3	[01]*	01	10	Day to select Passover lamb (*years refer to exodus)
8	Exod 12:6	[01]	01	14	Passover sacrifice meal conducted
9	Exod 12:18		01	14–21	Unleavened Bread to be observed
10	Exod 13:3–4	[01]	01	[15]	Day of departure from Egypt to be remembered
11	Exod 16:1	[01]	02	15–21	Manna to be gathered each day, except the 7th
12	Exod 19:1	[01]	03	[?]	Arrival at Mount Sinai
13	Exod 40:1, 18	02	01	01	Tabernacle erected
14	Num 1:1, 17	02	02	01	God instructs Moses to conduct a census
15	Num 9:1–3	02	01	14	First tabernacle Passover observed
16	Num 9:11	[02]	02	14	Alternate tabernacle Passover appointed (and observed)
17	Num 10:11	02	02	20	Israel leaves Mount Sinai for Paran
18	Num 20:1	[?]	01	01	Israel leaves Paran
19	Num 33:3	[01]	01	15	Israel left Egypt
20	Num 33:38	40	05	01	Aaron dies on Mount Hor
21	Deut 1:3	40	11	01	Moses addresses the people on Canaan's eastern border

are more difficult to reconcile with one another. Van Goudoever concluded, "From such conflicting indications it is clear that the 'calendar' in the Torah is not consistent. There are either different traditions, which are not harmonized, or some alterations were made by writers or redactors which disturbed a 'calendar' which was originally consistent."[4] Unfortunately, there has been little attention to the dates of the Pentateuch as a whole since Van Goudoever.[5]

In this essay, each of the twenty-one dates recorded in the Pentateuch will be examined. The thesis that will emerge is that Van Goudoever's basic insight regarding the liturgical character of the Pentateuch's dates is correct, but that he was too quick to discount the other disparate dates as redactional vestiges. The Pentateuch's dates reveal an editorial interest, not only with Passovers but with the whole liturgical calendar of biblical Israel. Furthermore, the reason there are incongruities when the dates are related to one another as historical data does not indicate contradictory sources, as Van Goudoever presumed. Rather, dates in the Pentateuch are difficult to reconcile with one another because they are not intended as historical data; they are given for liturgical guidance. It is the imposition of the anachronistic concepts of the modern historian that evokes incongruities from the editorially harmonious use of dates within the liturgical concern of the Pentateuch.[6]

Dated Events in the Pentateuch

There are twenty-one dated events in the Pentateuch (see table 7.1).[7] In addition, there are five passages where dates for festivals are listed (Exod 23:10–17; 34:18–24; Lev 23:4–43; Num 28:18–29:40; Deut 16:1–17). Obviously, dates included in festival lists are provided for liturgical guidance. This chapter will focus on the twenty-one dates provided in narratives. Displaying these dates visually over the Hebrew liturgical calendar will make their congruence become evident (see table 7.2).

It is not surprising that, for example, the Passover night event in Exod 12:6 (no. 8 on the chart) would align with the date for Passover observance in the liturgical calendar. However, even the Pentateuch's nonfestival narratives (when

---

4. Van Goudoever, *Biblical Calendars*, 56.

5. Cf. Smith, *Pilgrimage Pattern*, 290–91; Jeremy Hughes, *Secrets of the Times: Myth and History in Biblical Chronology*, LHBOTS 66 (Sheffield: Sheffield Academic Press, 1990).

6. Norbert Elias traces the reification of time to the rise of modern science in the mathematical descriptions of Galileo, Newton, and their peers. Sacha Stern argues that the objectification of time can be traced further back, to the philosophical revolution of ancient Hellenism. In either case, the now pervasive and seemingly instinctual perception of time as an objective reality (a conception which relativity theory has only recently begun to unravel) was alien to the biblical world (Norbert Elias, *Time: An Essay* [Oxford: Blackwell, 1992], 106–7; Stern, *Time and Process*, 91–102).

7. Dates are based on the MT. The LXX gives some different dates. Gerhard Larsson has argued that the dates preserved in the MT are primary and those preserved in the LXX are later developments (Gerhard Larsson, "The Chronology of the Pentateuch: A Comparison of the MT and LXX," *JBL* 102, no. 3 [1983]: 401–9).

116   Michael LeFebvre

TABLE 7.2. Dates Displayed over Mosaic Festival Calendar

Notes: Each numbered circle corresponds to the same numbered date from table 7.1, above. The Hebrew festivals are noted by dark gray boxes, as follows: 1/10 = selection of Passover lamb; 1/14 (P) = Passover; 1/15 (F?) = Likely date for Firstfruits; 1/15–21 = Unleavened Bread; 2/14 = Alternate Passover; 3/8 (W?) = Approximation of date for Weeks; 7/1 (T) = Trumpets; 7/10 (A) = Atonement; and 7/15–22 = Feast of Booths. Additionally, the first day of each month was a New Moon (NM) feast. Some nuances of the Mosaic calendar are difficult to pin down. It is uncertain whether Firstfruits (see Lev 23:11) should be located on the day after Passover (P = 14; F = 15), after the first day of Unleavened Bread (UB = begins on 15; F = 16), or after a regular Sabbath during UB (F = floating date based on a Saturday during UB). (a) Similarly, it is uncertain when exactly Weeks occurred, since it was the fiftieth day after Firstfruits. (b) These uncertainties, as will be seen in the course of this essay, do not impact the present thesis. Furthermore, the light gray thirtieth day at the end of each

The Liturgical Function of Dates in the Pentateuch   117

month indicates the likelihood that Israel practiced monthly intercalation. That is, Israel did not have months of fixed length, but the length of each month varied from twenty-nine to thirty days depending on when a new moon was sighted. (c) Finally, the timing of the various festivals was dictated by cosmic realia and the agricultural seasons (Gen 1:14). As will be discussed in the course of this essay, festivals correspond with the timing of the various grain and fruit harvests.

    a. See discussion of various positions in Milgrom, *Leviticus 23–27*, 2056–63; Gordon J. Wenham, *The Book of Leviticus*, NICOT 3 (Grand Rapids: Eerdmans, 1979), 304. But see my own argument for the fifteenth of the month in n. 27, below.

    b. Milgrom, *Leviticus 23–27*, 1990–2003.

    c. Francesca Rochberg-Halton, "Calendars, Ancient Near East," in *ABD* 1:810.

given dates) are almost always aligned with festival days. There are only four dates that do not fall directly on festivals (nos. 1, 5, 11, and 17), and those four dates are all grouped within the same two-week window, between the fifteenth and twenty-seventh days of the second month. The fact that all the dated events that fall outside of specific festival dates are grouped together nonetheless suggests that there is a significance to that particular window as well, with respect to the festival calendar.

Table 7.2 visually demonstrates the thesis which the remainder of this essay will explore, examining each of the twenty-one dated events of the Pentateuch as they conform to Israel's liturgical calendar.

New Year's Day

There are four events in the Pentateuch with a stated date of New Year's Day:[8]

> It was on a New Year's Day that Noah removed the ark's cover and saw the ground was dry (Gen 8:13; no. 4 in tables 7.1 and 7.2).
>
> The month of the exodus was to be the first month of Israel's year, and thus its first day was New Year's Day (Exod 12:2; no. 6).[9]
>
> The tabernacle was set up and filled with God's glory on a New Year's Day (Exod 40:1, 17; no. 13. Cf. Num 7:1; 9:15).
>
> The transition from the exodus generation to the next began during the first month (New Year's Day?) of the year, with the death of Miriam and Israel's departure from the wilderness of Paran (Num 20:1; no. 18).

8. New Year's Day refers to the first day of the first month, at the beginning of spring (the month of the spring equinox). The retitling of the Feast of Trumpets in the seventh month as *Ro'š Haššānâ* is probably a postbiblical development (Milgrom, *Leviticus 23–27*, 2012–13).

9. The first day is not explicitly mentioned, but the text is clearly written from the perspective of the first day of the first month. In particular, the following verse (Exod 12:3) points to the tenth day of the month as still ahead.

118   Michael LeFebvre

It is easy to see why these events fit New Year's Day, since each marks a new beginning. What is hard to fathom is that these could be historically (rather than liturgically) intended. Van Goudoever regarded the dating of the tabernacle's inauguration (1 above) as the most obvious problem with the Pentateuch's calendar.[10] Exodus 12 dates Israel's departure from Egypt in the first month of that year. The erection of the tabernacle is dated to New Year's Day the very next year. It is unfathomable that this timing could be historical. But the problem is actually much more significant than even Van Goudoever realized.

According to Exodus, the people left Egypt on the fifteenth day of the first month (Exod 12:6, 29; Num 33:3). They arrived at Sinai during the third month (Exod 19:1). After their arrival at Sinai, there are a total of ninety days explicitly accounted for: three days preceding the Decalogue (19:16); seven days preparing for the elders to commune with God (24:15); forty days for Moses on the mountain to receive the tabernacle instructions (24:18); and another forty days for Moses on the mountain to receive the second set of tablets (34:28). In addition to those four timed events (totaling ninety days), Moses made at least four other trips up the mountain (19:20; 20:21; 32:31; 33:21; 34:2), he collected a national head tax (30:11–16), and he confronted the golden calf in the camp (32:1–35). If Moses spent ten days on the mountaintop for each of those four additional climbs (although forty days is the pattern set by the previous climbs), then another forty days are accounted for ($4 \times 10 = 40$). If another three days are added for the census (30:11–16), three days for destroying the golden calf and executing the three thousand perpetrators of that sin (32:28), along with another three days for the plague (32:35) and three days for mourning the dead (33:4–6; although thirty days seems to be typical, cf. Num 20:39; Deut 34:8), we would require another twelve days.

Even if we suppose all these events occurred at the rapid speeds suggested, nearly five more months (142 days $= 90 + 40 + 12$) would have elapsed between the people's arrival at Sinai and their beginning construction on the tabernacle. Even with such a rapid pace, construction could only have begun sometime during the eighth month. That would leave only five months to collect, sort, and organize all the gold, silver, yarns, skins, and other raw materials for the tabernacle (35:4–29); for Moses to communicate the instructions to Bezalel and Oholiab; for those master craftsmen to enlist, organize, and train their craftsmen teams (35:30–36:1); and for the actual construction of all the parts, furnishings, and utensils of the tabernacle to be completed—using whatever furnaces and other equipment they could assemble in the wilderness—all while observing a Sabbath rest each week. It would be remarkable for such a massive project to be completed so efficiently even with modern manufacturing and construction technologies![11]

---

10. Van Goudoever, *Biblical Calendars*, 56.

11. In the 1940s, H. G. Baldwin spent five years constructing a full-sized replica of the tabernacle (Scott Taylor Hartzell, "Man's 1948 Creation Followed Divine Plan," *St. Petersburg Times*, May

The author could have described the speed of these accomplishments as a mark of special divine help. However, there is no suggestion in the text of supernatural assistance in the tabernacle's construction. If the text intended the tabernacle inauguration date as a historical datum, it seems the text would extol the supernatural help of the Lord to accomplish so much in such a remarkable period of time. The narratives elsewhere draw attention to divine help on behalf of the nation during their wanderings (e.g., Exod 16:35; 34:38; Deut 29:5). Since the author of the text does not show any need to explain the rapidity of these dates, it seems the author never intended the dates to be calculated the way a modern historian would.

Modern historians commonly explain such problems as the result of incompatible sources that redactors failed to resolve. However, in view of the pervasive interest in festival dates in the Pentateuch and the author's lack of concern for the historical problems (for modern historians) created by them, another explanation is more plausible. Dates in the Pentateuch are not intended as historical data; they are liturgical markers that relate the events recounted to the festival dates observed by the listening audience.

Each event dated to a New Year's Day marks God's care for his people as they enter a new era. It is particularly significant that the flood narrative dates the first sight of dry ground after the flood (Gen 8:13, no. 4), and not the beginning of the flood itself, to the date when Hebrews would later be celebrating the first New Moon feast looking ahead into a new year.

Passover and Unleavened Bread Dates

There are seven dates in the Pentateuch associated with Passover and unleavened bread. Most of these events are from the original Passover and unleavened bread narratives. Two of these dates mark the first ritual observance of Passover in the year after the exodus:

The tenth day of the first month is appointed for the Hebrews in Egypt to select the lambs that will become the original Passover sacrifices (Exod 12:3, no. 7).
The first Passover meal was eaten on the fourteenth day of the first month, Passover night (Exod 12:6, no. 8).
The unleavened bread of the exodus generation is memorialized in a week-long observance from the evening of the fourteenth day to the twenty-first day of the first month (Exod 12:14–20, no. 9).

9, 2001, http://www.sptimes.com/News/050901/news_pf/SouthPinellas/Man_s_1948_creation_f .shtml). Presumably the work could be done much more rapidly with a larger construction team.

120   Michael LeFebvre

On "this day . . . in the month of Abib" when Israel left Egypt, Moses instructed them to eat no leavened bread and prescribed future observance of the same date with unleavened bread (Exod 13:3–4, no. 10).

On the fourteenth day of the first month, on the year after the exodus (year 2), Moses led Israel in their first ritual celebration of Passover (Num 9:1–3, no. 15).

During the first ritual celebration of Passover (above), "certain men . . . were unclean" and unable to participate. Therefore, Moses appointed an alternate Passover on the fourteenth day of the second month (Num 9:11, no. 16).

In Moses's review of Israel's journeys, the date of the departure from Egypt (the fifteenth day of the first month) is repeated (Num 33:3, no. 19).

The first four of these dates all appear in Exod 12–13. The profusion of dates in that narrative is striking, since no other dates appear in Exodus prior to that point. In fact, apart from the flood narrative in Gen 6–9, there are no dates in the Pentateuch prior to the Passover night in Exod 12. Exodus 12 not only gives the first series of dates, it also states the liturgical purpose of those dates. In other words, the thesis of this essay—that dates are given for liturgical (not historical) instruction—is made explicit in the opening series of dates in Exod 12–13.

The exodus night narrative begins with the calendrical instruction "This month shall be for you the beginning of months. It shall be the first month of the year for you" (Exod 12:2). After that, the entire Passover event is described in alternating voices, switching between original Passover night instructions and future observance prescriptions. For example, in Exod 12:3–13 God speaks to the people *of Moses's generation*: "Tell all the congregation of Israel . . . I will pass over you, and no plague will befall you to destroy you, when I strike the land of Egypt." Then, in verses 14–20, the Lord speaks *to later generations*: "This day shall be for you a memorial day, and you shall keep it as a feast to the LORD throughout your generations." This pattern of alternating address continues, back and forth, through the text as shown in table 7.3.

This beginning of the exodus story shows the liturgical purpose of these narratives. The narrative is being recounted in order to instruct later Israel's understanding of their worship calendar, beginning with the first month of the year (so, Exod 12:25–27; 13:8–10, 12–16).

Numbers 9:1–3 gives the date of the first tabernacle Passover: the fourteenth day of the first month, the next year. For the same reasons rehearsed earlier with respect to the tabernacle's construction, it is difficult to conceive historically of the first Passover taking place in a fully functioning tabernacle so soon after the congregation's departure from Egypt. By dating the first ritual Passover to the same dates as the original Passover events one year later, the Pentateuch

The Liturgical Function of Dates in the Pentateuch 121

TABLE 7.3. Alternating Passover Event and Passover Rite Instruction

Ref.	Date (M | D)		Passover Night Instruction	Passover Rite Instruction
12:1–2	01			The month of the exodus is to be the first month of the year.
12:3–12	01	10	Select lambs for Passover.	
	01	14	Offer the Passover sacrifice and eat the Passover meal.	
12:14–20	01	15–21		Liturgical instructions for keeping the Feast of Unleavened Bread.
12:21–23	[01]	[14]	Put sacrifice blood over door.	
12:24–27				Observe this rite in all generations, teaching its meaning to your children.
12:28–41	[01]	[14–15]	That night ("at midnight," v. 29), the Lord struck Egypt, so that Egypt urgently compelled Israel to leave (i.e., predawn and into the 15th).	
12:42–49	[01]	[14]		"So this same night is . . . kept to the LORD . . . throughout their generations."
12:50–13:1	[01]	[15]	The Lord brought them out and told Moses to consecrate all Israel's firstborn to him.	
13:3–16	01	[15–21]		Instructions for keeping the Feast of Unleavened Bread in Canaan (vv. 3–10) and the consecration to the Lord of every firstborn born in Canaan (vv. 11–16).

is establishing a parallel in which later generations participate.[12] Worshiping Hebrews were being taught to regard each year's festivals as a parallel rehearsal of the original exodus events. Dates are employed in the Pentateuch to serve that liturgical purpose.

---

12. Cf. Amos Frisch's conclusion regarding dates in 1 Kings: "This very system of dating comes to demonstrate a relationship between two events" (Amos Frisch, "The Exodus Motif in 1 Kings 1–14," *JSOT* 87 [2000]: 6).

122   Michael LeFebvre

Feast of Weeks

There is one event specifically dated to the Festival of Weeks: "In the third month after the people of Israel went out from the land of Egypt, on that day (*bayyôm hazzeh*) they came to the wilderness of Sinai" (Exod 19:1, a.t.). It has long been a puzzle of pentateuchal scholarship why this passage provides no antecedent for "on that day" (*bayyôm hazzeh*). The only date given is "the third month" (*baḥōdeš haššělîšî*), yet the audience is expected to have a specific day (*bayyôm hazzeh*) of that month in mind.

Some scholars speculate that scribes miscopied the original and lost the day number on which the people arrived at Mount Sinai. There may once have been an exact day of the third month indicated, like "on *the first day of* the month (*bĕ°eḥād laḥōdeš*)" (cf. Num 1:1) or "on the new moon day (*bĕyôm haḥōdeš*)" (cf. Ezek 46:1).[13] There is no textual evidence, however, for this omission. Some argue that the expression "on the third moon" refers to the third new moon *day*, although it is unusual to indicate the new moon day in this manner.[14] Others suggest that "day" is used here in its generic sense and should be translated "in that time" rather than "on that day" (cf. Gen 2:4; Pss 20:1; 137:7; Isa 9:4; Ezek 30:9). However, the best explanation seems to be that the text is pointing to a specific day known to the audience by its association with the third month, without need of a stated antecedent.[15] The audience is expected to understand the Feast of Weeks as "that day," which was observed in the third month. Indeed, a long history of interpretation confirms the identification of this passage with the Feast of Weeks day.[16]

A specific day could easily have been recorded if the author wanted to complete a historical timeline. However, if the author's concern was to identify the event with the day of the audience's festival observance, then the date reference actually makes sense as it presently stands without a specific day of the month noted.[17] The Feast of Weeks was not fixed to a specific date in the third month; it was always determined by counting seven weeks from the Feast of Firstfruits

---

13. August Dillman, *Die Bücher Exodus und Leviticus* (Leipzig: S. Hirzel, 1880), 190–91; Bruno Bäntsch, *Exodus-Leviticus-Numeri* (Göttingen: Vandenhoeck & Ruprecht, 1903), 170–72.

14. Brevard S. Childs, *The Book of Exodus: A Critical, Theological Commentary*, OTL (Louisville: Westminster John Knox, 1974), 342.

15. Cf. Sejin Park, *Pentecost and Sinai: The Festival of Weeks as a Celebration of the Sinai Event*, LHBOTS 342 (New York: T&T Clark, 2008), 55.

16. 2 Chr 15:10–15; Acts 2:1–4; Park, *Pentecost and Sinai;* Van Goudoever, *Biblical Calendars,* 139–44; James C. VanderKam, "Covenant and Pentecost," *CTJ* 37 (2002): 239–54. Cf. Ronald Hendel, "Sacrifice as a Cultural System: The Ritual Symbolism of Exodus 24:3–8," *ZAW* 101, no. 3 (1989): 373; Moshe Weinfeld, "The Uniqueness of the Decalogue and Its Place in Jewish Tradition," in *The Ten Commandments in History and Tradition*, ed. Ben-Tsiyon Segal, trans. Gershon Levi (Jerusalem: Hebrew University, 1987), 21–27; Smith, *Pilgrimage Pattern*, 62–65.

17. Van Goudoever, *Biblical Calendars,* 139; Smith, *Pilgrimage Pattern*, 292. Cf. Park, *Pentecost and Sinai,* 55.

(Lev 23:15). It was, therefore, "the day" which always took place in the third month but was not identified by a specific day number. Exodus 19:1 therefore avoids giving a specific day number in keeping with the liturgical calendar. The unusual date form in Exod 19:1 supports the thesis of this essay. The Pentateuch is not concerned with precise historical dates, but with assigning dates that connect historical events with the liturgical calendar.

Feast of Booths

The Pentateuch makes only one date assignment to the seventh-month festivals. It is in the flood narrative: "In the seventh month, on the seventeenth day of the month, the ark came to rest on the mountains of Ararat" (Gen 8:4, no. 2). This date is liturgically significant since the ark was a mobile sanctuary carrying Noah's family through the "watery wilderness" to its final resting place on Mount Ararat, a sacrificial site (Gen 8:20).[18] Booths was a festival to recall the safe journey of God's people through the wilderness—living in booths around God's booth—to their settlement in the promised land (Lev 23:39–43). Noah's safe journey through the flood, with his "sanctuary" finally settled securely on its mount of sacrifice, serves the Booths liturgy well.

Apart from the settlement of Noah's ark, there are no events in the Pentateuch dated to the seventh month. Since the telos of Booths was only achieved with the construction of the Temple,[19] it is not surprising that the Pentateuch lacks other events suitable to that festival.[20]

New Moon Days

There are four events dated to New Moon feast days in the Pentateuch (besides the New Year's Day events discussed earlier):

18. Steven W. Holloway, "What Ship Goes There: The Flood Narratives in the Gilgamesh Epic and Genesis Considered in Light of Ancient Near Eastern Temple Ideology," *ZAW* 103, no. 3 (1991): 328–54; C. T. R. Hayward, "Sirach and Wisdom's Dwelling Place," in *Where Shall Wisdom Be Found? Wisdom in the Bible, the Church, and the Contemporary World*, ed. Stephen C. Barton (Edinburgh: T&T Clark,1999), 31–46, esp. 37; Meredith G. Kline, *Kingdom Prologue* (South Hamilton: Gordon-Conwell Theological Seminary, 1989), 105; G. K. Beale, *The Temple and the Church's Mission: A Biblical Theology of the Dwelling Place of God*, New Studies in Biblical Theology (Downers Grove, IL: IVP Academic, 2004), 104; Joseph Blenkinsopp, *Creation, Un-creation, Re-creation: A Discursive Commentary on Genesis 1–11* (New York: T&T Clark, 2011), 137–40.

19. Notably, 1 Kgs 6:1 also gives the Feast of Booths as the date for the establishment of Solomon's Temple on Mount Zion (Karl William Weyde, *The Appointed Festivals of YHWH: The Festival Calendar in Leviticus 23 and the Sukkot Festival in Other Biblical Texts*, FAT, 2nd ser., no. 4 [Tübingen: Mohr Siebeck, 2004], 155–56; Frisch, "Exodus Motif," 5–6).

20. Smith, *Pilgrimage Pattern*, 307n46.

124   Michael LeFebvre

As Noah's flood was receding, the mountaintops became visible on the New Moon day of the tenth month (Gen 8:5, no. 3).

On the New Moon day of the second month of the second year, the Lord instructed Moses to conduct a census of the nation (Num 1:1, 18, no. 14).

On the New Moon day of the fifth month, during the final year of the exodus generation (the fortieth year after leaving Egypt), Aaron ascended Mount Hor and died (Num 33:38, no. 20).

Exactly six months after Aaron's death, on the New Moon day of the eleventh month of the fortieth year, Moses preached the book of Deuteronomy to the people prior to his own death (Deut 1:3, no. 21).

The first of these New Moon dates (Gen 8:5; no. 3) belongs to the flood narrative, when the waters began to recede and the mountaintops became visible. Noah's flood had begun during the spring harvest season (Gen 7:11, no. 1); the ark came to rest on Mount Ararat during the autumn harvest festival (Gen 8:4, no. 2); the mountaintops began to be visible on the New Moon festival of the tenth month; then the water disappeared during the spring harvest season of the following year (Gen 8:13–14, nos. 4–5). Dating the appearance of the mountaintops to the New Moon feast of the tenth month fits the festival cadence of the entire narrative. That date is a feast day at the exact midpoint between the final harvest festival of the flood year (the seventh month, when the ark landed) and the first harvest festival of the new year (the first month, when the waters disappeared).

There is no historical reason for the events of the flood to be given such precise dates, especially since dates are an unusual aspect of pentateuchal narratives, as noted at the beginning of this essay. Furthermore, since the launching and landing of the ark took place at a location far removed from Canaan, there is no evident historical reason for the Lord to have brought about those events at times aligned with *Canaan*'s planting and harvest schedules. If, however, these dates are provided to relate the flood events to the liturgical observances of Israel at the time of their settlement in Canaan, then the flood dates are sensible.

The second New Moon event is the Lord's instruction to Moses to complete a census of the people at Mount Sinai (no. 2). The purpose of that census was to prepare the people to leave Sinai. It took place on the next New Moon day after the inauguration of the mobile sanctuary (Exod 40:1, 18). In fact, the text indicates that the entire census was conducted and completed in one assembly of the congregation on that very day: "and on the first day of the second month, they assembled the whole congregation together, who registered themselves by clans" (Num 1:18–19). It is remarkable to imagine such an efficient registration of such a large number of warriors (Num 1:46) and Levites (Num 3:39)! The text

The Liturgical Function of Dates in the Pentateuch 127

wheat harvest was presented. The relationship between these two grain festivals is further indicated by determining the date of Weeks based on a count of seven Sabbaths from Firstfruits.

The second month was the center point between the grain harvests, at the middle of the spring festival season. The date of the alternate Passover (2/14) was both the final remembrance of Passover and the full-moon midpoint of the second month; it likely provided a conceptual center point to the spring harvest season. This could explain why that single week (immediately following the alternate Passover) was populated with three of the four second-month dates (1, 2, and 3 above).[24]

The dating of the week of manna collection in Exod 16:1–36 (no. 11) fits well in this location theologically. Beginning on the fifteenth day of the second month, the Lord provided daily gifts of manna for Israel with instruction to rest on the seventh day. While this pattern was for Israel's instruction all through the year, its poignancy fits particularly well at the heart of the grain harvest season. The analogy between gathering manna and gathering grain would make memorable the lesson to trust the Lord to bless the harvest even if laborers abstain from collecting on the Sabbath. The date of the manna story makes its lesson especially fitting for later Israel's observance during the grain harvest season, which "was the most intensive major operation of the agricultural year."[25] The temptation to continue daily harvesting on Sabbaths would have been most keen during the urgency of the grain harvest period, precisely the time which the manna story targets with its guidance to stop gathering on the Sabbath each week.

Genesis dates both the beginning of the flood (Gen 7:11, no. 1) and the final drying of the ground (Gen 8:14, no. 5) to the second month. As historical data, it is hard to fathom such a dramatic deluge beginning and completely drying within a mere year. Agriculturally, however, the start and end dates make sense. The rainy season in Canaan occurred between autumn and spring (cf., Deut 11:14; Jer 25:4; Joel 2:23–24);[26] and grain harvest took place during the return of dry weather the next spring (cf. 2 Sam 21:10). Although it was normal for the Jordan River to flood its banks during the grain harvest due to the winter rainfall on the surrounding hills and mountains (Josh 3:15), an unseasonably

---

24. In fact, if it could be demonstrated that the alternate Passover included a weeklong observance of a second Week of Unleavened Bread as well, then three of the four second-month dates would fall *directly* on festival dates. However, there is no indication for an alternate Week of Unleavened Bread following the alternate Passover.

25. David Hopkins, *The Highlands of Canaan: Agricultural Life in the Early Iron Age*, SWBA 3 (Decatur, GA: Almond, 1985), 224.

26. Ibid., 87.

128   Michael LeFebvre

heavy rainfall during the grain harvest could damage the field crops. In fact, a thunderstorm during grain harvest was regarded as a sign of God's judgment (1 Sam 12:17–18; cf. Prov 26:1). The flood narrative draws upon the fear of God's judgment starting with the first harvest of the year, eclipsed by his mercy starting with the beginning of the harvest season the following year.

Another second month date is given in Num 10: "In the second year, in the second month, on the twentieth day of the month, the cloud lifted from over the tabernacle and the people of Israel set out by stages from the wilderness of Sinai" (Num 10:11, no. 17). Israel was to remember their departure from Sinai at the heart of the grain harvest festivals that began the year, in anticipation of celebrating their arrival at Mount Zion with the pilgrimage festival of Booths during the seventh month.

The cumulative evidence of these second-month dates all occurring within the same window, and fitting the theology of the spring harvest festivals, is impressive. It is striking that the only dates in the Pentateuch not occurring directly on festival dates are all grouped here in the second month in between the spring harvest festivals.

Conclusions

Scholars such as Van Goudoever are correct to note the incongruity of the Pentateuch's various dates when compared as historical data. An argument could be made to maintain their historicity, but it would be difficult to sustain. One reason scholars have regarded the Pentateuch as a compilation of incongruous sources is because the dates do not fit well into a single timeline. However, in this essay we have outlined a pervasive liturgical interest behind the twenty-one dates spread through the Pentateuch. From this perspective it can be seen that there is, in fact, remarkable congruity among the Pentateuch's dates—but it is liturgical, not historical, congruity.

The exodus dates also present a liturgical pattern in their year assignments. Events assigned to the first year of the exodus are all "original" events: the antetype Passover, Unleavened Bread escape, Sinai arrival, and so forth. Events assigned to the second year were all ritual rehearsals of those prototype events: erection of the tabernacle, the first tabernacle Passover, the first alternate Passover, and so forth. There are no dates assigned to anything between the second year and the fortieth. The fortieth year marks the end of the exodus generation: the deaths of Miriam, Aaron, and Moses. The forty-first year is then picked up by Joshua with the new generation's first observances in the land of Canaan: the settlement generation crossed the Jordan on the tenth day of the first month of the forty-first year (the day when Passover lambs were traditionally selected;

The Liturgical Function of Dates in the Pentateuch 129

Josh 4:19); they celebrated the first Passover in the promised land on the fourteenth of the first month of that forty-first year (Josh 5:10); and the people ate the first fruits of the land (and the manna ceased) beginning on the fifteenth of the first month (the first day of Unleavened Bread).[27] Thus, the year assignments further support the text's liturgical interest in its dates, rather than an anachronistic interest in historical data.

It is also noteworthy that the only events in the Pentateuch with dates are sanctuary-construction narratives. It is only Gen 6–9 (the flood narrative) and the exodus history (Exod 12:1 through Deut 1:3) that have specific dates recorded. The flood narrative describes the construction of a floating sanctuary, in which the household of faith was delivered from an early judgment of the world and carried to a place of rest and worship.[28] Similarly, the exodus narrative is centered on Israel's encounter with God at the holy mountain in the wilderness (Sinai), where God provided them a mobile sanctuary (the tabernacle) to carry them on their pilgrimage to a place of rest and fruitfulness in the promised land.

From the findings in this essay, the liturgical interest of the Pentateuch's system of dates is evident. This discovery not only explains the dates, but also points to the importance of liturgical guidance (i.e., *tôrâ* in its early significance as cultic instruction)[29] behind the compilation of the Pentateuch as a whole. By mapping specific events to festival dates, the Pentateuch provides guidance for the faith and labors of Israel connected with those observances. Rather than the Pentateuch being an uncomfortable mix of narrative history and ritual laws,[30] the evidence of the dates located strategically throughout all five books of the Pentateuch suggests that the whole collection is shaped around liturgical concerns—including the histories (at least those narratives related to sanctuary construction).

These findings correspond with the self-reported purpose of the Pentateuch expressed in Deuteronomy's closing chapters: "Then Moses wrote this law and

---

27. That final fact—that Israel first ate the fruits of the land and the manna ceased on the fifteenth of the first month—might confirm that the Feast of Firstfruits was held on the fifteenth of the month (and that Passover was the Sabbath Firstfruits followed; Lev 23:11) since Israel was to eat the first grain from the new year's harvest and no longer had to live off winter stores on the Feast of Firstfruits day (Lev 23:14).

28. On the identification of Noah's ark as a sanctuary, see Holloway, "What Ship Goes There," 328–54; Hayward, "Sirach and Wisdom's Dwelling Place," 37; Kline, *Kingdom Prologue*, 105; Beale, *Temple*, 104; Blenkinsopp, *Creation, Un-creation, Re-creation*, 137–40.

29. E.g., Hag 2:11; Mal 2:6. Cf. Hermann Kleinknecht and Walter Gutbrod, *Law*, trans. Dorothea Barton, Bible Key Words from Gerhard Kittel's Theologisches Wörterbuch zum Neuen Testament 11 (London: Black, 1962), 45.

30. Cf. Frank Crüsemann, *The Torah: Theology and Social History of Old Testament Law*, trans. Allan Mahnke (Minneapolis: Fortress, 1992), 10; Samuel Greengus, "Law," in *ABD* 4:250.

130   Michael LeFebvre

gave it to the priests . . . and commanded them, 'At the end of every seven years, at the set time in the year of release, at the Feast of Booths, when all Israel comes to appear before the LORD your God at the place that he will choose, you shall read this law before all Israel in their hearing'" (Deut 31:9–13). Scholars generally understand that designation as originally referring only to Deuteronomy (at least chaps. 1–30),[31] although the final redaction likely intends it to define the entire collection. Moses compiled a book of *tôrôt* for liturgical instruction.[32] The narratives with dates, at least, conform to this purpose.

Jan van Goudoever's basic insight about the dates of the Pentateuch can therefore be accepted as correct: "The Torah *is* a Passover-story."[33] But the historical incongruities of the twenty-one dates throughout the Pentateuch do not arise from incoherent sources. Rather, they reflect a coherent liturgical interest in the Pentateuch's final compilation.

---

31. Peter C. Craigie, *The Book of Deuteronomy*, NICOT (Grand Rapids: Eerdmans, 1976), 370.
32. Cf. Ezra 7:6, 10; Neh 8:5.
33. Van Goudoever, "Liturgical Significance," 145; cf. Van Goudoever, *Biblical Calendars*, 54–61.

PART 2

Exegetical Studies

Chapter 8

In the Tradition of Moses:
The Conceptual and Stylistic Imprint of
Deuteronomy on the Patriarchal Narratives

Daniel I. Block
Wheaton College

A Survey of Approaches to the Relationship Between Deuteronomy and the Patriarchal Narratives

After two centuries of critical investigation, scholarly opinion on the relationship between Deuteronomy and the rest of the Pentateuch has reached no consensus. The options available today include the following.

1. Moses was the author of the entire Pentateuch. The Talmud represents this position,[1] and Christians generally accepted it until the Enlightenment. It is widespread among laypeople and still occasionally defended by conservative scholars,[2] though the latter often allow for geographical and historical updating.[3]

2. The Pentateuch's authority derives from a historical Moses, and it contains substantial materials he may have written (e.g., the speeches in Deuteronomy; cf. 31:9–13), but the books that make up this corpus were composed later.[4]

---

1. According to B. Bat. 14b, "Moses wrote his own book and the portion of Balaam and Job."

2. See Oswald T. Allis, *The Five Books of Moses* (Phillipsburg, NJ: Presbyterian & Reformed, 1943; repr., Eugene, OR: Wipf & Stock, 2001); Gleason Archer, *A Survey of Old Testament Introduction*, rev. ed. (Chicago: Moody, 2007), 89–26; Edward J. Young, *An Introduction to the Old Testament*, rev. ed. (Grand Rapids: Eerdmans, 1989), 42–46; Eugene H. Merrill, *Deuteronomy: An Exegetical and Theological Exposition of the Holy Scripture NIV Text*, NAC 4 (Nashville: Broadman & Holman, 1994), 22–23 (though technically Merrill comments only on the authorship of Deuteronomy).

3. Michael A. Grisanti, "Deuteronomy," in *Numbers to Ruth*, EBC, rev. ed., 2 (Grand Rapids: Zondervan, 2012), 459–61; Grisanti, "Josiah and the Composition of Deuteronomy," in *Sepher Torath Mosheh: Studies in the Composition and Interpretation of Deuteronomy*, ed. Daniel I. Block and Richard L. Schultz (Peabody, NJ: Hendrickson, 2017), 130n68.

4. For a premonarchic date for Deuteronomy, see Peter T. Vogt, "'These Are the Words Moses Spoke': Implied Audience and a Case for Pre-Monarchic Dating of Deuteronomy," in *For Our Good Always: Studies on the Message and Influence of Deuteronomy in Honor of Daniel I. Block*, ed. Jason S. DeRouchie, Jason Gile, and Kenneth J. Turner (Winona Lake, IN: Eisenbrauns, 2013), 61–80. For a date in the time of the United Monarchy, see Daniel I. Block, "Recovering the Voice of Moses: The Genesis of Deuteronomy," *JETS* 44 (2001): 385–408; repr. in *The Gospel According*

134   Daniel I. Block

3. The so-called Deuteronomic elements in the Pentateuch reflect the antiquity of Deuteronomistic style and theology ("proto-Deuteronomy"), which may be identifiable in the Decalogue and came to full bloom in Deuteronomy.[5]

4. The Pentateuch's production involved the combination of several sources (JEDP) that were produced separately but were combined serially by redactors.[6] Prior to the addition of the P material, a Deuteronomic/Deuteronomistic redactor inserted statements, phrases, and words into the patriarchal narratives that aligned with the vocabulary and theology of Deuteronomy. The most obvious and widely recognized Deuteronomic segments are Gen 18:17–19; 22:16–18; 26:4–5 (traditionally credited to E).[7] According to Blenkinsopp, "This kind of language is indistinguishable from the homiletic and hortatory style of the Deuteronomists. Similar language occurs at intervals throughout the ancestral history (e.g., 16:10; 26:24; 28:15; 35:1–4), allowing for the possibility that a D writer has edited narrative source material in a manner analogous to the presentation of prophetic narratives in Dtr, e.g., the stories about Elijah and Elisha."[8]

---

to Moses: Theological and Ethical Reflection on the Book of Deuteronomy (Eugene, OR: Cascade, 2012), 21–51. Gordon Wenham suggests that Genesis was not written much later than 950 BCE (Gordon J. Wenham, *Genesis 1–15*, WBC 1 [Waco: Word, 1987], xliv–xlv).

5. The foremost proponents of this view are Chris H. W. Brekelmans, "Die sogenannten deuteronomischen Elemente in Gen.-Num: Ein Beitrag zur Vorgeschichte des Deuteronomiums," in *Volume du Congrés Genève 1965*, VTSup 15 (Leiden: Brill, 1966), 90–96; Norbert Lohfink, "Die These vom 'deuteronomischen' Dekalog-anfang: Ein fragwürdiges Ergebnis atomistischer Sprachstatistik," in *Student zum Pentateuch: Walter Kornfeld zum 60. Geburtstag*, ed. Georg Braulik (Vienna: Herder, 1963), 99–109. For a helpful survey of the antecedents and successors to Brekelmans's and Lohfink's theories, see Hans Ausloos, "The 'Proto-Deuteronomist': Fifty Years Later," *OTE* 26, no. 3 (2013): 531–58.

6. Many have admitted the difficulty of distinguishing JE from D. See, e.g., Julius Wellhausen, *Die Komposition des Hexateuchs und der historischen Bücher des Alten Testaments*, 3rd ed. (Berlin: G. Reimer, 1899), 74, 86; indeed, Wellhausen grants the spiritual affinity between JE and Deuteronomy (Wellhausen, *Die Komposition*, 94n2).

7. According to Joel S. Baden, none of the expressions in 26:5 are Deuteronomic; the verse belongs to J. He suggests that J "typically uses clusters of legal terminology to signify general obedience to the will of Yahweh (since J has no law code to which it might refer). Indeed, there is no logical reason that a deuteronomic editor would insert references to obedience to actual laws, since in both Genesis 26:5 and Exodus 15:26 no laws have yet been given" (Joel S. Baden, *The Composition of the Pentateuch: Renewing the Documentary Hypothesis*, AYBRL [New Haven: Yale University Press, 2012], 139).

8. Joseph Blenkinsopp, *The Pentateuch: An Introduction to the First Five Books of the Bible*, AYBRL (New York: Doubleday, 1992), 122. Already in the nineteenth century John W. Colenso asserted that the D elements derive from the author who composed the book of Deuteronomy (John W. Colenso, *The Pentateuch and the Book of Joshua Critically Examined*, part III, 2nd ed. [London: Longman, 1879], 145). Although Erhard Blum departs significantly from classical forms of the Documentary Hypothesis represented by JEDP, he provides the most detailed presentation of this approach in his opus *Die Komposition der Vätergeschichte*, WMANT 57 (Neukirchen: Neukirchener Verlag, 1984). Dispensing with J and E, he argues that independent "Abrahamgeschichte" and "Jakobusgeschichte" were combined to create "die Vätergeschichte," and linked to narratives in the preceding chapters to create the first "deuteronomic" Pentateuch, to which the P materials were later

5. The author of Deuteronomy is the author of the Pentateuch. Rejecting the notion of a separate and coherent P narrative, Rolf Rendtorff observes that the first comprehensive Pentateuch bears a marked "Deuteronomistic stamp," and that the Deuteronomic theological school produced it.[9] While not arguing for a single author, H. H. Schmid suggests the Pentateuch was the result of an "[inner] jahwistischen Redaktion- und Interpretationsprozess." However, as a whole, Genesis–Numbers presents a highly developed Deuteronomic theology.[10] R. N. Whybray has proposed a single author for the entire Pentateuch, which was produced as part of a comprehensive national history, analogous to Herodotus's *Histories*.[11] Like the Greek work, the Pentateuch contains a mass of traditional and fictional material, yielding a sixth-century BCE "literary masterpiece."[12]

In recent decades, the results of computer-assisted research have also challenged source- and redaction-critical findings. Thirty years ago, Yehuda T. Radday and Haim Shore demonstrated on linguistic grounds that in Genesis the separation of J from E is groundless, and that evidence for P as a separate source should be attributed to differences in genre rather than to separate authors. They observed that the style and vocabulary suggest three sorts of discourse, but they bear no relationship to the traditional sources J, E, and P.[13] In Genesis three distinct registers of discourse are on display, linked specifically to words attributed to the narrator (N), human speakers (H), and the Deity (D), respectively.[14] Although many today recognize E as a phantom,[15] some resist this move,[16] and

---

added. For reviews of Blum's work, see R. N. Whybray, *The Making of the Pentateuch: A Methodological Study*, JSOTSup 53 (Sheffield: JSOT Press, 1994), 210–13; Mark A. O'Brien, "The Story of Abraham and the Debate over the Source Hypothesis," *ABR* 38 (1990): 1–17. Andrew D. H. Mayes argues that Genesis–Numbers never existed independently, but was composed as an introduction to an existent Deuteronomistic History (Andrew D. H. Mayes, *The Story of Israel Between Settlement and Exile: A Redactional Study of the Deuteronomistic History* [London: SCM, 1983], 141).

9. Rolf Rendtorff, *The Old Testament: An Introduction* (Minneapolis: Fortress, 1991), 162; and more fully, Rendtorff, *The Problem of the Process of Transmission in the Pentateuch*, trans. John J. Scullion, JSOTSup 89 (Sheffield: JSOT Press, 1990).

10. See Hans H. Schmid, *Der sogenannte Jahwist: Beobachtungen und Fragen zur Pentateuchforschung* (Zürich: Theologischer Verlag, 1976).

11. Herodotus, *Hist.* 4.117–20 (Godley, LCL).

12. Whybray, *Making of the Pentateuch*, 242.

13. For a summary of their conclusions, see Yehuda T. Radday and Haim Shore, *Genesis: An Authorship Study*, AnBib 103 (Rome: Pontifical Institute Press, 1985), 189–90. For more particular questions concerning a P narrative source as purportedly represented by Gen 1, 17, and 23, see 209–10.

14. For an analysis of these registers, see Chaim Rabin, "Linguistic Aspects," in Radday and Shore, *Genesis*, 218–24.

15. See Christoph Levin, "Righteousness in the Joseph Story," in *The Pentateuch: International Perspectives on Current Research*, ed. Thomas B. Dozeman, Konrad Schmid, and Baruch J. Schwartz, FAT 78 (Tübingen: Mohr Siebeck, 2011), 227–29.

16. See Jeffrey Stackert, "The Elohist Source: The End of Israelite Prophecy," in *A Prophet Like Moses: Prophecy, Law, and Israelite Religion*, ed. Jeffrey Stackert (Oxford: Oxford University Press, 2014), 70–125.

136   Daniel I. Block

P's place as a source in the narratives of Genesis is largely unchallenged.[17] Radday and Shore's pessimism regarding a scholarly hearing of their evidence has largely proven justified.[18]

Perhaps the new work by Israeli scholars under the rubric of "The Tiberias Project" will move computer-assisted source analysis forward.[19] However, if the first publication by scholars working on the project is any indication,[20] its participants are subject to the same temptation to negation, bisection, and suppression of evidence that characterizes two hundred years of source- and redaction-critical work.[21] The pressure from the academic guild is overwhelming.

The Evidence for a Relationship Between Deuteronomy and the Patriarchal Narratives

Although pentateuchal scholars have recognized links between Deuteronomy and the Tetrateuch, for more than 150 years they have also recognized the special lexical, linguistic, and stylistic characteristics of Deuteronomy.[22] In this essay my interest is not in the distinctive features of Deuteronomic style or

17.   Blum attributes the fragments 23, 27:46–28:9; 35:9–15; 48:3–7, as well as the larger block, chapter 17, to P (Blum, *Komposition der Vätergeschichte*, 420–58). He is less certain about chapter 23, which may represent an independent tradition (443–46). According to Baden, in the patriarchal narratives P is restricted to chapters 17 and 23 (Baden, *Composition of the Pentateuch*, 178).

18.   They write, "The conclusion that the two [J and E] . . . were one will predictably be repudiated. Such dysfunction is not unique in scholarship. Even scientists tend to shut their eyes to data liable to collide with an existing cherished theory." They cite the supposed discovery of Uranus by Sir William Herschel; although astronomers had seen this planet at least twenty times before, its existence had been suppressed as fact (Radday and Shore, *Genesis*, 217). Cf. Joshua Berman's note that critical scholars regularly try to secure dates for specific biblical texts by negating, bisecting, and suppressing contrary evidence (Joshua Berman, "Historicism and Its Limits: A Response to Bernard M. Levinson and Jeffrey Stackert," *JAJ* 4 [2013]: 297–309).

19.   For an introduction to the project, see https://www.youtube.com/watch?v=MDjx99KTMto.

20.   See Idan Dershowitz, Navot Akiva, Moshe Koppel, and Nachum Dershowitz, "Computerized Source Criticism of Biblical Texts," *JBL* 134 (2015): 253–71.

21.   According to Dershowitz et al., the computer analysis of Gen 1:1–2:4a "places the section in the predominantly non-P cluster, despite Bible scholars' nearly unanimous agreement that it is Priestly in origin." Their explanation is awkward: it may have been thrust into the non-P cluster by the dominance of the words אלהים and ויאמר and the particle כי, which are typical of non-P materials. They conclude, "It may therefore be worth considering our method's results in the light of the questions surrounding the literary history of Gen 1:1–2:4a" (ibid., 269). Should they not rather have said: It may therefore be worth considering the questions surrounding our understanding of the literary history of Gen 1:1–2:4a in light of the method's results?

22.   For catalogues of distinctively Deuteronomic/Deuteronomistic elements, see Moshe Weinfeld, *Deuteronomy and the Deuteronomic School* (Winona Lake, IN: Eisenbrauns, 1992), 320–65; Samuel R. Driver, *A Critical and Exegetical Commentary on Deuteronomy*, 3rd ed., ICC (Edinburgh: T&T Clark, 1902), lxxvii–xcv; Colenso, *Pentateuch and the Book of Joshua*, 391–406. Colenso discusses not only expressions that never occur in the Tetrateuch and are therefore unique to and/ or typical of D but also expressions that are common in the Tetrateuch but absent from D (cf. also Driver, *Deuteronomy*, lxxxiv).

vocabulary, but the opposite—Deuteronomy's links with the Abraham, Isaac, and Jacob narratives, spanning Gen 11:27–35:29, and identified internally as the תּוֹלְדֹת of Terah (11:27–25:11) and Isaac (25:19–35:29).[23] This is not to say that the links with Deuteronomy are limited to the patriarchal narratives, but that this study is limited to this segment of the Tetrateuch. As I observe occasionally below, many of the shared features also occur in other parts of the Hexateuch.

When I began this project, I did not expect to find many links between D and PN, beyond those snippets of patriarchal text that scholars had already identified as Deuteronomic/Deuteronomistic) (cf. above). However, having marinated in Deuteronomy for the past fifteen years, my eyes and ears have been sensitized not only to Deuteronomy's diction, but also to the book's conceptual world. When I returned to the biblical accounts of Abraham, Isaac, and Jacob with these "Deuteronomic lenses," what I discovered caught me by surprise.

I have divided the links between D and PN into eight categories, moving from the most explicit (specific lexemes) to the vaguest (conceptual) connections: (1) morphological links; (2) individual lexemes; (3) idioms involving more than one lexeme; (4) toponyms; (5) ethnicons; (6) verbal formulas involved in the promises to / covenant with the ancestors; (7) the human responses of faith and obedience; and (8) other theological motifs. These categories are not exhaustive. For example, one should also identify the syntactical and other literary features of the respective texts. But that presupposes a detailed discourse linguistic analysis of both texts, which time and space preclude. Boundaries separating the categories identified are rarely crisp, but for heuristic purposes this will serve as an organizing taxonomy. The first few categories are listed more or less in alphabetic order. Obviously each entry in the list deserves further discussion, but limitations of space mean we must concentrate on cataloguing the data. The purpose of this essay is to invite readers to assess the evidence cited and to begin the discussion.

Morphological Links

1. הָאֵל in place of הָאֵלֶּה, "these" (Gen 19:8, 25; 26:3, 4; Deut 4:42; 7:22; 19:11).[24]
2. הוּא for הִיא, 3rd fem. sing. pronoun.[25] Whereas in the rest of the Hebrew Bible this pronoun is always הִיא, in the Pentateuch this form occurs only eighteen times (never in D).[26] By contrast, the otherwise unusual

---

23. Curiously, in neither case is the תּוֹלְדֹת named after the dominant character.

24. The long form occurs eighty times in the Pentateuch; the short form occurs once in the rest of the Pentateuch (Lev 18:27), but is not found elsewhere in the Hebrew Bible.

25. For a full, if dated, study of this phenomenon, see Gary Rendsburg, "A New Look at Pentateuchal HW," Bib 63 (1982): 351–69.

26. Genesis 14:2; 19:20; 20:5; 26:7; 38:25; 40:10; Exod 1:16; Lev 5:11; 11:39; 13:6, 10, 21; 16:31; 20:17, 18; 21:9; Num 5:13, 14. Rendsburg overlooks Gen 19:20; 26:7; 40:10; Exod 1:16; Lev 5:11; 13:6;

138   Daniel I. Block

form הוּא appears almost two hundred times, being distributed among all five books (with Genesis having more than fifty and D thirty-five). That it occurs in all of the purported JEDP sources, but never outside the Pentateuch, seriously undermines long-standing critical theories for the growth of the Pentateuch.[27]

Shared Lexemes

In addition to the examples given here from PN, see also from the Joseph story, תּוֹעֵבָה, "abomination," in Gen 43:32; 46:34; cf. Deut 7:25, 26 + 15× (also in Exod 8:22; Lev 18:22–30; 20:13).

3. אָהַב, "to love." The lexeme אָהַב occurs fourteen times in Genesis, but is never used of God's love for human beings.[28] By contrast, in D two-thirds of the circa two dozen occurrences involve either YHWH's love for people (the ancestors, 4:37; 10:15; Israel, 7:8, 13; 23:6[5]; sojourn-ers, 10:18) or Israel's love for YHWH (5:10; 6:5; 7:9; 10:12; 11:1, 13, 22; 13:4[3]; 19:9; 30:6, 16, 20). Horizontally, it is used of the Israelites' love for sojourners (10:19), a servant for his master (15:16, cf. Exod 21:5), and a husband for his wife (21:15–16). The last reference is especially sig-nificant, providing guidance in bigamous cases where the husband loves one wife more than the other, as was the case in Jacob's relationship with Leah and Rachel (Gen 29:30–32). The scarcity of אָהַב in Exodus–Num-bers (only Exod 20:6 [Deut 5:10]; 21:5; Lev 19:18, 34) reinforces the sense of linkage between D and PN.

4. הָפַךְ, "to overthrow" (Gen 19:21, 25, 29; Deut 29:22[23]).

5. חָשַׁק, "to love" [heartfelt impassioned love] (Gen 34:8; Deut 21:11; used theologically of YHWH's love for Israel in Deut 7:7; 10:15).[29]

6. מַעֲשֵׂר, "tithe" (Gen 14:20; 28:20–22; Deut 14:22; 26:12; cf. 12:6, 11, 17; 14:23, 28). Tithes are mentioned in Leviticus (27:30–32) and Numbers

---

20:18. הֲהָיא never occurs (Rendsburg, "New Look," 351 n. 1).

27. According to Rendsburg, this represents an early form of the language before the adoption of a distinctive third feminine singular pronoun, הִיא, which he sets in the Davidic or Solomonic period (Rendsburg, "New Look," 365).

28. Of a parent's love for a child (Abraham/Isaac, 22:2; Isaac/Esau and Rebekah/Jacob, 25:28; Jacob/Joseph, 37:3, 4; 44:20); of a husband's love for his wife (Isaac/Rebekah, 24:67; Jacob/Rachel, 29:18, 30; and Leah's hope that Jacob will love her, 29:32); an unmarried man for an unmarried woman (Shechem/Dinah, 34:3); a man's love of food (Isaac, 27:4, 9, 14).

29. The word is rare, appearing elsewhere as a verb only in 1 Kgs 9:19 [2 Chr 8:6]; Ps 91:14; Isa 21:4; 38:17, and as a noun חֵשֶׁק only in 1 Kgs 9:1, 19; 2 Chr 8:6). For discussion of this word, see Jon D. Levenson, *The Love of God: Divine Gift, Human Gratitude, and Mutual Faithfulness in Judaism* (Princeton: Princeton University Press, 2016), 40–42, 167–68, 176–77.

(18:21–28), but by linking the tithe with the creed-like declaration naming the Aramean ancestor (Deut 26:12), D forges a link with Genesis.

7. נָבִיא, "prophet" (Gen 20:7; Deut 13:2–6[1–5]; 18:15–22; 34:10).[30]
8. עֵד, an object as "a witness" to a covenant (Gen 31:44, 48, 52; Deut 31:21, 26).
9. עֲקָרָה, "to be barren" (Gen 11:30; Deut 7:14).[31]
10. פָּלֵא, "to be difficult, beyond one's ability" (Gen 18:14; Deut 17:8; 30:11).[32]
11. הִשְׁחִית, "to destroy" (Gen 18:28; 19:13–14).[33]
12. שׁמד, meaning "to be destroyed, to destroy," of populations (Gen 34:30; Deut 1:27).[34]

Shared Phrases/Idioms

In addition to the examples given below from PN, from the Joseph story, note also (1) עֵינְכֶם אַל־תָּחֹס, "your eye shall not pity," Gen 45:20 (toward inanimate objects); cf. לֹא־תָחוֹס עֵינְךָ, Deut 7:16; 13:9[8]; 19:13, 21; 25:12 (toward humans); (2) לֹא יוּכַל, "to be unable," Gen 43:32; cf. Deut 21:16; 22:19, 29; 24:4.

13. אֱלֹהֵי [הַ]נֵּכָר, "foreign gods" (Gen 35:2, 4; Deut 31:16; 32:12).[35]
14. בֵּרֵךְ וְהִרְבָּה, "to bless and multiply" (Gen 17:20; 22:17; 26:4, 24; 28:3; Deut 7:13; 30:16).[36]
15. דָּגָן וְתִירֹשׁ, "grain and wine" (Gen 27:28, 37; Deut 7:13; 11:14; 12:17; 14:23; 18:4; 28:51; 33:28).[37]

---

30. The word also occurs in Exod 7:1; Num 11:29; 12:6, but Abraham's intercessory responsibility was embodied most dramatically by Moses after the golden calf debacle (Deut 9:8–21, 25–29).

31. Elsewhere only in Exod 23:26.

32. The root occurs elsewhere in the Pentateuch (Exod 3:20; 34:10; Lev 22:21; 27:2; Num 6:2; 15:3, 8; Deut 28:59), but never with this sense.

33. In Exodus–Numbers the form מַשְׁחִית occurs twice (Exod 12:13, 13), where it concerns YHWH's judgment of Egypt at the time of Israel's first Passover.

34. Cf. Deut 1:27; 2:12, 21, 22, 23; 4:3, 26; 6:15; 7:4, 23, 24; 9:3, 8, 14, 19, 20, 25; 12:30; 28:20, 24, 45, 48, 51, 61, 63; 31:3, 4; 33:27. Elsewhere in the Tetrateuch only in Lev 26:30 and Num 33:52, but of pagan cult installations.

35. אֱלֹהֵי הַנֵּכָר occurs outside Genesis only in Josh 24:23; Judg 10:16; 1 Sam 7:3; 2 Chr 33:15. The expression אֱלֹהִים אֲחֵרִים, "other gods," is much more common, occurring eighteen times in D (Deut 5:7; 6:14; 7:4; 8:19; 11:16, 28; 13:3, 7, 14 [2, 6, 13]; 17:3; 18:20; 28:14, 36, 64; 29:25 [26]; 30:17; 31:18), and frequently in the Deuteronomistic History. While rooted in the Decalogue (Exod 20:3; Deut 5:7), it occurs only once more in Exodus–Numbers (Exod 23:13); cf. the abbreviated version, אֵל אַחֵר, in Exod 34:14.

36. The combination "bless and multiply" never occurs in Exodus–Numbers.

37. Except for the poetic occurrence (Deut 33:28), in D this pair always occurs with יִצְהָר, "olive oil," and they always occur in this order: grain, wine, oil. None of these is the common word for the commodity. Whether or not the expressions imply a special quality of the product, D's usage in place of לֶחֶם, יַיִן, and שֶׁמֶן involves a subtle anti-idolatry polemic. See Daniel I. Block, "Other Religions

140   Daniel I. Block

16. טַל הַשָּׁמַיִם, "dew of heaven" (Gen 27:28, 39; Deut 33:13, 28).[38]

17. יִיטַב לְ, "to go well for/with [you]" (Gen 12:13; cf. also 40:14; Deut 4:40).[39]

18. יָרַד מִצְרַיְמָה לָגוּר שָׁם, "To go down to Egypt to sojourn there" (Gen 12:10; Deut 26:5).

19. עָשָׂה חֶסֶד, "to demonstrate steadfast love" (Gen 19:19; 20:13; 21:23; 24:12, 14, 49 [divine חֶסֶד]32:11; [חֶסֶד]; cf. 40:14; 47:29; Deut 5:10 [Exod 20:6] [divine חֶסֶד]).[40]

20. הִרְחִיב אֶת־גְּבֻלְךָ, "to extend your borders" (Gen 26:22; Deut 12:20; 19:8). Here the verb הִרְחִיב, "to extend, expand [space]," provides the only lexical connection between PN and D. Despite the addition of "as he promised you" (כַּאֲשֶׁר דִּבֶּר־לָךְ) in Deut 12:20 and "as he swore to your ancestors" (כַּאֲשֶׁר נִשְׁבַּע לַאֲבֹתֶיךָ) in 19:8, PN never speak about the ancestors' or their descendants' future גְּבוּל. The closest we get is Gen 23:17–18, which declares that the Hittites deeded the entire area (גְּבוּל) around the cave at Machpelah over to Abraham. Nevertheless, the expansion of Isaac's *Lebensraum*, memorialized in the new toponym Rehoboth (רְחֹבוֹת), presents a microcosm of the territorial expansion defined in Gen 15:18 and anticipated elsewhere (12:7; 13:14–17; 15:7–21; 26:4; 28:13; 35:12). However, the first explicit promise to expand Israel's גְּבוּל occurs in Exod 34:24.

21. שָׁמַע אֶל־עָנִי, "to hear/listen to [someone's] afflictions" (Gen 16:11; Deut 26:7).[41]

Toponymic Links

The terms differ, but in this context note also Edom's possession (אֲחֻזָּה) of land (Seir, Gen 36:43); Deut 2:12 uses יְרֻשָּׁה and characterizes the land as granted (נָתַן) to them by YHWH.

---

in Old Testament Theology," in *Gospel According to Moses*, 208–209. The combination of דָּגָן and תִּירֹשׁ occurs elsewhere in the Tetrateuch only in Num 18:12, albeit in reverse order.

38. D casts the idiom in different form, clarifying טַל הַשָּׁמַיִם, but Moses's benediction of the tribes is linked with Isaac's blessing of Jacob (and virtual curse of Esau). These words do not appear together elsewhere in the Tetrateuch.

39. Cf. Deut 1:23; 4:40; 5:16, 29; 6:3, 18; 8:16; 12:25, 28; 22:7; 28:63. The idiom occurs in Deut 5:16, but is missing in the Exodus version of the Decalogue (Exod 20:12).

40. Otherwise the idiom is missing in the Tetrateuch. Elsewhere D speaks of "keeping the covenant and the steadfast love" (שָׁמַר הַבְּרִית וְהַחֶסֶד, 7:9, 12).

41. The envoy's statement in Gen 16:11 appears to be poetic shorthand for "YHWH has heard your cry and seen your affliction." Cf. also Exod 3:7.

22. אֵלוֹ[ן] מוֹרֶה, "the oak[s] of Moreh" (Gen 12:6; Deut 11:30). Given the importance of the ancestors in D,[42] remarkably D never names the sites most important in PN (Shechem, Hebron, Beersheba, Bethel). The location of Mounts Gerizim and Ebal אֵצֶל אֵלוֹנֵי מֹרֶה, "beside the oaks of Moreh," is as close as we get. The expression אֵלוֹ[ן] מוֹרֶה, "the oak[s] of Moreh," occurs in the Hebrew Bible only in these two texts.[43] The geographic note in Deut 11:30 suggests that by entering Canaan from across the Jordan the Israelites could quickly reach the site where both Abraham (12:6) and Jacob (33:18–20) had celebrated YHWH's fulfillment of his promises and staked their divinely based claim to this land by building altars.[44] That the Israelites as the people of YHWH would cement their claim to this land there is especially significant,[45] since Jacob had renamed the place אֵל אֱלֹהֵי יִשְׂרָאֵל, "El, the God of Israel" (Gen 33:20).[46]

23. אֶרֶץ הַכְּנַעֲנִי, "land of the Canaanite" (Gen 12:6; cf. 50:11; Deut 11:30). Although Genesis lacks the construct phrase, the collocation of the gentilic כְּנַעֲנִי with אֶרֶץ links these texts. Note also references to the Canaanite in the land in 13:7; 24:3; and 34:30. Remarkably, in contrast to D, PN never hints at a Canaanite moral or religious problem.[47] If anything, the narrator casts them as more righteous than the ancestors. First, Melchizedek ("Malki is righteous" or "My king is Zedek[Zaddik]"),[48] the king of Salem, was priest of El Elyon (אֵל עֶלְיוֹן), whom Abraham acknowledged as his political and priestly superior. Second, in 20:1–18 God characterizes Abimelek, king of Gerar, as a man of internal piety (תָּם לֵבָב)[49] and external ethical morality (נִקְיוֹן כַּף, vv. 5–6),[50] in contrast to the

---

42. On this subject, see Jerry Hwang, *The Rhetoric of Remembrance: An Investigation of the "Fathers" in Deuteronomy*, Siphrut 8 (Winona Lake, IN: Eisenbrauns, 2012).

43. גִּבְעַת הַמּוֹרֶה, "Teacher's Hill," in Judg 7:1 refers to a different site.

44. Both texts locate Shechem "in the land of Canaan" (12:5; 34:18).

45. On the significance of the ceremony at Gerizim and Ebal, see Daniel I. Block, "What Do These Stones Mean? The Riddle of Deuteronomy 27," *JETS* 56 (2013): 17–41; republished in *The Triumph of Grace: Literary and Theological Studies in Deuteronomy and Deuteronomic Themes* (Eugene, OR: Cascade, 2017), 126–51.

46. Jacob had departed the land as Jacob ("trickster"), but he returned with a new name and a new relationship with the patron deity.

47. Abraham's warning to his servant not to allow Isaac to marry a woman "from the daughters of the Canaanites" (Gen 24:3, 37) appears contradictory to our point, but the prohibition is not grounded in ethical or theological considerations. As a first-generation immigrant, Abraham may have been concerned about maintaining contact with his roots (מוֹלֶדֶת). Cf. Gen 11:28; 12:1; 24:4, 7; 31:3, 13; 32:10.

48. "מַלְכִּי־צֶדֶק," *HALOT*, 1:593.

49. El Shadday's charge to Abram to be "blameless" in 17:1 involves the etymologically related term תָּמִים.

50. This expression occurs elsewhere only in Pss 26:6 and 73:13.

142   Daniel I. Block

self-serving patriarch (vv. 2, 11–13). Third, the narrator casts the Hittites of Kiriath-Arba (Hebron), located "in the land of Canaan" (אֶרֶץ כְּנָעַן; cf. 33:18), as profusely generous to Abraham (23:3–9). Fourth, Shechem's rape of Dinah was reprehensible (34:2), but in the rest of the chapter the Hivites of Shechem behave more honorably than Jacob's family, who are "odious (הַבְאִישׁ) among the inhabitants of the land, the Canaanites and Perizzites" (v. 30). Fifth, after his own duplicitous actions, Judah acknowledged that the Canaanite Tamar was more righteous (צָדְקָה) than he. These characterizations give credence to the divine statement in 15:16 and betray the narrator's own context, which contrasts with Abraham's time when the iniquity of the Amorites was not yet full.[51]

24. צֹעַר, "Zoar" (Gen 13:10; 14:2, 8; 19:22, 23, 30; Deut 34:1b–3).[52]

25. סְדֹם וַעֲמֹרָה, "Sodom and Gomorrah" (Gen 13:10; Deut 29:11[23]; 32:32).[53]

26. שַׁעַר הָעִיר, "gate of the/his/their town" (Gen 23:10, cf. v. 18; 34:20;[54] Deut 22:24; cf. 21:19; 22:15).[55]

27. The maximalist definition of the promised land (Gen 15:18; Deut 1:17; 11:24).[56]

Ethnicons

28. [הָ]אֲרַמִּי, "[the] Aramean" (Gen 25:20; 28:5; 31:20, 24; Deut 26:5).[57]

29. הָאֵמִים, "the Emmites" (Gen 14:5; Deut 2:10–11).

30. הַחֹתִי[ם] בְּשֵׂעִיר/בְּהַרְרָם שֵׂעִיר, "the Horite[s] in Seir/the mountains of Seir" (Gen 14:6; 36:20, 21, 29, 30; Deut 2:12, 2:22).

---

51. It seems he intentionally associated Amorites, rather than Canaanites, with the evil (עָוֹן).

52. Zoar is never named in Exodus–Numbers and appears elsewhere only in Isa 15:5 and Jer 48:34.

53. Neither Sodom nor Gomorrah is mentioned in Exodus–Numbers.

54. Cf. Gen 19:2, which refers to "the gate of Sodom" (שַׁעַר־סְדֹם). On the use of שַׁעַר in the Pentateuch, see Ellen van Wolde, *Reframing Biblical Studies: When Language and Text Meet Culture, Cognition, and Context* (Winona Lake, IN: Eisenbrauns, 2009), 81–86.

55. Deuteronomy 21:19 speaks of "the elders of his town" at "the gate of his place" (זִקְנֵי עִירוֹ וְאֶל־שַׁעַר מְקֹמוֹ), and 22:25 of taking the accused "to the elders of the town at the gate" (אֶל־זִקְנֵי הָעִיר הַשַּׁעְרָה). "Gate" and "town" are never conjoined elsewhere in the Tetrateuch.

56. On which see Daniel I. Block, "The Theology of Land in Deuteronomy," in *Lexham Geographic Commentary on the Pentateuch*, ed. Barry J. Beitzel (Bellingham, WA: Lexham, forthcoming).

While the specification of the great Euphrates River (הַנָּהָר הַגָּדֹל נְהַר־פְּרָת) as the northern boundary, and assumption of the "River of Egypt" (נְהַר מִצְרַיִם) as the southern border, are absent in Exodus–Numbers, the maximalist definition appears in slightly modified form in Exod 23:31 and Josh 1:4.

57. Elsewhere the Tetrateuch never mentions Arameans.

31. הַזּוּזִים/זַמְזֻמִּים, "the Zuzites/Zamzummites" (Gen 14:5; Deut 2:20–21). The identification of the Zuzim of Genesis with the Zamzummim of D is not in doubt.[58]

32. רְפָאִים, "Rephaim" (Gen 14:5; 15:19–21; Deut 2:11, 20; 3:11, 13).[59]

33. The lists of peoples occupying the promised land (Gen 15:19–21; Deut 7:1; 20:17). Whereas Deut 20:17 follows the stereotypical listing by naming six Canaanite nations,[60] Deut 7:1 (also Josh 3:10; 24:11) completes the quota of seven by adding the Girgashites, and links this text directly to God's promise to Abraham in Gen 15:1–21.

34. רְאוּבֵן, "Reuben" (Gen 35:22; Deut 33:6). "Reuben" serves as a personal name in Gen 35:22 but as a tribal name in Deut 33:6. However, while the first part of the latter is a benediction of sorts, the second half functions as a not-so-subtly veiled curse, alluding to Reuben's immoral act with his father's concubine, Bilhah.[61] Jacob's "blessing" for Simeon and Levi in Gen 49:5–7 is actually a "curse," expressly linked to their violence against the people of Shechem in Gen 34. This contrasts with how the "Blessing of Moses" treats these tribes. Whereas Levi's defense of YHWH at Massah eclipses his involvement at Shechem, Simeon is forgotten.

Formulas Relating to the Ancestral Promises/Covenant

Here I have arranged the items logically, rather than alphabetically.

35. אֲנִי יְהוָה אֲשֶׁר הוֹצֵאתִיךָ מִן, "I am YHWH who brought you out of . . ." (Gen 15:7; Deut 5:6; 13:6). While the statements in D follow post-exodus

---

58. So already Symmachus and the Genesis Apocryphon 21:29. Greek reads ἔθνη ἰσχυρά, "a strong people."

59. Remarkably, none of these three ethnicons (Rephaim, Emmim, Zamzummim) appears in Exodus–Numbers, while Genesis is silent on עֲנָק/בְּנֵי עֲנָקִים/עֲנָקִים, another common ethnicon for the aboriginal population of Canaan.

60. So also, Exod 3:8, 17; 23:23; 33:2; 34:11; Josh 9:1; 11:3; 12:8; Judg 3:5. Exodus 13:5 omits Perizzites. Numbers 13:29 heads a list of four with Amalekites (a nonautochthonous Edomite group (Gen 36:12, 16), located in the Negeb, followed by Hittites, Jebusites, and Amorites, who occupy the hill country, and concluding with Canaanites ("lowlanders"), who occupy the coastal region and the Jordan valley. For discussion of these lists, see Tomoo Ishida, "The Structure and Historical Implications of the Lists of Pre-Israelite Nations," *Bib* 60 (1979): 461–90. Assuming that the list has grown gradually, because the Genesis list is the longest, Westermann concludes that this is the oldest list (Westermann, *Genesis 12–36*, 230). On the fallacy of this sort of reasoning, see Benjamin Kilchör, *Mosetora und Jahwetora: Das Verhältnis von Deuteronomium 12–26 zu Exodus, Levitikus und Numeri*, BZABR 21 (Wiesbaden: Harrassowitz, 2015), 39–40, 90–92, 101–2, 201–2, 292.

61. Compare the explicit link in Jacob's "blessing" for Reuben in Gen 49:3–4.

144   Daniel I. Block

convention,[62] the adaptation of the formula to Abraham's migration from Ur is extraordinary. The narrator (and the character YHWH) hereby casts Abraham as a devotee of the God of the exodus.

36. וְהָיִיתִי לְךָ/לָהֶם לֵאלֹהִים, "I will be your/their God" (Gen 17:7, 8; Deut 26:17–19). This is the first half of the two-part "covenant formula": "I will be your God, and you shall be my people" (Exod 6:7; Lev 26:12). Even though the pure form of the first part of the formula never occurs in D, the three hundred–plus occurrences of suffixed forms "your God" and "our God" assume it, and rituals underlying the book of Deuteronomy celebrate the fulfillment of YHWH's promise in Gen 17:7–8 to be the God of Abraham's descendants. The significance of the ceremonies suggested by Deut 26:17–19 is reinforced in 27:9b–10: "Keep silence and hear, O Israel: *This day you have become the people of* YHWH *your God.* You shall therefore listen to the voice of YHWH your God, keeping his commands and his statutes, which I command you today."

37. [אָנֹכִי/אֲנִי] יְהוָה אֱלֹהֵי אָבִיךָ/אֲבֹתֶיךָ/אֲבֹתֵיכֶם, "[I am] YHWH the God of your father[s]" (Gen 26:24; 28:13; Deut 10:22; Deut 26:7).[63]

38. כָּרַת בְּרִית, "to cut [make] a covenant" (Gen 15:18;[64] Deut 4:23; 5:2, 3; 9:9; 28:69; 29:11, 24 [12, 25]; 31:16.).[65]

39. הֵקִים בְּרִית, "to establish/confirm a covenant" (Gen 17:7, 19, 21; Deut 8:18).[66]

40. God's promise to multiply (הִרְבָּה) the descendants (זֶרַע) "like the stars of the sky" (כְּכוֹכְבֵי הַשָּׁמַיִם; Gen 22:17; 26:4; Deut 1:10; 10:22; 28:62).[67] Note also the references to the numerable nature of Jacob's descendants who went to Egypt in Gen 46:6–7 and Deut 26:5.

---

62. Exodus 6:7; 20:2; 29:46; Lev 19:36; 22:33; 25:38, 42, 55; 26:13, 45; Num 15:41. An alternative form of the divine introduction/deliverance formula uses the verb עָלָה (Hiphil), "to bring up" (Deut 20:1; Lev 11:45; note also the perverse adaptation of the formula to the golden calf, Exod 32:4).

63. Cf. also Deut 4:1; 6:3; 12:1; 27:3; 29:24 [25]. Note especially Exod 3:6, "I am the God of your father, the God of Abraham, the God of Isaac, and the God of Jacob." Also, Exod 3:13, 15–16; 4:5; 15:2 (sing.); 18:4 (sing.).

64. The idiom is used elsewhere of human covenants (21:27, 32; 26:28; 31:44).

65. However, this covenant is never specified as the covenant made with Abraham. The idiom is used of YHWH's covenant with Israel elsewhere in the Tetrateuch (Exod 24:8; 34:10, 27). Exodus 23:32 and 34:12, 15 respectively forbid making covenants with other gods and with the Canaanites.

66. The formula also occurs in Exod 6:4 and Lev 26:9. Related conceptually to Deut 4:31, the latter speaks of YHWH's fidelity to his covenant in the distant future. However, instead of confirming the covenant, in Deut 4:31 Moses declares that YHWH will "not forget" (לֹא יִשְׁכַּח) the covenant with Israel's ancestors. לֹא יִשְׁכַּח אֶת־בְּרִית is equivalent to זָכַר אֶת־הַבְּרִית in Gen 9:15, 16; Exod 2:24, 6:5; Lev 26:42, 45, casting doubt on Weinfeld's claim that the latter is a mark of P (Weinfeld, *Deuteronomy and the Deuteronomic School*, 230).

67. Cf. also Exod 32:13. Remarkably, only Genesis uses the comparative idioms "like the sand of the sea[shore]" (22:17; 32:12) and "like the dust of the earth (13:16; 28:14).

41. God's promise to make a great nation (גּוֹי גָּדוֹל) of Abraham and his descendants (Gen 12:2; 18:18; cf. 46:3;[68] Deut 4:7–8; 26:5).

42. God's sworn promise (נִשְׁבַּע) to give land to Abraham's offspring (Gen 24:7; 26:3;[69] Deut 1:8; 11:9; 34:4; cf. also 31:21).

In the following, the lexical links are less precise, but the conceptual connections are apparent.

43. God's election of Abraham and his descendants (Gen 18:19, with יָדַע, "to know"); Deut 4:37; 7:6–7; 10:15; 14:2, all with בָּחַר, "to choose").

44. God's promise to make Abraham and his descendants a blessing to the nations (Gen 12:3; 18:18; 22:18; 26:4; 28:14; Deut 4:6–8; cf. 26:19).

45. Outsiders recognizing YHWH or being blessed because of Israel's blessed status (Gen 21:22; 26:28–29; 30:30; Deut 28:10).

46. The promise of divine protection (Gen 15:1; 26:24; Deut 7:21; 20:3–4; 31:6; 31:8).

47. Israel's dominance over outsiders (Gen 22:17; 24:60; 27:29, 37; Deut 26:19; 28:1, 10, 13).

48. Claiming the land (Gen 13:17;[70] Deut 11:24).

49. Israel's sojourn (גּוּר) in the foreign land of Egypt (Gen 15:13; Deut 10:19).[71]

50. Divine terror/dread striking those who encounter the ancestors and their descendants (Gen 35:5;[72] Deut 2:25; 11:25).[73]

51. The brotherhood of Jacob/Israel and Esau/Edom (Gen 25:23–34; 32:4[3]; Deut 23:7[6]).

---

68. Cf. also 35:11. God gave the same promise to Ishmael in Gen 17:20; 21:8. Twice in Exodus–Numbers YHWH threatened to transfer the promise from Abraham's descendants to Moses (Exod 32:10; Num 14:12).

69. Cf. Gen 50:24. References to the sworn grant of land also occur in Deut 4:31; 6:10, 18, 23; 7:8, 12, 13; 8:1, 18; 9:5; 11:9, 21; 26:3; 28:11; 30:20; 31:7, as well as in Exod 13:5; 32:13; 33:1; Num 14:16. The forms of the promises of land vary. Gen 12:2 and 28:13 omit references to an oath. The remainder alternate between variations of the collocation נָתַן . . . נִשְׁבַּע, "he swore . . . to give," and elliptical statements without נָתַן.

70. הִתְהַלֵּךְ carries overtones of "staking one's claim," or "acting as one who already held title [to the land]." Thus Donald J. Wiseman, "Abraham in History and Tradition, Part 1: Abraham the Hebrew," BSac 134 (1977): 126; cf. Wiseman, "Abraham Reassessed," in Essays on the Patriarchal Narratives, ed. A. R. Millard and D. J. Wiseman (Leicester: Inter-Varsity, 1980), 147 and 155n31.

71. According to Deut 23:8 [7], the memory of Israel's sojourn in Egypt was to temper their treatment of the Egyptians; they had served as their hosts at a critical time in their history. This motif is memorialized in the name of Moses's son Gershom (Exod 2:22; 18:3) and surfaces elsewhere as motivation for ethical living (Exod 22:20; 23:9; Lev 19:4).

72. In Gen 31:42 פַּחַד functions as an epithet of the God of Isaac (before Laban the Aramean).

73. The motif of divine terror going before the Israelites surfaces in Exod 15:16 (אֵימָתָה וָפַחַד) and 23:27 (אֵימָה). The root פחד occurs three times in Deut 28:66–67, denoting Israel's fear of the nations.

146   Daniel I. Block

52. God's blessing (ברך) of Abraham and the ancestral families (Gen 12:2; 14:19–20; 17:16, 20; 22:17; 26:3, 12; 24; Deut 12:7; 14:24, 29; 15:4, 6, 10, 14, 18; 16:10, 15; 23:21; 24:12; 26:15; 28:1–24; 30:16; 33:11, 13, 24).[74]

53. Demonstrating covenant lovingkindness and faithfulness (חֶסֶד וֶאֱמֶת) to the ancestors (Gen 24:12, 14, 27, 49; 32:10; cf. Deut 7:9, which characterizes YHWH as "the faithful God who keeps covenant and lovingkindness [הָאֵל הַנֶּאֱמָן שֹׁמֵר הַבְּרִית וְהַחֶסֶד]"; 32:4 [אֵל אֱמוּנָה]).

54. God "doing good" to (הֵטִיב, hiphil of יטב; i.e., bestowing covenant benefactions on) the ancestors (Gen 32:10, 13[9, 12]; Deut 8:16; 28:63; 30:15).[75]

Dispositional and Ethical Responses to God/YHWH

55. Generic fear of God (יְרֵא אֱלֹהִים/יִרְאַת אֱלֹהִים) with ethical implications[76] (Gen 20:11, cf. 42:18; Deut 25:18).[77]

56. The fear (יָרֵא, trusting awe) of YHWH (Gen 22:12; Deut 4:10; 31:12–13).[78]

57. Trust in YHWH (הֶאֱמִין בַּיהוה) (Gen 15:6; Deut 1:32; 9:23).[79]

58. "To listen to the voice, obey" (שָׁמַע לְקוֹל/שָׁמַע בְּקוֹל) (Gen 22:18; 26:5; 4:30; Deut 26:17; 28:1–2).[80]

59. To swear by YHWH, or by his name (נִשְׁבַּע בִּשְׁמוֹ) (Gen 24:3;[81] Deut 6:13; 10:20).

60. To walk/stand before YHWH (הִתְהַלֵּךְ/עָמַד לִפְנֵי יהוה) (Gen 17:1; 18:22;[82] Gen 24:40; Deut 10:8; 18:5). D does not use the verb הִתְהַלֵּךְ, but the idiom עָמַד לִפְנֵי יְהוָה, "to stand before YHWH," presupposes the person has been

---

74. See also Gen 24:1; 24:31, 35; 25:11; 26:29; 27:27; 28:3; 32:27, 29 [26, 28]; 32:26, 29; 35:9. Here I distinguish YHWH blessing the ancestors and their descendants from them being a blessing to the world (#45 above), and other humans blessing the ancestors or their progeny, including the ancestors blessing their children (Gen 24:60; 27:4—28:28:6; 32:1 [31:55]).

75. Cf. also the frequent references to it going well for Israel (יָטַב in qal): 4:40; 5:16, 29; 6:3, 18; 12:25, 28; 22:7.

76. Although the divinity is specifically identified as YHWH, the notion also appears in Lev 19:14, 32; 25:15, 36, 43.

77. Cf. Exod 1:17, 21.

78. This use of יָרֵא is frequent in D: Deut 4:10; 5:29; 6:2, 13, 24; 8:6; 10:12, 17, 20; 13:5 [4]; 14:23; 17:19; 25:18; 28:58; 31:12, 13.

79. On הֶאֱמִין, "to believe, demonstrate trust," in the Tetrateuch, see also Exod 4:1, 5, 8, 9, 31; 19:9; Num 14:11; 20:12.

80. Cf. Deut 8:20; 9:23; 13:5 [4], 19 [18]; 15:5; 21:18, 20 (of a son to parents); 26:14; 27:10; 28:15, 45, 62; 30:2, 8, 10, 20.

81. Cf. Gen 21:23–24, where Abraham swears before Abimelech by God (בֵּאלֹהִים). The notion of swearing specifically by YHWH's name appears elsewhere in the Tetrateuch only in Lev 19:12.

82. The idiom also involves lesser persons standing before human superiors. See Gen 41:46; 43:15; 47:7.

In the Tradition of Moses   147

invited to the presence of God. Whereas הִתְהַלֵּךְ אֶת־הָאֱלֹהִים, "to walk
with God," speaks of intimate communion, "to walk before YHWH"
implies access to the divine court and service as YHWH's commissioned
agent. This notion is on display in Gen 18, where Abraham intercedes for
Sodom and Gomorrah.[83] The idea of appearing before YHWH is explicit
in the D texts, which speak of YHWH choosing the Levitical priests "to
serve him and bless [the people] in his name."

61. Prostration before (הִשְׁתַּחֲוָה לְ) deity (Gen 22:5; 24:48; 5:9; 26:10). The
verb הִשְׁתַּחֲוָה denotes a physical gesture of prostration in submission
and homage before a superior.[84] Although Genesis frequently reports
mundane prostration before a human superior,[85] D only employs the
word theologically, and except for 26:10, in keeping with the demand for
exclusive devotion to YHWH, it always occurs in prohibitions of prostra-
tions before other deities (8:19; 11:16; 17:3; 29:25[26]; 30:17).

62. שָׁמַר דֶּרֶךְ יהוה/הָלַךְ בְּדֶרֶךְ יהוה, "to keep/walk in the way of YHWH" (Gen
18:19; Deut 5:33; 8:6; 10:12; 11:22; 13:6[5]; 19:9; 26:17; 28:9; 30:16). "To
keep/walk in the way/ways of YHWH" is ambiguous, meaning either "to
walk" (i.e., conduct one's life) as YHWH does (cf. 10:18–19), or "to walk"
as YHWH commanded one to walk. Texts that speak of keeping the com-
mands/ordinances "by walking in the way of YHWH" (5:33; 8:6; 11:22;
13:6[5]) render the latter sense explicit. Since "keeping the commands"
is frequently linked with "walking in the way of YHWH," the charge to
"keep the way of YHWH" in Gen 18:19 may represent intentional shorthand conflation of the Deuteronomic expressions. In any case, this text
clarifies the idiom with לַעֲשׂוֹת צְדָקָה וּמִשְׁפָּט, "by practicing righteousness
and justice," which involves thoroughly Deuteronomic vocabulary.[86]
However, the characterization of "the Judge of all the earth" as one who
"executes justice" (יַעֲשֶׂה מִשְׁפָּט) in Gen 18:25 blurs the boundary between
keeping God's commands and imitating him.

63. Righteousness / a righteous person / to be righteous / to demonstrate
righteousness / to declare someone righteous (צֶדֶק/צְדָקָה/צַדִּיק/צָדַק/הִצְדִּיק)
(Gen 15:6; 18:19, 25; cf. 38:26; Deut 6:25; 16:20; 25:1). Of the links

83. Verse 22 is text-critically problematic. While MT and all the versions have Abraham standing before YHWH, this is one of the eighteen alleged *tiqqune sopherim*. The Masorah in *BHS* claims
the original reading had YHWH standing before Abraham. Cf. "R. Simon said: 'This is a correction
of the Scribes for the *Shekinah* was waiting for Abraham'" (*Gen. Rab.* 49.7). However, Emanuel Tov
deems it unlikely that the original would have had YHWH standing before Abraham (Emanuel Tov,
Textual Criticism of the Hebrew Bible, 3rd ed. [Minneapolis: Fortress, 2012], 60–61).

84. For fuller discussion, see Daniel I. Block, *For the Glory of God: Recovering a Biblical
Theology of Worship* (Grand Rapids: Baker Academic, 2014), 12–17.

85. Genesis 18:2; 19:1; 23:7, 12; 27:29; 33:3, 6, 7; 37:7, 9, 10; 42:6; 43:26, 28; 47:31; 48:12; 49:8.

86. Cf. Deut 6:25; 33:21; 2 Sam 8:15; 1 Kgs 10:19.

148   Daniel I. Block

between Genesis and D, this may be the most remarkable of all. The root צדק occurs forty-six times in the Pentateuch, only nine of which occur in Exodus–Numbers. These are limited to three contexts,[87] and each recalls corresponding texts in PN or D.[88] Genesis and D employ the root צדק with a similar range of meaning,[89] and both use the root as a verb and in at least two forms of the noun.[90]

64. The prohibition on intermarriage with Canaanites (Gen 24:3; 28:1; 34:9–10, 16–17, 21; Deut 7:2–4, 16). As noted earlier, the positive picture of Canaanites the author of PN paints is striking, and raises questions concerning the rationale behind Abraham's demand that Isaac's wife be from the Aramaeans in Haran, Isaac and Rebekah's problems with Esau's Hittite wives (26:34–35), and Rebekah's rejection of a potential Hittite wife for Jacob (27:46). Would this have been an issue had YHWH later not prohibited such intermarriage? The case of Shechem is especially significant, because Jacob's sons speak expressly of becoming one people with the Shechemites through intermarriage (וְהָיִינוּ לְעַם אֶחָד, Gen 34:16). The entire chapter seems to be narrated in the light of the later prohibition.[91]

65. The motif of testing (נסָּה) (Gen 22:1; Deut 8:2, 16; 13:4[3]). This motif is not unique to PN and D (cf. Exod 15:25; 16:4; 20:20), but it is more fully developed in D than elsewhere, including the prohibition against Israel testing YHWH (6:16; 33:8; cf. Exod 17:2, 7; Num 14:22).

66. שָׁמַר בְּרִית, "to keep a covenant" (Gen 17:9–10; Deut 7:9; 29:8[9]; 33:9).[92]

67. הֵפִיר הַבְּרִית, "to break a covenant" (Gen 17:14; Deut 31:16, 20).[93]

---

87. Exodus 9:27 (הַצַּדִּיק), צֶדֶק [×2], 23:7–8 (צַדִּיק); Lev 19 (צֶדֶק, v. 15, 4× in v. 36).

88. Compare Exod 9:27 with Gen 38:26; Exod 23:7–8 with Deut 25:1; Lev 19:15 with Deut 1:16 and 16:18; and Lev 19:36 with Deut 25:15.

89. Compare Gen 15:6 and Deut 6:25; 24:13 (צְדָקָה); the juxtaposing of צַדִּיק with רָשָׁע, Gen 18:23 and Deut 9:4–5; 25:1; exercising justice (עָשָׂה מִשְׁפָּט/שָׁפַט) with righteousness (Gen 18:25; Deut 1:16; 16:18; cf. 25:1); righteousness in economic assessments (Gen 30:33; Deut 25:15); divine righteousness/administration of righteousness (Gen 15:6; Deut 6:25; 9:4–6; 24:16; 32:4; 33:21).

90. Verb: צָדְקָה, Gen 38:26 (Qal); נִצְטַדָּק, 44:16 (Hithpael); וְהִצְדִּיקוּ, Deut 25:1 (Hiphil); Nouns: צֶדֶק, Deut 1:16; 16:18, 20; 25:15; 33:19; צְדָקָה, Gen 15:6; 18:10; 30:33; Deut 6:25; 9:4–6; 24:13; 33:21; צַדִּיק, 18:23–28 (6 ′); 20:4 (cf. also 6:9; 7:1).

91. This concern is not unique to Deut 7:2–4, but rooted in Exod 34:15–16.

92. Precisely, Deut 29:9 [10] speaks of "keeping the words of this covenant and doing them" (וּשְׁמַרְתֶּם אֶת־דִּבְרֵי הַבְּרִית הַזֹּאת וַעֲשִׂיתֶם אֹתָם). According to Weinfeld, P's equivalent to שָׁמַר הַבְּרִית is זָכַר הַבְּרִית, "to remember the covenant" (cf. Gen 9:15), in which case vv. 9–10 should be deleted from chapter 17 as a non-P insertion in a pericope that is universally applied to P (Weinfeld, *Deuteronomy and the Deuteronomic School*, 330). See, e.g., Blum, *Komposition der Vätergeschichte*, 420–32; Claus Westermann, *Genesis 12–36: A Commentary*, trans. John J. Scullion (Minneapolis: Augsburg, 1985), 251–71. Against this interpretation, the computer analysis of Dershowitz et al. ("Computerized Source Criticism," 266) identified Gen 16:2–19:22 all as non-P.

93. The idiom also occurs in Lev 26:15, 44; Judg 2:1.

In the Tradition of Moses   149

68. שָׁמַר מִשְׁמֶרֶת, "to keep [God's] charge" (Gen 26:5; Deut 11:1).[94]

69. שָׁמַר מִצְוֺתַי/מִצְוֺתָיו, "to keep God's commands" (Gen 26:5; Deut 13:5 [4]).[95]

70. שָׁמַר חֻקּוֺתַי/חֻקּוֺתָיו, "to keep [God's] ordinances" (Gen 26:5; Deut 6:2).[96]

71. הִשָּׁמֶר לְךָ/לָכֶם פֶּן, "guard yourself/yourselves lest . . ." (Gen 24:6; 31:24; Deut 4:9, 23; 6:12; 8:11; 11:16; 12:13, 19, 30; 15:9.[97]

72. שָׁמַר תּוֺרֹתַי/הַתּוֺרָה, "to keep my instructions / the Instruction" (Gen 26:5; Deut 17:19). While Gen 26:5 shares תּוֺרָה with D, Exod 16:28 provides the closest analogue to this text (the plural refers to divine instructions generically). This usage is missing in D, but the articular form, הַתּוֺרָה, occurs twenty times. Except for 32:46, it always functions as a formal title to the body of Moses's instruction.[98]

Shared Theological Motifs

While many lexical and idiomatic links are relatively easy to establish, exploration of the relationship between PN and D needs to include questions of ideology and theology. Some evidence we have tracked above borders on this, such as the relationship between Shechem in PN and Ebal and Gilgal in Deut 11 and 27. However, the phrase אֵלוֺן [י']מוֺרֶה, "the oak[s] of Moreh," links these texts. Here I shall consider two additional issues: the portrayal of Egypt and the characterization of Abraham.

73. The Portrayal of Egypt

Both PN and D present an ambivalent picture of Egypt, namely as a house of slavery for Israel and as a gracious host of the ancestors. Not surprisingly, the proportion of strokes devoted to each is reversed. While Egypt's role as the "house of slavery" (בֵּית עֲבָדִים) dominates D,[99] it receives only passing and

---

94. The expression links D and PN, but it occurs only here in both books. The phrase occurs frequently in Leviticus–Numbers: Lev 8:35; 18:30; 22:9; Num 1:53; 3:7, 8, 28, 32, 38; 8:26; 9:19, 23; 18:3, 4, 5; 31:30, 47.

95. Cf. also Deut 11:22; 13: 19 [18]; 19:9; 26:17, 18; 27:1; 28:9, 45; 30:10, 16.

96. See also Deut 8:11; 10:13; 11:1; 28:15, 45; 30:10, 16. However, the phrase also occurs in Exodus–Numbers: Exod 13:10; Lev 18:4, 5, 26; 19:19, 37; 20:8, 22. Remarkably, שָׁמַר מִשְׁפָּטִים, "keep the judgments," never occurs in Genesis.

97. The idiom occurs nowhere else in the Tetrateuch.

98. Deuteronomy 1:5; 4:8, 44; 17:11, 18, 19; 27:3, 8, 26; 28:58, 61; 29:20, 28 [21, 29]; 30:10; 31:9, 11, 12, 24, 26; 32:46. The poetic statement in 33:4 lacks the article on תּוֺרָה, but it obviously identifies a body of instruction, rather than individual teachings. In 33:10, the suffixed form תּוֺרָתְךָ, "your Torah," is definite. הַתּוֺרָה represents a body of teaching elsewhere only in Exod 24:12, where it refers to the Decalogue, which is expressly described as something to be taught (לְהוֺרֹתָם), rather than legislated.

99. בֵּית עֲבָדִים occurs in Deut 5:6; 6:12; 7:8; 8:14; 13:6, 11 [5, 10]. See also 5:15; 6:21; 15:15; 16:12; 24:11, 18, 22.

150   Daniel I. Block

veiled attention in Gen 15:13–14, which anticipates both Israel's enslavement and their exodus from Egypt. The reference to four hundred years makes little historical sense apart from the narratives in Exodus,[100] and limited theological sense without reference to D.

On the other hand, Genesis highlights Egypt's role as gracious host to the patriarchs in times of crisis (Gen 12:10–20; 37–50) and as the context in which the family of seventy individuals (Gen 46:27) became an innumerable population (cf. Exod 1:7).[101] This positive role receives scant attention in D. We may hear an allusion in Deut 10:19, "You shall love the alien (גֵּר), for you were foreigners (גֵּרִים) in Egypt." Most interpret the statement negatively—"Don't treat the alien the way you were treated in Egypt"—but the statement is ambiguous and may also be understood positively—"Love the alien, remembering how the Egyptians treated you." Verse 22 strengthens this possibility, noting the outcome of Israel's sojourn in Egypt, namely the mushrooming of Israel's population in fulfillment of yhwh's repeated promise to the ancestors (13:16; 22:16–17; 26:4; 28:14; 32:12).[102] The only explicit Deuteronomic reference to Egypt's positive role in Israel's history occurs in 23:8b[7b]: "You shall not treat an Egyptian as contemptible, because you were an alien in his land." In contrast to the harsh treatment prescribed against Ammonites and Moabites in verses 4–7[3–6], once the Israelites have settled in the land, they are to welcome third-generation Egyptians even to the assembly of yhwh (קְהַל יְהוָה, vv. 8–9 [7–8]). This awareness probably accounts both for the detail in the narrator's description of Jacob and his family's descent into Egypt (Gen 37–50) and for the inclusion of the otherwise unflattering story of Abraham's descent (Gen 12:10–20). Abraham's moral compromises in the face of the Egyptians reinforce the impression of faithlessness in response to the famine in Canaan. Nevertheless, his journey with Sarah anticipates Jacob's later divinely sanctioned descent (Gen 46:1–7).

74. The Characterization of Abraham

Because many of the comments relating to the patriarch's character in PN are cast with a Deuteronomic flavor, critical scholars see these as secondary interpolations. However, their ubiquity calls for another look. The following "baker's dozen" represent a few significant literary brushstrokes of Abraham:

---

100. Note the incomplete sentence in Exod 2:28: וַיַּרְא אֱלֹהִים אֶת־בְּנֵי יִשְׂרָאֵל וַיֵּדַע אֱלֹהִים, "God saw the people of Israel—and God knew . . ." Knew what? Presumably that the time to carry out what was promised in Gen 15:13–14 had come.

101. The roles are reversed. Whereas Gen 12:10–20 portray Pharaoh as more righteous than the patriarch, 21:10–13 portray Abraham and Sarah as exploitative owners of Hagar the Egyptian.

102. Genesis 15:14 only hints at this dimension of the Egyptian experience; yhwh declares they will emerge with great wealth (יֵצְאוּ בִּרְכֻשׁ גָּדוֹל).

a. Abraham was chosen (יָדַע) by YHWH (18:19; cf. the election [בָּחַר] of Israel in Deut 4:37; 7:6–7; 10:15; 14:2).

b. Abraham was a paragonic "God-fearer" (יְרֵא אֱלֹהִים אַתָּה, 22:12; cf. Deut 4:10; 31:12–13).[103]

c. Abraham trusted in YHWH (וְהֶאֱמִן בַּיהוָה], 15:6; cf. Deut 1:32; 9:23).

d. Abraham listened to the voice of God (עֵקֶב אֲשֶׁר שָׁמַעְתָּ בְּקֹלִי, 22:18; אֲשֶׁר־שָׁמַע אַבְרָהָם בְּקֹלִי, 26:5; cf. Deut 4:30; 26:17; 28:1–2).

e. Abraham swore by YHWH's name (אַשְׁבִּיעֲךָ בַּיהוָה אֱלֹהֵי הַשָּׁמַיִם וֵאלֹהֵי הָאָרֶץ, 24:3; cf. Deut 6:13; 10:20).

f. Abraham walked before YHWH (יְהוָה אֲשֶׁר־הִתְהַלַּכְתִּי לְפָנָיו, 17:1; הִתְהַלֵּךְ לְפָנָיו, 24:20; cf. Deut 10:8; 18:5).

g. Abraham did physical obeisance before YHWH (וְנִשְׁתַּחֲוֶה וְנָשׁוּבָה אֲלֵיכֶם, 22:5 [cf. 24:48]; cf. Deut 5:9; 26:10).

h. Abraham kept/walked in the way of YHWH (יְדַעְתִּיו לְמַעַן אֲשֶׁר יְצַוֶּה אֶת־בָּנָיו וְאֶת־בֵּיתוֹ אַחֲרָיו וְשָׁמְרוּ דֶּרֶךְ יְהוָה, 18:19; cf. Deut 5:33; 8:6; etc.).

i. Abraham demonstrated that he was a righteous man (וַיַּחְשְׁבֶהָ לּוֹ צְדָקָה, 15:6; cf. Deut 6:25; 16:20; 25:1).

j. Abraham refused to let his son Isaac marry a Canaanite (לֹא־תִקַּח אִשָּׁה לִבְנִי מִבְּנוֹת הַכְּנַעֲנִי, Gen 24:3;[104] cf. Deut 7:2–4).

k. Abraham passed the test of his faith (וְהָאֱלֹהִים נִסָּה אֶת־אַבְרָהָם, Gen 22:1; cf. Deut 8:2, 16; 13:3[2]).

l. Like his offspring, Abraham was charged to keep the covenant (וְאַתָּה אֶת־בְּרִיתִי תִשְׁמֹר אַתָּה וְזַרְעֲךָ אַחֲרֶיךָ לְדֹרֹתָם; cf. Deut 29:9 [8]; 33:9; cf. Deut 17:19 and Exod 16:28).

m. Abraham kept YHWH's charge, commands, ordinances, and the *torahs* (Gen 26:5; וַיִּשְׁמֹר מִשְׁמַרְתִּי מִצְוֹתַי חֻקּוֹתַי וְתוֹרֹתָי; cf. Deut 6:2; 11:1; 13:5 [4]). This correlation is most remarkable of all. Although the patriarchal narratives never attribute love for YHWH to the three ancestors,[105] Deut 11:1 glosses love for YHWH with keeping his charge, his commands, his *torahs*, and his judgments. To be sure, the lexemes appear in a different order, but strikingly three of the four match: מִצְוֹתַי/ מִשְׁמַרְתּוֹ/מִשְׁמַרְתִּי;

---

103. For detailed discussion of the semantic range of the root ירא, see Daniel I. Block, "The Fear of YHWH: The Theological Tie That Binds Deuteronomy and Proverbs," in *Triumph of Grace*, 283–311. For a modified version of this essay, see Block, "The First Principle of Wisdom in Deuteronomy: The Fear of YHWH as Allegiance to YHWH Alone," in *Interpreting the Old Testament Theologically: Essays in Honor of Willem A. VanGemeren*, ed. Andrew T. Abernethy (Grand Rapids: Zondervan, 2018), 150–64.

104. Similarly, Isaac (Gen 28:1, but cf. 34:9–10).

105. Cf. Isa 41:8 and 2 Chr 20:7, which identify Abraham as "my/your beloved" (אֹהֲבִי/אֹהַבְךָ, respectively). While most translations treat the suffix as a subjective genitive (Abraham was the object of YHWH's love; cf. Isa 48:14), morphologically the Hebrew construction could also be interpreted objectively, "who loves me/you."

152   Daniel I. Block

חֻקֹּתָיו/חֻקּוֹתַי ;מִצְוֹתָיו. The only exception is תּוֹרֹתַי, "my instructions," which Deuteronomy replaces with מִשְׁפָּטָיו, "his judgments.[106]

Some have tried to drive a spiritual and ethical wedge between Abraham and Moses. Interpreting Exodus–Deuteronomy generically as a biography of Moses *sub lege* (under the law) in contrast to the Genesis biography of Abraham, who lived *ante legem* (before the law), John Sailhamer has argued that Abraham embodied the divinely approved pattern of a life of faith, while Moses demonstrated the inevitable failure of a life driven by law.[107] The data cited above expose the flaws in this approach. To the narrator of Genesis Abraham was the paragon of faith and righteousness as defined by YHWH's covenant with Israel generally and laid out in detail in D.

The watchword of the Torah of Moses is צֶדֶק צֶדֶק תִּרְדֹּף, "Righteousness, only righteousness you shall pursue" (Deut 16:20). As elsewhere in D, here צְדָקָה/צֶדֶק denotes the vassals' loyalty before their Suzerain, demonstrated in response acceptable to the Suzerain.[108] In Gen 15:6 Abraham exhibited צְדָקָה by trusting (הֶאֱמִן) in YHWH, and in 22:12 he demonstrated awed trust in YHWH (יְרֵא אֱלֹהִים) by radical obedience in the face of a preposterous divine demand.[109] Abraham's conversation with YHWH over the fate of Sodom and Gomorrah in Gen 18:16–33 demonstrated that for him "righteousness" was neither theoretical nor hypothetical, but profoundly ethical, in keeping with YHWH's expressed goal of his election: "I have singled him out, that he may instruct his children and his posterity to keep the way of YHWH by doing what is righteous (צְדָקָה) and just (מִשְׁפָּט), in order that YHWH may fulfill for Abraham what he has promised him" (18:19). Except for the single ordinance of circumcision (Gen 17:10–14),[110] and the general charges to "walk before me, and be blameless" (הִתְהַלֵּךְ לְפָנַי וֶהְיֵה תָמִים, Gen 17:1),[111] we have no record of YHWH revealing to him what "righteousness" and "justice" might entail. Even so, in Gen 26:5 YHWH explicitly credited Abraham with precisely the response demanded of Israel by YHWH himself at Sinai, and

---

106. For further discussion, see Jon D. Levenson, *Inheriting Abraham: The Legacy of the Patriarch in Judaism, Christianity, and Islam* (Princeton: Princeton University Press, 2012), 142–44.

107. John H. Sailhamer, "Appendix B: Compositional Strategies in the Pentateuch," in *Introduction to Old Testament Theology: A Canonical Approach*, John H. Sailhamer (Grand Rapids: Zondervan, 1999), 272–89.

108. On the meaning of צֶדֶק/צדקה in Deuteronomy and extrabiblical inscriptions, see Daniel I. Block, "The Grace of Torah: The Mosaic Prescription for Life (Deut 4:1–8; 6:20–25)," in *How I Love Your Torah, O LORD! Studies in the Book of Deuteronomy* (Eugene, OR: Cascade, 2011), 15–17.

109. Sirach 44:20 interprets Abraham's "fear" in this instance as "faith" (πιστός).

110. The act of circumcision is here cast within divine speech (וַיֹּאמֶר אֱלֹהִים אֶל־אַבְרָהָם), rather than legislation. Cf. 17:23, which describes Abraham's obedience in nonlegal terms: "as God has spoken with him" (כַּאֲשֶׁר דִּבֶּר אִתּוֹ אֱלֹהִים).

111. Also cast as divine speech (וַיֹּאמֶר אֵלָיו) rather than legislation.

that Moses had called for on the Plains of Moab: "He has listened to my voice and kept my charge (מִשְׁמַרְתִּי), my commands (מִצְוֹתַי), my ordinances (חֻקּוֹתַי), and my instructions (תּוֹרֹתָי)." This is the righteousness of which Moses spoke in Deut 6:25, and this is the wisdom of which Ben Sira wrote in the second century BC: "Abraham was the great father of a multitude of nations, and no one has been found like him in glory. He kept the Torah of the Most High (νόμον ὑψίστου), and entered into a covenant with him; he certified the covenant in his flesh, and when he was tested he proved faithful (Sir 44:19–20; NRSV modified)."[112]

Deuteronomistic Features in the Patriarchal Narratives and the Composition of the Pentateuch

I follow scholarly consensus in acknowledging that the form, style, and intent of D differ dramatically from both the pentateuchal narratives and the other constitutional documents (the Decalogue, Book of the Covenant, Instructions on Holiness, and regulations governing worship and the priesthood).[113] My goal in this essay has been to demonstrate that despite D's distinctive features, the book exhibits a plethora of tight lexical, stylistic, and conceptual links with PN. However, as our occasional forays into the narratives of Joseph, the exodus, and the desert wanderings and our references to Israel's other constitutional documents have shown, Deuteronomic features are scattered throughout the Pentateuch. How do we best account for these interconnections?

If we follow prevailing scholarly reconstruction of the Pentateuch's composition, we will probably treat these common elements as protodeuteronomic features that later inspired the author of D or as editorial amendments to earlier documents postdating the composition of D. Benjamin Kilchör has recently argued in convincing detail in *Mosetora und Jahwetora* that the order of the constitutional documents in the Pentateuch reflects the order of the composition of these respective documents.[114] The internal biblical evidence suggests that the Decalogue (Exod 20:2–17; Exod 31:18; 34:28–29; Deut 4:13; 5:6–22; 10:1–5),

---

112. Although Jacob's removal of foreign gods (Gen 35:2–4) recalls Deut 7:3–5, as men of faith/righteousness, both Isaac and Jacob appear as flatter figures than Abraham. Both the Deuteronomistic Historian and the Chronicler pick up the collocation הָסֵר אֶת־אֱלֹהִים הַנֵּכָר (Josh 24:14, 23; Judg 10:16; 1 Sam 7:3; 2 Chr 33:15). However, there is no need here to follow Second Temple Jewish literature that claims that Abraham actually had access to the laws of the Torah centuries before Moses (cf. Baruch 3:36b–4:4). For full discussion of this matter, see Levenson, *Inheriting Abraham*, 113–75.

113. With Raddday and Shore these differences are best attributed to distinctions in genre than to different authors (Radday and Shore, *Genesis*, 189–90). What I identify as "constitutional documents" mostly refer to as the legal material. I find the latter characterization generically misleading.

114. See note 60 above.

154   Daniel I. Block

the Book of the Covenant (Exod 20:22–23:19; cf. 24:4), the speeches of Moses in D (31:9–13), and the concluding song (31:19, 22) were committed to writing almost immediately after their promulgation. Proof of the separate textual existence of the Instructions on Holiness is less clear. The seventeen occurrences of the narrative heading וַיְדַבֵּר יְהוָה אֶל־מֹשֶׁה לֵּאמֹר, "And YHWH spoke to Moses saying," suggest that Leviticus 17–27 consists of at least seventeen (or eighteen) discrete pronouncements.[115] Leviticus 26:46 suggests that at one stage this verse may have been a colophon for a written collection of divine "ordinances, judgments, and instructions" (הַחֻקִּים וְהַמִּשְׁפָּטִים וְהַתּוֹרֹת), perhaps commencing with Lev 17:1.[116] But the author of the Pentateuch has intentionally embedded these documents in narratives recounting the divine hand on the ancestors, their descent into and exodus from Egypt, the covenant making events at Sinai, the desert wanderings, and in Deuteronomy their imminent entry into Canaan, in fulfillment of the covenant promises to the ancestors and reiterated to the exodus generation (Gen 15:13–21; Exod 2:24; 3:9; 6:6–8; 23:20–31).

Concerning what kinds of sources underlie the ancestral and exodus narratives, we may only speculate. Regarding the latter, Exod 17:14 and Num 33:2 suggest that while the Israelites journeyed from Egypt to the promised land they kept a written diary of their experiences. While the literacy assumed here need not apply to the time of the patriarchs, at least four centuries earlier,[117] it is unlikely that memories of YHWH's call of Abraham and oversight of the lives of the ancestors would not have been treasured and at least passed on orally from generation to generation, perhaps until the time of the exodus. The formula אֵלֶּה תּוֹלְדֹת, "These are the generations," followed by the personal name of the line whose history follows, either in the form of a genealogy or a narrative,[118] hints at records of some sort. The reference to a "document" (סֵפֶר) in Gen 5:1 (זֶה סֵפֶר תּוֹלְדֹת אָדָם) suggests that written sources may underlie these narratives.[119] It is plausible that, along with their more explicitly sacerdotal responsibilities, after the Levites' installation to priestly service at an early stage some of them assumed the role of custodians of Israel's patriarchal traditions, that these traditions were passed on orally for centuries, and were finally committed to writing

---

115. Leviticus 17:1; 18:1; 19:1; 20:1; 21:16; 22:1, 17, 26; 23:1, 9, 23, 26, 33; 24:1, 13; 25:1; 27:1. To these we should probably add וַיֹּאמֶר יְהוָה אֶל־מֹשֶׁה, in 21:1, which introduces a speech for the priests (vv. 1–15).

116. Note the colophon-like ending to chapter 16.

117. But see the essay in this volume by Richard S. Hess, "Second-Millennium BC Cuneiform from the Southern Levant and the Literature of the Pentateuch."

118. Gen 2:4; 5:1; 6:9; 10:1; 11:10, 27; 25:12, 19; 36:1, 9; 37:2; Num 3:1.

119. Many scholars assign these *tôlĕdōt* formulas to the Priestly layer, some viewing them as the skeleton for the original Priestly narrative. See Blum, *Komposition der Vätergeschichte*, 432–46.

on separate documents, some of which are identifiable by this תּוֹלְדת formula.[120] Having committed these memories to writing, the Levites would have had these documents in hand when the Israelites crossed the Jordan into the promised land. These records represent the sources of the PN as we now have them in Genesis.

If this hypothetical reconstruction is correct, then documents the Israelites carried across the Jordan would have included sacred narratives, legal constitutional material from Sinai, Moses's hortatory valedictory addresses, as well as commemorative songs and hymns. Whether or not the people treasured these separate documents as scripture and used them in worship we cannot know. However, we know this was true of Moses's Torah—which he charged the Levites to read before the entire assembly at the festival of Sukkoth every seven years (Deut 31:10–12, 24–26)—and of the "Song of YHWH"—which was to function as a sort of national anthem.[121] We do not know what use Israelites made of the other pentateuchal documents in early worship, though tradition has it that the Israelites recited the Decalogue at Shavuoth in commemoration of YHWH's establishment of his covenant with Israel at Sinai.[122]

But when were these disparate documents collected, arranged, and integrated into the composition we know as the Pentateuch? Whybray has made a strong case for interpreting the entire Pentateuch as a coherent document, composed by a single author, à la the Greek historian Herodotus. While his extremely late dating of the Pentateuch is dubious, his impression that the author was a profoundly gifted historian is sound. Indeed, Martin Noth's assessment of the Deuteronomistic History applies here as well: this composition is the product of an author, not an editor, who "brought together material from highly varied traditions and arranged it according to a carefully conceived plan."[123] Based on anticipatory statements in earlier texts (e.g., Gen 17:7–8; Exod 3:12), the proportion of text devoted to getting Jacob's family into Egypt (Gen 37–50), and from there to Sinai (Exod 1–18), and especially the amount of text space involving Israel's experiences at Sinai, the core focus is striking.[124] As Jacob Milgrom

---

120. Cf. Duane Garrett, *Rethinking Genesis: The Source and Authorship of the First Book of the Pentateuch* (Grand Rapids: Baker, 2001).

121. On which see Daniel I. Block, "The Power of Song: Reflections on Ancient Israel's National Anthem (Deuteronomy 32)," in *How I Love Your Torah, O* LORD, 162–88.

122. See Moshe Weinfeld, "The Decalogue: Its Significance, Uniqueness, and Place in Israel's Tradition," in *Religion and Law: Biblical-Judaic and Islamic Perspectives*, ed. E. B. Firmage, B. G. Weiss, and J. W. Welch (Winona Lake, IN: Eisenbrauns, 1990), 12–15.

123. Martin Noth, *The Deuteronomistic History*, 2nd ed., JSOTSup 15 (Sheffield: JSOT Press, 1991), 26; trans. of *Überlieferungsgeschichtliche Studien*, 2nd ed. (Tübingen: Max Niemeyer, 1957), 1–110.

124. Assuming ca. 280 years for the patriarch's lives (Abraham was 100 years old when Isaac was born [Gen 17:1]; Isaac was ca. 50 when Jacob was born [25:20–21]; Jacob was 130 when he

156   Daniel I. Block

has recognized, the heart of the narrative is obviously YHWH's establishment of his covenant with Israel at Sinai (Exod 19–Lev 26; cf. figure 8.1).[125]

Making the most of the sources available to him, the author has created an impressive narrative, equal if not superior in literary quality to anything the Greek historians Herodotus and Thucydides produced in the fifth century BCE. The pervasive links between PN and D suggest that the author was thoroughly schooled in the Torah of Moses, and that he wrote from the perspective of the promises to the ancestors having been fulfilled. The composer of Israel's first comprehensive Scripture perceived the covenant ratification rituals at Sinai as the establishment (הֵקִים בְּרִית) of the covenant made with Abraham (Gen 17:7, 19; Exod 6:4–7), and the incorporation of his descendants into the mission announced at the outset (Gen 12:1–3; cf. Exod 19:5–6).

Whenever the entire pentateuchal project was completed, the compiled vale-dictory addresses of Moses (D) apparently constituted the תּוֹרַת מֹשֶׁה that pro-vided the basis of David's charge to Solomon in 1 Kgs 2:2–4, that Josiah's men discovered in the temple in 621 (2 Kgs 23:3–16), and that Ezra read before the assembled gathering of returned exiles in Jerusalem (Neh 8:1–18).[126] The person responsible for the narrative stitching in D may well have been the author of the entire Pentateuch. While Hosea's use of D suggests the early eighth cen-tury BC as the *terminus ad quem* for the entire project,[127] it may have been completed centuries earlier.[128] Eventually, in recognition of the literary unity

---

went to Egypt [47:9–28]), a 430-year sojourn in Egypt (Exod 12:41), and 40 years from the time of the exodus to Moses's death (Deut 1:3; the "biography of Moses" [Exod 1:1–Deut 34:12] spans 120 years [Deut 34:7]), 16 percent of historical time (120/750 years) takes up 78 percent of narrated time (Exodus–Deuteronomy = 59,369 words / Gen 12:27–Deut 34:12 = 76,276 words). Even more dramatic, 0.13 percent of historical time (less than 1 year at Sinai; cf. Exod 19:1; Num 10:11) takes up 28 percent of narrated time (Exod 19:1–Lev 27:34 = 21,393 words/Gen 12:27–Deut 34:12 = 76,276 words). The figures are even more impressive when we consider that a segment of Moses's first address in Deuteronomy (4:9–31), and the entire second (4:44–11:32) and third (12:1–26:19; 28:1–69 [Eng 29:1]) addresses represent commentary on Israel's Sinai experience. Therefore, we must add 9,522 words to the 21,393 above, yielding 30,915 words: 41 percent of the text is devoted to 0.13 per-cent of the historical time. These figures are based in part on the statistics provided in the "Statistical Appendix" to *Theological Lexicon of the Old Testament*, ed. Ernst Jenni and Claus Westermann, trans. Mark E. Biddle (Peabody, MA: Hendrickson, 1997), 3:1444–45.

125. Note the concluding colophons at Lev 26:46 and 27:34. Figure 8.1 is inspired by Jacob Milgrom's diagram of "The Theological-Literary Structure of the Hexateuch," in *Numbers: The Traditional Hebrew Text with the New JPS Translation*, JPS Torah Commentary (Philadelphia: Jewish Publication Society, 1990), xviii.

126. Contra Michael L. Saltow (*How the Bible Became Holy* [New Haven: Yale University Press, 2014], 77–78), who suggests that "the 'law of Moses' was composed of some subset of P and D materials in not quite the version that we now possess."

127. For convincing defense of the chronological priority of D vis-à-vis Hosea, see Carsten Vang, "When a Prophet Quotes Moses: On the Relationship Between the Book of Hosea and Deu-teronomy," in Block and Schultz, *Sepher Torath Mosheh*, 277–303.

128. With the possible exception of Juha Pakkala's last argument (for which there is a better explanation than he proposes), his nine arguments for a Persian date for D all fit much more naturally

In the Tradition of Moses 157

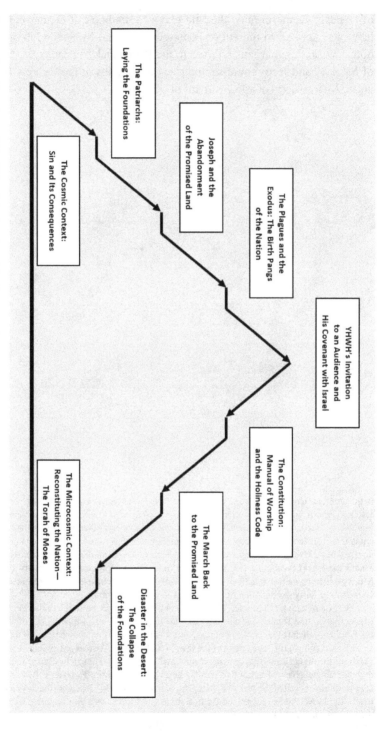

FIGURE 8.1. The place of Sinai/Horeb in the plot of the Pentateuch.

158   Daniel I. Block

of Genesis–Deuteronomy, the title given to the book of Deuteronomy (תּוֹרַת מֹשֶׁה) was applied to the entire Pentateuch, so that by Second Temple times both Jews and Samaritans referred to the Pentateuch as תּוֹרַת מוֹשֶׁה , "the Torah of Moses," and Jesus could summarize the contents of the Hebrew Bible as ὁ νόμος Μωσέως καὶ οἱ προφῆται καὶ οἱ ψαλμοί.[129]

---

in the premonarchic period (Juha Pakkala, "The Date of the Oldest Edition of Deuteronomy," *ZAW* 121, no. 3 [2009]: 394–95). This impression is reinforced by the virtual absence of theophores involving *Yah* or *Yeho* in the Pentateuch. יוֹכֶבֶד (Moses and Aaron's mother, Exod 6:20), יְהוֹשֻׁעַ, and יוֹאָשׁ (Judg 6:11–12) are the only exceptions. However, Num 13:16 credits Moses with changing Joshua's name from הוֹשֵׁעַ to יְהוֹשֻׁעַ (in the wake of the revelatory events associated with the exodus and the Sinai experience). According to Carsten Vang (in private communication, February 26, 2016), the paucity of YHWH names in the Pentateuch suggests the patriarchal stories incorporated in the Pentateuch were fairly fixed written traditions prior to the tenth century.

129. Luke 24:44. Of course, Jesus was not alone in referring to the entire Pentateuch as ὁ νόμος, that is, "the Torah." See also the Prologue to Ecclesiasticus, which speaks of "the Law and the Prophets and the other books of our ancestors," and 1 Macc 1:56, which refers to the Pentateuch as τὰ βιβλία τοῦ νόμου, "the books of the law." The Letter of Aristeas (ca. 200 BCE) refers to the Torah as "the divine Law" (§3) or simply "the Law" (§§309–16). Though the Samaritans recognized that the Pentateuch consisted of five scrolls, they viewed the entire Torah as a continuous text that later traditionists called the תורה שומרונית, "the Samaritan Torah." Josephus did not call the Pentateuch "the Law," but he recognized the five "books of Moses" as a unit, separate from the rest of the Hebrew canon (*Against Apion* 1.8).

CHAPTER 9

Was Moses the Last Prophet? An Analysis of a Neo-Documentarian Interpretation of Document E

Duane A. Garrett
Southern Baptist Theological Seminary

The Current State of the Documentary Hypothesis

The survival of the Documentary Hypothesis is in doubt. Many pentateuchal scholars treat it as having already perished, although it still has its defenders. Richard Friedman, for example, promotes a version of the classic presentation of the hypothesis, one in which the four source documents (J, E, D, and P) were combined in a two-stage redactional process.[1] Yet every aspect of the Documentary Hypothesis is disputed.[2] From almost the inception of the hypothesis, scholars have questioned the independent existence of E. More recently, J and P seem to be dissolving before scholars' eyes. Much credit for this development goes to the pentateuchal studies of Rolf Rendtorff, especially to his influential and controversial book *The Problem of the Process of the Transmission of the*

---

1. Richard Elliott Friedman, "Three Major Redactors of the Torah," in *Birkat Shalom: Studies in the Bible, Ancient Near Eastern Literature, and Post-biblical Judaism Presented to Shalom M. Paul on the Occasion of His Seventieth Birthday*, ed. Chaim Cohen, Victor Avigdor Hurowitz, Avi M. Hurvitz, Yochanan Muffs, Baruch J. Schwartz, and Jeffrey H. Tigay, 2 vols. (Winona Lake, IN: Eisenbrauns, 2008), 1:31–44. For a full presentation of his views, see Friedman, *The Bible with Sources Revealed: A New View into the Five Books of Moses* (San Francisco: HarperSanFrancisco, 2005). He gives a fairly standard presentation of evidence for the Documentary Hypothesis on pp. 7–31. Friedman could be considered to be part of the "Neo-Documentarian" movement described below, but his adherence to the notion of a JE redaction belongs more to the classic Documentary Hypothesis.

2. One can observe this even in studies that are friendly to traditional source criticism and to subsequent developments in scholarship. See, for example, Jonathan Huddleston, "Recent Scholarship on the Pentateuch: Historical, Literary, and Theological Reflections," *ResQ* 55, no. 4 (2013): 197–201. He states, "Without an assured Documentary Hypothesis, exegetes lack the neat classification of the Pentateuch into four coherent voices" (201). For another brief overview of the current state of scholarship, see Anselm C. Hagedorn, "Taking the Pentateuch to the Twenty-First century," *Expository Times* 119, no. 2 (2007): 53–58. See also William Johnstone, review of *A Farewell to the Yahwist? The Composition of the Pentateuch in Recent European Interpretation*, ed. Thomas B. Dozeman and Konrad Schmid, *JSS* 54, no. 1 (2009): 276–77.

159

160   Duane A. Garrett

Pentateuch (1977).[3] In the aftermath of this study, a large number of European scholars, including Konrad Schmid, Jan Christian Gertz, Albert de Pury, and Erhard Blum, have abandoned document J (E having already been jettisoned).[4] Other scholars (mostly North American), such as Thomas Dozeman, John Van Seters, David Carr, and (from Europe) Christoph Levin, hold to the existence of some kind of non-Priestly source text. Van Seters explicitly defends the existence of the Yahwist.[5] None of these scholars, however, holds to the classical Documentary Hypothesis, and all of them assert that the major source documents, if one may still use that term, are exilic or postexilic. Other scholars (mostly Jewish), following in the tradition of Yeḥezkel Kaufmann, hold to the existence of P but (against the classic formulation of the Documentary Hypothesis) treat it as a

---

3. See in particular his concluding remarks: *The Problem of the Process of Transmission in the Pentateuch*, trans. John J. Scullion, LHBOTS 89 (Sheffield: JSOT Press, 1990), 178.

4. For a succinct history of the problem of J in scholarship, see Thomas Römer, "The Elusive Yahwist: A Short History of Research," in *A Farewell to the Yahwist? The Composition of the Pentateuch in Recent European Interpretation*, ed. Thomas B. Dozeman and Konrad Schmid, SBLSS 34 (Atlanta: SBL, 2006), 9–27. For more specific studies, see Konrad Schmid, "The So-Called Yahwist and the Literary Gap Between Genesis and Exodus," in *Farewell to the Yahwist?*, 29–50; Schmid, *Genesis and the Moses Story: Israel's Dual Origins in the Hebrew Bible*, trans. James Nogalski, LTHS 3 (Winona Lake, IN: Eisenbrauns, 2010); Erhard Blum, "The Literary Connection Between the Books of Genesis and Exodus and the End of the Book of Joshua," in *Farewell to the Yahwist?*, 89–106; Blum, "Pentateuch-Hexateuch-Enneateuch? Or: How Can One Recognize a Literary Work in the Bible?," in *Pentateuch, Hexateuch, or Enneateuch? Identifying Literary Works in Genesis Through Kings*, ed. Thomas B. Dozeman, Thomas Römer, and Konrad Schmid, AIL 8 (Atlanta: Society of Bibilical Literature, 2011), 43–72; Jan Christian Gertz, "The Transition Between the Books of Genesis and Exodus," in *Farewell to the Yahwist?*, 73–88; Albert de Pury, "The Jacob Story and the Beginning of the Formation of the Pentateuch," in *Farewell to the Yahwist?*, 51–72; Thomas Römer, "How Many Books (Teuchs): Pentateuch, Hexateuch, Deuteronomistic History, or Enneateuch?," in Dozeman, Römer, and Schmid, *Pentateuch, Hexateuch, or Enneateuch?*, 25–42.

5. See Thomas B. Dozeman, *God at War: Power in the Exodus Tradition* (Oxford: Oxford University Press, 1996); Dozeman, "The Commission of Moses and the Book of Genesis," in *Farewell to the Yahwist?*, 107–29; Dozeman, "The Authorship of the Pentateuch," *Dialogue* 32, no. 4 (1999): 87–112; Christoph Levin, "The Yahwist: The Earliest Editor in the Pentateuch," *JBL* 126, no. 2 (2007): 209–30; Levin, "The Yahwist and the Redactional Link Between Genesis and Exodus," in *Farewell to the Yahwist?*, 131–42; Levin, "The Text of the Yahwist's History," in *Re-reading the Scriptures: Essays on the Literary History of the Old Testament*, FAT 87 (Tübingen: Mohr Siebeck, 2013), 25–50; Levin, "Israel and Canaan: The Origins of a Fictitious Antagonism," in *Re-reading the Scriptures*, 143–64; John Van Seters, *Abraham in History and Tradition* (New Haven: Yale University Press, 1975); Van Seters, *In Search of History: Historiography in the Ancient World and the Origins of Biblical History* (New Haven: Yale University Press, 1983); Van Seters, *The Yahwist: A Historian of Israelite Origins* (Winona Lake, IN: Eisenbrauns, 2013); Van Seters, "An Ironic Circle: Wellhausen and the Rise of Redaction Criticism," *ZAW* 115, no. 4 (2003): 487–500; Van Seters, "The Report of the Yahwist's Demise Has Been Greatly Exaggerated!," in *Farewell to the Yahwist?*, 143–58; Seters, *The Edited Bible: The Curious History of the "Editor" in Biblical Criticism* (Winona Lake, IN: Eisenbrauns, 2006); David McLain Carr, *Reading the Fractures of Genesis: Historical and Literary Approaches* (Louisville: Westminster John Knox, 1996); Carr, "What Is Required to Identify the Pre-Priestly Narrative Connections Between Genesis and Exodus? Some General Reflections and Specific Cases," in *A Farewell to the Yahwist?*, 159–80; Carr, *The Formation of the Hebrew Bible: A New Reconstruction* (Oxford: Oxford University Press, 2011).

Was Moses the Last Prophet? 161

preexilic document.[6] A few scholars, such as Mark O'Brien and Antony Campbell, have proposals that are true outliers, holding neither to the Documentary Hypothesis, nor to a version of current critical scholarship, nor to a traditional view of the origin of the Pentateuch.[7]

Against this turbulent backdrop, it may come as a surprise to discover that some scholars, the "Neo-Documentarians," argue that one can detect in an almost pristine condition the four separate pentateuchal source texts of the Documentary Hypothesis. Joel Baden is a prominent member of this group. In *J, E, and the Redaction of the Pentateuch* (2009) and *The Composition of the Pentateuch* (2012), he seeks to take source criticism back to the theory that the Pentateuch is made up of four distinct documents: J, E, D, and P.[8] In some respects, his interpretation of the four source theory has a purity and simplicity that surpasses the classical Documentary Hypothesis. He argues that the four documents coexisted independently until they were all combined into the Pentateuch in a single redaction. Against the traditional Documentary Hypothesis, he does not believe that there ever was a combined document JE. He believes that the Deuteronomist knew J and E as separate documents, but that the Priestly writer wrote independently, knowing neither J nor E (as such, there is no reason to consider P the latest document). Rather than representing different stages in the evolution of Israelite religion, he believes the four documents represented the religious beliefs of different but contemporary communities within Israel. The redaction of the four documents took place in the postexilic period, perhaps in the time of Ezra.[9]

Other scholars have published similar analyses of the Pentateuch. Philip Yoo, in a study of the narrative of the death of Moses in Deut 34, argues from the Neo-Documentarian perspective that the account contains the recognizable remnants of J, E, D, and P. His contribution generated a flurry of published

---

6. See Yehezkel Kaufmann, *From the Babylonian Captivity to the End of Prophecy*, vol. 4 of *History of the Religion of Israel* (New York: Ktav, 1977), 175–200. Against this, see Joseph Blenkinsopp, "An Assessment of the Alleged Pre-Exilic Date of the Priestly Material in the Pentateuch," *ZAW* 108, no. 4 (1996): 495–518. But in defense of an early P, see Jacob Milgrom, "The Antiquity of the Priestly Source: A Reply to Joseph Blenkinsopp," *ZAW* 111, no. 1 (1999): 10–22; Menahem Haran, "Ezekiel, P, and the Priestly School," *VT* 58, no. 2 (2008): 211–18; Israel Knohl, "Nimrod, Son of Cush, King of Mesopotamia, and the Dates of P and J," in Cohen et al., *Birkat Shalom*, 1:45–52.

7. Mark A. O'Brien and Antony F. Campbell, *Rethinking the Pentateuch: Prolegomena to the Theology of Ancient Israel* (Louisville: Westminster John Knox, 2005).

8. Joel S. Baden, *J, E, and the Redaction of the Pentateuch*, FAT 68 (Tübingen: Mohr Siebeck, 2009); Baden, *The Composition of the Pentateuch*, AYBRL (New Haven: Yale University Press, 2012).

9. Baden, *J, E, and the Redaction of the Pentateuch*, 305–13. His analysis of the Pentateuch has some resemblance to the original conception of the Deuteronomistic Historian, an exilic or early postexilic author who combined various sources to create a theological epic, as described in Martin Noth, *The Deuteronomistic History*, JSOTSup 15 (Sheffield: JSOT Press, 1981).

162   Duane A. Garrett

responses in the *Journal of Biblical Literature*.[10] Jeffrey Stackert, another Neo-Documentarian, proposes in *A Prophet Like Moses* that a specific theological agenda lies behind the documents. Using Stackert's study as a test case, this essay will consider how well or how poorly a Neo-Documentarian approach lends itself to a study of the history of Israelite religion.

Jeffrey Stackert's Proposal Regarding Israelite Religion

Stackert argues that E, D, and P each create a "political allegory" conveying the message that Moses was the last true prophet and that henceforth religious authority proceeds from priestly elders who preserve and interpret Torah.[11] In this manner, the texts carry out a "rationalization of charisma" bringing about "a transition from nonlegal to legal Israelite socio-religious organization."[12] He dates all four documents to around the seventh century,[13] and believes that E, D, and P all support the same antiprophetic agenda, although they employ different rhetorical strategies. The authors of the documents favored the permanence of written law over the ad hoc nature of prophecy.[14] Their arguments against prophetic religion were not effective, however, and prophecy continued to flourish in the seventh century and afterward.[15] For Stackert, E is the real fountainhead of this ideology, and thus I will focus my brief review on his treatment of E.

For the purposes of his study, the E texts that are directly relevant include the following: Exod 3:1, 4b, 6a, 9–15, 21–22; 4:17–18, 20b; 18:1–27; 19:2b–9a, 16aβ–17, 18aβ, 18bβ*, 19; 20:1–23:33; 24:3–8, 12–15a, 18b; 31:18*–32:14, 15*–25, 30–35; 34:1, 4*, 5aα, 28*–29*; 33:6b–11; Num 11:11–12, 14–17, 24b–30; 12:1aα, 2–15; Deut 34:10–12.[16] The call narrative in the E material of

---

10. The original paper is Philip Y. Yoo, "The Four Moses Death Accounts," *JBL* 131, no. 3 (2012): 423–41. The initial response is Serge Frolov, "The Death of Moses and the Fate of Source Criticism," *JBL* 133, no. 3 (2014): 648–60. This was in turn followed by David McLain Carr, "Unified Until Proven Disunified? Assumptions and Standards in Assessing the Literary Complexity of Ancient Biblical Texts," *JBL* 133, no. 3 (2014): 677–81; Shawna Dolansky, "Deuteronomy 34: The Death of Moses, Not of Source Criticism," *JBL* 133, no. 3 (2014): 669–76; Philip Y. Yoo, "The Place of Deuteronomy 34 and Source Criticism: A Response to Serge Frolov," *JBL* 133, no. 3 (2014): 661–68.

11. Jeffrey Stackert describes the documents as "political allegories" (Jeffrey Stackert, *A Prophet Like Moses: Prophecy, Law, and Israelite Religion* [Oxford: Oxford University Press, 2014], 29). Stackert devotes less than a page to the analysis of J, which, he says, had little interest "in the legal and prophetic issues that E, D, and P engage" (ibid., 191).

12. Ibid., 196.

13. Ibid., 32–33.

14. Ibid., 54.

15. Ibid., 28.

16. Ibid., 56, 92, 117. The transposition of Exod 33:6b–11 to directly before Num 11 is deliberate, as will be explained below.

Exod 3–4 establishes that Moses was a genuine prophet.[17] Furthermore, since E contains most of Exod 19–24, including the Decalogue and the Book of the Covenant, it promotes the supremacy of the Law. Implicitly, the stage is set for E's ostensible argument: Moses, the great prophet of YHWH, has given us a definitive statement of YHWH's will, and therefore there is no more need for prophecy.[18]

Adding further support to his hypothesis, Stackert analyzes the ministry of Moses at the Tent of Meeting as described by E. In the unified Pentateuch, the small tent of Exod 33 is the precursor to the more elaborate tent that the Israelites constructed in Exod 35–40. In E, however, the small tent is the *only* Tent of Meeting, the large tent being a creation of P. Stackert transposes Exod 33:6b–11 from its current position in the Pentateuch to directly before Num 11:11–12 (both are E texts). Since the small tent is E's Tent of Meeting, Stackert believes that Exod 33:6b–11 belongs in the wilderness narrative, and thus he feels justified in claiming that it was originally situated just before Num 11. He thinks that the compiler of the pentateuchal documents moved 33:6b–11 to its current position in Exodus.[19]

He also asserts that Exod 33:6b (מֵהַר חוֹרֵב, "from [the time of] Mount Horeb") properly begins verse 7 and does not belong with verse 6a. He justifies this with an appeal to a journal article written by Joel Baden.[20] Thus, he translates verses 6b–7, "6b From the time of Mount Horeb, 7 Moses would take a tent and pitch it outside of the camp at some distance from the camp, and he would call it a 'Tent of Meeting,' and everyone desiring to make an inquiry of YHWH would go out to the Tent of Meeting that was outside of the camp."[21] He believes that in the original E the Exodus verses "are a preface to the appointment of the elders in Num 11."[22]

In the original E, therefore, this version of how Moses would go to the (small) tent to receive direction from YHWH (Exod 33:6b–11) was immediately followed by Moses's complaint that he was unable to bear the burden of this people (Num 11:11–12). YHWH then instructed Moses to bring to him seventy elders; they would receive the Spirit and help Moses with his duties (Num 11:16–17). Stackert draws the following conclusion: "Within E's chronology, Moses in Num 11* has only recently begun his Tent of Meeting service, but he is already overwhelmed by it. He is thus dismayed at the prospect of bearing this load *throughout the wilderness journey*."[23] In E, therefore, the process of

---

17. Ibid., 56–57.

18. Ibid., 77.

19. Ibid., 83–91.

20. Joel S. Baden, "On Exodus 33,1–11," *ZAW* 124, no. 3 (2012): 336–39.

21. Stackert, *Prophet Like Moses*, 82.

22. Ibid., 84.

23. Ibid., 98 (emphasis original). We might note that at this stage in the narrative there is no reason for Moses to suppose that the time in the wilderness will be lengthy, and it thus seems odd that this would be troubling to him.

164   Duane A. Garrett

transferring leadership from the charismatic prophet to a body of elders was already begun in Moses's lifetime. As Stackert portrays it, E's message is that a continuing prophetic ministry is unnecessary (since the great prophet Moses has already provided Israel with the definitive statement of YHWH's will in the Book of the Covenant), unworkable (since even Moses could not bear the burden of being Israel's charismatic leader), and obsolete (since elders will assume religious leadership in Israel).

A Critique

It goes without saying that Stackert's proposal depends entirely on the reality of document E. If, as most pentateuchal scholars believe, a separate E never existed, any analysis of that document's religious outlook is obviously meaningless.

Setting that aside, however, his thesis has many flaws. The first and most obvious problem is that neither E nor any other alleged source document asserts that prophecy is obsolete. Stackert deals with this by his claim that the documents are political allegories, by which he means that they conceal their message and that one must read between the lines of the text.[24] To the contrary, the pentateuchal texts are not allegories at all. For true political allegory in the Bible, we have the example of the parable of Jotham (Judg 9:8–15). E never states, even in the legislation of the Book of the Covenant, that prophecy in Israel is illegitimate. Stackert thus appears to use the word "allegory" to mean "a text that does not explicitly state its central lesson." But this does not work. Even Jotham's allegory is quite transparent about the lesson it intends to drive home. When the trees look about for a king and settle for a bramble, the meaning is not concealed between the lines.

Far from asserting that prophesying is illegitimate, Num 11:25 implies that the prophetic gift, or at least a genuine prophetic experience, is a prerequisite for assuming leadership in Israel: "And YHWH descended in the cloud and spoke to [Moses], and he took some of the Spirit that was on [Moses] and put it on the seventy, [on] each of the elders. And it came about that as soon as the Spirit rested on them, they prophesied (וַיִּתְנַבְּאוּ), although they did not repeat [the experience]." Dealing with this text, Stackert argues that the hithpael of נבא, "they prophesied," implies that the person who had the prophetic ecstasy was not a genuine prophet. The verb "indicates a behavior recognizable as prophet-like that was being performed by actors *who are not themselves prophets and who do not actually offer a prophetic message*."[25] It is certainly true that the hithpael

24. Ibid., 29.
25. Ibid., 101 (emphasis original).

of נבא is sometimes used of pseudoprophets (for example, the prophets of Baal in 1 Kgs 18:29, and the opponents of Jeremiah in Jer 14:14—although in both cases the individuals claimed to be prophets). Most famously, Saul sometimes went into a mantic rage or ecstasy (1 Sam 10:5–11; 18:10). While we, from our perspective, might conclude that Saul exhibited mantic behavior even though he was not really a prophet, this was not true of the observers at the time, who wondered if he was a prophet (1 Sam 10:11). Nothing in the narratives suggests that the hithpael of נבא carries the implied meaning that the subject is not really a prophet. Most significantly, the verb can be used of genuine prophets in the process of giving a word from YHWH (e.g., Micaiah the son of Imlah in 1 Kgs 22:8 [יִתְנַבֵּא]; Ezekiel the son of Buzi in Ezek 37:10 [וְהִנַּבֵּאתִי]). The verb is neutral with regard to the status of the person doing the prophesying. In the case of the seventy elders, the text asserts that they prophesied in response to the same Spirit that had rested on Moses. If Moses was a prophet, they obviously partook of the prophetic experience.

In addition, Eldad and Medad, two elders who were back in the camp, received the Spirit and prophesied, much to the dismay of Joshua (Num 11:26–28). In response, Moses declared (v. 29b):

וּמִי יִתֵּן כָּל־עַם יְהוָה נְבִיאִים כִּי־יִתֵּן יְהוָה אֶת־רוּחוֹ עֲלֵיהֶם

> But I wish that all of YHWH's people were prophets—[I wish] that YHWH would set his Spirit on them!

Moses implies that the elders were "prophets" (נְבִיאִים), a direct falsification of Stackert's claims. In response, Stackert makes two arguments.

First, he says that Eldad and Medad, like the rest of the seventy, did not prophesy again and therefore were not really prophets.[26] But whether they prophesied again is irrelevant; the only issue in the text is that they prophesied after receiving a portion of Moses's Spirit. This was a prerequisite for assuming their new duties. In that sense, at least, they were prophets.

Second, Stackert says that, rightly understood, Num 11:29b actually means, "Would that all YHWH's people were prophets, *with the result that* YHWH would put his spirit upon them!"[27] This translation makes little sense, as it indicates that Moses wants the people *first* to prophesy and *then* receive the Spirit (contrast the sequence in Joel 2:28 [MT 3:1]). Stackert, however, explains it as follows: "Moses's desideratum is *not* that all Israelites would be made prophets like the elders were" (in Stackert's interpretation they were not prophets at all).[28] He

---

26. Ibid., 104–5.
27. Ibid., 106 (emphasis original).
28. Ibid., 106.

166 Duane A. Garrett

continues, "[Moses's] wish is that all Israelites, including the elders, would be appointed prophets, *as he was*, so that they too might receive the divine spirit regularly, *as he does*."[29]

To support his translation of Num 11:29b, he provides examples of interrogative statements in which the second clause begins with כִּי and (in his view) is sequential or resultative (Judg 9:28aα; Isa 22:1b; 22:16a; Ps 8:5; Gen 20:9a; Exod 3:11).[30] The last example is typical: מִי אָנֹכִי כִּי אֵלֵךְ אֶל־פַּרְעֹה, "Who am I that I should go to Pharaoh?" However, none of his examples is truly parallel to Num 11:29, which has מִי יִתֵּן, a clause that formally is interrogative but functionally is desiderative (as Stackert acknowledges by translating it "Would that!"). A more helpful parallel is Jer 9:1a (Eng. 2a):

מִי־יִתְּנֵנִי בַמִּדְבָּר מְלוֹן אֹרְחִים וְאֶעֶזְבָה אֶת־עַמִּי וְאֵלְכָה מֵאִתָּם

Would that I had in the wilderness a travelers' lodge, and then I could abandon my people and go from them!

Here, the clause expressing purpose or subsequent outcome is introduced with a *weyiqtol* (וְאֶעֶזְבָה), as one would expect, and not by כִּי (cf. Judg 9:29; Jer 8:23 [Eng. 9:1]; Ps 55:7 [Eng. 6]). In addition, in Stackert's examples the clauses with כִּי do not mean what he suggests. They do not describe a result or subsequent action. After all, how could there be an action subsequent to "Who am I," a rhetorical question? Instead, the clauses with כִּי provide explanatory exposition. Thus, when Moses asks, "Who am I that (כִּי) I should go to Pharaoh?," the clause with כִּי explains the significance of the question, indicating that when Moses asks, "Who am I," his point is that he did not have the prestige to stand before the king of Egypt. In the same manner, when he says, "But I wish that all of YHWH's people were prophets—[I wish] that YHWH would set his Spirit on them!," the second clause gives exposition of the first; it does not describe a subsequent, resulting action. Stackert's translation of Num 11:29 is not possible.

Finally, Moses's desire for the people, כִּי־יִתֵּן יְהוָה אֶת־רוּחוֹ עֲלֵיהֶם, "that YHWH would set his Spirit on them," employs the same idiom (using נתן and עַל) that Num 11:25 uses to describe what actually happened to the elders: וַיִּתֵּן עַל־שִׁבְעִים, "And [YHWH] set [his Spirit] on the seventy." Clearly, and against Stackert, Moses believes that the elders experienced a prophetic gift by the Spirit of God, and his "desideratum" is that the common people should also receive the Spirit and have a prophetic experience like the elders.

---

29. Ibid., 106–7 (emphasis original).
30. Ibid., 105–6.

Stackert also argues that another E passage, Num 12:1aα, 2–8, supports his case. In the text, Miriam and Aaron complain, "Has YHWH in fact spoken through Moses alone? Has he not also spoken by us?" (v. 2). YHWH responds (vv. 6b–8a),

> If you have a prophet, [says] YHWH,[31]
> In a vision I make myself known to him;
> In a dream I speak to him.
> My servant Moses is not like that!
> In all my household he is [the most] trustworthy.
> Mouth to mouth I speak with him,
> And [he sees me] visibly, and [I do] not [speak] in riddles.
> And he beholds the form of YHWH!

YHWH ends the oracle with a prose question: "Why were you not afraid to speak against my servant Moses?" (v. 8b).

It appears that Miriam and Aaron claim to have a prophetic gift like Moses and thus are jealous of him since they, too, are entitled to be regarded as leaders in Israel. Stackert, however, argues that this misreads the text: their complaint is actually directed against the newly created governance by nonprophetic elders. He paraphrases the complaint as "Why is such a drastic innovation necessary to deal with Moses's exhaustion? Why shouldn't other prophets—like us!—step in to assist him? Do we not have something to offer?"[32]

In fact, nothing indicates that Miriam and Aaron are unhappy about the seventy elders. YHWH regards their complaint as an attack on Moses (v. 8b), not on the seventy. Verse 1, moreover, explicitly states that Miriam and Aaron were motivated by anger over Moses's marriage to a Cushite (Stackert avoids this difficulty by excluding v. 1aβ–b from E on the grounds that it "cannot be correlated with the surrounding narrative").[33] To the contrary, there is nothing peculiar about a story in which personal animosity enflames religiously framed criticism—one need only recall Michal's response to David's dancing (2 Sam 6:20).

In addition, Stackert translates YHWH's response in Num 12:6–8 as past tense, rendering v. 6b as "whenever you have had a prophet, I have revealed myself

---

31. The Hebrew of this line (אִם־יִהְיֶה נְבִיאֲכֶם יְהוָה) is difficult. I take אִם־יִהְיֶה נְבִיאֲכֶם to be equivalent to אם יהיה נביא לכם and regard יהוה as elliptical for either אמר יהוה or נאם יהוה, expressions that are common in oracles.

32. Stackert, *Prophet Like Moses*, 108.

33. Ibid., 108n92. It is not clear where he thinks these words came from; it is hard to imagine how they might fit in another document. If he thinks they are a secondary interpolation, it is curious to see a Neo-Documentarian resorting to a redactor in order to save his reconstruction.

(אֶתְוַדָּע) to him in a vision; in a dream I would speak with him."[34] He regards the *yiqtol* verbs, such as אֶתְוַדָּע, as describing repeated past actions. His translation suggests that for E, all legitimate prophets were in the past; with the coming of Moses, the prophetic order is finished. While it is true that the *yiqtol* can have a frequentative past-tense meaning in Hebrew prose narrative, this is not the function of the *yiqtol* verbs in this text, which is an oracle of YHWH. The oracle speaks of the nature of Moses (present tense) and of the nature of the prophets (a present, or better, atemporal reality). In the oracle, it is simply a timeless truth that prophets receive a limited encounter with YHWH; it is not an account of what used to happen.[35] We should note that verse 8, referring to YHWH's encounters with Moses, uses the *yiqtol* אֲדַבֶּר, "I speak." Inconsistent with his treatment of the *yiqtol* verbs in verse 6, Stackert correctly translates this example in the present tense: "From (my) mouth to (his) mouth do I speak through him."[36] Nothing in the Hebrew text suggests that verse 6 and verse 8 are in different time frames.

To summarize: in Num 12, God does not suggest that Moses is the last prophet, but he does assert that Moses is superior to anyone else of any time who might hold the prophetic office. This is not antiprophetic polemic. It establishes the preeminence of Moses, but does not exclude the possibility that other people (now or in the future) might be genuine prophets of YHWH.

Stackert's treatment of Exod 33:6b is also implausible. Recall that, following Baden, he detaches 33:6b from its context and moves it to verse 7, and then moves all of Exod 33:6b–11 to just before Num 11:11–12. From this, he concludes that the burden of being Israel's charismatic leader was too heavy for Moses, and this led to the appointment of the seventy.[37]

The arrangement of the passage in the MT is quite different. In Exod 33:1–6, YHWH declares that he will not journey with Israel to Canaan. The people mourn this and, as a sign of their submission, remove their jewelry. Verse 6 (as the MT has it) concludes the narrative:

וַיִּתְנַצְּלוּ בְנֵי־יִשְׂרָאֵל אֶת־עֶדְיָם מֵהַר חוֹרֵב

So the Israelites went without their jewelry, [starting] from [the time at] Mount Horeb.[38]

---

34. Ibid., 111.

35. The *yiqtol* verbs in Num 12:6 describe what is characteristic in the experience of prophets. This is analogous to the timeless aphorisms we see often in Proverbs, as at Prov 12:3, "A good man obtains (יָפִיק) favor from YHWH; / but [YHWH] condemns (יַרְשִׁיעַ) a cunning man."

36. Stackert, *Prophet Like Moses*, 111.

37. Ibid., 82–91.

38. More literally, "And the Israelites stripped themselves of their jewelry from [the time at] Mount Horeb."

Baden considers the connection between the *wayyiqtol* וַיִּתְנַצְּלוּ and the phrase מֵהַר חוֹרֵב to be intolerable, saying that the verb "hardly lends itself to such a meaning of continuous stativity."[39] In fact, Baden is imposing unwarranted constraints on the language. We can see elsewhere a perfective verb (both *qatal* and *wayyiqtol* are perfective) with a temporal מִן functioning analogously to Exod 33:6. For example, in 1 Sam 12:2, הִתְהַלַּכְתִּי לִפְנֵיכֶם מִנְּעֻרַי could be translated literally as "I have walked before you from my youth," but in our terms it actually means "I have been a public figure before you ever since my youth." Job 38:12, הֲמִיָּמֶיךָ צִוִּיתָ בֹּקֶר, is literally "From your days have you commanded morning?" It means, "Have you been in charge of morning throughout the days of your life?"

Nevertheless, having declared the syntax of the MT to be unacceptable, Baden proposes moving verse 6b to verse 7, so that it reads, מֵהַר חוֹרֵב וּמֹשֶׁה יִקַּח אֶת־הָאֹהֶל. This produces the ungrammatical "From [the time of] Horeb *and* Moses would take the tent" (emphasis added). The presence of the conjunction in וּמֹשֶׁה is obviously strange, but Baden justifies it by appeal to three texts (Num 16:5; Gen 22:1; 1 Sam 3:2).[40] Based on these analogies, he essentially argues that we can disregard the conjunction.

The latter two examples employ a protasis-apodosis construction, in which וַיְהִי introduces the protasis and the וְ with a noun introduces the apodosis. Thus, 1 Sam 3:2 states, וַיְהִי בַּיּוֹם הַהוּא וְעֵלִי שֹׁכֵב בִּמְקֹמוֹ (And it happened on that day that Eli was lying in his place). The protasis clause begins with וַיְהִי and the apodosis clause with וְעֵלִי; also, the verse describes a specific episode. However, this is not a genuine analogy to Baden's proposed text. Exodus 33:6 is a single clause, it has no protasis-apodosis construction, and it concerns habitual activity.

His other example, Num 16:5, is set in the confrontation between Moses and the sons of Korah. Moses gives the rebels the terse message בֹּקֶר וְיֹדַע יְהוָה אֶת־אֲשֶׁר־לוֹ. This is elliptical language, and it reflects the anger and conflict of the narrative. It is literally "Morning! Then YHWH will make known who belongs to him!" בֹּקֶר conveys the implied meaning "[Wait until] morning!" Furthermore, וְיֹדַע has the conjunction on the verb and not on the subject, יהוה. This, too, is different from Baden's proposal for Exod 33:6b–7.[41]

In reality, the conjunction וְ in וּמֹשֶׁה of Baden's proposal has no function, and the result is as ungrammatical in Hebrew as it is in English.[42] We do not have sufficient reason to alter the MT arrangement of the verses, and this means that Stackert's entire thesis regarding the setting and significance of Exod 33:6b–11 is founded on an improperly delineated text.

---

39. Baden, "On Exodus 33,1–11," 336–37.

40. Baden, "On Exodus 33,1–11," 338 nn28,29.

41. It may be that the MT of Num 16:5 is not correct. The Greek has Ἐπέσκεπται καὶ ἔγνω for the MT וְיֹדַע בֹּקֶר, prompting the *BHS* (note a) to suggest reading בֹּקֶר וַיֵּדַע. If this is valid, it removes Baden's example completely, although I prefer to leave the MT as is.

42. See the translation in Stackert, *Prophet Like Moses*, 82. He simply omits the conjunction.

170   Duane A. Garrett

Finally, Stackert looks to E's account of the death of Moses (Deut 34:10–12) to support his thesis, and once again he relies upon an eccentric translation. He renders verses 10–11a as "Never again did a prophet arise in Israel, as Moses (did), the one whom YHWH selected directly for all of the signs and wonders that YHWH sent him to perform in the land of Egypt before Pharaoh." A more conventional translation is "Never since has there arisen a prophet in Israel like Moses, whom the LORD knew face to face. He was unequaled for all the signs and wonders that the LORD sent him to perform in the land of Egypt" (NRSV). Stackert's translation indicates that Moses was the last true prophet, implying that all others since him have been spurious. The conventional translation only asserts that the Israelites have not seen Moses's equal among the prophets.

Stackert's version depends upon two novel interpretations. First, he must treat כְּמֹשֶׁה as an adverbial modifier of the verb קָם ("arise . . . as Moses [did]"), and not as creating a comparison with נָבִיא ("a prophet like Moses"). Second, he must set aside the conventional understanding of the "prophet . . . whom YHWH knew face to face" and contend that the text actually means that Moses was the last prophet whom God appointed.

Regarding the first matter: it is true that כ with a noun can modify a predicate, as in the examples that Stackert cites (Isa 11:9, 61:11; Ps 42:2). Thus, Isa 61:11 begins כִּי כָאָרֶץ תּוֹצִיא צִמְחָהּ ("For as the earth brings forth its new growth"). In each example, however, the prepositional phrase (כ plus noun) is followed by an explicit predicate, and its function is not open to question. But in Deut 34:10a, we have וְלֹא־קָם נָבִיא עוֹד בְּיִשְׂרָאֵל כְּמֹשֶׁה. No predicate follows כְּמֹשֶׁה, and the obvious inference is that it refers back to נָבִיא: "a prophet . . . like Moses." Stackert can only suggest that an implied קָם follows כְּמֹשֶׁה.[43] While this interpretation may be technically possible, it is unlikely. One should not infer an ellipsis where the explicit text is intelligible.

Regarding the second matter: Deut 34:10b reads, אֲשֶׁר יְדָעוֹ יְהוָה פָּנִים אֶל־פָּנִים ("whom YHWH knew face to face"). The idiom פָּנִים אֶל־פָּנִים appears five times in the Hebrew Bible (Gen 32:31 [Eng. 30]; Exod 33:11; Deut 34:10; Judg 6:22; Ezek 20:35). In three cases (Gen 32:31; Exod 33:11; Judg 6:22) God visibly and in some sense corporally appears in the presence of the person with whom he speaks. In Ezek 20:35, it is metaphorical (YHWH will judge Jerusalem face-to-face), but even there the force of the metaphor is lost if one sets aside the "face-to-face" nature of the encounter.[44] For Deut 34:10, the most relevant text is Exod 33:11, which says that YHWH spoke to Moses "face to face, as a man might speak to his friend." Against this, Stackert interprets פָּנִים אֶל־פָּנִים in Deut 34:10 as a more abstract adverb, "directly," obscuring the implication of personal encounter.

---

43. Ibid., 119.

44. Ezekiel 20:35 may in fact be an ironic allusion to Exod 33:11 and Deut 34:10, contrasting YHWH's relationship to Jerusalem with his relationship to Moses.

This effectively disregards all other uses of the idiom, and it should therefore be viewed as unlikely.

Also, he connects ידע from verse 10 to לְכָל־הָאֹתוֹת ("for all the signs") in verse 11. He argues that ידע plus ל means "to select for (a task)," and so translates the relevant words as "whom YHWH selected (ידע) directly (פָּנִים אֶל־פָּנִים) for (ל) all of the signs." He cites several verses where ידע has the nuance of "choose" (Gen 18:19, Exod 33:12, 17; Jer 1:5; Amos 3:2). In all of these cases, however, ידע implies personal love and loyalty; it is more than a synonym for "choose." In Deut 34:10, the implication of intimacy and devotion between YHWH and Moses is the prominent idea implied by ידע, not choosing. And Stackert has no evidence that ידע plus ל can mean "to select for (a task)." His only parallel text is Jer 1:5c (נָבִיא לַגּוֹיִם נְתַתִּיךָ),[45] which is not a true parallel since it uses נתן instead of ידע. Although it could legitimately be translated "I appointed you as prophet to the nations," it is more literally "I gave you as a prophet to the nations." This example does not validate Stackert's claims for ידע plus ל, and there is no basis for setting aside the conventional understanding of Deut 34:10. Thus, his entire interpretation is unconvincing.

Stackert's analysis of E depends heavily on novel interpretations of the Hebrew text, but none of his distinctive translations is compelling. In addition, his claims about the religious and social provenance of E and of the other source documents are perplexing. In his conclusion, he makes a number of surprising statements:

> The evidence suggests, however, that the views of E, D, and P are prospective expressions of the religious imagination, not implemented religious programs or reflections of widespread developments in real Israelite religious practice or ideology. . . . This means that even if the Torah sources advocate a transition from prophetic religion to legal religion, they must be recognized as doing so on a *literary* level. . . . Neither their characterizations of the views and practices that they oppose nor their portrayals of their own preferred religious perspectives and practices can be taken as accurate depictions of real, practiced religion in ancient Israel and Judah.[46]

It is difficult to know what to make of this. I can only assume that in Stackert's view the Elohist, Deuteronomist, and Priestly writers were theologians whose religious programs were no more than literary thought experiments.

---

45. Stackert, *Prophet Like Moses*, 120–22. Jeremiah 1:5a has the verb ידע, but it is in a different clause and is thus irrelevant.

46. Stackert, *Prophet Like Moses*. The first sentence is from p. 197 and the latter two are from p. 199 (emphasis original).

172   Duane A. Garrett

They apparently worked in isolation from their social context, since no conflict between priestly and prophetic religion actually existed in their day and their writings had no impact on contemporary religious practice. As a proposed description of the theological agenda of the source documents, this is as astonishing as it is implausible.[47] As a vindication for the methods and results of Neo-Documentary analysis, it fails.

In my view, the Neo-Documentary approach to the Pentateuch is unpersuasive. In this essay, however, I have not sought to engage the arguments for the existence of the four source documents as set forth by Baden and others. I have instead tried to show, by engaging Stackert, that the fruits of an analysis based in Neo-Documentary theory are not satisfactory.

---

47. As the reader will recognize, Stackert's thesis significantly revises and redates the proposals regarding prophecy and priestly law found in Julius Wellhausen, *Prolegomena to the History of Israel* (Edinburgh: Black, 1885). See Stackert, *Prophet Like Moses*, 6–19, 197. But Stackert's reconstruction is quite different from Wellhausen's, and it stands or falls on its own. Thus, in this essay I have not made reference to Wellhausen's views.

CHAPTER 10

Revisiting the Literary Structure(s) of Exodus

Richard Davidson, Tiago Arrais, and Christian Vogel
Andrews University

Introduction and Literature Review

The focus of this essay is to revisit the topic of the literary structure of the book of Exodus.[1] Modern interpretation of the book of Exodus—as with any other book within Torah—has been heavily influenced by the Documentary Hypothesis.[2] Within critical contexts, discussion relating to the literary structure of Exodus is normally set against the backdrop of the more detailed developments and theories concerning the sources scholars assert to be present within the book. What Umberto Cassuto long ago observed in his evaluation of the history of interpretation of Exodus is still valid to a large extent: "the study of sources takes precedence over that of the book as we have it."[3] Despite the literary turn in recent decades toward the final form of the text, it is still true that

---

1. This essay reflects the results of a joint effort toward the understanding of the literary structure of Exodus by Richard Davidson and two of his doctoral students, Christian Vogel and Tiago Arrais (both have now graduated with PhDs in Old Testament studies). We do not consider the findings presented here to be the final word on how Exodus presents itself as a literary unit. Rather, we understand that this is a work in progress and reflects where we are in our continuing research on this important topic.

2. From the publishing of Brevard S. Childs's *The Book of Exodus: A Critical, Theological Commentary*, OTL (Louisville: Westminster John Knox, 1974) to newer commentaries such as Thomas B. Dozeman's *Exodus*, ECC (Grand Rapids: Eerdmans, 2009), the majority of critical studies on Exodus follow the general tenets of the Documentary Hypothesis (and its various permutations). For a brief review of how scholars understand the composition of Exodus, see Duane A. Garrett, *A Commentary on Exodus*, Kregel Exegetical Library (Grand Rapids: Kregel Academic, 2014), 15–20. Garrett is among the few (mainly evangelical) scholars who reject the Documentary Hypothesis as the framework in which to understand the contents of the book. He writes, "Continually flogging the dead horse of the documentary hypothesis is pointless" (20). For more on Garrett's position on the Documentary Hypothesis, see Duane A. Garrett, *Rethinking Genesis: The Source and Authorship of the First Book of the Pentateuch* (Grand Rapids: Baker, 1991). Other representative examples of those who question the authoritative function of the Documentary Hypothesis as the framework in which to understand Torah include Umberto Cassuto, *The Documentary Hypothesis and the Composition of the Pentateuch: Eight Lectures* (Jerusalem: Shalem, 2006); and Isaac M. Kikawada and Arthur Quinn, *Before Abraham Was: The Unity of Genesis 1–11* (Nashville: Abingdon, 1985).

3. Umberto Cassuto, *A Commentary on the Book of Exodus*, trans. Israel Abrahams (Jerusalem: Magnes, 1967; Skokie, IL: Varda, 2005), 1.

174   Richard Davidson, Tiago Arrais, and Christian Vogel

consideration of an intentional literary macrostructure of the book as a whole
has not often been entertained. Mark Smith summarizes the situation: "Over
the last century scholarly discussion of Exodus has revolved largely around the
character and date of sources, their relation to one another, and their tradition
histories. . . . Diachronic analysis has rarely been joined to a discussion of the
synchronic arrangement of the book. . . . To date, diachronic discussions have
generated relatively few attempts to describe the literary character of the book."[4]

Scholars generally organize the final form of the book either by its evident
geographical markers (e.g., Egypt—Wilderness—Sinai); or by theological
subheadings (e.g., Redemption—Covenant/Law—Tabernacle). From these
two general choices, the contents of Exodus are organized in an outline with a
varying number of parts and varying demarcation points for sections. Below is
a fairly comprehensive survey of the various organizational structures suggested
by scholars for the final form of Exodus.[5]

Two-Part (Bifid) Structures

Jacob simply divides the book into a "first half" (1–19) and "second half"
(20–40), based on geography.[6] Johnstone also uses this subdivision, but based
on themes: 1–19 (freedom from slavery) and 20–40 (revelation of the Law).[7]
Propp divides the book differently, also based on theological themes: 1–15
(double revelations to Moses and Israel) and 16–40 (double covenant).[8] Enns

---

4. Mark S. Smith, "The Literary Arrangement of the Priestly Redaction of Exodus: A Preliminary Investigation," *CBQ* 58 (1996): 25–26, 29.

5. The following outlines are drawn from the major commentaries on the book of Exodus and
select Old Testament theologies and dictionaries, as well as dissertations/articles. An earlier version
of this essay included the full titles of each subdivision in all the book outlines surveyed, but due
to space constraints it has been necessary to include only the essential information, with inclusion
of subdivision titles only selectively when they are particularly striking or unique in their wording
or concepts. The major presentation of a given outline is placed in the main text, and later similarly
divided and similarly labeled outlines are placed in the footnotes.

6. Benno Jacob, *The Second Book of the Bible: Exodus* (Hoboken, NJ: Ktav, 1992), xxxv,
1083–87. Jacob proposes that each half has three sections.

7. William Johnstone, *Exodus*, 2 vols., SHBC 2 (Macon, GA: Smyth & Helwys, 2014), passim.
This same twofold division is followed by Eduardo C. Schenkel, "Indicios literarios y narratológicos
para estructurar e interpretar el libro de Éxodo: Una propuesta," *DavarLogos* 11, no. 2 (2012): 137–56.
See below for his further analysis of the linear structure of the book into seven sequences based on
alternating literary genres.

8. William H. Propp, *Exodus 1–18: A New Translation with Introduction and Commentary*, AB
2 (New York: Doubleday, 1999), 37–38. Propp in a footnote remarks that "the two halves of Exodus
are to a degree structurally symmetrical. The first panel features double revelations to Moses and
Israel, the second revelation (chaps. 6–7) more efficacious than the first (chaps. 3–4). The second
panel features two covenants, the first abortive (chaps. 19–23) and the second permanent (chaps.
33–34)" (38n17). This same bipartite division is also supported by R. J. Clifford, "Exodus," in *The
New Jerome Biblical Commentary*, ed. R. E. Brown, Joseph A. Fitzmyer, and Roland E. Murphy
(Englewood Cliffs, NJ: Prentice-Hall, 1990), 45.

Revisiting the Literary Structure(s) of Exodus   175

follows the same textual markers but with a geographical justification for his structure.[9]

Keil and Delitzsch suggest a slightly different bifid structure based upon a theological scheme: 1:1–15:21 (liberation) and 15:22–40:38 (adoption).[10] Thomas Dozeman follows the same textual division but under the twin theological themes of divine power and divine presence.[11] Willem Gispen also divides the book with the same textual markers, combining geographical descriptions with theological themes,[12] while Mark Smith follows the same textual markers but with consistent geographical subheadings.[13]

Carol Meyers proposes at least two ways in which to organize the material of Exodus in bifid structures. The first is through descriptive-theological themes: 1–15 (slavery to freedom) and 16–40 (Sinai experience). The second is through geographical markers: 1–18 (Midian–Jethro frame) and 19–40 (theophany at Sinai).[14]

Three-Part (Tripartite) Structures

Umberto Cassuto organizes the book according to a tripartite thematic scheme: 1–17 (bondage—liberation), 18–24 (Torah—precepts), and 25–40 (tabernacle—services).[15] Martin Noth divides the final form of Exodus into three different sections, arranged geographically according to Israel's itinerary: 1:1–15:21; 15:22–18:27; and 19:1–40:38.[16] John Durham also divides the book into three

---

9. Peter Enns, *Exodus*, NIV Application Commentary (Grand Rapids: Zondervan, 2000), 33. Enns suggests also a separation of the second part into two, making a three-part outline: 1–15, 16–24, and 25–40 (33).

10. Carl F. Keil and Franz Delitzsch, *Biblical Commentary on the Old Testament: The Pentateuch*, trans. James Martin, 6 vols. (Edinburgh: T&T Clark, 1864), 1:416–17. Each of these two main sections is seen to have seven sections.

11. Dozeman, *Exodus*, 52. Each of these two sections is divided into three episodes.

12. Willem H. Gispen, *Exodus* (Grand Rapids: Zondervan, 1982), 29, 153.

13. Mark S. Smith, *The Pilgrimage Pattern in Exodus* (Sheffield: Sheffield Academic Press, 1997), passim; Smith, *Exodus*, New Collegeville Bible Commentary 3 (Collegeville, MN: Liturgical Press, 2010), 3.

14. Carol L. Meyers, *Exodus*, NCBC (Cambridge: Cambridge University Press, 2005), 17–18. Meyers also mentions other possibilities, and actually outlines her book under three sections (1:1–15:21; 15:22–24:18; and 25:1–40:38), while acknowledging that it "does not claim to represent an arrangement intrinsic to the ancient Hebrew text" 18). Paul Wright shares the textual markers of Meyer's second two-part scheme following two major theological concepts; Paul A. Wright, "Exodus 1–24 (A Canonical Study)" (PhD diss., University of Vienna, 1993). This same basic structure is followed by Bruce K. Waltke and Charles Yu, *An Old Testament Theology* (Grand Rapids: Zondervan, 2007), 346–452.

15. Cassuto, *Commentary on the Book of Exodus*, 11–16.

16. Martin Noth, *Exodus: A Commentary*, OTL (Philadelphia: Westminster, 1962), 5–12. For others who follow this same basic structure, see Brevard S. Childs, *Introduction to the Old Testament as Scripture* (Philadelphia: Fortress, 1979), 170; Terence E. Fretheim, "Exodus, Book of,"

176   Richard Davidson, Tiago Arrais, and Christian Vogel

geographical sections, but with slightly different boundaries: 1:1–13:16; 13:17–18:27; and 19:1–40.[17] J. Alec Motyer divides the book into a slightly different three-part outline focused on God's character: 1:1–13:16 (Savior), 13:17–24:11 (Companion), and 24:12–40:38 (Indweller).[18] Walter C. Kaiser Jr. divides his tripartite structure based on God-related actions: 1–18 (redemption), 19–24 (morality), and 25–40 (worship).[19]

Four-Part Structures

John Oswalt divides the book into four parts, which are a mix of thematic and geographical sections, focusing on attributes/actions of Yahweh: 1:1–15:21 (deliverance), 15:22–18:27 (providence), 19:1–24:18 (principles), and 25:1–40:38 (person).[20] R. Alan Cole likewise provides a mixture of geographical and theological-descriptive headings in his four-part literary structure of Exodus: 1–11:10 (Egypt), 12–18 (Exodus to Sinai), 19–31 (law—covenant), and 32–40 (rebellion—revival).[21] Gerald Janzen organizes the content of the book into four parts (1–24, 25–31, 32–34, 35–40) around the two main themes of covenant and presence.[22]

Five-Part Structures

Claus Westermann divides the book into five sections that highlight divine action and human response: 1:1–14:31 (God's deliverance), 15:1–21 (human

---

in *Dictionary of the Old Testament: Pentateuch*, ed. T. Desmond Alexander and David W. Baker (Downers Grove, IL: InterVarsity, 2003), 250–51); and Nahum M. Sarna, *Exodus: The Traditional Hebrew Text with the New JPS Translation*, JPS Torah Commentary (Philadelphia: Jewish Publication Society, 1991), xii.

17. John I. Durham, *Exodus*, WBC 3 (Waco: Word, 1987), v–x. Durham also notices a centerpiece of Yahweh's Presence, and "the Book of Exodus may be seen as a series of interlocking concentric circles spreading outwards from the narratives of the coming of Yahweh" (xxi).

18. J. Alec Motyer, *The Message of Exodus: The Days of Our Pilgrimage*, The Bible Speaks Today (Downers Grove, IL: InterVarsity, 2005), 24.

19. Walter C. Kaiser Jr., "Exodus," in *Genesis–Leviticus*, EBC, rev. ed., 1 (Grand Rapids: Zondervan, 2006), 344–46 and passim. Tremper Longman follows the same textual markers and a similar theological descriptive scheme (Tremper Longman III, *How to Read Exodus* [Downers Grove, IL: IVP Academic, 2009], passim). Randall Bailey follows the same textual markers and offers a similar outline (Randall C. Bailey, *Exodus*, College Press NIV Commentary [Joplin, MO: College Press, 2007], 39–42).

20. John N. Oswalt, "Exodus," in *Genesis–Exodus*, Cornerstone Biblical Commentary 1 (Carol Stream, IL: Tyndale, 2008), 282–83.

21. R. Alan Cole, *Exodus: An Introduction and Commentary*, Tyndale Old Testament Commentaries (Downers Grove, IL: InterVarsity, 1973), 52.

22. Gerald J. Janzen, *Exodus*, Westminster Bible Companion (Louisville: Westminster John Knox, 1997), passim.

praise), 15:22–18:27 (God's preservation), 19:1–31:18 (human obedience), and 32:1–40:38 (transgression—renewal).[23] J. P. Fokkelman proposes a different five-section outline based on a mix of theological and geographical features: 1:1–6:27; 6:28–15:21; 15:22–18:27; 19:1–31:18; and 32:1–40:38.[24] Paul House follows yet another five-part outline, based on major contents: 1–18 (Exodus), 19–24 (covenant), 25–31 (tabernacle), 32–34 (golden calf), and 35–40 (tabernacle).[25]

Six-Part Structures

James Bruckner outlines the book in six parts under descriptive geographical and theological terms: 1–14, 15–18, 19–24, 25–31, 32–34, and 35–40.[26] David Dorsey divides the book into six (chiastically arranged) topical sections: 1:1–13:16; 13:17–19:2; 19:3–20:14; 20:22–24:11; 24:12–34:28; and 34:29–40:38. Sections 1 and 2 are placed at the end of the chiastic "Historical Prologue" to the Book of the Law of Moses, which stretches from Gen 1:1 to Exod 19:2, while sections 3–6 are placed first in the chiastic "Treaty at Sinai," which stretches from Exod 19:3–Num 10:10.[27]

Seven-Part Structures

Douglas Stuart follows a seven-part thematic outline in his commentary, divided as follows: 1:1–2:25; 3:1–7:7; 7:8–11:10; 12:1–13:16; 13:17–19:25; 20:1–31:18; and 32:1–40:38.[28] Victor Hamilton suggests a different seven-part thematic division: 1:1–6:1; 6:2–15:21; 15:22–18:27; 19:1–24:18; 25:1–31:18; 32:1–34:35; and 35:1–40:38.[29] Duane Garrett organizes the book into still different seven main sections, with noteworthy catchy titles: "Until Moses"

---

23. Claus Westermann, and Robert Henry Boyd, *Handbook to the Old Testament* (Minneapolis: Augsburg, 1967), passim.

24. J. P. Fokkelman, "Exodus," in *The Literary Guide to the Bible*, ed. Robert Alter and Frank Kermode (Cambridge, MA: Belknap, 1987), 57–58.

25. Paul R. House, *Old Testament Theology* (Downers Grove, IL: InterVarsity, 1998), 87–125.

26. James K. Bruckner, *Exodus*, Understanding the Bible Commentary Series 2 (Peabody, MA: Hendrickson, 2008), 2. Ross W. Blackburn sees a similar six-part division of Exodus in his structure of the book and organizes the contents similarly to Bruckner (Ross W. Blackburn, *The God Who Makes Himself Known: The Missionary Heart of the Book of Exodus* [Downers Grove, IL: Apollos, 2012], 7–8).

27. David A. Dorsey, *The Literary Structure of the Old Testament: A Commentary on Genesis–Malachi* (Grand Rapids: Baker Academic, 1999), 70–77.

28. Douglas K. Stuart, *Exodus: An Exegetical and Theological Exposition of Holy Scripture*, NAC 2 (Nashville: Broadman & Holman, 2006), 50–52.

29. Victor P. Hamilton, *Exodus: An Exegetical Commentary* (Grand Rapids: Baker Academic, 2011), vii–x.

178   Richard Davidson, Tiago Arrais, and Christian Vogel

(1:1–2:10), "Unlikely Savior" (2:11–7:7), "The Twelve Miracles of the Exodus" (7:8–15:21), "The Journey to God" (15:22–19:25), "The Sinai Covenant" (20:1–24:11), "The Worship of God" (24:12–31:18), and "Sin and Restoration" (32–40).[30]

Eduardo Schenkel divides the book into two basic parts as noted above, but also uniquely goes beyond the various thematic analyses of other scholars (who give little or no attention to genre in their proposals of structure) by recognizing seven sequences based solely upon the alternation of literary genres throughout the book, highlighting the theophany and Decalogue of Exod 19–20 at the center of the book: narrative followed by genealogy (1:1–6:27); narrative followed by laws (6:28–13:16); narrative followed by poetry (13:17–15:21); narrative (15:22–18:27) followed by theophany and the Decalogue (19:1–20:26); law followed by narrative (20:27–24:18); law (25:1–31:18) followed by narrative (32:1–34:28); and execution of laws followed by narrative (34:29–40:38).[31]

Multipart Structures

Terence Fretheim (in his earlier commentary) presents a nine-part detailed outline of the book, with organization based upon geography and theological themes: 1–2; 3:1–7:7; 7:8–11:10; 12:1–15:21; 15:22–18:27; 19–24; 25–31; 32–34; and 35–40.[32] John Sailhamer organizes the contents of Exodus into ten sections based upon descriptive theological themes: 1; 2; 3–4; 5:1–15:21; 15:22–18:27; 19–24; 25–31; 32; 33–34; and 35–40.[33]

Göran Larsson suggests a thirteen-part outline/structure, with very creative titles: "The Prelude" (1), "The Discovery" (2), "The Master, the Mission and the Means" (3:1–4:17), "The Return" (4:18–6:30), "Ten Strikes Less One" (7–11), "The Liberation Prepared" (12:1–13:16), "The Liberation" (13:17–15:21), "Stumbling Steps Toward Freedom" (15:22–18:27), "The Miracle of Pentecost" (19–20), "The Book of the Covenant" (21–23), "The Confirmation" (24), "The Sanctuary of Freedom" (25–31; 35–40), and "The Fall and the New Covenant" (32–34).[34] Finally, Victor Hamilton suggests a compact fifteen-part outline/structure that covers the main scenes within the book under single-word alliterative headings: "Oppression" (1–2), "Trepidation" (3–4), "Rejection" (5), "Reaffirmation" (6), "Confrontation" (7:1–12:30), "Liberation" (12:31–14:31), "Celebration"

---

30. Garrett, *Commentary on Exodus*, 135–36.

31. Schenkel, "Indicios literarios y narratológicos," 150.

32. Terence E. Fretheim, *Exodus*, Interpretation: A Bible Commentary for Preaching and Teaching (Louisville: John Knox, 1991), ix–xii.

33. John H. Sailhamer, *The Pentateuch as Narrative: A Biblical-Theological Commentary* (Grand Rapids: Zondervan, 1992), 241–322.

34. Göran Larsson, *Bound for Freedom: The Book of Exodus in Jewish and Christian Traditions* (Peabody, MA: Hendrickson, 1999), vii and passim.

Revisiting the Literary Structure(s) of Exodus 179

(15:1–21), "Itineration" (15:22–17:15), "Administration" (18), "Legislation" (19–24), "Specifications" (25–31), "Deviation" (32–33), "Reconciliation" (34), "Construction" (35:1–40:33), and "Glorification" (40:34–38).[35]

Preliminary Observations

It is apparent from the survey of literature regarding the structure of Exodus that no consensus has emerged. Almost all of these analyses of contents of the book of Exodus utilize descriptive geographical markers or theological themes as an organizing scheme of its contents, but they rarely, if ever, provide any inner reasoning of why the structure is in such particular form in the text, nor do they present any textual support to show authorial intentionality (even if this intentionality would come from a final redactor). Thus, they are more "outlines" than literary structures.[36]

Furthermore, almost all of these analyses describe linear schemes of the book's arrangement, with little attention to possible parallel structural schemes created by repetition. Recent research on other areas of Scripture shows a widespread use of such nonlinear structural schemes as block parallelism and reverse/symmetrical parallelism (chiastic structures), and the interpretive value of recognizing these structures.[37] Thus, there seems to be need for further work, with greater attention given to the literary artistry of Exodus as a whole and the literary markers of the sections and interrelations within its literary structure, both on a microstructural and macrostructural level.

New (Tentative) Proposals for the Literary Structure of Exodus: An Overview

The ideas proposed in this essay were perceived and developed in community. Davidson identifies seven consecutive and contiguous microstructures within the book, each made up of either a chiastic or block parallelism (panel writing).

---

35. Hamilton, *Exodus*, xxviii–xxix.

36. A major exception is the recent study in Spanish by Eduardo Schenkel, referred to above, who proceeds beyond this basic twofold division between "narrative" and "legal" sections of the book to examine the alternation of literary genres in the book, which highlights the Decalogue at the center of the book (see his charts in Schenkel, "Indicios literarios y narratológicos," 142, 150). However, his structure is still a linear one, with little attention to possible parallel structures.

37. For discussion of literary structure, see esp. Dorsey, *Literary Structure*, 15–44. Dorsey provides a very helpful treatment of the history of research on literary structure of biblical material; identifying markers of literary units; the arrangement of literary units, especially highlighting parallel patterns such as block parallelism and chiastic structures, and how to recognize these patterns by recurring terminology, grammatical-syntactical structure, themes/concepts/motifs, and structural features; the relationship between structure and meaning; and the purpose and value of literary structural analysis.

Viewed together, these may be regarded as moving in the direction of a macrostructure of the book, with the apex of the middle chiasm (Exod 14:30–31) pointing to the microstructural center of the book (see discussion below). These structures, revised from their original presentation in the annual meetings of the Evangelical Theological Society and Adventist Theological Society in 2013,[38] are displayed as structure 1 in this essay, accompanied by brief comments.

Christian Vogel proposes a parallel-panel macrostructure of Exodus that displays the similarities and differences between the life of Moses and the life of the Israelites,[39] as well as between the physical exodus from Egypt and the spiritual exodus from sin. Vogel's macrostructural research utilizes as its starting point the striking parallels between the *introduction* of the book and its *midpoint*, and is displayed as structure 2 of this essay, accompanied by brief comments.[40]

Davidson's parallel-panel macrostructure (not microstructures as described above) utilizes as its starting point the striking parallel between the *conclusion* of the book and its *midpoint*: the book concludes with the imagery of God's presence in a cloud filling the tabernacle and leading the people onward (Exod 40:34–38), and the middle of the book (Exod 13:20–22) presents the same imagery and terminology. This macrostructure was presented as part of his paper at the ATS/ETS meetings in Baltimore,[41] and an updated, modified (and still-in-progress) summary of this structure (incorporating insights from Vogel and Tiago Arrais) is displayed as structure 3 of this essay, accompanied by brief comments.[42]

It will be argued that these separate structures are actually complementary and have significant implications for authorship and unity of the book of Exodus.

38. Richard M. Davidson, "Literary Structure in the Book of Exodus: A Case Study in the Aesthetic Nature and Theological Function of Scripture" (paper presented at the ATS/ETS Annual Meeting, Baltimore, November 19, 2013).

39. Others have recognized this parallel between Moses's life and the structure of Exodus. See John D. Currid, *Exodus*, 2 vols., Evangelical Press Study Commentary (Grand Rapids: Evangelical Press, 2000), 1:19; Fretheim, *Exodus*, 41–46; and Enns, *Exodus*, 83. None of these scholars, however, utilizes these parallels as part of the full macrostructure of the book of Exodus.

40. A few clarifying footnotes to structure 2 are added by Davidson, in response to queries by the editors. This structure was first posted on Christian Vogel's blogsite The Word, "The Structure of Exodus," https://fascinatedbytheword.wordpress.com/2013/04/14/the-structure-of-exodus/.

41. Davidson, "Literary Structure."

42. Building upon the individual insights and parallel-panel structures of Davidson and Vogel, Arrais charted the contents of the book to find further textual confirmations for these ideas and to reorganize points from both Vogel's and Davidson's macrostructures according to the natural literary development of the book. This more lengthy structure, which follows the overall panel arrangement of Davidson but diverges somewhat in the latter half, is displayed in his doctoral dissertation: Tiago Arrais, "A Study on the Influence of Philosophical Presuppositions Relating to the Notion of the God–Human Relation upon the Interpretation of Exodus" (PhD diss., Andrews University, 2015), 164–256. Some of the most significant unique insights from Arrais's proposed macrostructure are noted in the footnotes dealing with structure 3.

Structure 1: Microstructural Analysis of Exodus

Seven consecutive and contiguous microstructures emerge from a close reading of the book of Exodus:

I. **Yahweh Prepares for Israel's Exodus and Reveals His Name to Moses: 1:1–6:27 (Chiasm)**
   A. Genealogy ("These are the names. . .") (1:1–7)
      B. Oppression by Pharaoh, but deliverance is brought by midwives (1:8–22)
        • "heavy work" (*siblōt*), "toil" (*'ăbōdāh*), making "bricks" (*ləbēnîm*)
        • "taskmasters" (*śārê missîm*) "set" (*śîm*) over Israel
        • Pharaoh says, "Behold, the people (*ām*) are too many (*rāb*)
         C. Moses's birth and coming to Pharaoh's house as a child (2:1–10)
           • Pharaoh's daughter sends (*šālaḥ*) her maiden
           D. Moses flees from *Egypt* to *Midian* (2:11–25)
             • Moses "sees" (*rā'āh*) a "kinsman" (*'aḥ*)
             • Moses "kills" (*hārag*) the Egyptian; Pharaoh "seeks" (*bāqaš*) to "kill" (*hārag*) Moses
             • Moses flees to *Egypt* from *Midian;* marries *Zipporah; Gershom born*
             E. Call of Moses: a divine sign (*'ôt*) (3:1–12)
               F. Center: Yahweh reveals his Name to Moses: "I AM" (3:13–15)
             E'. Call of Moses: divine signs (*'ôt*) (3:16–4:17)
           D'. Moses returns from *Midian* to *Egypt* (4:18–31)
             • Moses wishes to "see" (*rā'āh*) how his "kinsmen" (*'aḥ*) are faring
             • Pharaoh who "sought" (*bāqaš*) his life is dead; Yahweh "seeks" (*bāqaš*) to "kill" (*hārag*) him on the way
             • Moses returns to *Egypt* from *Midian* with *Zipporah* and *Gershom*
         C'. Moses comes to Pharaoh's house as an adult (5:1–4)
           • Pharaoh asked to "send" (*šālaḥ*) Israelites into the wilderness
      B'. Oppression by Pharaoh worsens, but deliverance is promised (5:5–6:13)
        • "heavy work" (*siblōt*), "toil" (*'ăbōdāh*), making "bricks" (*ləbēnîm*)
        • "taskmasters" (*śārê missîm*) "set" (*śîm*) over Israel
        • Pharaoh says, "Behold, the people (*ām*) are too many (*rāb*)
   A'. Genealogy ("These are the heads . . .") (6:14–27)

182   Richard Davidson, Tiago Arrais, and Christian Vogel

II. Yahweh Performs Signs and Wonders (The Ten Plagues): 6:28–11:10 (Chiasm)

A. Yahweh promises to bring "signs and wonders [*môptîm*]" to Pharaoh and deliver Israel (6:28–7:7)
- Yahweh promises to "harden" Pharaoh's heart

B. Yahweh's first sign (*môpēt*): Aaron's miraculous rod (7:8–13)
- Pharaoh's heart is hardened

C. The first three plagues, on Egyptians and Israelites (7:14–8:19)
- Pharaoh's heart is hardened after each plague

D. Center: Yahweh's presence: "I, the Lord, am in the midst of the land" (8:20–23)

C'. The next six plagues, only on Egyptians (8:24–10:29)
- Pharaoh's heart is hardened and/or Yahweh hardens his heart after each plague

B'. Yahweh's final sign (*môpēt*): death of the firstborn announced (11:1–8)

A'. "Moses and Aaron did all these wonders [*môptîm*] before Pharaoh" (11:9–10)
- Yahweh hardens Pharaoh's heart

III. Yahweh Gives Instructions About Passover and Firstborn and Brings His Hosts Out of Egypt: 12–13 (Panel)

A. Instructions for Passover (*pesaḥ*) and Feast of Unleavened Bread (*hammaṣôt*) (12:1–28)

B. Tenth plague realized: firstborn (*bəkôr*) of Egypt slain (12:29–30)

C. Yahweh's "hosts" (*ṣib'ôt*) go out from Egypt after 430 years' sojourn (12:31–42)

A'. Additional Passover (*pesaḥ*) / [Unleavened Bread] instructions (12:43–50)

C'. Yahweh brings the children of Israel out of Egypt by their "hosts" (*ṣib'ôt*) (12:51)[43]

B' Instructions about the firstborn (*bəkôr*) (13:1–2)

A". Additional [Passover] / Unleavened Bread (*maṣôt*) regulations (13:3–10)

B". Instructions about the firstborn (*bəkôr*) (13:11–16)

C". Yahweh leads the children of Israel up out of Egypt "in orderly ranks" (*ḥămūšîm*) and goes before them in the pillar of cloud/fire (13:17–22)

---

43. Note that in this microstructure the C' member is placed in between A' and B', in contrast to the other two triplets of members, ABC and A"B"C", where the C member comes at the end. It is suggested that this switch in the middle triplet allows the theme of YHWH bringing Israel out of Egypt to be placed exactly in the center of the microstructure of this section.

Revisiting the Literary Structure(s) of Exodus   183

IV. Yahweh Delivers Israel from the Egyptians at the Red Sea: 14:1–15:22a (Chiasm)

A. Israel comes to the *Red Sea* (*Yām Sûp*) (14:1–2)

  B. Narrative of Yahweh's deliverance of Israel from the Egyptians at the Red Sea (14:2–29)

    C. Center: "Yahweh saved [*yāšaʿ*] Israel . . . the people feared Yahweh and believed Yahweh" (14:30–31) = Microstructural apex of the whole book

  B'. Poetic recital of Yahweh's work of deliverance: Song of Moses and Miriam (15:1–21)

A'. Israel leaves the *Red Sea* (*Yām Sûp*) (15:22a)

V. Yahweh Provides for Israel's Needs in the Wilderness Journey: 15:22b–18:27 (Panel)

A. Israel comes to the wilderness (*midbār*) of Shur (15:22b)

  B. The people murmur (*lûn*) (for lack of water) (15:23–24)

    C. Yahweh provides water for Israel (at Marah and Elim) (15:25–27)

A'. Israel comes to the wilderness (*midbār*) of Sin (16:1)

  B'. The people murmur (*lûn*) (for lack of food) (16:2–3)

    C' Yahweh provides manna and reiterates the Sabbath (16:4–36)

A''. Israel comes to *Rephidim* (17:1)

  B''. The people murmur (*lûn*) (for lack of water) (17:2–3)

    C''. Yahweh provides water for Israel (from the rock in Horeb) (17:4–7)

      D. Yahweh gives victory over the Amalekites at *Rephidim* (17:8–16)[44]

        E. Jethro comes to Moses in the wilderness (*midbār*) and gives advice to Moses (18:1–27)

VI. Yahweh Establishes a Covenant with Israel at Sinai (19:1–24:11) (Chiasm)

A. Narrative: Yahweh offers the covenant (*bərît*) to Israel at Sinai (19:1–25)

  • People's response: "All that Yahweh has spoken, we will do" (v. 8)

  • Theophany: Yahweh invites the entire nation to come up (*ʿālāh*) the mountain (v. 13)

  B. Laws: Decalogue (20:1–17)

    C. Narrative/Laws: People fear God's presence; law of *sacrificial altar* (20:18–24a)

---

44. The last two members of this panel structure could also be analyzed as a continuation/expansion of member C'', Yahweh's further provisions for Israel in the wilderness.

184 Richard Davidson, Tiago Arrais, and Christian Vogel

      D. Center: God's presence—"I will come to you and I will bless you" (20:24b)

    C'. Law: *sacrificial altar* (20:25–26)

  B'. Laws: Judgments amplifying the Decalogue (21–23)

  A'. Narrative: Yahweh ratifies the covenant (*bərît*) with Israel (24:1–11)

- People's response: "All that Yahweh has said we will do, and be obedient" (v. 7)
- Theophany: Yahweh invites leaders of Israel to come up (*'ālāh*) the mountain (vv. 1, 9)

VII. Yahweh Provides Israel a Sanctuary Filled with His Glory and Reveals His Name to Moses (24:12–40:38) (Chiasm)

  A. Moses goes up to God on the mountain; God's glory (*kābôd*) rests (*šākan*) on the mountain (24:12–18)

    B. Instructions for constructing the tabernacle (*miškān*) (25:1–31:11)

      C. Sabbath (*Šabbāt*) legislation (31:12–18)

        D. Covenant (*bərît*) broken with worship of the golden calf (32:1–29)

          E. Moses's mediation for the sins (*ḥatta't*) of the people (32:30–33:11)

            F. Center: Yahweh proclaims his Name to Moses (33:12–34:7)

          E'. Moses's mediation for the sins (*ḥatta't*) of the people (34:8–9)

        D'. Covenant (*bərît*) renewal with a "cultic Decalogue" (34:10–35)

      C'. Sabbath (*Šabbāt*) legislation (35:1–3)

    B'. Construction of the tabernacle (*miškān*) (35:4–40:8)

  A'. Moses goes into the tabernacle to anoint it; the cloud rests (*šākan*) upon and God's glory (*kābôd*) fills the tabernacle, and leads his people in their journeys (40:9–38)

Comments

Several features of the microstructures may be noted. First, the boundary markers of each structure are clearly indicated in the text, and these boundary markers have been recognized in various outlines presented in the survey of literature above. Microstructure I is bounded by framing genealogies; microstructure II encompasses the ten plagues; microstructure III is framed by divine instructions regarding Passover/firstborn; microstructure IV encompasses the narrative and song about God's deliverance of Israel at the Red Sea; microstructure V encompasses the wilderness journey to Sinai; microstructure VI is the "Book of the Covenant"; and microstructure VII is the section dealing with the sanctuary.

Second, in terms of literary style, the structures alternate symmetrically between chiastic structures and parallel-panel structures. Moreover, the first two and last two structures are chiastic, the third and fifth are panel, and the middle (fourth) structure is chiastic:

I. Chiasm
II. Chiasm
III. Parallel-panel
IV. Chiasm
V. Parallel-panel
VI. Chiasm
VII. Chiasm

Third, the literary apex of each microstructure features some element of the character/power/presence of Yahweh, and in general follows a thematically chiastic arrangement:

I. Yahweh reveals his name to Moses (3:13–15)
II. Yahweh is present in the midst of the land of Egypt (8:20–23)
III. Yahweh acts to bring the people out of Egypt (12:51)
IV. Yahweh saves Israel at the Red Sea (14:30–31)
V. Yahweh acts to provide manna and reintroduce the Sabbath (16:4–36)
VI. Yahweh promises to be present with Israel in every place where he causes his name to be remembered (20:24)
VII. Yahweh reveals his name to Moses (33:13–34:9)

Fourth, the matching microstructures (I and VII, II and VI, III and V) echo each other in terms of both form and content. Structures I and VII are both chiastic, both highlight the motif of preparation, and both have a literary apex focusing upon the revelation of God's name. Structures II and VI are both chiastic, and both have a literary apex focusing specifically upon the promise of God's presence in the midst of his people. Structures III and V are both panel structures, both consisting of three panels in block parallelism, and the threefold emphasis of both structures is upon Yahweh's mighty actions: in bringing Israel out of Egypt (structure III) and providing for their needs in the wilderness (structure V).

Finally, the book's central microstructure IV is chiastic, with its parallel members making prominent Yahweh's deliverance of Israel at the Red Sea. The midpoint of this central microstructure, and thus of the entire book—using the verb "save" (*yāšaʿ*) to describe Yahweh's action for the first time in Torah

186   Richard Davidson, Tiago Arrais, and Christian Vogel

and the only time in Exodus[45]—proclaims, "Yahweh saved Israel!" And "the people . . . believed Yahweh and Moses His servant" (14:30–31).

Structure 2: Parallel-Panel Structure of Exodus (Arising from Parallels Between the *Beginning* and Middle of the Book)

In this proposed structure, as with the other structures in this essay, the general flow of items listed is in canonical order, but there is no claim that all the features mentioned occur exactly in order within each section.

Part 1: In Egypt Serving Pharaoh: Deliverance from Slavery (1:1–12:36)

A *Sons of Israel* (*bǝnê yiśrā'ēl*) come to Egypt (1:1–22)

- 70 people (1:5)

- *Ramses* mentioned (1:11)
- Lest . . . they *go up* (*'ālāh*) from the land (1:10)
- Pharaoh's rules regarding foreigners (1:9–14)
- Pharaoh's rules regarding Israelite males (1:15–22)

B Rescue of Moses out of the water at the *reeds* (*sûp*) of the Nile (2:1–10)

- Daughter of Pharaoh and her servants rescue Moses out of the water and stay alive
- Moses's sister Miriam mentioned

C Suffering and rescue (2:11–25)

- Israel suffering
- Moses challenged by fellow Israelite (2:14)
- Moses provides water (2:17)

- *Bread* (*leḥem*) for Moses (2:20)

Part 2: In the Wilderness and at the Mountain Serving YHWH[a]: Deliverance from Sin (12:37–40:38)

A' *Sons of Israel* (*bǝnê yiśrā'ēl*) leave Egypt (12:37–13:22)

- 600,000 men plus women and children (12:37)
- *Ramses* mentioned (12:37)
- A great mixed multitude *went up* (*'ālāh*) with them (12:38)
- YHWH's rules regarding foreigners (12:43–51)
- YHWH's rules regarding firstborn males (13)

B' Rescue of Israel out of the water at the Sea of *Reeds* (*sûp*) (14:1–15:21)

- Pharaoh and his servants pursue Israel into the water and are killed

- Moses's sister Miriam mentioned

C' Suffering and rescue (15:22–18:27)

- Israel suffering
- Moses challenged by fellow Israelites (15:24; 17:3)
- YHWH/Moses provide water (15:25; 17:1–7)
- *Bread* (*leḥem*) for Israel (16)

---

45. The verb is only used once before this, to describe Moses's work of "saving" the seven daughters of Jethro from being harassed (Exod 2:17), revealing that Moses is performing the very work Yahweh will do at the Exodus.

• Moses as *ruler* (*śar*) and *judge* (*š-p-ṭ*) (2:11–15)	• Moses as *judge* (*š-p-ṭ*), installs *rulers* (*śar*) (18:13–27)
• Jethro and family (2:18–22)	• Jethro and family (18)

D Moses at Sinai (3–4) **D'** Israel at Sinai (19–24)

• YHWH appears (3:1–13)	• YHWH appears (19:1–24:11)
• YHWH reveals his name (3:13–15)	• YHWH reveals his law (20–23)
• Moses and the elders worship (*hištaḥawâ*) YHWH (4:29–31)	• Moses and the elders worship (*hištaḥawâ*) YHWH (24:1–11)

E YHWH speaks through Moses to Pharaoh (5–11) **E'** YHWH speaks through Moses to Israel (24:12–39:43)

• Pharaoh's building project	• YHWH's building project
• People forced to provide material (5:6–6:1)	• People invited to provide material voluntarily (25:2)
• Rebellion of Pharaoh (hard heart)	• Rebellion of Israel (stiff neck)
• YHWH *smites* (*nāgap*) Egypt (8:2; 12:13, 23, 27)	• YHWH *smites* (*nāgap*) Israel (32:35)
• Allusions to creation: Plagues are de-creation	• Allusions to creation: Building of sanctuary reminds of creation[b]

F Instructions for Passover (12:1–28) **F'** Instructions for setting up of the sanctuary (40:1–16)

• In the first month (12:2, 18)	• In the first month (40:1)
• Passover reminds of slavery and deliverance (12:26–27)	• Sanctuary reminds of sin and deliverance (40:3–15; typology of furniture and priestly ministry)[c]
• Closes with: "The sons of Israel did as YHWH had commanded Moses and Aaron, thus they did" (12:50)	• Closes with: "Moses did as the YHWH had commanded him, thus he did" (40:16)

G Climax of de-creation: Tenth plague (12:29–36) **G'** Climax of creation: Setting up of the sanctuary (40:17–38)

• YHWH visits Egypt (negative)	• YHWH visits Israel (positive)
• Go serve the Lord—the end of service to Pharaoh (12:31)	• Moses finishes the work of erecting the sanctuary and YHWH fills it with His glory (40:33–38)

a. In this structure, worked out by Vogel, his preferred display of the Tetragrammaton as YHWH is preserved, while in the rest of the paper the personal name for Israel's God is spelled out as Yahweh.

b. See Richard M. Davidson, "Earth's First Sanctuary: Genesis 1–3 and Parallel Creation Accounts," *AUSS* 53, no. 1 (2015): 65–89.

c. The basic typology of the sanctuary and its services is already indicated in Exod 25:9, 40 by the use of the Hebrew term *tabnît*, and the major features of the sanctuary building and priestly service are summarized in Exod 40:3–15. See Richard M. Davidson, *Typology in Scripture: A Study of Hermeneutical Τύπος Structures*, AUSDS 2 (Berrien Springs, MI: Andrews University Press, 1981), 367–88.

188   Richard Davidson, Tiago Arrais, and Christian Vogel

Significance

The structure alerts the reader to several things the author wants to highlight:

1. *The contrast between service to Pharaoh and service to God.* The first part of the book focuses on Israel's period of time in Egypt serving Pharaoh. The second part of the book focuses on Israel's period of time in the wilderness and at the mountain serving God.

- The service to Pharaoh is bondage. The service to God is freedom.
- Pharaoh commands the Israelite males to be killed. God commands the firstborn to be killed but then provides a way out by way of redemption.
- The building project of Pharaoh is for his own glory and is made possible through hard labor. The building project of God is so that he can dwell among his people and save them from sin and is made possible through free-will offerings.
- Pharaoh oppresses, God rescues.
- In the end, Pharaoh is powerless against God.

2. *The story of Moses foreshadows the story of Israel.* Moses is rescued from the water just as Israel is rescued from the water. He flees from Pharaoh just as Israel flees from Pharaoh. He meets God at Sinai just as Israel meets God at Sinai. As Moses had to learn patience and trust in the wilderness, so Israel had to learn patience and trust in the wilderness. As one who has gone the way before them, he is perfectly equipped to lead them on the same journey.

3. In both panels there is a *movement from imminent death to rescue to worship through ritual.* The order is important: first God rescues, then he asks people to worship him in a way that symbolizes and commemorates the rescue. Regarding the motif of worship, in both panels there is rebellion and counter-worship. Pharaoh refuses to worship God, Israel worships another god. In both cases there is judgment that follows from the false worship, yet only those stubbornly refuse to side with God end up losing their lives.

4. *The connection between slavery and sin.* In the first panel, God appears at Sinai and speaks to Pharaoh in order to take care of the slavery problem. In the second panel, God appears at Sinai and speaks to Israel to take care of the sin problem. Thus, the exodus from slavery becomes an illustration for the exodus from sin. This also shows that God is interested in more than simply getting his people out of Egypt. In the end, he wants to take care of their sin problem. The solution is provided in the climax of each of the two panels: through the Passover, where God spares his people because of the blood of the Lamb, and through the tabernacle and its rituals, which make provision for atonement for sin.[46]

---

46. Atonement (*kippēr*) is mentioned several times in Exodus (29:33, 36, 37; 30:10, 15, 16; 32:30) and becomes a central focus in the book of Leviticus (where the term appears nearly fifty times,

Revisiting the Literary Structure(s) of Exodus   189

5. In both panels *God reveals himself*: to Moses, to Pharaoh, to the Egyptians, to Israel. He appears to Moses at Sinai and to Israel at Sinai. He speaks to and through Moses throughout the whole book. He thus reveals himself both through words and through actions. The book climaxes in the building of the Tabernacle so that God may dwell among his people and thus reveal himself most fully. At the same time God reveals himself through Moses who passes on to Pharaoh and to Israel what God has told him.

Structure 3: Parallel-Panel Structure of Exodus (Arising from Parallels Between the *End* and Middle of the Book)

Part I: Yahweh Delivers Israel from Slavery (*'ābad*) in Egypt (1–13)

Part II: Yahweh Brings Israel to Himself That They May Serve/ Worship (*'abad*) Him (14–40)

A. Children of Israel come to Egypt and are oppressed by Pharaoh (1:1–2:10)

A'. Children of Israel depart from Egypt and are delivered from Pharaoh (14:1–15:27) .

- "Children of Israel" (*bənê yiśrā'ēl*) come to Egypt (1:1–7)

- "Children of Israel" (*bənê yiśrā'ēl*) leave Egypt and come to the Red Sea (14:1–2)

- Pharaoh tries to destroy Israel/Moses (1:8–22)

- Pharaoh tries to destroy Israel (14:3–10)

- Moses is saved in water (2:1–10)

- Israel is saved in water (14:11–15:21)

B. Moses goes into the wilderness (2:11–25)

B'. Israel goes into the wilderness (15:27–18:27)

- Israel is suffering (2:11–12)

- Israel is suffering (15:22–23; 17:1)

- Moses is challenged (2:13–15)

- Moses is challenged (15:24; cf. 16:2–3; 17:2–3)

- Moses provides water (2:16–20)

- God/Moses provide water (15:25; cf. 17:4–7)

- God hears the cry of his people (2:23–25)

- God hears the cry of his people (16:10–12)

- Jethro (2:16, 18), Zipporah (2:21), Gershom (2:22); "eat bread" (*'ākal leḥem*) (2:20)

- Jethro (18:1), Zipporah (18:2), Gershom (18:3–4); "eat bread" (*'ākal leḥem*) (18:12)

---

often in the context of atoning for sin through the sanctuary rituals). Note also that microstructural apex of the book of Exodus (Exod 14:30–31), as displayed in the previous section of this essay, focuses upon God's salvation (*yāša'*) of Israel and their response of faith. This theme is set at the chiastic apex of the book because, among other reasons, it is the focus both of Yahweh's salvation of his people from Egyptian slavery in the first half of the book, and also his work of salvation in the second half of the book, including his actions in the sanctuary.

C. Yahweh remembers his covenant (3:1–6:27)	**C′. Yahweh makes a covenant with Israel (19–24)**
• Moses comes to Horeb (3:1)	• Israel comes to Horeb (19:1–2)
• God appears in theophany and promises to deliver his people (3:2–12)	• God appears in theophany and promises to make a covenant with his people (19:3–25)
• God reveals his name "I AM" (3:13–15)	• God reveals his Law (20:1–23:19)
• Promised signs of God's presence (3:16–4:17)	• Promise of the angel's presence (23:20–33)
• Covenant neglected: cutting (*kārat*) foreskin and blood (*dām*) (4:24–26)	• Covenant established: cutting (*kārat*) covenant and blood (*dām*) (24:4b–8)
• Moses returns to Egypt and with the elders to worship (*hištaḥawâ*) God (4:18–31)	• Moses and elders worship (*hištaḥawâ*) God (24:1, 9–11)
• Moses introduces *Shabbat* (*šābat*) to the people (5:4, 5)[a]	• Moses ascends to the top of the mountain on "the seventh day" (*Shabbat*) (24:16; cf. 31:12–18; 34:21; 35:1–3)
• Yahweh remembers his covenant (*bərît*) with Abraham, Isaac, and Jacob (6:1–8)	• Yahweh ratifies his covenant (*bərît*) with Israel (24:3–8)

D. Plagues of judgment ("de-creation") (6:28–11:10)	**D′. Plans for building the sanctuary ("creation") (25–31)**
• Pharaoh's building project (cf. 1:11; 5:4–21) derailed (6:28–7:13)	• God's building project detailed (25:1–9)
• Language of "[de]creation" from Gen 1–2: references to all six days of creation in the ten plagues (7:14–11:10)	• Language of creation from Gen 1–2: rhythm of six sections followed by the Sabbath (25:10–31:18)
• God's presence "in the midst" of the land (8:22)	• God's presence "in the midst" of his people (25:8)
• Plagues as "signs" (*'ôt*) (7:3; 8:19; 10:1–2)	• Sabbaths as a "sign" (*'ôt*) (31:13)

E. Feast of Passover and Unleavened Bread (12:1–28)	**E′. Counterfeit feast and worship of the golden calf (32:1–34:10)**
• "Feast [*ḥāg*] to the Lord" (12:14; 13:6)	• "Feast [*ḥāg*] to the Lord" (32:5)
• Instructions regarding Yahweh's feast (12:1–28)	• Description of the idolatrous feast (32:5, 6, 19, 25)
• Yahweh executes judgment against the false gods of Egypt and their worshipers (12:12)	• Moses executes judgment against the false god of Egypt and its worshippers (32:20–28)
• Yahweh "passes through" (*'ābar*) the land and spares those covered by the blood of the lamb, revealing himself as deliverer (12:12, 23, 27)	• Yahweh "passes before" (*'ābar*) Moses, who is covered by Yahweh's hand (33:19, 2), and reveals his name/character (34:6–7)

Revisiting the Literary Structure(s) of Exodus 191

- the people "bowed their heads and worshipped" (*hištaḥawâ*) (12:27)

F. "Decreation": The tenth plague and the exodus from Egypt (12:29–13:16)

- Yahweh acts in "de-creation": he strikes all the firstborn in the land of Egypt not under the blood of the lamb (12:29)

- Yahweh completes the ten plagues of "de-creation" (12:29–35)

- Yahweh gives Israelites favor in sight of the Egyptians and the women borrow *gold* (*zāhāb*), *silver* (*kesep*), and other articles and plunder the Egyptians (12:36; cf. 3:21–22)

- At the *end* (*qēṣ*) of the time predicted Yahweh brings Israel out of the land of Egypt (12:37–41)

- Dateline for Exodus: end of 430 years (12:40–41)

- Repetition of instructions regarding Passover (*pesaḥ*) and Unleavened Bread (*maṣṣōt*) (12:43–13:10)

- Legislation regarding firstborn (*peṭer*) (13:11–16)

G. The presence of Yahweh in the cloud leads his people on their journey (13:17–22)

- Yahweh's presence in the cloud guides Israel in their journey (13:20, 22)

- pillar of cloud (*'ammûd 'ānān*) by day (*yômâm*) and pillar of fire (*'ammûd 'ēš*) by night (*laylâ*) (13:21–22)

- Moses "bowed his head . . . and worshipped" (*hištaḥawâ*) (34:8)

F'. "Creation": The new covenant and the construction of the tabernacle (34:10–40:33)[b]

- "Yahweh acts in "new creation": he makes ("I will make, do" 2 ′) a new covenant with his "first-born" son, Israel (34:10–13; cf. 4:22–23)

- Yahweh gives the ritual Ten Commandments (34:14–28); cf. the sanctuary "creation" completed in ten steps (36:18–39:31)

- Yahweh gives Israelites a willing spirit and they donate *gold* (*zāhāb*), *silver* (*kesep*), and other articles for the building of the sanctuary (35:1–36:7)

- The children of Israel *finish* (*kālā*) the work on the sanctuary as God has commanded (39:32, 43)

- Dateline for erection of the tabernacle: first day of first month (40:2, 17)

- Repetition of instructions regarding Passover (*pesaḥ*) and Unleavened Bread (*maṣṣōt*) (34:18, 25)

- Repetition of legislation regarding firstborn (*peṭer*) (34:19–20)

G'. The presence of Yahweh in the cloud leads his people on their journeys (40:34–38)

- Yahweh's presence in the cloud guides Israel in their journeys (40:36–38)

- cloud (*'ānān*) by day (*yômâm*) and fire (*'ēš*) by night (*laylâ*) (40:38)

---

a. See Mathilde Frey, "Sabbath in Egypt? An Examination of Exodus 5," *JSOT* 39 (2015): 249–63.

b. The items in §F' do not all match in precise canonical order with their parallels in §F, but the inclusion of major unique items from the parallel section is striking. The repetition of instructions regarding Passover and Unleavened Bread and firstborn come at the end of §F and near the beginning of §F', counterbalancing each other.

192   Richard Davidson, Tiago Arrais, and Christian Vogel

Comments

The macrostructure proposed above (structure 3) emerges respecting essentially the same text markers and boundaries as in the seven microstructures (structure I), but builds its double-seven (fourteen-part) structure by subdividing microstructures I and III into three parts each and microstructure VII into four parts.[47]

Many of the same theological insights pointed out by Vogel with regard to his panel structure of the book apply equally well to this structure, inasmuch as the two proposed structures complement one another, even overlapping at many points. In addition to the significant observations arising from the structure Vogel has recognized, the structure that emerged from Davidson's close reading of the book (augmented by Arrais's insights) highlights other features more clearly:

1. The parallel between God's remembering of the covenant in part I of the book (3:1—6:27) and God's ratification of the covenant in the "Book of the Covenant" of part II (19–24);
2. The parallel between God's revelation of his "name"/character "I Am" (3:13–15) and his revelation of the Ten Words (the transcript of his character) and their application (20:1—23:19);
3. Pharaoh's rejection of *Shabbat* in his "building project" (5:4, 5);[48] versus God's implementation of *Shabbat* in his sanctuary-building project (20:8–11; 23:12; 31:12–18; 35:1–3);[49]
4. The theme of "de-creation" in the plagues (6:28; 11:10; 12:29–13:16) contrasted with the "creation" motif in God's building project (25–31; 34:10–40:33);[50]

---

47. These additional divisions are supported by textual markers, and are recognized in various outlines presented in the survey of literature above.

48. See Frey, "Sabbath in Egypt?" 249–63.

49. In Arrais's modified/revised development of this structure in his dissertation, which takes a slightly different path of structural parallels, a potent parallel is noted (Arrais, "Interpretation of Exodus," 223–24). Pharaoh's building project involves seven commands and seven verbs (or verb pairs), beginning with Pharaoh's rejection of the Shabbat (5:4–9), and God's building project is likewise divided into seven sections, divided by the phrase "The Lord spoke to Moses" (seven times), with the last section about the Shabbat (25:1–31:18), paralleling the six days of creation followed by the Shabbat (cf. Gen 1:1–2:4a).

50. In Arrais's adaption of this panel structure (Arrais, "Interpretation of Exodus," 242), the section dealing with De-creation Through Plagues (7:14–12:32) matches the section dealing with Re-creation Through the Tabernacle (35:1–40:33), and the ten plagues are matched with ten steps in the construction of the tabernacle: construction step 1, curtains (36:8–19); step 2, boards, sockets, and veil (36:20–38); step 3, the ark (37:1–9); step 4, the table (37:10–16); step 5, the lampstand (37:17–24); step 6, the altar of incense (37:25–29); step 7, the altar of burnt offering (38:1–7); step 8, the laver of bronze (38:8); step 9, the court items (38:9–20); and step 10, the priestly garments (39:1–31).

Revisiting the Literary Structure(s) of Exodus   193

5. The contrast between Yahweh's feast (*ḥāg*) and true worship (12:1–28) and Israel's counterfeit feast (*ḥāg*) to the Lord in the worship of the golden calf (32:1–34:10);

6. The parallel between Yahweh "passing through" (*'ābar*) the land as Redeemer of those under the blood of the lamb (12:12, 23), and his "passing before" (*'ābar*) Moses to reveal his "name," his "goodness" (33:19, 23; 34:6–7); and

7. Emphasis (by its central placement in the midpoint transition of the block parallelism) upon God's leading his people by his presence in the cloud by day and night (13:17–22; 40:34–38).

Tentative Conclusions and Implications

A close reading of the book of Exodus reveals seven microstructures that span the book, with the middle microstructure pointing toward a theological and thematic apex of the entire book: the saving presence of Yahweh (and Israel's response of faith). The seven microstructures alternate symmetrically between chiastic and panel structures, and also match each other in both form and content, highlighting different aspects of the character, actions, and presence of God.

From a close reading of Exodus also emerge two detailed and overlapping parallel-panel macrostructures encompassing the entire book, one arising from striking parallels between the *beginning* of the book and its midpoint, and the second arising from striking parallels between the *end* of the book and its midpoint.

As we have seen above, the apex of the central microstructure is found in Exod 14 (vv. 30–31). The midpoint break of the panel structure arising from the parallels between the beginning and middle of the book comes in Exod 12 (vv. 37–41). And the panel structure arising from the parallels between the end and middle of the book has its midpoint break in Exod 13 (vv. 17–22). All three of these midpoints, suggested by the three slightly different approaches to the literary structure of the book, focus on one of three major passages in the description of Yahweh's bringing of his people out of Egypt, one at the beginning of the actual exodus (12:37–41), one in the process (13:21–22), and one after the final deliverance at the Red Sea (14:30–31). All three structures are needed to present the complete picture. All of them are interrelated, complementing and supplementing each other, and all highlight the same central theological point of the book: Yahweh's presence to deliver his people.

Besides exegetical and theological considerations, and perhaps most important for the issue of the composition of the Torah, these literary structures may provide a more reliable platform from which to evaluate the presence or absence of the different sources critical scholars generally identify within the book, namely J, E, and P (and their different variations). The exquisite literary artistry that is displayed in the structuring of this book seems to provide potent evidence of the overarching unity and single authorship of the book of Exodus.[51] It seems highly unlikely that a later redactor or redactors would have been able to modify various existing strands of earlier material to produce such exquisite, complex literary artistry and symmetry. What William Shea wrote some years ago regarding the literary structure of the flood narrative seems applicable to the book of Exodus as a whole: "As it stands, the structure could only have come from the hand of one author. Its precise design far transcends any modifications that might have been introduced to mold such sources together by a later editor."[52] What is stated about the flood narrative seems to be even more applicable to the book of Exodus, since the latter combines not one but several intricate interconnected structures that continuously intersect within the book.

This study does not deny the legitimacy of other possible literary macrostructures/outlines in Exodus, based upon theological themes, geographical location, or, particularly, alternation of literary genres, as surveyed in the first section of this essay. But this research is offered as a case study in how more detailed aesthetic literary structuring may inform the theology of Scripture, as well as providing evidence for the unity of its composition.

---

51. Note that this article argues for a single author for the book of Exodus, but it is not the intent of this study to identify this author nor date the authorial work.

52. William H. Shea, "The Structure of the Genesis Flood Narrative and Its Implications," *Origins* 6, no. 1 (1979): 29. Cf. Kikawada and Quinn, *Before Abraham Was*, 83–106.

CHAPTER II

Was Leviticus Composed by Aaronide Priests to Justify Their Cultic Monopoly?

Roy E. Gane
Andrews University

Introduction

Scholars who accept the Documentary Hypothesis maintain that Leviticus reflects the perspectives and interests of the priests who composed it, whether before, during, or after the Babylonian exile.[1] Thus, Joseph Blenkinsopp correlates the nature of the dominant Jerusalem priesthood during the Second Temple period—"a restrictive caste, jealously protective of its privileges and perquisites"—with the "P" legislation—"the self-interested nature of many priestly regulations, for example, those concerning tithes and the allocation of cuts from sacrificed livestock." He notes, "Such self-protective measures, however, characterize practically all skilled professions to this day."[2]

James W. Watts has contributed to historical-critical theory by proposing that the persuasive rhetoric of Lev 1–16 indicates that it was composed by Aaronide priests, using pseudonymous attribution to Moses as a mask, to justify their cultic monopoly, which was first implemented during the Second Temple period.[3] I responded to Watts's proposal in "Didactic Logic and the Authorship

---

1. E.g., Julius Wellhausen, *Prolegomena to the History of Israel* (Edinburgh: Black, 1885; repr., Atlanta: Scholars Press, 1994), 404–5; "An Aaronid priest, or at least someone who was representing the Aaronid priests' interests" (Richard E. Friedman, *Who Wrote the Bible?* [New York: Summit, 1987; repr., New York: HarperOne, 1997], 188); Jacob Milgrom, *Leviticus 1–16: A New Translation with Introduction and Commentary*, AB 3 (New York: Doubleday, 1991), 13. For a summary of critical views regarding the composition and dating of P, including Leviticus, see Roy E. Gane, "Leviticus, Book of," in *Dictionary of Biblical Interpretation*, ed. John H. Hayes (Nashville: Abingdon, 1999), 2:56–58.

2. Joseph Blenkinsopp, *Sage, Priest, Prophet: Religious and Intellectual Leadership in Ancient Israel*, LAI (Louisville: Westminster John Knox, 1995), 67.

3. James W. Watts, *Ritual and Rhetoric in Leviticus: From Sacrifice to Scripture* (Cambridge: Cambridge University Press, 2007), 143–50; cf. Watts, "The Torah as the Rhetoric of Priesthood," in *The Pentateuch as Torah: New Models for Understanding Its Promulgation and Acceptance*, ed. Gary N. Knoppers and Bernard M. Levinson (Winona Lake, IN: Eisenbrauns, 2007), 320. Christophe Nihan similarly argues for dating Leviticus during the period of "the return from exile and the first decades of the Persian period" (Christophe Nihan, *From Priestly Torah to Pentateuch: A Study in the*

of Leviticus.[4] My essay identifies ten logical didactic strategies in Leviticus, which "leave no reasonable doubt that a calculated didactic orientation played a key role in shaping the final form of the book."[5] Indeed, Leviticus is a book of instruction (תּוֹרָה). Watts is right that Leviticus contains persuasive rhetoric, but this rhetoric serves a didactic purpose by encouraging all Israelites, both priests and nonpriests, to follow the instructions.

My "Didactic Logic" essay did not find adequate support within Leviticus for priestly authorship of this book, including chapters 1–16:

> In the final form of Leviticus, all Israelites (priests and laity) are responsible for knowing and following YHWH's authoritative teachings, which mandate much more than cultic domination by a priestly dynasty. The exclusive right of the Aaronides to perform potentially hazardous officiation (Lev 8–9; 10:1–2; 16:1–2; cf. Num 18:1–3), for which they receive "agents' commissions" as support for their service (Lev 6:9, 11, 19, 22; 7:6–10, 31–36; 10:17–18), is not primarily to benefit the Aaronides themselves (contra Watts). Rather, the priestly role is part of a tightly controlled ritual system that makes it possible for holy YHWH to reside among and be accessible to his faulty and often impure people for their benefit without harming them (e.g., 9:5–6, 22–24; 10:3, 10–11; 15:31; 16:16b; cf. Num 18:4–5). . . .

> There is no question that Leviticus can be regarded as "priestly" in the sense that much of its teaching concerns matters that involve priests. However, it is less certain that the author(s) belonged to the priestly profession, or at least primarily wrote in a priestly capacity. It is true that in Leviticus the priests are responsible for teaching laws to the other Israelites, but the priests receive these laws from Moses, whose reception of them from YHWH is what makes them authoritative (e.g., 10:11). In the didactic rhetoric of Leviticus, it is Moses, not a priest, who is the

---

Composition of the Book of Leviticus, FAT, 2nd ser., no. 25 [Tübingen: Mohr Siebeck, 2007], 383–94) and arrives at basically the same overall conclusion: "the depiction of Israel's cult in Lev 1–16 also serves to establish the legitimacy, and to some extent even the supremacy, of the priestly class within the temple community. This is apparent, in particular, in the careful and gradual construction of the figure of Aaron, the high priest, as co-leader of the community alongside Moses" (392; cf. 393–94).

4. Roy E. Gane, "Didactic Logic and the Authorship of Leviticus," in *Current Issues in Priestly and Related Literature: The Legacy of Jacob Milgrom and Beyond*, ed. Roy E. Gane and Ada Taggar-Cohen, RBS 82 (Atlanta: SBL, 2015), 197–221.

5. Gane, "Didactic Logic," 214. The ten strategies are (1) providing necessary background to new information, (2) linking units of information through shared terminology or concepts, (3) comparing and contrasting, (4) introducing concepts for later development, (5) organizing items of information in recognizable progressions, (6) providing perspective through logical hierarchy, (7) reinforcing by repetition, (8) simplifying by separating elements of legislation, (9) simplifying by abbreviating, and (10) illustrating (202–14).

paramount human authority and teacher. The present exploration of didactic logic in Leviticus points away from the idea that the composition of the book took place within a strictly priestly scribal matrix during or originally directed toward the postexilic period.[6]

The present essay continues the discussion with Watts by exploring the topics of priestly monopoly as didactic background in Leviticus, evidence for preexilic control by Aaronide priests and early authority of some instructions in Leviticus, and problems with pseudonymous authorship of Leviticus. I am grateful to Watts for stimulating my thinking and for his gracious clarifying responses to drafts of my earlier "Didactic Logic" essay and the present essay.[7]

Priestly Monopoly as Didactic Background in Leviticus

Given that the purpose of Leviticus is to teach, it makes sense to ask, "Who was trying to teach what and to whom by writing this book?"[8] I could only begin to address this question in my "Didactic Logic" essay with some preliminary observations by distinguishing between didactic background, which a teacher assumes or just mentions because the students already know about it, and didactic foreground, which the teacher presents in detail and/or with emphasis as the new contribution to the students' understanding. The most significant foreground topics in Leviticus as a whole, including chapters 1–16, are (1) establishing and regulating a new sanctuary cult of YHWH to worship him and maintain his presence among his faulty people, including by expiating their sins and physical ritual impurities, (2) the character of YHWH, and (3) bringing all of YHWH's people "into harmony with himself, commanding them to live holy lives in terms of their diet, ethical behavior, and religious practices because he is holy and makes them holy."[9]

By itself, the concept that priests would have a monopoly over the cult in which they serve would be didactic background. Exclusive authorization to perform cultic duties and to receive remuneration from this work has been inherent

6. Ibid., 219–21. Regarding the question of who receives the benefit, cf. Joshua A. Berman's point that the covenant between God and the Israelite people was not for the benefit of any particular group within Israel (including kings, priests, and prophets) or even the Israelite state overall (Joshua A. Berman, *Created Equal: How the Bible Broke with Ancient Political Thought* [Oxford: Oxford University Press, 2008], 47).

7. See esp. Gane, "Didactic Logic," 199. Watts explains that he is not primarily concerned with the issue of authorship and does not think "who wrote the Pentateuch makes so much difference either historically or literarily" (personal communication).

8. Ibid., 216, echoing Watts's question regarding rhetoric (Watts, *Ritual and Rhetoric*, xv).

9. Gane, "Didactic Logic," 218.

198   Roy E. Gane

in the priestly role from early times, so there would be no need for priests who are recognized as such to engage in persuasive strategies to assert these prerogatives. For example, when Abram returned from defeating several kings and recovering possessions and people that they had captured, no doubt along with other spoil, he was met by Melchizedek, "king of Salem" and "priest of God Most High." This priest "brought out bread and wine" and blessed Abram, whereupon Abram "gave him a tenth of everything" (Gen 14:18–20).

Elsewhere in the ANE during the second millennium BC, the Hittite "Instructions to Priests and Temple Officials" command cultic functionaries to properly serve the god all of his food and drink by laying it out before him as a presentation offering. After he is regarded as having consumed it in some sense, they are to secondarily eat and drink it.[10]

According to tablets prescribing rituals for the fourth day of the second millennium Hittite Ninth Year festival of the god Telipinu,[11] the crown prince, assisted by other ritual participants, makes an offering of one bovine and two sheep to the god Telipinu. They lay aside the livers and hearts, roast them, and set them before the god, accompanied by libations of beer and wine. Later, only the four priests of Kašḫa eat the livers and hearts.[12]

A second-millennium text from Emar that prescribes procedures for "The Installation of the Storm-God's High Priestess" specifies payments of silver shekels or animal portions for certain ritual functionaries on that occasion, especially the "diviner."[13] The high priestess herself receives thirty bushels of barley in a good year, but only fifteen bushels of barley in a bad year. Her yearly salary from the temple ("House of the Gods") includes "six hundred (shekels) of wool, two jars of oil, one juglet of oil, four hundred (shekels) of aromatics, five storejars of wine, two racks of grapes, two racks of apples, two racks of apricots, one pot of milk, one large (pot) of soured milk, one bushel of emmer, one bushel of aromatics, three quart jars of malt beer, two pairs of sandals, two pairs of boots, two gazelles, two fish, and four pigeons—per annum."[14]

10. "If [you are able] to eat (and) drink [everyth]ing on that day, eat and drink it. If, however, you are unable to do so, eat and drink [it within] three days. The *piyantalla*-bread, however, [you may not give] to your wives, children, (or) female or male servants. The beer and wine is not to [cross] the threshold of the gods" ("Instructions to Priests and Temple Officials," trans. Gregory McMahon [*COS* 1.83:218], §6). Compare the two-day limit for Israelites to eat from their well-being offerings in Lev 7:16–18; 19:6–8.

11. Of the Hittite tablets prescribing the rituals of the Ninth Year festival of Telipinu, one belongs to the Old or Middle Hittite period and the others are Late Hittite (Piotr Taracha, "Zum Festritual des Gottes Telipinu in Ḫanḫana und in Kašḫa," *AoF* 13 [1986]: 180).

12. Roy E. Gane, *Ritual Dynamic Structure*, GD 14, R2 (Piscataway, NJ: Gorgias, 2004), 247–48, 358–59.

13. "The Installation of the Storm-God's High Priestess," trans. Daniel Fleming (*COS* 1.122:427–28, 430–31).

14. Ibid., 1.122:431.

Thus, priests are like the servants of a human king, who have special access to him in order to perform duties for him and receive support from him that includes eating from his food. In this light, it is to be expected that Israelite priests should receive compensation from offerings and dedications to YHWH at his sanctuary (esp. Num 18),[15] including portions of sacrifices (e.g., Lev 7:34).

Didactic foreground information in the Pentateuch builds on the commonly understood background regarding the general role of priests in the ANE. The foreground identifies the Israelite priests and provides specifics regarding their duties and entitlements within the context of the new cult.

The book of Exodus singles out Aaron and his sons as the original members of the priestly dynasty to serve YHWH (esp. Exod 28–29). Leviticus incorporates this information as background and builds on it in the foreground by describing the consecration (Lev 8) and inauguration (Lev 9) ceremonies that initiate the priestly function of the Aaronides, and by instructing them regarding ritual activities, their portions of offerings brought by the Israelites, religious rules that they need to know and teach, and priestly lifestyle (esp. Lev 1–17; 21:1–24:9; 27). The identity of the priests continues as a foreground topic in the book of Numbers, where Korah and his fellow Levites challenge the exclusive authorization of Aaron and his sons (Num 16). Significantly, the rebels do not question the prerogatives of priesthood; they assume this as background, but want to be priests too so that they can have these prerogatives.

It is true that identification of some specific offering portions that belong to the priests is part of the foreground in Leviticus (2:3, 10; 6:9–11, 19, 22 [16–18, 26, 29]; 7:6–10, 31–36), and also in Num 18. But if priests authored their own job descriptions and remuneration plans, one could wonder why they would claim only the breast and right thigh of the well-being offering for themselves (Lev 7:31–34)[16] when more could be desirable for them, as shown by the behavior of Eli's sons (1 Sam 2:13–16; on which see below). Much more significantly, why would the priests forgo an inheritance of agricultural territory in the land of Israel for themselves and their Levite kinsmen (Num 18:20, 23–24; 26:62; Deut 10:9; 12:12; 14:27, 29; 18:1–2), thereby severely limiting their ability to amass wealth?

One could counter that priestly authors may have deliberately established limits for themselves and sought to display altruism in order to gain and maintain

---

15. Ada Taggar-Cohen finds that Num 18 "seems to suggest clearly the special covenantal status of both groups, priests and Levites, indicating their relations with the divine. In this regard, biblical priesthood shares similar characteristics with the Hittite institution" (Ada Taggar-Cohen, "Covenant Priesthood: Cross-Cultural Legal and Religious Aspects of Biblical and Hittite Priesthood," in *Levites and Priests in Biblical History and Tradition*, ed. Mark Leuchter and Jeremy M. Hutton, AIL 9 [Atlanta: SBL, 2011], 17–18; for comparisons between biblical and Hittite priesthood, see 17–21).

16. Cf. "the shoulder and the two cheeks and the stomach" (Deut 18:3).

200   Roy E. Gane

the popular support on which they depended.[17] But surely they could have asked for more, given the high requirements of some other ancient Near Eastern cults from their constituents.[18]

Thus far, we have found that Leviticus assumes that Aaron and his descendants are to have a cultic monopoly, so establishing this fact cannot be the primary purpose of this book, including its first sixteen chapters (contra Watts). Within the topical flow of the Pentateuch in its canonical form, the concern of Leviticus regarding the priests is to provide important details of their exclusive role.

Preexilic Cultic Control by Aaronide Priests

Watts has concluded that Lev 1–16 was applied to the Aaronide hierocracy that developed during the early Second Temple period.[19] This is undeniably true, but is it the first time that we find evidence of Aaronide control over the Israelite cult?

First Samuel 2, almost certainly a preexilic text,[20] reports the following priestly behavior at the premonarchic temple in Shiloh:

17. Leviticus begins with instructions for the burnt offering (chap. 1), which can be regarded as expressing a selfless ideal. Here Watts finds additional support for his theory, suggesting that the priestly authors placed the burnt offering there to mask "the economic claims and religious authority of Aaronide priests" (Watts, *Ritual and Rhetoric*, 72).

18. Berman compares the modest economic support of Israelite priests and Levites to the privileges and resources of priests in some other ANE cults, who aggressively demanded religious taxes and controlled vast lands and resources (Berman, *Created Equal*, 93–94).

19. Watts, *Ritual and Rhetoric*, 149–50.

20. Gary N. Knoppers views 1 and 2 Samuel, with their emphasis on the ark of the covenant, as significantly earlier than the Deuteronomistic History, which shifts the focus to the temple and is most likely preexilic for several reasons (Gary N. Knoppers, "The Historical Study of the Monarchy: Developments and Detours," in *The Face of Old Testament Studies: A Survey of Contemporary Approaches*, ed. David W. Baker and Bill T. Arnold [Grand Rapids: Baker Academic, 1999], 213–14). Ralph W. Klein regards 1 Sam 2 as antedating the composition of the "Deuteronomistic History" (Ralph W. Klein, "Samuel, Books of," *DBI* 2:432). Moshe Garsiel concludes regarding 1 and 2 Samuel: "The book of Samuel contains ancient and original materials, and both main versions were composed as early as the tenth century BCE" (Moshe Garsiel, "The Book of Samuel: Its Composition, Structure and Significance as a Historiographical Source," *JHebS* 10, no. 5 (2010): 1–42, doi: 10.5508/jhs.2010.v10.a5, url: http://www.jhsonline.org/Articles/article_133.pdf. Some scholars attribute the speech of the "man of God" in 1 Sam 2:27–36 to the Deuteronomistic Historian(s): P. Kyle McCarter Jr., *1 Samuel: A New Translation with Introduction and Commentary*, AB 8 (Garden City, NY: Doubleday, 1980), 92–93; Susan Ackerman, "Who Is Sacrificing at Shiloh? The Priesthoods of Ancient Israel's Regional Sanctuaries," in Leuchter and Hutton, *Levites and Priests*, 26. Marc Brettler suggests that the speech was composed by an exilic Dtr editor, partly because it shows some signs of Late Biblical Hebrew (Marc Brettler, "The Composition of 1 Samuel 1–2," *JBL* 116 [1997]: 609–12). However, Gary Rendsburg argues against Brettler's ideas that vv. 27–36 are an addition to the main narrative and that the language is exilic. Rather than LBH, Rendsburg

Now the sons of Eli were worthless men. They did not know the LORD. The custom of the priests with the people was that when any man offered sacrifice, the priest's servant would come, while the meat was boiling, with a three-pronged fork in his hand, and he would thrust it into the pan or kettle or cauldron or pot. All that the fork brought up the priest would take for himself. This is what they did at Shiloh to all the Israelites who came there. Moreover, before the fat was burned, the priest's servant would come and say to the man who was sacrificing, "Give meat for the priest to roast, for he will not accept boiled meat from you but only raw." And if the man said to him, "Let them burn the fat first, and then take as much as you wish," he would say, "No, you must give it now, and if not, I will take it by force." Thus the sin of the young men was very great in the sight of the LORD, for the men treated the offering of the LORD with contempt (vv. 12–17).

Eli the priest was descended from Aaron.[21] His sons, Hophni and Phinehas, were functioning as priests of YHWH (1 Sam 1:3). As such, they clearly held and enforced some exclusive prerogatives. The passage just quoted (1 Sam 2:12–17) focuses on two abuses of their priestly duties that were sinful. First, the wrongful practice (מִשְׁפַּט)[22] of these particular priests with זֶבַח sacrifices, from which the offerers could eat (cf. Gen 31:54; Lev 3; 7:11–36—well-being offering), was to take meat that belonged to the offerers while the latter were boiling it for their sacred meal (1 Sam 2:13–14).[23] Also, they would demand their priestly portions before the fat was separated out and burned on the altar (1 Sam 2:15–16).

---

finds evidence of the preexilic northern Israelian Hebrew (IH) dialect, which fits the setting of 1 Sam 1–2 in the territory of Ephraim (Gary Rendsburg, "Some False Leads in the Identification of Late Biblical Hebrew Texts: The Cases of Genesis 24 and 1 Samuel 2:27–36," *JBL* 121 [2002]: 35–45).

21. Scholars have developed different reconstructions of the lineage of Eli, who was the great-grandfather of Ahimelech, the priest in the time of David who was murdered at the command of Saul (cf. 1 Sam 14:3; 22:9, 11, 20; 1 Chr 24:3). But it is quite clear that Eli was descended from Aaron (cf. 1 Sam 2:27–28) because 1 Chr 24:1, 3 tells us that Aaron was the ancestor of an Ahimelech who was likely the grandson of the Ahimelech whom Saul murdered.

22. Cf. 1 Sam 27:11 for this usage of מִשְׁפַּט.

23. Here the well-being offering "was boiled (and probably eaten) on the sanctuary premises, and the priests received their remuneration not from the raw but from the boiled meat. The latter practice is actually attested for the boiled shoulder, the priestly perquisite from the Nazirite's ram (Num 6:19), and the former—the tradition of cooking the meat of the well-being offering in the sanctuary courtyard—is attested in Ezekiel's blueprint for the temple (Ezek 46:26 sic v. 24) and in the recorded practice of the Second Temple (*m. Mid.* 2:5)" (Milgrom, *Leviticus 1–16*, 223). "In this passage, the priest's perquisite is not fixed, but is 'whatever the fork brought up.' In this respect the Shilonite custom differed from that of P" (Milgrom, *Leviticus 1–16*, 479). Blenkinsopp similarly points out that there is nothing in P "corresponding to the 'lucky dip' method by which the priest-sons of Eli secured their share of the sacrificial meat (1 Sam 2:13–17)" (Blenkinsopp, *Sage, Priest, Prophet*, 70). He uses this as support for his argument against a preexilic date of P, exemplifying

202   Roy E. Gane

Interpreters have noted the apparent lack of priestly officiation activity at the Shiloh temple. There is no mention of the priests performing applications of blood to the altar (cf. 1 Sam 1:25), and, on the basis of grammatical ambiguity in 1 Sam 2:15–16, some scholars have questioned whether the priests themselves were supposed to burn the fat on the altar.[24] Richard D. Nelson has suggested that 1 Sam 2 describes an early stage of Israelite cult in which "Eli and his sons were primarily guardians of the ark and temple at Shiloh and played no special role in the sacrificial ritual except to collect their tariff (1 Sam. 2:13–14)."[25]

However, the concern of 1 Sam 2 is to point out some particularly egregious cultic abuses regarding sacrificial portions, for which Eli's sons were responsible. Apparently blood manipulation was not such an issue, so it is not mentioned. The fact that 1 Samuel refers to laypersons offering sacrifices, including performing sacrificial slaughter (1:3–4, 21, 25; 2:13) as offerers, is no evidence that the priests did not possess the right to act as officiants.[26] Even if the phrase "Let them burn the fat first" in 1 Sam 2:16 could refer to someone other than the priests burning the fat,[27] this would not require the conclusion that it was not the duty of the priests to perform this activity. The point here could be that the priests should at least allow YHWH's fat to be burned for him, even if they would not do it themselves.

Taking the above considerations into account, the sons of Eli controlled the Shiloh cult to the extent that they could do whatever they wanted, even against the will of the people and their duty to YHWH. So 1 Sam 2 provides evidence for a kind of preexilic Aaronide priestly monopoly (cf. 1 Sam 14:3). The passage quoted above (1 Sam 2:12–17) and the prophetic rebuke by "a man of God" later in the same chapter (vv. 27–36) do not question the legitimacy of Aaronide cultic control per se. The problem was that Eli's sons were abusing this control.

---

his point that "practices alluded to in texts generally thought to be preexilic rarely, if ever, confirm the antiquity of practices described in P and are often quite different" (ibid.). However, he ignores the reason for the difference that is clearly expressed in 1 Samuel: the sons of Eli were breaking YHWH's rules.

24. Georg Braulik, "Were Women, Too, Allowed to Offer Sacrifices in Israel? Observations on the Meaning and Festive Form of Sacrifice in Deuteronomy," *HvTSt* 55 (1999): 921; Ackerman, "Who Is Sacrificing at Shiloh?" 27–28.

25. Richard D. Nelson, *Raising Up a Faithful Priest: Community and Priesthood in Biblical Theology* (Louisville: Westminster John Knox, 1993), 46–47; cf. 11. Ackerman has proposed that the temple at Shiloh may have been only a regional sanctuary, which was not bound by all the protocols of the central shrine (Ackerman, "Who Is Sacrificing at Shiloh?" 29–43), but this possibility is ruled out by the fact that the ark of the covenant was at Shiloh (1 Sam 3:3; 4:3–4).

26. Aalred Cody did not adequately distinguish between the cooperative roles of offerer and officiant (cf. Lev 3; 7:29–36) when he wrote that "the priesthood at Shiloh was a priesthood of sanctuary attendants. They had no monopoly on sacrifice, for we know that Samuel's father Elkanah sacrificed as a pilgrim to the sanctuary they frequented (1 Sam. 1:3)" (Aalred Cody, *A History of Old Testament Priesthood*, AnBib 35 [Rome: Pontifical Biblical Institute, 1969], 72).

27. "4QSam*a* *yqtr hkwhn*, 'let the priest burn,' shows an explicating expansion" (McCarter, *I Samuel*, 79).

Other biblical passages also indicate the right of the Aaronide priests to control the cult before the exile. First Kings 8, recounting the dedication of the First Temple, describes the priests as performing special duties that require unique access to the cult (vv. 3–4, 6, 10–11).

In 2 Kgs 12, King Jehoash (Joash) orders the priests to repair the temple (v. 6 [5]) with "all the money of the holy things that is brought into the house of the LORD, the money for which each man is assessed—the money from the assessment of persons—and the money that a man's heart prompts him to bring into the house of the LORD" (v. 5 [4]). These donations to YHWH from the people that were flowing into the temple (cf., e.g., Lev 27) were controlled by the priests.

When the repair work was not done because the priests were keeping the contributions to the temple for themselves, "Jehoiada the priest took a chest and bored a hole in the lid of it and set it beside the altar on the right side as one entered the house of the LORD. And the priests who guarded the threshold put in it all the money that was brought into the house of the LORD" (v. 10 [9]). Here priests had the duty of guarding the entrance to the temple in order to control access to it.[28]

Second Kings 12:17 [16] refers to another category of sacred funds: "Now as for the money for compensation and purification offerings, it wasn't brought to the LORD's temple. It belonged to the priests" (CEB).[29] This money was not for repairs because it was to purchase sacrifices, apparently from animals owned by the temple.[30]

Jeremiah 33 offers a message of hope: "For thus says the LORD: David shall never lack a man to sit on the throne of the house of Israel, and the Levitical priests shall never lack a man in my presence to offer burnt offerings, to burn grain offerings, and to make sacrifices forever" (vv. 17–18). As the Davidic kings were to rule the nation, the priests were to be YHWH's ministers, operating and controlling the cult. Verses 20–21 reinforce these promises by affirming the immutability of the divine covenants with David and the priests.

The passages cited in this section provide evidence for the preexilic origin of exclusive Aaronide governance of the cult, with its responsibilities, entitlements,

---

28. See also 2 Kgs 22:4, in the context of the temple repair ordered by Josiah: "Go up to Hilkiah the high priest, that he may count the money that has been brought into the house of the LORD, which the keepers of the threshold have collected from the people." In 2 Kings, "keepers of the threshold" also appear in 23:4; 25:18.

29. The "compensation and purification offerings" were the אָשָׁם, "reparation offering" (so-called "guilt offering"; cf. Lev 5:14–26 [6:7]; 7:1–7), and חַטָּאוֹת (pl. of חַטָּאת), "purification offerings" (so-called "sin offerings"; cf. 4:1–5:13), respectively.

30. Milgrom, Leviticus 1–16, 287–88. For the idea that money could be brought for sacrifices, cf. Lev 5, where the reparation offering is convertible into silver: "an individual would bring the equivalent in silver shekels, and the priests would provide the required animal (5:15)" (Milgrom, Leviticus 1–16, 287).

204 Roy E. Gane

and sources of remuneration.[31] Therefore, it was not the adoption of Lev 1–16 as normative Scripture during the Persian and Greek periods that initiated the Aaronide hierocracy (contra Watts). Either the priestly monopoly developed in the preexilic era apart from Leviticus, or at least some of the instructions in this book played a role in establishing Aaronide priestly control before the exile. The next section argues for the latter.

Evidence for Early Authority of Some Instructions in Leviticus

In 1 Sam 2, on what basis could the author of the book and a "man of God" critique the ritual activities of the Aaronide priests? The ritual rules that Hophni and Phinehas were violating are found in Leviticus, especially 7:28–34:

> The Lord said to Moses: "Say to the Israelites: 'The one who offers his shared sacrifice of well-being to the Lord will bring his offering for the Lord from his shared sacrifice of well-being. His hands will bring the Lord's food gifts. He will bring the fat with the breast, to have the breast raised as a raised offering before the Lord. The priest will turn the fat into smoke on the altar, but the breast will belong to Aaron and his sons. You will give the right thigh as a contribution to the priest from your shared sacrifices of well-being. The right thigh will be the portion of the one among Aaron's sons who offers the blood and fat of the well-being offering. For I have taken the raised offering breast and the contribution thigh from the Israelites, from their shared sacrifices of well-being, and have assigned them to Aaron the priest and to his sons as a permanent portion from the Israelites.'"[32]

Here the priest must burn the fat/suet of the well-being offering on the altar as a "food gift" for the Lord (cf. Lev 3:5, 11, 16) before taking the breast and right thigh as the portions allocated to the priests,[33] leaving the remainder of the meat for the offerer to eat as a sacred meal (cf. Lev 7:15–21). By not first burning the fat, the sons of Eli were invalidating the sacrifice and showing contempt for God. If they were not even burning the fat later, even though all of it belonged to YHWH ("All fat is the Lord's," Lev 3:16), they were committing deliberate

---

31. See also the preexilic role of priests in the reform of Hezekiah, recounted postexile in 2 Chr 29, and the way in which priests withstood King Uzziah when he was about to burn incense in the temple, thereby asserting their exclusive Aaronide prerogatives (2 Chr 26:18).

32. Trans. Roy E. Gane and William Gilders, draft of "Leviticus" translation for CEB.

33. Cf. Deut 18:3: "the shoulder and the two cheeks and the stomach."

sacrilege by stealing from God, for which there was no remedy through expiatory sacrifice.[34]

By greedily extorting meat that belonged to the offerers, Hophni and Phinehas diminished their sacred meal with the Lord, which was the point of bringing a well-being offering.[35] If the sacrifice was invalidated and the people could not fully enjoy their meal, they had little or no incentive to bring such an offering to YHWH at all.

So what is the relationship between 1 Sam 2 and Leviticus? Obviously, these sources belong to different literary genres and relate to the Israelite cult in different ways at different times. Nevertheless, we have found that where the ritual concerns of 1 Sam 2 and Leviticus overlap, they are in basic agreement regarding procedures that should be followed. We cannot prove that the final form of Leviticus was already functioning as authoritative, canonical Scripture in the days of Eli and his sons. However, at least some of the people who suffered under their regime knew that they were violating existing cultic norms, as shown by a man's response to the priest's assistant in 1 Sam 2:16: "Let them burn the fat first, and then take as much as you wish."

The first part of the speech of the "man of God" to Eli in 1 Sam 2 expresses the belief that the Aaronide priesthood and its regulations originated from God when the Israelites departed from Egypt, in agreement with the books of Exodus and Leviticus.[36] The man announced:

This is what the LORD says: I revealed myself very clearly to your father's household when they were slaves in Egypt to the house of Pharaoh. I chose your father from all of Israel's tribes to be my priest, to go up onto my altar, to burn incense, and to wear the priestly vest in my presence. I also gave all of the Israelites' food offerings to your father's household. Why then do you kick my sacrifices and my offerings—the very

---

34. Only inadvertent sacrilege is expiable by a reparation offering (Lev 5:14–16). If they left the fat in the meat that they took and consumed, Hophni and Phinehas also violated the prohibition in Leviticus against eating the fat of sacrificeable animals (Lev 3:16–17; 7:22–25), thereby incurring the terminal divinely administered penalty of "cutting off" (*niphal* of the root כ.ר.ת), i.e., extirpation (Lev 7:25).

35. Bill T. Arnold is on target: "The specific nature of the sins of Hophni and Phinehas has to do with their rights as priests. The Old Testament law provided proper and just ways for priests to share in certain meat portions of animals offered at the tabernacle (Lev. 7:28–36; Deut. 18:3). But Eli's sons at Shiloh have devised their own system, using a fork to pilfer the choicest meat, including the fat usually burned entirely for Yahweh. If the worshiper does not yield to the grasping priests, Eli's sons threaten to take it by force. The narrator summarizes their great sin as 'treating the Lord's offering with contempt' (2:17)" (Bill T. Arnold, *1 & 2 Samuel*, NIV Application Commentary [Grand Rapids: Zondervan, 2003], 71).

36. For references to some scholars who maintain that this speech was an editorial addition by the Deuteronomistic Historian(s) or Dtr editor, see above.

206   Roy E. Gane

ones I commanded for my dwelling place? Why do you respect your sons more than me, getting fat off the best parts of every offering from my people Israel? Because of all that, this is what the LORD, the God of Israel, declares: I had promised that your household and your father's household would serve me forever. But now—this is what the LORD declares: I'll do no such thing! No. I honor those who honor me, and whoever despises me will be cursed" (vv. 27–30 CEB).

This understanding of the priesthood does not support the idea that one or more priests composed Leviticus, or traditions incorporated into it, in order to mandate an Aaronide monopoly over the cult. The priests were subject to rules of a higher authority that they had no right to make or change, whether for their own benefit or anyone else's. Their exclusive rights were to carry out special duties, and their entitlements had strict limits.

A number of prophets from the preexilic era through the exile and into the postexilic Persian period followed in the footsteps of the "man of God" and Samuel (1 Sam 2:27–36; 3:10–18) by rebuking priests in the name of YHWH (Isa 28:7; Jer 2:8; 5:31; 6:13; 23:11; Ezek 22:26; Mic 3:11; Zeph 3:4; Mal 1:6-2:9), holding them accountable to standards set by him. There is no hint that the prophets held the priests accountable to compliance with rules that the priests themselves had made.

Problems with Pseudonymous Authorship of Leviticus

Adherents of the Documentary Hypothesis generally regard Moses as legendary or fictional.[37] If they are right, biblical attribution of Leviticus to Moses is pseudonymous in order to imbue legislation produced by priestly tradents with authority in order to encourage people to comply with their agenda.[38] Thus, this

---

37. E.g., "indeed, the whole presentation of Moses in the Pentateuch in its present form may be described as the religious fiction of a later time" (Roger N. Whybray, *The Making of the Pentateuch: A Methodological Study*, JSOTSup 53 [Sheffield: JSOT Press, 1987], 240).

38. Thus, Watts maintains that priestly authors disguised their role "by hiding behind God and Moses, and casting their speeches in the distant past" in order to "use the voice of God and the actions of Moses to legitimize the role and authority of the Aaronide priests" (Watts, *Ritual and Rhetoric*, 150); cf. "It is historical only in form; the history serves merely as a framework on which to arrange the legislative material, or as a mask to disguise it" (Wellhausen, *Prolegomena*, 7); cf. "it tries hard to imitate the costume of the Mosaic period, and, with whatever success, to disguise its own" (9). "Watts does not think of the priestly authors as especially 'deceptive,' but regards their persuasive rhetoric as typical of ancient Near Eastern priestly rhetoric in general, which places priestly and temple prerogatives in the mouths of kings or, less often, gods" (Gane, "Didactic Logic," 199, citing James W. Watts, "Ritual Rhetoric in Ancient Near Eastern Texts," in

theory rejects the explicit pentateuchal narrative and replaces it with a hypothetical scholarly one.

Of course, nobody can prove that Moses or another prophet or a group of priests wrote Lev 1–16 or other parts of the Pentateuch. Conversely, however, neither can anyone definitively rule out any of these possibilities as an assured result of scholarship. In this section, I probe some weaknesses of the pseudonymous authorship theory in relation to the question of a historical Moses. My goal here is to question the confidence of those who assume that the pentateuchal narrative could not possibly be factual.

First, why do ANE scholars accept the historicity of Gudea, the ruler of Lagash about 2100 BC,[39] but biblical scholars reject the historicity of Moses, whom the biblical narrative framework places over half a millennium later? A detailed Sumerian composition on two cylinders of Gudea recounts his building and dedication of a new Eninnu temple for the god Ningirsu,[40] in which he claims to have received communication from his deity Ningirsu to build a temple.[41] This does not make him legendary or fictional[42] or use of his name pseudonymous. So what is the difference between him and Moses, who is said to have received analogous information from his deity YHWH (Exod 25:8–9, 40)?[43] To be consistent, this should not be enough to neutralize or diminish the

---

Ancient Non-Greek Rhetorics, ed. Carol Lipson and Roberta Binckley, Lauer Series in Rhetoric and Composition [West Lafayette, IN: Parlor, 2009], 39–66, and personal communication).

39. E.g., Michael Roaf, *Cultural Atlas of Mesopotamia and the Ancient Near East* (New York: Facts on File, 1990), 99–100; Dominique Charpin, "The History of Ancient Mesopotamia: An Overview," in *Civilizations of the Ancient Near East*, ed. Jack M. Sasson, 4 vols. (New York: Charles Scribner's Sons, 1995), 2:811; Amélie Kuhrt, *The Ancient Near East, c. 3000–330 BC*, Routledge History of the Ancient World (London: Routledge, 1995), 1:58; "The Cylinders of Gudea," trans. Richard E. Averbeck (*COS* 2.155:417).

40. "Cylinders of Gudea," *COS* 2.155:417–33. There are notable similarities between the Gudea cylinders and other ANE sanctuary/temple building accounts, including those in Exod 25–40, 1 Kgs 5–9, and Ezek 40–48 (2.155:417; Victor Hurowitz, "The Priestly Account of Building the Tabernacle," *JAOS* 105 [1985]: 21–30 [esp. 25–26]; Victor Hurowitz, *I Have Built You an Exalted House: Temple Building in the Bible in Light of Mesopotamian and North-West Semitic Writings*, JSOTSup 115 [Sheffield: Sheffield Academic Press, 1992], esp. 56, 109–10; D. M. Sharon, "A Biblical Parallel to a Sumerian Temple Hymn? Ezekiel 40–48 and Gudea," *JANES* 24 [1996]: 103–5).

41. He says that he received the commission and vision for the temple in dreams (Cyl. A i.15–21 and A ix.5–xii.11; "Cylinders of Gudea," *COS* 2.155:419, 423–24).

42. Cf. Benjamin R. Foster, "Transmission of Knowledge," in *A Companion to the Ancient Near East*, ed. Daniel C. Snell, Blackwell Companions to the Ancient World (Malden, MA: Blackwell, 2007), 262.

43. Cf. YHWH giving David the plan for Solomon's temple in 1 Chr 28:11–19. Another historical figure who claimed that there was divine revelation concerning a cultic matter was the Hittite king Ḫattušili III (1267–ca. 1240 BC): "(Now,) Ištar, My Lady, sent Muwatalli, my brother to Muršili, my father, through a dream (saying): 'For Ḫattušili the years (are) short, he is not to live (long). Hand him over to me, and let him be my priest, so he (will) live" ("Apology of Ḫattušili III," trans. Th. P. J. van den Hout [*COS* 1.77:199]). Compare YHWH's communication through Moses to designate Aaron and his sons as his priests (Exod 28:1).

real existence of Moses as a historical person.[44] There have been plenty of other prophets or alleged prophets from biblical times up to the present who are readily accepted as historical.

It is true that we have the original cylinders that date to the time of Gudea and other early artifacts pertaining to him, most notably a number of well-crafted black diorite inscribed statues of this ruler.[45] By contrast, "currently there are no existing nonbiblical contemporary sources that specifically mention Moses and the exodus. Furthermore, the Pentateuch lacks the type of information that contemporary historians demand: a clear witness to the use of sources close to the period described (i.e., annals, chronicles, inscriptions) and a backing of chronology that lines up with contemporary material."[46] So a case could be made against the historicity of Moses on the basis of silence, but this kind of argument is logically weak. As is often said, "absence of evidence is not evidence of absence."

Second, the argument for silence against the historicity of Moses is weakened by the fact that there are several plausible explanations for lack of earlier extant evidence for him. For one thing, it is likely that early written copies of pentateuchal books or portions of what is now the Pentateuch would have been relatively few. This could partly explain the importance of the discovery of the "Book of the Law (תּוֹרָה)" in the temple by Hilkiah the high priest during the reign of Josiah (2 Kgs 22:8, 10–11; 23:2–3, 21, 24). The few texts would have been vulnerable because they were likely written on papyrus, parchment (e.g., Jer 36:22–23), or other materials that would not survive for centuries and could easily be destroyed by fires, such as those kindled by invading armies.[47]

Moreover, the Bible and archaeology attest to widespread departure from the religion mandated by the Pentateuch throughout much of the preexilic era. There is abundant archaeological evidence of idolatry during this period, and 2 Kgs 23 reports concerning the Passover that was observed in Jerusalem in the eighteenth year of Josiah (v. 23): "For no such Passover had been kept since the days of the judges who judged Israel, or during all the days of the kings of Israel or of the kings of Judah" (v. 22; cf. 2 Chr 35:18).[48] It appears that the few

---

44. Cf. Kenneth A. Kitchen, *On the Reliability of the Old Testament* (Grand Rapids: Eerdmans, 2003), 300.

45. Kuhrt, *Ancient Near East*, 1:58; Marie-Henriette Gates, "Archaeology and the Ancient Near East: Methods and Limits," in Snell, *Companion to the Ancient Near East*, 67; Marian H. Feldman, "Mesopotamian Art," in Snell, *Companion to the Ancient Near East*, 313–15.

46. Mark W. Chavalas, "Moses," *DOTP* 571.

47. Kitchen, *On the Reliability*, 305; Garsiel, "Book of Samuel," 28.

48. Second Chronicles 30 records a Passover celebration during the reign of Hezekiah, but the whole event was delayed from the fourteenth day of the first month (Lev 23:5) to the fourteenth day of the second month (2 Chr 30:15; cf. Num 9:11), and most of the people were ritually impure (2 Chr 30:18; contrast Num 9:6–13). Second Chronicles 30:26 reports that "since the time of Solomon the son of David king of Israel there had been nothing like this in Jerusalem."

existing copies of parts of the Pentateuch were neglected, as indicated by the fact that the Book of the Law found by Hilkiah had been lost in the temple during the previous years of apostasy.

It appears that this neglect could at least partly explain the paucity of evidence in the historical and prophetic writings of the Hebrew Bible for the impact of Lev 1–16 on Israelite life during the preexilic period. Other explanations are less convincing. It is true that the priests were the custodians of the ritual legislation, which was idealistic and applied to the inner world of the cult.[49] However, this body of instruction was not intended to be a priestly secret, as ritual knowledge was in at least some other ancient Near Eastern cults.[50] Much of it was addressed to all Israelites (Lev 1:2; 4:2; 7:23, 29, etc.), and the priests were to teach it to them (Lev 10:11).[51]

Third, the historical plausibility (although not proof) of the pentateuchal witness to Moses is supported by analogues with Late Bronze Age textual and archaeological materials.[52] Kenneth A. Kitchen has observed that

to explain what exists in our Hebrew documents we need a Hebrew leader who had had experience of life at the Egyptian court, mainly in the East Delta (hence at Pi-Ramesse), including knowledge of treaty-type documents and their format, as well as of traditional Semitic legal/social usage more familiar to his own folk. In other words, somebody distressingly like that old "hero" of biblical tradition, Moses, is badly needed at this point, to make any sense of the situation as we have it. Or somebody in his position of the same or another name. On the basis of the series of features in Exodus to Deuteronomy that belong to the late second millennium *and not later*, there is, again, no other viable option.[53]

49. Menahem Haran (*Temples and Temple-Service in Ancient Israel: An Inquiry into Biblical Cult Phenomena and the Historical Setting of the Priestly School* [Winona Lake, IN: Eisenbrauns, 1985], 9–12) and Israel Knohl (*The Sanctuary of Silence: The Priestly Torah and the Holiness School* [Minneapolis: Fortress, 1995], 203) have cited these factors to counter the assumption of the classical Documentary Hypothesis (Wellhausen, etc.) that because the priestly writings lacked influence on Israel's life during the preexilic era, they did not yet exist.

50. Contra Haran, *Temples and Temple-Service*, 143–44; and Chaim Cohen, "Was the P Document Secret?" *JANESCU* 1 (1969): 39–44—with Mesopotamian examples, arguing for the similar secrecy of the P document to explain P's apparent lack of preexilic influence.

51. Cf. "It is telling that the Bible never depicts priests or scribes as jealous or protective of their writing skills. The notion of scribes feeling . . . that it is a tragedy if divine knowledge falls into the wrong hands, as Ipuwer put it in the Egyptian Middle Kingdom . . . , is alien to biblical thought" (Berman, *Created Equal*, 116). As pointed out in my "Didactic Logic" essay, it is difficult to imagine why the author(s) of Lev 1–16 would have this legislation address laypersons as well as priests, thereby making priests vulnerable to critique, if the authors themselves were priests concerned with establishing their own authority (Gane, "Didactic Logic," 199, 221).

52. Chavalas, "Moses," 571–77; Kitchen, *On the Reliability*, 295–99. On Deuteronomy as interpretation of actual history, see ibid., 300–304.

53. Kitchen, *On the Reliability*, 295.

Fourth, it is true that the earliest extant copies of the pentateuchal texts that refer to Moses, including Leviticus, were discovered at Qumran and date to the Second Temple period.[54] However, the Dead Sea Scrolls are canonical texts. Determining the date of composition of a canonical text that is preserved only in late copies is notoriously challenging, but scholars do not hesitate to acknowledge that such an ANE text, such as the Seleucid-era tablets of the Babylonian New Year (*Akītu*) festival, may go back to much earlier originals.[55] In the case of the Pentateuch, William M. Schniedewind cites two important factors indicating that it was composed before the Exile: the language is classical Hebrew, not late Hebrew, and it gives a prominent role to the northern tribes of Israel.[56]

An important piece of evidence for earlier origin of the Babylonian New Year festival tablets is their inclusion of a prominent ritual role for the king of Babylon,[57] an office that was gone before the Seleucid period. However, biblical scholars struggle to dismiss internal evidence for the reverse in the Pentateuch: there is a surprising lack of a ritual role for a monarch anywhere in the Israelite cult, and the legislation of Deut 17:14–20 explicitly indicates that a king is only a future possibility, in harmony with the pentateuchal narrative. Therefore, it appears that at least this portion of Deuteronomy was authored before the period of the Israelite monarchy. Ezekiel, the priestly prophet, gives a ritual role to a postexilic "prince" (44:3; 45:16–17, 22; 46:2, 4, 12), so why shouldn't Leviticus—if it knew of a monarch?

Fifth, in agreement with the narrative in Exodus–Deuteronomy, according to which Moses transmitted instructions from YHWH to the Israelites, other biblical books consistently attribute the foundation of Israelite law to Moses (e.g., Josh 8:30–35; 11:14–15; 13:14, 33; 1 Kgs 2:3; 8:9; 2 Kgs 14:6; 18:6, 12; 21:8;

---

54. See, e.g., Martin Abegg Jr., Peter Flint, and Eugene Ulrich, *The Dead Sea Scrolls Bible: The Oldest Known Bible Translated for the First Time into English* (New York: HarperSanFrancisco, 1999). For translation of DSS manuscripts of the pentateuchal books, with manuscript references, see 3–195 (Leviticus: 77–107). Also, "Astonishingly, every chapter of the book of Leviticus is referenced somewhere in the nonbiblical scrolls" (Abegg, Flint, and Ulrich, *Dead Sea Scrolls Bible*, 78).

55. "The program described may go back to a much earlier time" ("Temple Program for the New Year's Festival at Babylon," trans. A. Sachs [*ANET*, 331]). On the antiquity and long history of such *Akītu* festivals in Mesopotamia, see Mark E. Cohen, *The Cultic Calendars of the Ancient Near East* (Bethesda, MD: CDL, 1993), 400–453. Cf., regarding a Hittite text: "The copies date to the Empire period, but the text itself seems to go back to the pre-New Hittite period, before the reign of Šuppiluliuma I" ("Instructions to Priests and Temple Officials," *COS* 1.83:217). On the dating of this text, Ada Taggar-Cohen notes, "All the fragments of CTH 264 are written in the New Hittite script of the New Kingdom, but their language, . . . indicates possible Middle Kingdom sources" (Ada Taggar-Cohen, *Hittite Priesthood*, THeth 26 [Heidelberg: Universitätsverlag Winter, 2006], 34).

56. William M. Schniedewind, *How the Bible Became a Book: The Textualization of Ancient Israel* (New York: Cambridge University Press, 2004), 82–83; cf. Milgrom's arguments for preexilic composition of P, although with some possible exilic supplementation and redaction (Milgrom, *Leviticus 1–16*, 3–13).

57. "Temple Program for the New Year's Festival at Babylon," *ANET*, 334.

23:25). If such attribution was pseudonymous, how would it have infected these books, especially if the Pentateuch was written later, as many critics claim? But if the Pentateuch was written before the Exile, where is evidence that pseudepigraphical literature was already developing in Israel during that period?[58]

Sixth, the point of utilizing the name or persona of a famous individual, as in a pseudepigraphical composition, is to capitalize on that person's established reputation in order to gain credibility or authority. However, if a historical Moses never existed, at least not as a man who interacted with YHWH and received important communications from him, how would he have acquired such a significant reputation as a man of God that ancient writings, such as Leviticus, would use him so prominently as a mask for authorship by one or more others? After the Pentateuch established Moses's towering credentials, a later composition, such as the *Testament of Moses* (probably early first century AD), could hitch onto it. But Leviticus is part of the Pentateuch, on which Moses's reputation is based.

It could be argued that a mask of Moses in Leviticus draws on the personality of this character portrayed in an earlier book, such as Exodus. But then the question of historicity versus persuasive pseudonymity simply shifts to that book, and if he is historical there, why not in Leviticus? Authority must be established somewhere before it can be credibly extended by pseudonymity, especially when so much weight is placed on the authority.

Conclusion

This essay has continued discussion with James W. Watts, who has proposed that Lev 1–16 was composed by Aaronide priests, using pseudonymous attribution to Moses as a mask, to justify their cultic monopoly, which was first implemented during the Second Temple period. Against Watts's theory, we have found that the priestly prerogatives of the Aaronides are only didactic background in Leviticus;

---

58. Pseudepigraphical literature is abundantly attested in Jewish Second Temple period writings (James H. Charlesworth, ed., *The Old Testament Pseudepigrapha*, 2 vols. [Peabody, MA: Hendrickson, 1983]) and also elsewhere in the ancient Near East (Tremper Longman III, *Fictional Akkadian Autobiography: A Generic and Comparative Study* [Winona Lake, IN: Eisenbrauns, 1991]. Cf. Watts, "Ritual Rhetoric," 39–66. Watts summarizes: "Prevailing rhetorical norms, however, hid the role of priests and even prophets behind the voice and authority of kings or, sometimes, of gods. For example, though Egyptian ritual texts were always under the control of lector priests in the temple libraries, over time they were increasingly credited to the authorship of the god Thoth" (48). Because Watts believes that P most likely was produced during the Second Temple period, when pseudepigraphical literature flourished, he can continue: "The Pentateuch's presentation of priestly texts through a divine voice exhibits Israel's distinctive manifestation of this widespread convention of ancient priestly rhetoric to hide behind royal and divine voices" (48).

already in preexilic times there is evidence for Aaronide cultic control and functioning authority of some instructions in Leviticus; and there are significant weaknesses in the theory that Moses appears in Leviticus as a fictional character rather than a historical figure.

Even if Watts were right in concluding that the primary purpose for writing Lev 1–16 was to establish a cultic monopoly for priests descended from Aaron, it would not necessarily follow that the beneficiaries of the persuasive rhetoric in Leviticus were its authors, that is, Aaronide priests. Some kinds of persuasion are used by one party for the benefit of others.[59] For instance, the rhetoric of genuine biblical prophets was communicated for the best interests of others, often to the detriment of the prophets' own well-being. When they critiqued priests (Isa 28:7, etc.; see above), they did so for the benefit of their people, not for themselves.

The role of prophets was to convey messages from YHWH, to whom priests were accountable, and Leviticus claims that its divine speeches originated with him. So it is at least theoretically possible that the core authorship of Lev 1–16 was prophetic rather than priestly.

To acknowledge the uncertainty of excluding the possibility that Lev 1–16 was authored by a historical Moses, functioning as a prophet,[60] is not to adopt unscholarly, credulous faith in tradition over true critical, scholarly science. This uncertainty is simply a matter of fact and logic, objectively acknowledging the limits of available historical evidence regarding a canonical ancient Near Eastern composition.

---

59. E.g., intercession, such as in prayers of Moses (Exod 32:11–13; Num 14:13–19).

60. According to Deut 34:10, Moses was a uniquely great prophet. Blenkinsopp refers to prophets continuing "the role and activity of Moses the protoprophet" (Blenkinsopp, *Sage, Priest, Prophet*, 120). Of course, Moses also fulfilled a kind of priestly role before the Aaronides were fully authorized to function as priests (Exod 24:6; Lev 8).

Chapter 12

The Reception of Priestly Laws in Deuteronomy and Deuteronomy's Target Audience

Benjamin Kilchör
Staatsunabhängige Theologische Hochschule Basel

> In the fifth [book] . . . Moses repeats the whole law, with the story of all that has happened to them (except what concerns the priesthood), and explains anew everything that belongs either to the bodily or to the spiritual government of a people.
> —Martin Luther, *Prefaces to the Books of the Bible* (*Vorreden zur Heiligen Schrift*)

In my book *Mosetora und Jahwetora*, I argue that the Deuteronomic law presupposes Exodus, Leviticus, and Numbers more or less in their present shape and in quasicanonical prestige. While it is widely acknowledged that there is an intertextual relationship between the Deuteronomic law and the Covenant Code,[1] and also between the Deuteronomic law and the Holiness Code[2] (regard-

---

1. See, e.g., Samuel R. Driver, *A Critical and Exegetical Commentary on Deuteronomy*, 2nd ed., ICC (Edinburgh: T&T Clark, 1896), iii–xix; Benjamin Kilchör, "Frei aber arm? Soziale Sicherheit als Schlüssel zum Verhältnis der Sklavenfreilassungsgesetze im Pentateuch," *VT* 62 (2012): 381–97; Kilchör, "The Direction of Dependence Between the Laws of the Pentateuch," *ETL* 89 (2013): 1–14; Kilchör, *Mosetora und Jahwetora: Das Verhältnis von Deuteronomium 12–26 zu Exodus, Levitikus und Numeri*, BZABR 21 (Wiesbaden: Harrassowitz, 2015); Bernard M. Levinson, *Deuteronomy and the Hermeneutics of Legal Innovation* (Oxford: Oxford University Press, 1997); Levinson, "The Manumission of Hermeneutics: The Slave Laws of the Pentateuch as a Challenge to Contemporary Pentateuchal Theory," in *Congress Volume Leiden 2004*, ed. André Lemaire, VTS 109 (Leiden: Brill, 2006), 281–324; Norbert Lohfink, "Fortschreibung? Zur Technik von Rechtsrevisionen im Deuteronomischen Bereich, Erörtert an Deuteronomium 12, Ex 21,2–11 und Dtn 15,12–18," in *Das Deuteronomium und Seine Querbeziehungen*, ed. Timo Veijola, SFEG 62 (Helsinki: Finnische Exegetische Gesellschaft, 1996), 127–71; John Van Seters, *A Law Book for the Diaspora: Revision in the Study of the Covenant Code* (Oxford: Oxford University Press, 2003).

2. See, e.g., Georg Braulik, "Die Dekalogische Redaktion der deuteronomischen Gesetze: Ihre Abhängigkeit von Levitikus 19 am Beispiel von Deuteronomium 22,1–12:24,10.22, 25,13–16," in *Bundesdokument und Gesetz: Studien zum Deuteronomium*, ed. Georg Braulik, HBS 4 (Freiburg: Herder, 1995), 1–25; Braulik, "Weitere Beobachtungen zur Beziehung zwischen dem Heiligkeitsgesetz und Deuteronomium 19–25," in Veijola, *Das Deuteronomium und seine Querbeziehungen*, 23–55; Alfred Cholewiński, *Heiligkeitsgesetz und Deuteronomium*, AnBib 66 (Rome: Biblical Institute, 1969); Driver, *Deuteronomy*, iii–xix; Sara Japhet, "The Relationship Between the Legal Corpora in the Pentateuch in Light of Manumission Laws," in *Studies in Bible*, ed. Sara Japhet,

214   Benjamin Kilchör

less of the direction of dependence), already Samuel R. Driver noted concerning the connection between the Priestly laws and Deuteronomy, "There are *no* verbal parallels between Dt. and P; much that is of central significance in the system of P is ignored in Dt., while in the laws which touch common ground, great, and indeed irreconcilable, discrepancies often display themselves: hence the legislation of P cannot be considered in any degree to have been one of the sources employed by the author of Dt."[3]

In this essay, I will argue that the Priestly laws are presupposed in the Deuteronomic law indeed. However, since the target audience of Deuteronomy is the common people rather than the priests, Deuteronomy adapts Priestly legislation only as far as necessary for the people.

Deuteronomy 24:8 as a Hermeneutical Key for the Relationship Between P and D

We find the clearest reference to Priestly legislation in the Deuteronomic law in Deut 24:8: "Take care, in a case of leprous disease, to be very careful to do according to all that the Levitical priests shall direct you. As I commanded them, so you shall be careful to do" (ESV).

First, it is very clear that the common people are addressed in distinction from the Levitical priests. Second, it is also clear that Priestly legislation is presupposed ("As I commanded them"—כַּאֲשֶׁר צִוִּיתִם). Norbert Lohfink rightly states that, as a matter of course, Deuteronomy here presupposes legislation between Sinai and Moab.[4] And Moshe Weinfeld notes, "It [i.e., Deut 24:8] is doubtless referring to the instructions relating to the various forms of leprosy as they appear in Lev 13–14."[5] For the open and unbiased reader who does not know any pentateuchal theory, it is indeed very clear that Deut 24:8 refers to Lev 13–14. However, due to pentateuchal theory, scholars do not consider that Lev

---

ScrHier 31 (Jerusalem: Magnes VIII, 1986), 63–90; Kilchör, "Frei aber arm?"; Kilchör, "Direction of Dependence"; Kilchör, *Mosetora*; Kilchör, "Levirate Marriage in Deuteronomy 25:5–10 and Its Precursors in Leviticus and Numbers: A Test Case for the Relationship Between P/H and D," *CBQ* 77 (2015): 429–40; Levinson, "Manumission"; Jacob Milgrom, *Leviticus 17–22: A New Translation with Introduction and Commentary*, AB 3A (New Haven: Yale University Press, 2000), 1357–61; Christophe Nihan, *From Priestly Torah to Pentateuch: A Study in the Composition of the Book of Leviticus*, FAT, 2nd ser., no. 25 (Tübingen: Mohr Siebeck, 2007), 401–544; Eckart Otto, "Innerbiblische Exegese im Heiligkeitsgesetz Levitikus 17–26," in *Levitikus als Buch*, ed. Heinz-Josef Fabry and Hans-Winfried Jüngling, BBB 119 (Berlin: Philo, 1999), 125–96; Jeffrey Stackert, *Rewriting the Torah: Literary Revision in Deuteronomy and the Holiness Legislation*, FAT 52 (Tübingen: Mohr Siebeck, 2007).

3. Driver, *Deuteronomy*, xi–xii.

4. Norbert Lohfink, "Prolegomena zu einer Rechtshermeneutik des Pentateuchs," in *Das Deuteronomium*, ed. Georg Braulik, ÖBS 23 (Frankfurt am Main: Lang, 2003), 21.

5. Moshe Weinfeld, *Deuteronomy 1–11*, AB 5 (New York: Doubleday, 1991), 30.

The Reception of Priestly Laws in Deuteronomy   215

13–14 can be familiar to the author of Deut 24:8. Dieter Skweres, for example, writes in his monograph on back-references in Deuteronomy that Deut 24:8 refers to an ancient collection of laws that has been adapted by P.[6] With the assumption that P adapts an older law collection, Skweres avoids the conclusion that D here presupposes P in a direct way. More recently, scholars often choose another explanation in suggesting a post-Priestly redaction of Deuteronomy. This is indeed what Harald Samuel proposes for Deut 24:8. This leads him, however, to the somewhat awkward conclusion that the term "Levitical priests" (which according to him is otherwise a pre-Priestly term in Deuteronomy) here has another function than in the other appearances in Deuteronomy.[7] Samuel gives no explanation why a post-Priestly redactor should have inserted Deut 24:8–9 here.[8] Yet whoever is not willing to follow the Wellhausian dogma that D must be older than P can take the most obvious possibility, that Deut 24:8 does indeed refer to Lev 13–14 (and, even more explicitly, Deut 24:9 refers to Num 12).

If we now take a look at Lev 13:1–14:32, we find a twofold speech introduction. In 13:1 YHWH is speaking to Moses and Aaron, while in 14:1 he is speaking to Moses alone. In many speech introductions in Leviticus (e.g., 11:2; 12:2) Moses (and Aaron) are told to whom they shall pass on the instructions of YHWH, but there is no such hint in Lev 13–14. According to Lev 13:2 and 14:2, a person with leprous disease shall be brought (*hophal*) to Aaron and his sons. In both cases the following verbs then have the priest as subject (13:3 and 14:3), with instructions for the priests rather than for the persons with diseased skin. The instructions in Lev 13–14 hence perfectly fit the back-reference in Deut 24:8bβ.

Due to this clear back-reference, Deut 24:8 can serve as a hermeneutical key for the adaptation of Priestly legislation in the Deuteronomic law. The Deuteronomic law is aware that detailed instructions for the priests exist, but it is written for common people. However, the common people do not have to be informed about the details of these priestly instructions. They are just advised to go to the priests and to observe their instructions. The priests will know what they have to do.

This raises the question about whether the hermeneutical key of Deut 24:8 fits the relationship between D and other Priestly laws.

---

6. Dieter E. Skweres, *Die Rückverweise im Buch Deuteronomium*, AnBib 79 (Rome: Biblical Institute Press, 1979), 194.

7. Harald Samuel, *Von Priestern zum Patriarchen: Levi und die Leviten im Alten Testament*, BZAW 448 (Berlin: De Gruyter, 2014), 146.

8. "Auch wenn es für die These, dass die Verse nachgetragen seien, eine gewisse Hypothek darstellt, dass das Ziel der Einfügung an Ort und Stelle nicht befriedigend geklärt werden kann, scheinen mir alles in allem hinreichende Gründe vorzuliegen, die These dennoch zu vertreten" (Samuel, *Von Priestern zum Patriarchen*, 129–30). I have argued that the motives of Lev 13–14 and the strongly related text in Num 12 are already subtly present in Deut 23 (see Kilchör, *Mosetora*, 277–78).

216   Benjamin Kilchör

The Sacrifices (Lev 1–7)

In the Deuteronomic law we do not find any detailed explanations or instructions for the different types of sacrifices as in Lev 1–7. In comparison with Lev 1–7 the Deuteronomic law uses only the two terms עֹלָה (12:6, 11, 13, 14, 27) and זֶבַח (12:6, 11, 27; 18:3). Both terms are used for blood sacrifices; עֹלָה designates the sacrifice where the whole animal is burned, while זֶבַח designates any type of blood sacrifice which is partly eaten by the people (see Deut 12:27). These two types of sacrifices are found in Lev 1 (עֹלָה) and 3 (זֶבַח שְׁלָמִים). The other two blood sacrifices that are treated in Lev 1–7 are the חַטָּאת and the אָשָׁם. It seems likely that Deut 12 does not mention the חַטָּאת and the אָשָׁם because "the flesh of these two sacrifices was to be consumed by priests only (Lev 6:24ff. [MT Lev 6:18ff.]; 7:1ff.; Num 18:9."[9] With regard to the fact that Deut 12:15–27 deals with the question of the consumption of meat by the people, it is clear that the consumption of meat by the priests is not of relevance for Deuteronomy. Only in the law of the priests and Levites is the consumption of meat by the priests briefly mentioned (Deut 18:1–8). The formulation in verse 3 is telling: "And this shall be the right (מִשְׁפַּט) of the priests *from the people* (מֵאֵת הָעָם) who are offering a sacrifice (זֶבַח)." This law is not directed to the priests but to the people. They are informed about the right of the priests regarding the meat of their זֶבַח sacrifices. Unlike Num 18, Deut 18:3 does not instruct the priests about what they can eat from these sacrifices, but it instructs the people about what they are obliged to give to the priest (נָתַן לַכֹּהֵן, v. 3b). From the three stated parts that shall be given to the priest, the first (הַזְּרֹעַ, arm) corresponds to the instruction in Lev 7:32 for the זֶבַח שְׁלָמִים, where the right leg (שׁוֹק הַיָּמִין) is determined for the priests. The latter two parts seem to be Deuteronomic additions. Note also that with regard to the right of the priests and the Levites, Deut 18:1 uses the very general term אִשֶּׁה (food gift),[10] which is a term used for all kind of sacrifices (except for the purification offering) throughout Lev 1–7.[11]

---

9. J. Gordon McConville, *Law and Theology in Deuteronomy*, JSOTS 33 (Sheffield: JSOT Press, 1984), 54. The same distinction can also be found in Ezek 40:38–43 and 42:13. On the one hand, the זֶבַח is partly eaten by the people. On the other hand, the עֹלָה is completely sacrificed to YHWH. The חַטָּאת and the אָשָׁם, however, are most sacred offerings like the עֹלָה, but they are partly to be eaten by the priests. But like most sacred offerings, the priestly parts must not leave the holy area; they shall be kept away from the people (see Walther Zimmerli, *Ezechiel 25–48*, BKAT, vol. 13, no. 2 [Neukirchen-Vluyn: Neukirchener Verlag, 1969], 1063).

10. For the translation "food gift" instead of "fire offering" see Jacob Milgrom, *Leviticus 1–16: A New Translation with Introduction and Commentary*, AB 3 (New Haven: Yale University Press, 1991), 161–62.

11. The term is used throughout Exod 29–30 and both the books of Leviticus and Numbers. Otherwise it is attested in the Old Testament only in Deut 18:1; Josh 13:14; and 1 Sam 2:28. The latter two verses are quoting Deut 18:1. Thus it is clearly a "Priestly" term.

The Reception of Priestly Laws in Deuteronomy 217

In Deut 12, we find further allusions to the sacrifice laws of Leviticus, especially in light of the concern of Deut 12. According to Norbert Lohfink, the main corpus of Deut 12 consists of four laws that are logically built upon each other:[12]

12:4–7	A single sanctuary for Israel
12:8–12	Time of entry into force
12:13–19	Distinction of sacrifice and slaughter
12:20–28	Limitation of permission to slaughter; dealing with blood

In these four laws, detailed instructions regarding the performance of sacrifices are not the focus. The first main issue is the place of God's dwelling. In the repeated and varied formulas regarding the place, there are lists of sacrifices, duties, and gifts that shall be brought there. None of them are explained, but they are presupposed as known. I have argued elsewhere that all items of these lists (except the primogeniture) are established in Priestly texts.[13]

Another issue of interest here is the distinction between sacrifice and slaughter.[14] While Lev 17 distinguished between sacrificial animals that must always be brought to the sanctuary for slaughter and wild animals that can be slaughtered for profane use, Deut 12 introduces the profane slaughter of sacrificial. It raises the question as to whether these animals should be slaughtered according to the rules of sacrificial animals (Lev 3) or according to the rules of wild animals (Lev 17:13–14). There are two main distinctions between these sets of rules. First, according to Lev 3:17, it is forbidden to eat any fat or blood from sacrifices, while according to Lev 17:13, only the consumption of blood is forbidden for wild animals. Second, according to Lev 3, the blood of sacrifices always belonged to the altar, while according to Lev 17:13, the blood of wild animals was to be poured out on the ground and covered with earth. Within this focus, Deut 12:16a quotes Lev 3:17 to answer the question:

Lev 3:17b	All fat and all blood you must not eat
Deut 12:16a	Only the blood you must not eat

---

12. See Lohfink, "Fortschreibung?" 130 (thereby he is following Georg Braulik, *Die deuteronomischen Gesetze und der Dekalog: Studien zum Aufbau von Deuteronomium 12–26*, SBS 145 [Stuttgart: Katholisches Bibelwerk, 1991], 23–24 and 29–30). This challenges the widespread theory that sees different redactional additions in Deut 12, whereby the oldest law is to be found in Deut 12:13–18/19 (see, e.g., Simeon Chavel, "The Literary Development of Deuteronomy 12: Between Religious Ideal and Social Reality," in *The Pentateuch: International Perspectives on Current Research*, ed. Thomas B. Dozeman, Konrad Schmid, and Baruch J. Schwartz, FAT 78 [Tübingen: Mohr Siebeck, 2011], 303–26; Thomas Römer, *The So-Called Deuteronomistic History: A Sociological, Historical and Literary Introduction* [London: T&T Clark, 2007], 56–65). In the inner logic of Deut 12, it is clear that Deut 12:13–18 presupposes Deut 12:4–12. However, even if one assumes Deut 12:13–18 is the oldest part of Deut 12, it is striking that it is exactly this sequence out of Deut 12 that presupposes the legislation of Lev 3 and 17.

13. Kilchör, *Mosetora*, 82–83.

14. For the following see ibid., 84–88.

218   Benjamin Kilchör

As Deut 12:15 states, profane slaughter of sacrificial animals shall be done according to the rules of the gazelle and deer. These rules are given in Lev 17:13–14. Thus, according to Deut 12:16b, the blood does not belong to the altar but is to be poured out like water, as commanded in Lev 17:13.

The third main focus in reference to these sacrifices is the insistence that the blood from sacrifices (both עֹלָה and זֶבַח) must be brought to the altar, as commanded several times in Lev 1–7.

Finally, Deut 21:1–9 is a further instance where the Priestly laws concerning sacrifices are possibly presupposed, dealing with the case of residual murder. As I have argued,[15] Num 35:33–34, where it is stated that only the blood of the murderer can make atonement for the land, might be the background behind Deut 21:1–9. The latter provides a rite in case the blood of the murderer is unavailable due to lack of knowledge of the murderer's identity, formulated as לֹא נוֹדַע, "it is not known." The verb ידע plays an important role in Lev 4 (vv. 14, 23, 28) and 5 (vv. 1, 3, 4, 17, 18), especially in the instructions on the חַטָּאת. In the case of Deut 21:1–9, atonement is necessary, but it cannot be done in the usual way. Deuteronomy 21:8 uses the term כפר for atonement, which is only used here in the Deuteronomic law (but also in Deut 32:43), in contrast to sixty-eight times in P/H (ten times in Lev 4–5). The context of this verse (Deut 21:1–9) gives instructions for the elders and judges who are responsible for the processing. The shed blood was to be atoned by the blood of a young cow (עֶגְלָה), a term that is never used in the sacrificial laws of Leviticus.[16] The atoning blood does not belong to the altar, but to the running water used to ritually rinse the shed blood out of the land. It is noteworthy that Deut 21:5 mentions the Levitical priests who shall come forward, for YHWH has chosen them to minister to him. Again, there are no instructions to the priests about what they are to do, but the elders are informed that the performance of the rite with the young cow is a priestly matter.

In summary, we see that the substance of Lev 1–7 influences Deut 12 and 18, and possibly also Deut 21:1–9, in several ways. However, the laws concerning the sacrifices in Leviticus are adapted just as far as they deal with the newly raised questions in Deuteronomy, and as far as they are relevant for the people apart from the detailed instructions for the priests.[17]

---

15. Kilchör, *Mosetora*, 242–43.

16. The cow can be understood in relation to Lev 4:27-35 and 5:6 (cf. Num 15:27), where a female flock animal is required for purification offerings for individual laypersons. For a group, a larger female animal is used (cf. Num 19). Deuteronomy 21:1–9 is not an offering but a ritual of elimination (see David P. Wright, "Deuteronomy 21:1–9 as a Rite of Elimination," *CBQ* 49 [1987]: 387–403. I thank Roy Gane for this reference).

17. It might be worth noting here that in Lev 1–7 the instructions for the people and for the priests are interwoven, although the task of each group is always clearly stated. This shows a clear awareness of the relevance of different laws for different addressees.

The Priests (Lev 8–10)

In Lev 8–10, the consecration of Aaron and his sons with their first sacrifices, and the tragic death of two of Aaron's sons, are situated as a narrative rather than a legal text. Nevertheless, in light of Lev 8–10, it is remarkable that among the Deuteronomic laws that deal with the different offices in Israel (Deut 16:18–18:22) there are none for the appointment of priest and Levites. In contrast, we do find instructions for the appointment of judges and officers (16:18–20) and for the appointment of a king (17:14–20). Moreover, God prohibits the people from choosing their own "prophets," who would be soothsayers and the like (18:9–14), and instead promises to appoint himself a prophet like Moses (18:15–18). The only offices without a word about their appointment are the offices of the priests and Levites. The best explanation for the lack of their appointment is, in my view, that they already have been appointed as a hereditary dynasty (Lev 8–10 and Num 3). A renewed instruction for their appointment in Deuteronomy would weaken the sense for their appointment, which is already affirmed in Numbers, for example, Num 17–18.[18] Nevertheless, the fact that the appointment of the different offices is such an important theme in Deut 16:18–18:22, shows again that the Deuteronomic law addresses the people, who are responsible for appointing their officials, and not the officials appointing themselves. Thus, Deut 18:1–8 clearly presupposes an appointment of priests and Levites that has already taken place.

If we look at the content of Deut 18:1–8, which is arranged similarly to the respective laws in Exodus, Leviticus, and Numbers, we see again that Deuteronomy is interested not in the functions and duties of the priests and Levites but only in the duty of the people in contrast to the priests and Levites. In fact, Deut 18:1–8 only informs the people about the right the priests and Levites have regarding the offerings of the people. The same concern is already in the focus of Deuteronomy's tithe and firstborn laws (Deut 14:22–29; 15:19–23), where the people are addressed. In contrast, in Num 18 the priests and Levites are addressed by these issues, which explains why Num 18 treats these things in more detail.

But can the appointment of priests and Levites, as we find it in the books of Leviticus and Numbers, really be presupposed in Deuteronomy? Does not Deuteronomy identify the priests with the Levites as Wellhausen already argued, and as the scholarly term "identity formula" for the wording לַכֹּהֲנִים הַלְוִיִּם כָּל־שֵׁבֶט לֵוִי ("the Levitical priests, the whole tribe of Levi"; Deut 18:1) suggests?[19] I cannot answer this issue in detail here but will give a few hints:

---

18. For the distinction in appointment of the different offices in Deuteronomy, see Joshua Berman, *Created Equal: How the Bible Broke with Ancient Political Thought* (Oxford: Oxford University Press, 2008), 51–80.

19. The term *Identitätsformel* was first introduced by Antonius H. J. Gunneweg, *Leviten und Priester: Hauptlinen der Traditionsbildung und Geschichte des israelitisch-jüdischen*

220 Benjamin Kilchör

1. There are many scholars who have argued with good reason that Deuteronomy does indeed distinguish between priests and Levites.[20]
2. Even scholars who think that in Deuteronomy all Levites are allowed to do full priestly service, and who think that the respective Deuteronomic texts predate Num 3 and 18, see in the "identity formula" an awareness in Deuteronomy of a distinction between priests and Levites. If no distinction existed, the whole formulation would be much too circuitous.[21]
3. As I have argued, it is possible to understand לַכֹּהֲנִים הַלְוִיִּם כָּל־שֵׁבֶט לֵוִי as meaning "the Levitical priests, [moreover] the whole tribe of Levi."[22] If this reading is correct, Deut 18:1 distinguishes between priests and Levites in the same sense as the book of Numbers does: the priests are a subset of the Levites. This distinction is then found in the subsequent law regarding priests and Levites. While Deut 18:1–2 is concerned with both priests and Levites, Deut 18:3–5 is explicitly concerned only with the priests, and 18:6–8 is concerned only with the Levites.
4. The distinction between the priests as Aaron's sons and the Levites as Aaron's brothers instituted in Num 3 can be terminologically seen in Deut 18:1–8 as well. While the priests are called sons (Deut 18:5), the Levites are called brothers (Deut 18:7).[23]

In summary, there are good reasons to suggest that Deut 18:1–8 indeed presupposes the texts regarding the appointment of priests and Levites in Leviticus and Numbers. However, they are not repeated verbatim, but Deuteronomy only addresses the issues of priests and Levites that pertain to the common people.

Clean and Unclean Animals (Lev 11)

In the introduction to this essay I quoted Samuel R. Driver's statement arguing for no verbal parallels between P and D. Yet he noted that this was not absolutely true when he wrote the following: "There is only one exception to what has been stated, viz. the law of clean and unclean animals in Dt. 14:3–20, which present undoubtedly, in the main . . . , a remarkable verbal parallel with Lev. 11:2–23 (if this is referred rightly to H, rather than to P): the section, it is plain, must

---

Kultpersonals, FRLANT 89 (Göttingen: Vandenhoeck & Ruprecht, 1965), 4.

20. See, e.g., Raymond Abba, "Priests and Levites in Deuteronomy," *VT* 27 (1977): 257–67; Rodney K. Duke, "The Portion of the Levite: Another Reading of Deuteronomy 18:6–8," *JBL* 106 (1987): 193–201; Kilchör, *Mosetora*, 215–20; McConville, *Law and Theology*, 124–53; G. Ernest Wright, "The Levites in Deuteronomy," *VT* 4 (1954): 325–30.

21. See, e.g., Samuel, *Von Priestern zum Patriarchen*, 16–147, for the respective formulations in Deuteronomy, and especially the summary on 142.

22. Kilchör, *Mosetora*, 218–19.

23. See ibid., 218.

The Reception of Priestly Laws in Deuteronomy   221

have been derived directly either from H, or from an older collection of Priestly *Tôrōth* . . . , the immediate source (in this case) of both H and Dt."[24]

The wording of Lev 11:1–20 and Deut 14:1–20 is largely identical.[25] Since Driver rejects a relationship between P and D otherwise, he feels pressed to connect Lev 11 with H instead of P. In any case, recently Christophe Nihan called Lev 11 and Deut 14 "the most remarkable instance of legislation shared by Priestly and non-Priestly legal traditions within the Torah."[26]

Because of this outstanding parallel, several scholars who otherwise argue for the priority of D in relation to P/H see here a post-Priestly addition in Deuteronomy, as with Deut 24:8–9.[27] According to Römer, for instance, the adaptation of Lev 11 in Deut 14 belongs to the Persian period and is "perhaps an indication that the Persian revision of the Deuteronomistic History paid already some attention to Priestly interest, preparing in a way the compromise that gave birth to the Torah."[28] In this scenario, the adaptation of Priestly material in Deuteronomy is exceptional. But if there was a revision of Deuteronomy and the Deuteronomistic history, with some sort of Priestly interest that led to large verbal quotations at one place in Deuteronomy, one might ask why there is no other Priestly legal material adapted in a similar way in Deuteronomy.

A close comparison between Lev 11 and Deut 14 shows that Lev 11 is more extensive in general, while Deut 14 only has a few passages that exceed the text of Lev 11. This has led Nihan and others to suggest that there is not a direct relationship between Lev 11 and Deut 14 but that, rather, both of them use a common source and extend it at some places.[29] The underlying assumption is some kind of *lectio brevior*: the longer text is an addition to the shorter, more original text. Achenbach, however, has argued that Lev 11 contains a more detailed version of the food-Torah for Priestly instructions, while Deuteronomy contains a simplified food-Torah for the common people.[30] Shortness can also be explained by simplification, not only by originality. This does fit perfectly with

24. Driver, *Deuteronomy*, xi.

25. See the synopsis in Kilchör, *Mosetora*, 97–98.

26. Christophe Nihan, "The Laws About Clean and Unclean Animals in Leviticus and Deuteronomy and Their Place in the Formation of the Pentateuch," in Dozeman, Schmid, and Schwartz, *Pentateuch*, 401.

27. Among these scholars are Reinhard Achenbach, Eckart Otto, and Thomas Römer. For a good short overview on the state of research, see Sias Meyer, "Leviticus 11, Deuteronomy 14 and Directionality," *Journal for Semitics* 23 (2014): 71–72.

28. Römer, *Deuteronomistic History*, 171.

29. Nihan, "Laws," 401–32. Others include, e.g., Walter Houston, *Purity and Monotheism: Clean and Unclean Animals in Biblical Law*, JSOTS 140 (Sheffield: Academic Press, 1993), 63–65; Naphtali Meshel, "Pure, Impure, Permitted, Prohibited: A Study of Classification Systems in P," in *Perspectives on Purity and Purification in the Bible*, ed. Baruch J. Schwartz, Naphtali S. Meshel, Jeffrey Stackert, and David P. Wright (New York: T&T Clark, 2008), 33.

30. Reinhard Achenbach, "Zur Systematik der Speisegebote in Leviticus 11 und in Deuteronomium 14," *BZABR* 17 (2011): 173. See also Kilchör, *Mosetora*, 97–108.

222   Benjamin Kilchör

the observations above, in that Deuteronomy is aware of the Priestly legislation but uses its laws only selectively as far as they are relevant for Deuteronomy's aim and focus on the common people. In this light, regarding the relationship of P and D, it is not at all surprising that Deut 14 treats the topic in a simplified and shorter way in comparison to Lev 11.

What is surprising and calls for an explanation is the extent to which Deuteronomy is still verbally quoting Lev 11. The key to understand why Deuteronomy adapts this law from Lev 11 can be found in Deut 14:4–5, an addition in comparison to Lev 11. While Lev 11 only lists the animals that are forbidden to eat, Deut 14:4–5 places a short list of animals that are allowed to be eaten before the list of the forbidden animals. First, the list of permitted animals names the three sacrificial animals: bull, ram, and goat. In the whole Old Testament, these three animals are listed together otherwise only in Lev 7:23; 17:3; 22:27; and Num 18:17, which are all texts with Priestly concerns.[31] Second, Deuteronomy lists several wild animals, starting with gazelle and deer, the two animals that are named in Deut 12, where the profane slaughter of sacrificial animals is introduced. Thus, due to the previous innovation of profane slaughter of sacrificial animals, Deut 14 sees the need to add an explication of allowed animals to the list of Lev 11. Since there is nothing new to be said about touching unclean animals, there is no need to quote the second half of Lev 11 in the Deuteronomic law.

Other Cases of Uncleanness (Lev 12–15)

While, as far as I can see, no reference to Lev 12 is found in the Deuteronomic law, Lev 13–14 is presupposed in Deut 24:8, as argued above. With regard to the topic of uncleanness, it is worth taking note of the term מִחוּץ לַמַּחֲנֶה, as it is used twenty-nine times in the Old Testament, twenty-six of these in Exod 29 and 33, Leviticus, and Numbers. The other three appearances are in Deut 23:11, 13 and Josh 6:23. The wilderness context is very important for this concept. Israel was camping around the sanctuary, and this means that there was a high risk that the sanctuary would be contaminated by uncleanness. Therefore, according to Lev 17:15, the sojourner as well as the native were forbidden to eat carrion. Later on, when the camp was abolished and Israel was in the land and not near to the sanctuary, they were allowed to slaughter sacrificial animals for profane use apart from the sanctuary as discussed above (Lev 17 and Deut 12), and the sojourner was also allowed to be unclean and eat carrion (Deut 14:21) since he did not live next to the sanctuary anymore.

---

31. See Achenbach, "Zur Systematik der Speisegebote," 178; Kilchör, *Mosetora*, 103.

The same principle is valid for other kinds of uncleanness, such as leprous disease (cf. Num 5:1–4). The unclean had to go out of the camp (מְחוּץ לַמַּחֲנֶה) until he was clean again (cf. Lev 13:46; Num 12:14–15). In the Deuteronomic law, the concept of מְחוּץ לַמַּחֲנֶה does not play a role, since the law is for the situation in the land where the people are not camping around the sanctuary anymore. However, there is one exception: when Israel went to war, they would live in camps again, and the ark would be with them. This is why Deut 23:15 states that in the situation of a war, the camp must be kept clean. Here the term מְחוּץ לַמַּחֲנֶה appears two times (Deut 23:11 and 13), when it is otherwise only attested in Priestly materials. Considering all this, it is not very surprising that Deut 23:11–12 takes up a case formulated in Lev 15:16, with verbal allusions to Lev 15:16 and Num 5:3.[32]

In summary, it becomes clear that the whole Priestly concept of cleanness and uncleanness was known to the writer of the Deuteronomic law. However, it was taken up only selectively, where Deuteronomy has something to say for a new situation and where it is of relevance for the common people.

The Day of Atonement (Lev 16)

Leviticus 16 is exclusively addressed to Aaron alone (v. 2). It is therefore no surprise that these instructions are neither explicitly nor implicitly mentioned in the Deuteronomic law.

Laws for the Priests in H (Lev 21–22)

The different laws in the Holiness Code have clear target audiences: Lev 17 addresses the priests and the people (v. 2); Lev 18–20 and 23–27 address only the people; and Lev 21–22 addresses the priests exclusively. It is striking that the Deuteronomic law has a substantial amount of allusions to the Holiness Code but no clear allusions to Lev 21–22.[33] This shows that there is no distinction in the use of P and H in principle, but laws that are relevant for the people are more intensively adapted than laws that are primarily given to the priests. The reason why the laws of H are much more frequently and more explicitly adapted in D than the laws of P is not because P and H are two different sources (whereby

---

32. See Kilchör, *Mosetora*, 260.

33. I have argued for the following few allusions: Lev 22:31–32 in Deut 14:1–1 (Kilchör, *Mosetora*, 104–7); Lev 22:18–25 in Deut 15:19–23 (Kilchör, *Mosetora*, 156–62); Lev 22:19–20 in Deut 17:1 (Kilchör, *Mosetora*, 211–12).

224   Benjamin Kilchör

P was not available to D), but simply because H contains issues of much more relevance for the target audience of the Deuteronomic law.

Conclusions

An examination of the allusions of Lev 1–16 in the Deuteronomic law shows that, except for Lev 12 and 16, the material of the Priestly Torah is indeed presupposed in the Deuteronomic law. In several places in Deuteronomy we can see that the concerns of the priests are not directly of interest for the Deuteronomic target audience of the people. Therefore, the allusions to the Priestly Torah only go as far as it is of relevance to the people. It is important to see that the same is also true for the Holiness Code. Thus, in the Deuteronomic law there are only a few allusions to H in the places where H addresses the priests. In my view, this leads to the following two conclusions for the composition of the Pentateuch:

1. It confirms the thesis of my book *Mosetora und Jahwetora* that the Deuteronomic law presupposes Exodus, Leviticus, and Numbers more or less in their present shape.
2. It shows that Deuteronomy in principle does not use P in another way than it uses H. This means that there is, at least on this point, no reason to assume that the Deuteronomic law used P and H as two distinct texts and under different hermeneutical viewpoints. Where H treats issues that are of Priestly concern, H is used in a way that is identical to the use of P.

Therefore, the reason for the different intensity in the use of P and H by D does not lie in a different ideology of P and H or in a different availability of the two sources, but in Deuteronomy's target audience. For the people, the contents of Priestly laws are, in general, of lower relevance than most of the contents of the Holiness Code.

Since the large majority of scholars predate D as against P, the question of the way in which D deals with P has not been much discussed. However, two giants in pentateuchal research have discussed the issue with different results, although both predated P in relation to D. Moshe Weinfeld argued for discontinuity between P and D, which he formulated in terms of "Demythologization and Secularization."[34] Jacob Milgrom, on the other hand, argued for continuity between P and D. He states, "If then D presupposes a crystallized (if not final)

---

34. Moshe Weinfeld, *Deuteronomy and the Deuteronomic School* (Oxford: Clarendon, 1972), 191–243; cf. Weinfeld, *Deuteronomy 1–11*, 28–29.

form of P, is it plausible to argue that its silence in respect to P's laws bespeaks their abolition? So Weinfeld claims. For example, on the basis of 20:14, he concludes that 'according to D all spoils of war accrue to the warriors, and there is no need to consecrate any of them to the Lord' (p. 239). This *ex silentio* deduction cannot be correct, because D never deprives God of His due."[35]

The present study confirms Milgrom's position. D does not compete against P in cultic concerns, but presupposes the Priestly Torah (Deut 24:8). Wherever we find allusions to P in D, it becomes clear that D presupposes that the priests obey the instructions they have already received; the people do not have to be informed about details pertaining to the Priestly office.

---

35. Jacob Milgrom, "Alleged Demythologization and Secularization in Deuteronomy," *IEJ* 23 (1973): 160.

CHAPTER 13

The Relevance of Ezekiel and the Samaritans for Pentateuchal Composition: Converging Lines of Evidence

John S. Bergsma
Franciscan University of Steubenville

> But although the Samaritans and Sadducees, who receive the books of Moses alone, would say that there were contained in them predictions regarding Christ, *yet certainly not in Jerusalem, which is not even mentioned in the times of Moses*, was the prophecy uttered.
> —Origen, *Against Celsus* 1.49 (*ANF* 4:418)

The purpose of this essay is to call attention to recent trends in (1) comparative studies of Ezekiel and the Pentateuch and (2) research on Samaritan origins, both of which shed a similar light on certain aspects of pentateuchal composition.

Comparative Studies of Ezekiel and the Pentateuch

The close relationship between Ezekiel and the Pentateuch, particularly the Holiness Code (H; Lev 17–26), has long been recognized. There are so many shared locutions between these documents that most scholars working on the topic have felt there must be a direct literary dependence between them.[1]

Without ever making a careful study of the matter, Wellhausen declared that Ezekiel reflected an early form of what would later become the Priestly Document, including the Holiness Code.[2] Wellhausen's view has been regarded as standard, at least until recently.

---

1. For discussion of the literature on Ezekiel and H through 2007, see John Bergsma, *The Jubilee from Leviticus to Qumran*, VTSup 115 (Leiden: Brill, 2007), 177–80. Recently, Menahem Haran has argued that P (including H) and Ezekiel do not know each other but stem from the same tradition (Menahem Haran, "Ezekiel, P, and the Priestly School," *VT* 58, no. 2 [2008]: 211–18).

2. See Michael A. Lyons, *From Law to Prophecy: Ezekiel's Use of the Holiness Code*, LHBOTS 507 (New York: T&T Clark, 2009), 37–39. "Wellhausen's literary analysis is so superficial that it cannot yield significant results" (39).

The Relevance of Ezekiel and the Samaritans for Pentateuchal Composition 227

Since 2000, at least two landmark studies of the relationship of Ezekiel to the Pentateuch have appeared. Facilitated by the availability of electronic resources for the study of the biblical text, these studies have been able *systematically* to identify and analyze shared locutions between Ezekiel and the different pentateuchal strata at a level of resolution beyond anything accomplished in nineteenth- and twentieth-century scholarship. The results of these studies have not confirmed Wellhausen's view that the Priestly materials of the Pentateuch (both P and H) are dependent on Ezekiel.

In a 2002 monograph, Risa Levitt Kohn examined ninety-seven terms occurring only in Ezekiel and the Priestly texts of the Pentateuch (including H), and an additional twenty-one terms shared by Ezekiel, Deuteronomy, and other Deuteronomistic literature (e.g., DtrH, Jeremiah).[3] Levitt Kohn demonstrated that, where a direction of dependence could be determined, it was always from P and D to Ezekiel (P/D → Ezekiel), on the basis of interpretability. In other words, where Ezekiel shares language with the pentateuchal sources, and the respective contexts are compared, it is typically not difficult to understand how Ezekiel might be reusing older authoritative locutions, but it is usually difficult to construct a plausible scenario in which the pentateuchal authors would be borrowing from Ezekiel.[4] Moreover, in many passages of Ezekiel (e.g., Ezek 20), clear evidence can be found of the conflation of unique P diction with unique D diction.[5] Therefore, of the three (P, D, and Ezekiel), Ezekiel is the conflationary text. As David Carr has pointed out, when faced with a text that conflates the diction characteristic of two or more distinct literary sources, one should conclude that the conflating text is later than, and dependent on, those literary sources.[6]

---

3. Risa Levitt Kohn, *A New Heart and a New Soul: Ezekiel, the Exile, and the Torah*, LHBOTS 358 (Sheffield: Sheffield Academic, 2002). See also Levitt Kohn, "A Prophet Like Moses? Rethinking Ezekiel's Relationship to the Torah," *ZAW* 114 (2002): 236–54; Milgrom, "Leviticus 26 and Ezekiel," in *The Quest for Context and Meaning*, ed. C. A. Evans and S. Talmon (Leiden: Brill, 1997), 57–62; and Milgrom, *Leviticus 17–22*, AB 3A (New York: Doubleday, 2000), 1362.

4. Particularly persuasive are Kohn's examples of "reversals" in Ezekiel's use of Priestly/ Holiness terminology, in which positive terminology from P/H is reused in a strikingly negative sense in Ezekiel:

Ezekiel parodies P language by using terms antithetically. It is virtually impossible to imagine that the Priestly Writer would have composed Israelite history by transforming images of Israel's apostasy and subsequent downfall from Ezekiel into images conveying the exceptional covenant and unique relationship between Israel and Yahweh. Indeed, it is difficult to imagine that the Priestly Writer could have turned Ezekiel's land of exile (אֶרֶץ מְגֻרֵיהֶם) into Israel's land of promise, Israel's enemies (קְהַל עַמִּים) into a sign of fecundity, or Israel's abundant sin (בִּמְאֹד מְאֹד) into a sign of Yahweh's covenant. It is, however, plausible that Ezekiel, writing in exile, re-evaluated P's portrayal of Israel's uniqueness, cynically inverting these images so that what was once a "pleasing odor to Yahweh" now symbolizes impiety and irreverence. (Kohn, *New Heart*, 77–78)

5. See ibid., 96–104.

6. David Carr, "Method in Determination of Direction of Dependence: An Empirical Test of Criteria Applied to Exodus 34, 11–26 and Its Parallels," in *Gottes Volk am Sinai: Untersuchungen zu Ex 32–34 and Dtn 9–10*, ed. M. Köckert and E. Blum (Gütersloh: Gütersloh, 2001), 124–26.

228   John S. Bergsma

To argue otherwise, as many scholars have, is a failure to follow the standard practices of literary analysis and constitutes a form of special pleading.

At the conclusion of her work, Levitt Kohn describes Ezekiel as the forerunner of R (the pentateuchal redactor) inasmuch as the prophet, like the later redactor, combined in one work the legal traditions of both P (including H) and D.

Seven years after Levitt Kohn's monograph appeared, Michael A. Lyons released the first exhaustive study of shared locutions between Ezekiel and the Holiness Code in the history of biblical scholarship.[7] Lyons concluded that, in virtually all instances where a direction of dependence can be demonstrated between Ezekiel and the Holiness Code, the evidence points to the priority of H.

Four years after the publication of Lyons's study, Jason Gile defended a dissertation under the direction of noted Ezekiel commentator Daniel I. Block, demonstrating that essentially the same literary relationship of creative reuse that Lyons found between Ezekiel and the Holiness Code also held true for Deuteronomy.[8] Gile pointed to overwhelming evidence of intentional literary reworking of themes and specific locutions of Deuteronomy in Ezek 8, 16, 20, and many other passages throughout the book. Tova Ganzel had already made a similar argument on a smaller scale.[9]

It is no longer controversial, therefore, to argue that Ezekiel represents a creative fusion of Deuteronomic and Priestly/Holiness concepts and language. For this reason, as noted above, Levitt Kohn suggested Ezekiel was the precursor of R, the redactor of the Pentateuch. But, for all Levitt Kohn's valuable insights, she and many other scholars have failed to recognize—or at least to call attention to—a seismic difference and distinction between Ezekiel and the pentateuchal redactor(s): *the embrace of Zion theology.*[10] Contra Levitt Kohn, Ezekiel is *not* the precursor of R, because Zion theology (albeit in a unique form) is pervasive in Ezekiel and completely absent from the text of the Pentateuch as we have it. Yes, Ezekiel does conflate D with P/H, on every level; but

---

7. Lyons, *From Law to Prophecy.*

8. Jason Gile, "Deuteronomic Influence on the Book of Ezekiel" (PhD diss, Wheaton College, 2013).

9. Tova Ganzel argues that Ezekiel combines D and P, and in fact knew nearly all of Deuteronomy in a written form (Tova Ganzel, "Transformation of Pentateuchal Descriptions of Idolatry," in *Transforming Visions: Transformations of Text, Tradition, and Theology in Ezekiel*, ed. William A. Tooman and Michael A. Lyons, PTMS 127 [Eugene, OR: Pickwick, 2010], 33–49).

10. On Zion theology generally, see Jon D. Levenson, *Sinai and Zion: An Entry into the Jewish Bible* (San Francisco: HarperOne, 1985), 89–217. On Zion theology in Ezekiel, see Thomas Renz, "The Use of the Zion Tradition in the Book of Ezekiel," in *Zion, City of Our God*, ed. Richard S. Hess and Gordon J. Wenham (Grand Rapids: Eerdmans, 1999), 77–103; Daniel I. Block, "Transformation of Royal Ideology in Ezekiel," in Tooman and Lyons, *Transforming Visions*, 208–46; Daniel I. Block, "Zion Theology in the Book of Ezekiel," in *Beyond the River Chebar: Studies in the Kingship and Eschatology in the Book of Ezekiel* (Eugene, OR: Cascade, 2013); Jon D. Levenson, *Theology of the Program of Restoration of Ezekiel 40–48*, HSM 10 (Missoula, MT: Scholars Press, 1976), 57–69.

there is more: he conflates them with Z, the concepts and language of the Zion tradition so characteristic of the Deuteronomistic History, the Psalms, and the other prophets. Ezekiel can be observed engaging in this conflationary activity on both what we may call a *microstructural* and *macrostructural* level. On the *microstructural level*, Ezekiel combines and conflates individual lexemes and phrases from D, P/H, and Z to create new oracles. On the *macrostructural level*, large sections of Ezekiel's book (e.g., the temple vision of chaps. 40–48) combine sizable blocks of text dominated by themes and motifs from these different literary-theological sources.

Fusion of H, D, and Z at the Lexical/Syntactical or Microstructural Level

On the microstructural level, I provide four examples of the fusion of P/H, D, and Z on the following pages. They demonstrate the literary dependence of Ezekiel on pentateuchal literary strata, modified by the incorporation of elements of Zion theology.

Example I. Covenantal Blessings Specified to Zion
(Lev 26:3–4 :: Ezek 34:26–27)

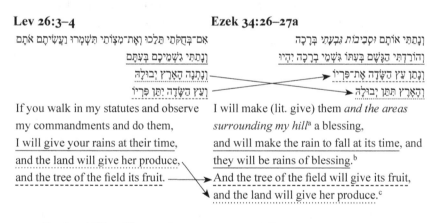

a. For "my hill" as Zion, see Isa 2:2, 10:32, 31:4, Mic 4:1.

b. Ezekiel expands his source text into a traditional Hebrew synonymous bicola. In the first colon he modifies the number of "rain" to the singular, but the plural of his source text reasserts itself in the second colon ("rains of blessing"). Observe the same literary technique in example II (Deut 30:3::Ezek 20:41), only applied to D.

c. Observe the so-called Seidel's law with the inversion of the quoted clauses from the Holiness Code.

230   John S. Bergsma

Example II. Zion as Deuteronomic Central Sanctuary (Ezek 20:39–41)

Pentateuchal Sources	**Ezek 20:39–40**

Lev 22:32; cf. 20:3

וְאַתֶּם בֵּית־יִשְׂרָאֵל כֹּה־אָמַר אֲדֹנָי יְהוִה אִישׁ גִּלּוּלָיו

<u>וְלֹא תְחַלְּלוּ אֶת־שֵׁם קָדְשִׁי</u>

לְכוּ עֲבֹדוּ וְאַחַר אִם־אֵינְכֶם שֹׁמְעִים אֵלָי

Deut 12:5–6

וְאֶת־שֵׁם קָדְשִׁי לֹא תְחַלְּלוּ־עוֹד

כִּי אִם־אֶל־הַמָּקוֹם אֲשֶׁר־יִבְחַר יְהוָה אֱלֹהֵיכֶם מִכָּל

בְּמַתְּנוֹתֵיכֶם וּבְגִלּוּלֵיכֶם

שִׁבְטֵיכֶם לָשׂוּם אֶת־שְׁמוֹ **שָׁם** *לְשִׁכְנוֹ תִּדְרְשׁוּ*

כִּי בְהַר־קָדְשִׁי בְּהַר מְרוֹם יִשְׂרָאֵל נְאֻם אֲדֹנָי יְהוִה

וּבָאתָ **שָׁמָּה** *וַהֲבֵאתֶם* **שָׁמָּה** *עֹלֹתֵיכֶם וְזִבְחֵיכֶם*

שָׁם יַעַבְדֻנִי כָּל־בֵּית יִשְׂרָאֵל כֻּלֹּה בָּאָרֶץ

וְאֵת מַעְשְׂרֹתֵיכֶם וְאֵת תְּרוּמַת יֶדְכֶם וְנִדְרֵיכֶם

שָׁם אֶרְצֵם **וְשָׁם** אֶדְרוֹשׁ

וְנִדְבֹתֵיכֶם וּבְכֹרֹת בְּקַרְכֶם וְצֹאנְכֶם

אֶת־תְּרוּמֹתֵיכֶם

וְאֶת־רֵאשִׁית מַשְׂאוֹתֵיכֶם בְּכָל־קָדְשֵׁיכֶם

Lev 22:32, cf. 20:3: <u>You shall not profane my holy name</u>
Deut 12:5–6: But *the place which the lord your God will choose out of all your tribes to put his name and make his habitation **there*** you shall seek*;*
there you shall go, and **there** you shall bring your burnt offerings and your sac-rifices, your tithes and the contributions of your hand, your votive offerings, your freewill offerings, and the firstlings . . .

As for you, O house of Israel . . . Go serve every one of you his idols . . . if you will not listen to me; but <u>my holy name you shall no more profane</u>[a] with your gifts and your idols.
For *on my holy mountain, the mountain height of Israel,*[b] says the Lord GOD, **there** all the house of Israel, all of them, shall serve me in the land; **there** I will accept them, and **there** <u>I will seek</u> your contribu-tions and the choicest of your gifts, with all your sacred offerings.[c]

a. This locution is common in H (Lev 20:3; 21:6; 22:2, 32). Leviticus 22:32 and 20:3 are the closest grammatical and conceptual parallels, respectively, to its use in Ezek 20:39.

b. For "my holy mountain" as Zion, see Ps 2:6; 3:5; 15:1; 24:3; 43:3; 48:1; 99:9; Isa 11:9; 56:7; 57:13; 65:11, 25; 66:20; Joel 2:1; 3:17; Obad 16; Zeph 3:11; Dan 9:16, 20; for the "mountain height of Israel" as Zion, see Ezek 17:23; cf. Ps 48:1–2; 68:16–17, 19; 78:68–69.

c. Ezekiel 20:40 reflects the concepts and diction of the cult-centralization com-mands of Deuteronomy, esp. Deut 12:5–6: note shared distinctive *triple repetition* of "there" (שָׁם), the verb "to seek" (דרשׁ), and the noun "(your) contributions" (תְּרוּמֹתֵיכֶם). The other terms for offerings in Ezek 20:40 can be paralleled in other cult-centralization passages of Deuteronomy: for קָדְשֵׁיכֶם cf. קָדְשֶׁיךָ in Deut 12:26 (only examples of קדשים + 2m suffix in MT); for רֵאשִׁית see Deut 26:2, 10. On Ezek 20:40 as reworking Deuter-onomy, see Greenberg, *Ezekiel 1–20*, 385.

The Relevance of Ezekiel and the Samaritans for Pentateuchal Composition 231

Example II (cont.). Zion as Deuteronomic Central Sanctuary
(Ezek 20:39–41)

Pentateuchal Sources   Ezek 20:41

Lev 26:31c

וְלֹא אָרִיחַ בְּרֵיחַ נִיחֹחֲכֶם   בְּרֵיחַ נִיחֹחַ אֶרְצֶה אֶתְכֶם

Deut 30:3d   בְּהוֹצִיאִי אֶתְכֶם

וְקִבֶּצְךָ מִכָּל־הָעַמִּים   מִן־הָעַמִּים וְקִבַּצְתִּי אֶתְכֶם

אֲשֶׁר הֱפִיצְךָ יְהוָה אֱלֹהֶיךָ שָׁמָּה   מִן־הָאֲרָצוֹת אֲשֶׁר נְפֹצֹתֶם בָּם

Num 20:12; cf. 27:14   וְנִקְדַּשְׁתִּי בָכֶם לְעֵינֵי הַגּוֹיִם

לְהַקְדִּישֵׁנִי לְעֵינֵי בְּנֵי יִשְׂרָאֵל

Lev 26:45

הוֹצֵאתִי־אֹתָם מֵאֶרֶץ מִצְרַיִם לְעֵינֵי הַגּוֹיִם

Lev 26:31: I will not smell your <u>pleasing odor</u> . . .

Deut 30:3: He will <u>gather you from all the peoples</u> where the lord your God <u>scattered you there</u>

Num 20:12: To <u>sanctify me in the eyes of the people of Israel</u>

Lev 26:45: I brought them forth from the land of Egypt <u>in the eyes of the nations</u>

As a <u>pleasing odor</u> I will accept you,[a] when I bring you out <u>from the peoples,</u> and <u>gather you</u> out of the countries where you have been <u>scattered;</u>[b] and I will <u>sanctify myself</u>[c] among you in the eyes of the nations.[d]

a. "Pleasing odor" occurs frequently in P/H and Ezekiel, but never elsewhere in MT. The preposition ב occurs on רֵיחַ in this phrase *only* in Ezek 20:41 and Lev 26:31, suggesting a specific literary connection.

b. "People" (עם), "gather" (קבץ), and "scatter" (פוץ) appear together in the MT only in Deut 30:3 and several verses of Ezekiel (11:17; 20:34, 41; 28:25; 29:13). Verbs קבץ and פוץ do not occur in H, but see Deut 4:27; 28:64; 30:4. Gile discusses Ezekiel's reuse of Deuteronomic terminology for Israel's scattering and regathering ("Deuteronomic Influence," 93–96, 197–236). Just as in example I (Lev 26:3//Ezek 34:26), Ezekiel expands a single clause of his source (Deut 30:3, "He will gather you from all the peoples") into a synonymous bicola ("I will bring you out from the peoples//and gather you out of the countries"). Thus, Ezekiel imposes the same literary techniques on both D and H texts.

c. "Sanctify in the eyes of" occurs only in Numbers (20:12; 27:14) and Ezekiel (20:41; 28:25; 36:23; 38:16; 39:27).

d. "In the eyes of the nations" occurs only in Lev 26:45; Ps 98:2, and Ezekiel (5:8; 20:9, 14, 22, 41; 28:25; 39:27).

232   John S. Bergsma

Example III. Jerusalem as Focus of Covenant Curses on Israel
(Ezek 4:13–17)

Pentateuchal Sources	**Ezek 4:13–14**

Deut 30:1c

וַהֲשֵׁבֹתָ אֶל־לְבָבֶךָ
בְּכָל־הַגּוֹיִם אֲשֶׁר הִדִּיחֲךָ יְהוָה אֱלֹהֶיךָ שָׁמָּה

Lev 22:8a

נְבֵלָה וּטְרֵפָה לֹא יֹאכַל לְטָמְאָה־בָהּ

Lev 19:7

וְאִם הֵאָכֹל יֵאָכֵל בַּיּוֹם הַשְּׁלִישִׁי **פִּגּוּל** הוּא לֹא יֵרָצֶה

וַיֹּאמֶר יְהוָה כָּכָה יֹאכְלוּ בְנֵי־יִשְׂרָאֵל
אֶת־לַחְמָם טָמֵא בַּגּוֹיִם אֲשֶׁר אַדִּיחֵם שָׁם
וָאֹמַר אֲהָהּ אֲדֹנָי יְהוִה הִנֵּה נַפְשִׁי
לֹא מְטֻמָּאָה וּנְבֵלָה וּטְרֵפָה לֹא־אָכַלְתִּי מִנְּעוּרַי
וְעַד־עַתָּה וְלֹא־בָא בְּפִי בְּשַׂר **פִּגּוּל**

Deut 30:1: And when all these things come upon you, . . . and you call them to mind among all the nations whither the LORD your God has driven you . . .

And the LORD said, "Thus shall the people of Israel eat their bread unclean, among the nations whither I will drive them."[a]

Lev 22:8: That which dies of itself or is torn by beasts he shall not eat, defiling himself by it: I am the LORD.

Then I said, "Ah Lord GOD! behold, I have never defiled myself; from my youth up till now I have never eaten what died of itself or was torn by beasts,[b]

Lev 19:7: If it is eaten at all on the third day, it is **foul**; it will not be accepted . . .

nor has **foul** flesh come into my mouth."[c]

a. The lemmas נדח, שׁם, and גוי + ב occur together only in Deut 30:1, Jer 29:14, 18; 43:5; 46:28; 49:36; and Ezek 4:13. The verb נדח never occurs in P/H. Since most scholars reject any direct literary dependence between Ezekiel and Jeremiah, it seems most likely that both Jeremiah and Ezekiel are dependent on Deut 30:1 for this phrase.

b. Ezek 4:14 is nearly a quotation of Lev 22:8: note five contiguous, identical lemmas, with minor syntactical rearrangement.

c. "Foul" (פִּגּוּל) occurs only in Lev 7:18; 19:7; Isa 65:4; and Ezek 4:14. Given that Ezekiel has just quoted Lev 22:8, Lev 7:18 (and/or 19:7) is the likely source for פִּגּוּל, since the prophet is affirming his heretofore compliance with the covenantal cleanliness laws.

The Relevance of Ezekiel and the Samaritans for Pentateuchal Composition   233

Example III (cont.). Jerusalem as Focus of Curses on Israel
(Ezek 4:13–17)

Pentateuchal Sources	**Ezek 4:16–17**
Lev 26:26	
בְּשִׁבְרִי לָכֶם מַטֵּה־לֶחֶם	וַיֹּאמֶר אֵלַי בֶּן־אָדָם הִנְנִי
וְאָפוּ עֶשֶׂר נָשִׁים לַחְמְכֶם בְּתַנּוּר אֶחָד	שֹׁבֵר מַטֵּה־לֶחֶם
וְהֵשִׁיבוּ לַחְמְכֶם בַּמִּשְׁקָל וַאֲכַלְתֶּם וְלֹא תִשְׂבָּעוּ	בִּירוּשָׁלַ͏ם
Deut 8:9	וְאָכְלוּ־לֶחֶם בְּמִשְׁקָל
אֶרֶץ אֲשֶׁר לֹא בְמִסְכֵּנֻת תֹּאכַל־בָּהּ	וּבִדְאָגָה וּמַיִם בִּמְשׂוּרָה
לֶחֶם לֹא־תֶחְסַר כֹּל בָּהּ	וּבְשִׁמָּמוֹן יִשְׁתּוּ
Lev 26:39	לְמַעַן יַחְסְרוּ לֶחֶם וָמָיִם וְנָשַׁמּוּ אִישׁ
וְהַנִּשְׁאָרִים בָּכֶם יִמַּקּוּ בַּעֲוֹנָם	וְאָחִיו וְנָמַקּוּ בַּעֲוֹנָם

Lev 26:26: When I break your staff of bread, ten women shall bake your bread in one oven, and shall deliver your bread again by weight, and you shall eat, and not be satisfied.	Moreover he said to me, "Son of man, behold, I will break the staff of bread *in Jerusalem*; they shall eat bread by weight[a] and with fearfulness; and they shall drink water by measure and in dismay.
Deut 8:9: A land in which without scarcity you will eat bread, you will not lack anything in it . . .	I will do this that they may lack bread and water,[b]
Lev 26:39: The remnant among you shall rot away in their iniquity.	and look at one another in dismay, and rot away in their iniquities.[c]

     a. Note the nearly contiguous occurrence of six identical lemmas (לֶחֶם [2×], שֹׁבֵר, מַטֵּה, אָכַל, בְּמִשְׁקָל). Ezekiel's unique contribution is to specify the location "in Jerusalem."

     b. Ezekiel constructs a curse by reversing the covenant blessing in Deut 8:9. "Lack bread" (חסר לחם) never occurs in P/H, yet it is not exclusive to D (cf. 2 Sam 3:29; Isa 51:14; Amos 4:6; Prov 12:9). Nonetheless, the context of Deut 8:9 (see 8:7–10), extolling abundant water (8:7) and food (8:8) of the promised land, provides the best semantic contrast with Ezek 4:16–17. Ezekiel's "lack food and water" can be understood as a merism for total lack of sustenance, in contrast to the promised total abundance (לֹא־תֶחְסַר כֹּל בָּהּ) of Deuteronomy.

     c. "To rot for iniquities" (מקק ב+עוֹן) occurs only in Lev 26:39, Ezek 4:17, and 24:23.

234   John S. Bergsma

Example IV. Jerusalem as the Center of the Nations (Ezek 5:5–17)

Pentateuchal Sources   Ezek 5:5–7

Deut 17:14

כִּי־תָבֹא אֶל־הָאָרֶץ אֲשֶׁר יְהוָה אֱלֹהֶיךָ נֹתֵן לָךְ . . .
וְאָמַרְתָּ אָשִׂימָה עָלַי מֶלֶךְ כְּכָל־הַגּוֹיִם אֲשֶׁר סְבִיבֹתָי

Lev 26:43

וּבְיַעַן בְּמִשְׁפָּטַי מָאָסוּ וְאֶת־חֻקֹּתַי גָּעֲלָה נַפְשָׁם

Lev 18:4a

אֶת־מִשְׁפָּטַי תַּעֲשׂוּ
וְאֶת־חֻקֹּתַי תִּשְׁמְרוּ לָלֶכֶת בָּהֶם

Lev 20:23a

וְלֹא תֵלְכוּ בְּחֻקֹּת הַגּוֹי אֲשֶׁר־אֲנִי מְשַׁלֵּחַ מִפְּנֵיכֶם

כֹּה אָמַר אֲדֹנָי יְהוִה זֹאת יְרוּשָׁלַ͏ִם
בְּתוֹךְ הַגּוֹיִם שַׂמְתִּיהָ וּסְבִיבוֹתֶיהָ אֲרָצוֹת
וַתֶּמֶר אֶת־מִשְׁפָּטַי לְרִשְׁעָה מִן־הַגּוֹיִם . . .
כִּי בְמִשְׁפָּטַי מָאָסוּ וְחֻקּוֹתַי לֹא־הָלְכוּ בָהֶם
לָכֵן כֹּה־אָמַר אֲדֹנָי יְהוִה יַעַן הֲמָנְכֶם מִן־הַגּוֹיִם
אֲשֶׁר סְבִיבוֹתֵיכֶם בְּחֻקּוֹתַי לֹא הֲלַכְתֶּם
וְאֶת־מִשְׁפָּטַי לֹא עֲשִׂיתֶם
וּכְמִשְׁפְּטֵי הַגּוֹיִם אֲשֶׁר סְבִיבוֹתֵיכֶם לֹא עֲשִׂיתֶם

Deut 17:14: When you come to the land which the LORD your God gives you, . . . and then say, 'I will set a king over me, like all the nations that are round about me'

Lev 26:43: But the land shall be left by them . . . because they spurned my ordinances, and their soul abhorred my statutes.

Lev 18:4: You shall do my ordinances, and keep my statutes and walk in them . . .

Lev 20:23: And you shall not walk in the customs of the nation which I am casting out before you . . .

Thus says the Lord GOD: "*This is Jerusalem*; I have set her in the center of the nations, with countries round about her.[a] And she has rebelled against my ordinances more than the nations . . . for they spurned my ordinances and did not walk in my statutes." Therefore thus says the Lord GOD: "Because you are more turbulent than the nations that are round about you, and have not walked in my statutes or done my ordinances,[b] but have acted according to the ordinances of the nations that are round about you . . ."[c]

     a. Interestingly, the lemmas אֶרֶץ, גּוֹי, שִׂים, אָמַר, and סָבִיב occur together in the same clause in the MT only in Ezek 5:5 and Deut 17:14. Jerusalem is the royal city among the nations. Polemic against "the nations round about" is not found in P/H, but *is* found in strategic texts of D and DtrH: Deut 6:24, 12:10, 13:7, 17:14; Judg 2:12; 2 Kgs 17:15.

     b. Observe "Seidel's law" here in the inversion of quoted clauses.

     c. The idea of "statutes of the nations" is very rare in the MT. It is absent from Deuteronomy. Leviticus 20:23 is the only legal text mentioning it. Arguably, Ezekiel changes Leviticus's חֻקַּת to מִשְׁפָּטִים to get a better contrast with the divine מִשְׁפָּטִים in the previous clause, and Leviticus's "nation I am casting out" becomes the Deuteronomism "nations round about" for the sake of relevance to Ezekiel's contemporary situation. Ezekiel's formulation is close to 2 Kgs 17:8, which itself reflects influence from Lev 20:23.

The Relevance of Ezekiel and the Samaritans for Pentateuchal Composition   235

Example IV (cont.). Jerusalem as the Center of the Nations
(Ezek 5:5–17)

Pentateuchal Sources   **Ezek 5:16–17**

Deut 32:23–24

. . . אַסְפֶּה עָלֵימוֹ רָעוֹת **חִצַּי** אֲכַלֶּה־בָּם מְזֵי **רָעָב**	בְּשַׁלְּחִי אֶת־**חִצֵּי הָרָעָב** הָרָעִים בָּהֶם

Deut 32:42

. . . אַשְׁכִּיר חִצַּי מִדָּם וְחַרְבִּי תֹּאכַל בָּשָׂר	אֲשֶׁר הָיוּ לְמַשְׁחִית אֲשֶׁר־אֲשַׁלַּח אוֹתָם לְשַׁחֶתְכֶם

Lev 26:26

. . . בְּשִׁבְרִי לָכֶם מַטֵּה־לֶחֶם	**וְרָעָב** אֹסֵף עֲלֵיכֶם וְשָׁבַרְתִּי לָכֶם מַטֵּה־לֶחֶם

Lev 26:22

וְהִשְׁלַחְתִּי בָכֶם אֶת־חַיַּת הַשָּׂדֶה וְשִׁכְּלָה אֶתְכֶם	וְשִׁלַּחְתִּי עֲלֵיכֶם **רָעָב** וְחַיָּה רָעָה וְשִׁכְּלֻךְ

Lev 26:25

וְהֵבֵאתִי עֲלֵיכֶם חֶרֶב נֹקֶמֶת נְקַם־בְּרִית	וְדֶבֶר **וָדָם** יַעֲבָר־בָּךְ
וְנֶאֱסַפְתֶּם אֶל־עָרֵיכֶם	וְחֶרֶב אָבִיא עָלָיִךְ
וְשִׁלַּחְתִּי דֶבֶר בְּתוֹכְכֶם	אֲנִי יְהֹוָה דִּבַּרְתִּי

Deut 32:23–24: "'And I will heap evils upon them; I will spend my **arrows** upon them, emptiness of famine . . .
Deut 32:42: I will make my **arrows** drunk with blood . . .
Lev 26:26: When I break your staff of bread . . .
Lev 26:22: And I will let loose the wild beasts among you, which will bereave you . . .
Lev 26:25: And I will bring a sword upon you, vengeance for the covenant; and if you gather within your cities I will send pestilence among you . . .

When I loose against you my deadly **arrows** of **famine**, **arrows** for destruction, which I will loose to destroy you, and when I heap **famine** upon you, and break your staff of bread. I will send famine and wild beasts against you, and they will bereave you; pestilence and **blood** shall pass through you; and I will bring the sword upon you. I the Lord have spoken.

Greenberg, Block, Gile, and others recognize Ezek 5:16–17 as a mosaic assembled from the covenant curses of Lev 26 and Deut 32 (Gile, "Deuteronomic Influence," 76–77). The bold terms in Ezek 5:16–17 above—famine, arrows, and blood—are absent from Lev 26, and appear borrowed from Deut 32. These three nouns occur together exclusively in Deut 32 and Ezek 5.

     To summarize these examples briefly: in example I (Ezek 34:26–27), Ezekiel modifies his source text to give it a Zion/Jerusalem focus. In Leviticus, the recipients of the covenant blessings are simply the people of Israel generally; in

236   John S. Bergsma

Ezekiel, they become Israel "*and the areas surrounding my hill*," an undoubted reference to Jerusalem (cf. Isa 10:32; 31:4).

Likewise, in example II (Ezek 20:39–41) we see that the prophetic author—in the midst of a passage drawing from H, P, and D—essentially rewrites the cult centralization command(s) of Deuteronomy as an eschatological prophecy of a restored cult on "my holy mountain, the mountain heights of Israel," a clear reference to Jerusalem.[11] The result is a fusion of Priestly and Deuteronomic thought with Zion theology.

In examples III (Ezek 4:13–17) and IV (Ezek 5:5–17), the author of Ezekiel has composed new oracles of judgment by splicing together locutions from legal material and covenant curses of both H and D and recentered the divine declarations of judgment not on Israel generally (as in his sources) but specifically on *Jerusalem*, which, in keeping with classic Zion theology, is conceived as the mystical center not only of the nation of Israel but of all nations generally (Ezek 5:5; cf. Ps 2:6–10; 48:2 and passim; 87:1–6, etc.). In example III (Ezek 4:13–17), Ezekiel takes the covenant curse of Lev 26:26 concerning the "breaking of the staff of bread" and specifies that this will take place *in Jerusalem* (Ezek 4:16). In example IV (Ezek 5:5–17), Ezekiel prefaces an oracle of judgment composed from various pentateuchal sources with the declaration: "This is Jerusalem!" (Ezek 5:5).[12]

Macrostructural Fusion of H, D, and Zion Theology

The fusion of P/H, D, and Z discovered in Ezekiel on the microstructural level also holds true on a macrostructural level: there are large literary structures in Ezekiel that incorporate extensive Zion themes into material otherwise modified from pentateuchal sources.

One of the best examples is Ezekiel's concluding Temple vision, Ezek 40–48. In this large unit, the prophet is taken up to a "very high mountain" and receives a vision of the dimensions of an ideal temple (chaps. 40–43), the details of a revised liturgical law code (chaps. 44–46), the supernatural river flowing from the temple (chap. 47:1–12), and the new division of the holy land (chaps. 47:13–48:35). Since Moses is the only other person in Israel's sacred history to ascend a mountain and receive a vision of the dimensions of the sanctuary, the specifics of liturgical law, and the boundaries of the divided land, scholars have always compared and contrasted the vision of Ezek 40–48 with parallel or analogous

---

11. Cf. Ps 2:6; 48:1; 87:1; 99:9; Joel 2:1; 4:17; Zeph 3:11; Isa 66:20; Dan 9:16, 20.

12. For brevity, example IV analyzes only the beginning (Ezek 5:5–7) and end (Ezek 5:16–17) of this oracle, to capture the strongest references to Zion (Ezek 5:5) and examples of dependence on D (Ezek 5:16–17) present in this unit. Ezekiel 5:8–15 are also rich in literary reuse of P, H, and D texts: see Moshe Greenberg, *Ezekiel 1–20*, AB 22 (Garden City, NY: Doubleday, 1983), 113–16.

The Relevance of Ezekiel and the Samaritans for Pentateuchal Composition   237

passages in the Pentateuch.[13] But rarely if ever have scholars called attention to a major—perhaps *the* major —point of distinction between Ezek 40–48 and pentateuchal parallels: Ezekiel *reflects the influence of the Zion tradition*:

- Ezekiel 40–43, the vision of the dimensions of the temple, is analogous to the instructions for the tabernacle in Exod 25–27, but also bears important similarities to the description of the Solomonic temple (1 Kgs 6–7), the sanctuary nonpareil of Zion theology.[14]
- Ezekiel 44–46, which largely concern regulations for temple personnel, draws strongly from various passages of P and H; but Ezekiel incorporates into this P/H legislation new regulations for the liturgical functions of the *nāśî*,[15] the Davidic monarch associated with Zion (cf. 37:24–26). The concept of the monarch as cultic functionary is foreign to all pentateuchal legislation, but characteristic of Zion theology.[16]
- Ezekiel 47–48 have obvious parallels to accounts of land division in the Hexateuch (Num 34–35; Josh 13–19), but also reveal the influence of Zion traditions. The river of life flowing from the temple (47:1–12) is not a Sinaitic or Mosaic motif at all. Instead, it develops the ancient Near Eastern concept of the divine river flowing from the primordial mountain of God, which Israelite tradition assimilated to Zion/Jerusalem and the Gihon spring (Gen 2:13; Ps 46:4; 1 Kgs 1:33, 38, 45).[17] Likewise, Ezekiel's division of the land in 47:13–48:35 reflects the significance Jerusalem gained during the Davidic monarchy. As Judah and Benjamin surrounded Jerusalem on

13. See Jacob Milgrom and Daniel I. Block, *Ezekiel's Hope: A Commentary on Ezekiel 38–48* (Eugene, OR: Cascade, 2012), 214–18.

14. Ezekiel's and Solomon's temples share the same dimensions of the Holy of Holies and the Holy Place (see 1 Kgs 6:16–20; Ezek 41:2, 4) over against the much smaller dimensions in the tabernacle (Exod 26). Moreover, Ezekiel sees a stone temple constructed on a holy mountain, and thus tied permanently to a single sacred site. This is more analogous to the Solomonic temple narratives (1 Kgs 6–8) and Zion theology than the material concerning the movable tabernacle, which implies a different theology of God's presence. On the similarities between Solomon's and Ezekiel's temples, see Paul Joyce, "Temple and Worship in Ezekiel 40–48," in *Temple and Worship in Biblical Israel*, ed. John Day (New York: T&T Clark, 2005), 145–63.

15. See Ezek 44:3; 45:7–9, 16–17, 22; 46:2, 4, 8, 10, 12, 16–18. Jon D. Levenson comments, "*Nasi* is a term from Sinai, most of whose attestations are from P narratives. . . . Ezekiel sought to bring the institution of the monarchy under the governance of the Sinaitic covenant" (Levenson, *Ezekiel 40–48*, 69), i.e., Ezekiel sought to situate Z within P/H, and that summarizes the agenda of most of Ezek 40–48. For further discussion, see Brian Boyle, "The Figure of the *Nasi* in Ezekiel's Vision of the New Temple (Ezekiel 40–48)," *ABR* 58 (2010): 1–16.

16. Ezekiel's *nāśî* is clearly a Davidide: see Ezek 34:24 and 37:25, and discussion in Levenson, *Ezekiel 40–48*, 57–69. Levenson points out, "The Zion traditions are inseparable from the institution of monarchy" (18–19).

17. See ibid., *Ezekiel 40–48*, 28–29; and Lawrence E. Stager, "Jerusalem and the Garden of Eden," in *Eretz-Israel: Archeological, Historical and Geographical Studies; Frank More Cross Festschrift*, vol. 26 of *Eretz-Israel: Archeological, Historical and Geographical Studies* (Jerusalem: Israel Exploration Society / Hebrew Union College, 1999), 183–94.

238   John S. Bergsma

each side, so Ezekiel sandwiches his temple city and environs between the territories of these two tribes (Ezek 48:22). By contrast, there is no hint in the tribal land divisions in the Hexateuch of the significance Jerusalem would gain later in the biblical narrative, or that the national capital would lie between Judah and Benjamin. In sum, Ezekiel's placement of the capital precinct between Judah and Benjamin (48:21–22) is the influence of the Zion tradition. By contrast, the Hexateuch's de facto capital of Israel is Shechem (Deut 11:29; 27:4, 13; Josh 24:1, 25, 32).

Thus, every major division of Ezekiel's temple vision—the sanctuary (40–43), the personnel (44–46), and the land (47–48)—shows the same pattern of conflation of pentateuchal motifs and instructions with material drawn from or inspired by the Zion traditions.

This contrast between Ezekiel and the Pentateuch highlights the absence of any specific concern for Zion, Jerusalem, or the temple in the Pentateuch. This is true no matter the position one takes on the direction of dependence. If Ezekiel is using the pentateuchal strata, then he is inserting into them Zion material that they lacked. But if one or more of the pentateuchal strata are drawing on Ezekiel—the Holiness Code, for example—then the Holiness redactors must have *intentionally edited out references to Zion/Jerusalem* in their Ezekielan source, such as "my hill" (Lev 26:3::Ezek 34:26) or "the mountain of my holiness" (Deut 12:5–6::Ezek 20:40). Such a procedure cannot be reconciled with the view that the final redaction of the Pentateuch was executed by Jerusalem priests in the Persian period as part of an effort to legitimize the Jerusalem temple cult, as posited by several current models of pentateuchal composition.[18]

Samaritan Origins and Their Implications for the Composition of the Pentateuch

If careful study of shared locutions between Ezekiel and the Pentateuch highlights the absence of Zion theology from the Pentateuch, Gary Knoppers's recent monograph on Samaritan origins also confirms this.[19]

---

18. E.g., "[The Priestly Document] is closely linked to the rebuilding of the Temple [and] the legitimation of the Second Temple community in *Jerusalem*. . . . The writing down of P also betrays the claims of the priestly class in *Jerusalem*" (Christophe Nihan, *From Priestly Torah to Pentateuch: A Study in the Composition of the Book of Leviticus*, FAT, 2nd ser., no. 25 [Tübingen: Mohr Siebeck, 2007], 614). Similarly, Ziony Zevit describes Deuteronomy as the work of a "Jerusalem Temple loyalist" (Ziony Zevit, "Deuteronomy and the Temple: An Exercise in Historical Imagining," in *Mishneh Todah: Studies in Deuteronomy and Its Cultural Environment in Honor of Jeffrey H. Tigay*, ed. Jeffrey H. Tigay, Nili Sacher Fox, David A. Glatt-Gilad, and Michael James Williams [Winona Lake, IN: Eisenbrauns, 2009], 217).

19. Gary Knoppers, *Jews and Samaritans: The Origins and History of Their Early Relations* (New York: Oxford University Press, 2013).

The Relevance of Ezekiel and the Samaritans for Pentateuchal Composition   239

Knoppers points out that Yahwism was alive and well in Samaria throughout the entire (Judean) Second Temple period, and that a Yahwistic sanctuary was operational on Mount Gerizim from the first half of the fifth century (ca. 450 B.C.) forward. The prevalence of Yahwistic religious indicators in Samaria from the fifth century on is too widespread to be explained as a sudden development, and Knoppers points to indications that Yahwism was practiced in Samaria long before the Judean Babylonian exile. Moreover, from the sixth through fourth centuries, Samaria was wealthier and more powerful than Jerusalem and Judah/Yehud to the south. Thus, *there never was a time in the Second Temple period when the referent of the phrase "the place which the* LORD *your God will choose" could be considered uncontested.*

How, then, can we explain that both the Samaritans and the Judeans came to share the Pentateuch as their foundational sacred text? Older views regarded the Pentateuch as a Judean textual product begun in the exile and finalized in early postexilic Jerusalem, aimed at legitimizing the Jerusalem temple and its cult. It was then brought to Samaria and adopted by the Samaritans at some point in the (Judean) Second Temple period, perhaps by Manasseh, the renegade scion of the high priestly family who left Jerusalem to take charge of the Gerizim sanctuary in the late fourth century.[20]

But how likely is it that the "Samarian" Yahwistic community,[21] sometime in the fifth through fourth centuries BCE, would have discarded their own sacred texts and priestly writings—for surely they would have had some—in order to embrace wholesale a sacred document produced by the smaller, more impoverished, and socially/politically weaker Yahwistic community centered around Jerusalem? I submit that this is historically implausible. Therefore, the Pentateuch is unlikely to be a product of the postexilic Jerusalem priesthood. As Terence Fretheim observed over fifty years ago, "It is incredible that a document promulgated by a priesthood that had been entrenched in Jerusalem for over three hundred years, and so closely bound up with the monarchy and 'Zion theology,' would be completely devoid of so much as an allusion to the David-Zion traditions."[22]

Knoppers demonstrates that there is nothing specifically Jerusalemite about the Pentateuch, and it can be read to support Samarian cultic claims just as easily as Judean ones.[23] Jerusalem (יְרוּשָׁלַם), Zion (צִיּוֹן), and the temple (הֵיכָל) are never mentioned in it, which is an odd literary strategy if it was meant to legitimize the Jerusalem temple. By contrast, the Samaritan sanctuary city of

---

20. See Josephus, *Ant.* 11:7, §2; 11:8, §2–4; 12:4, §1.

21. Knoppers employs the term "Samarian" to describe people of Israelite heritage living in the territory later associated with the Samaritans, but before a clear "Samaritan" identity was established.

22. Terence Fretheim, "The Priestly Document: Anti-Temple?" *VT* 18 (1968): 319.

23. Knoppers, *Jews and Samaritans*, 194–219.

240   John S. Bergsma

Shechem, nestled by Mounts Ebal and Gerizim, receives much more attention than Jerusalem.[24] Furthermore, the phrase "the place which the LORD your God will choose" does not necessarily indicate Zion: as Knoppers states, "It would not have been difficult for the framers of Deuteronomy (or the editors of the Pentateuch) to clarify Yhwh's choice if they wanted to do so."[25] Finally, we observe that the Pentateuch portrays the claimed ancestor of the Samarians (Joseph) more favorably—and grants him greater blessings—than the claimed ancestor of the Judeans (Judah).[26]

These pro-Samarian features of the Pentateuch and its embrace by the Samarian people and priesthood can only be explained if the Pentateuch represents non-Judean-specific and non-Jerusalem-specific Israelite traditions whose compilation as a document extends back before the sixth century.[27] This agrees with the witness of the book of Ezekiel, which—if its sixth-century dating is accepted[28]—testifies to the existence already of a completed Pentateuch or at least several important parts of the Pentateuch in written form by the time of the late Judean monarchy at the latest.

Concluding Observations: Ezekiel Research and the Composition of the Pentateuch

We may conclude with the following observations:

24. Gen 12:6; 33:18; 34:2–26; 35:4; Deut 11:29; 27:4, 12–13; cf. also Josh 8:30–33; 21:21; 24:1, 25, 32.

25. Knoppers, *Jews and Samaritans,* 212.

26. Contrast the final blessings of both tribes (Deut 33:7 vs. 33:13–17), and consider Jacob's blessing of Joseph's sons (Gen 48:1–22). Genesis portrays Judah as the betrayer of Joseph into slavery (37:27), who begets most of his descendants through incestuous fornication (38:12–30). Joseph's descendants receive the Israelite heartland as their inheritance (Josh 16–17), whereas Judah's territory is mostly the southern desert (Josh 15:20–63).

27. Thomas L. Thompson has recently endorsed this view as well: "I do not sincerely believe that Wellhausen's thesis, as argued, will stand, not least because of the chronological priority of a Samaritan Pentateuch, a temple on Gerizim and, especially, the known history of a non-Jewish Israel" (Thomas L. Thompson, "On Myths and Their Contexts: An Issue of Contemporary Theology? A Response to Jeffrey Morrow," The Bible and Interpretation, http://www.bibleinterp.com/articles/2017/01/tho418030.shtml).

28. Recent English-language commentators such as Moshe Greenberg, Daniel I. Block, Jacob Milgrom, and Paul Joyce have understood the book of Ezekiel as a sixth-century document largely shaped by the prophet himself. Marvin Sweeney writes, "In contrast to the heavily edited books of Isaiah and Jeremiah, Ezekiel displays only light editing. Most of the book, including its literary structure, appears to derive from the prophet himself" (Marvin Sweeney, "Dating Prophetic Texts," *HS* 48 [2007]: 67). Likewise, Lawrence Boadt asserts: "Both books [of Jeremiah and Ezekiel] were put together within a relatively short period of time. Ezekiel perhaps not much after *571, since there is no evidence of any awareness of the world of Second Isaiah after 547;* and Jeremiah perhaps in the 550's after Jehoiachin's release" (Lawrence Boadt, "Do Jeremiah and Ezekiel Share a Common View of the Exile?" paper presented at the SBL Annual Meeting, Atlanta, November 2003, 40, emphasis added).

1. Since Ezekiel shows a closer literary relationship to both the Holiness Code and Deuteronomy than *either of these law codes show towards each other*,[29] it is no longer legitimate, methodologically, to explore the question of the relationship of the Holiness Code and Deuteronomy in the absence of the data from Ezekiel. In fact, theories of pentateuchal composition need to incorporate consideration of Ezekiel at the ground level of the study, and not only as an afterthought in which Ezekiel is typically stratified and redated in such a way as to conform to the individual scholar's opinions about pentateuchal development.

Studies claiming to demonstrate the dependence of H on D by Bernard Levinson, Jeffrey Stackert, Mark Leuchter, and many others have ignored the evidence of Ezekiel, and have been unable to produce any examples of literary borrowing from D into H as clear and convincing as the several examples of Ezekiel's dependence on H and D presented in this essay.[30]

2. Since Ezekiel is the conflate text relative to H and D, it follows, by standard literary-critical methodology, that Ezekiel is the relatively later text than both those documents.[31] If Ezekiel is dated to the sixth century—perhaps circa 571 BCE according to Lawrence Boadt[32]—then it follows that both H and D are substantially preexilic, as Jan Joosten, Michael Lyons, Israel Knohl, Jacob Milgrom, and many others have held and argued for decades now.[33]

---

29. See John Bergsma, "The Biblical Manumission Laws: Has the Literary Dependence of H on D Been Demonstrated?" in *A Teacher for All Generations: Essays in Honor of James C. VanderKam*, ed. E. F. Mason et al., 2 vols. (Leiden: Brill Academic, 2012), 1:65–89.

30. For example, Bernard Levinson, "The Manumission of Hermeneutics: The Slave Laws of the Pentateuch as a Challenge to Contemporary Pentateuchal Theory," in *Congress Volume Leiden 2004*, ed. André Lemaire, VTSup 109 (Leiden: Brill, 2006), 281–324; Jeffrey Stackert, *Rewriting the Torah: Literary Revision in Deuteronomy and the Holiness Legislation*, FAT 52 (Tübingen: Mohr Siebeck, 2007), 113–64; to a lesser extent, Christophe Nihan, *From Priestly Torah to Pentateuch*, 496–535; and Eckart Otto, "Innerbiblische Exegese im Heiligkeitsgesetz Levitikus 17–26," in *Levitikus als Buch*, ed. H.-J. Fabry and H.-W. Jüngling, BBB 119 (Berlin: Philo, 1999), 125–96. I have responded in detail to Levinson's arguments in Bergsma, *Jubilee from Leviticus to Qumran*, 138–42; and to Stackert's in my review of his book (John S. Bergsma, review of *Rewriting the Torah: Literary Revision in Deuteronomy and the Holiness Legislation*, by Jeffrey Stackert, *Bib* 92 [2011]: 123–27). The arguments of Levinson and Stackert have been endorsed by Mark Leuchter, "The Manumission Laws in Leviticus and Deuteronomy: The Jeremiah Connection," *JBL* 127 (2008): 635–53.

31. So David Carr, "Method in Determination," 126.

32. Boadt, "Do Jeremiah and Ezekiel," 40.

33. Jan Joosten, *People and Land in the Holiness Code: An Exegetical Study of the Ideational Framework of the Law in Leviticus 17–26*, VTSup 68 (Leiden: Brill, 1996); Lyons, *From Law to Prophecy*; Israel Knohl, *The Sanctuary of Silence: The Priestly Torah and the Holiness School* (Minneapolis: Fortress, 1995); Yehezekel Kaufmann, *The Religion of Israel: From the Babylonian Captivity to the End of Prophcy*, trans. and abridg. Moshe Greenberg (Chicago: University of Chicago Press, 1972), 166–200; Richard E. Friedman, *Who Wrote the Bible?* (New York: HarperOne, 1987), 161–216; Moshe Weinfeld, *Deuteronomy and the Deuteronomic School* (Oxford: Clarendon, 1972), 179–89; Milgrom, *Leviticus 17–22*, 1357–64.

242   John S. Bergsma

3. The literary dependence of the Priestly tradition of the Pentateuch (P and/ or H) on Ezekiel is no longer a tenable position.[34] Ezekiel is not the precursor of P/H, but its receptor.[35] Dependence of a Persian-period P/H on Ezekiel would involve the highly implausible scenario of a fifth-century Jerusalem priest-scribe(s) disentangling and excising the locutions of Ezekiel from their Zion motifs and Deuteronomisms in order to create P/H, a fictional law code projected into Israelite antiquity; a law code that, in any event, did nothing to legitimize the Jerusalem temple, to which the supposed priestly scribe(s) was so attached. Why would such a writer excise the mentions of Jerusalem from Ezekiel's oracles,[36] and how (and why) would he recognize all the Deuteronomisms in Ezekiel in order to purge them from the text of his priestly composition? If he was opposed to the presence of Zion and Deuteronomistic theologies in Ezekiel, why did he nonetheless revere the prophet so highly as to borrow so extensively from his diction?

4. The final form of the Pentateuch contains no Zion theology. This fact is often not realized, because scholars have become accustomed to reading Zion theology into the Pentateuch in passages where it is not actually present—for example, by taking "the place which the LORD your God will choose" as a transparent reference to Zion. Nonetheless, the absence of Zion theology in the Pentateuch leaves us with only two viable options for dating the final redaction of the document: either the Pentateuch must have reached something close

34. The priority of Ezekiel to P/H is falling out of favor even in German scholarship, according to Michael Konkel, "Ezekiel 40–48 and P: Questions and Perspectives," paper presented at the Theological Perspectives on Ezekiel Seminar, SBL Annual Meeting, San Diego, November 22, 2014.

35. Our position on this issue, developed out of careful study of the intertextual relationship between these two literary corpora, agrees well with the linguistic studies of Avi Hurvitz: "Linguistic Observations on the Priestly Term 'Edah and the Language of P," *Imm* 1 (1972): 21–23; Hurvitz, "Evidence of Language in Dating the Priestly Code: A Linguistic Study in Technical Idioms and Terminology," *RB* 81 (1974): 24–56; Hurvitz, *A Linguistic Study of the Relationship Between the Priestly Source and the Book of Ezekiel: A New Approach to an Old Problem*, CahRB (Paris: Gabalda, 1982); Hurvitz, "Dating the Priestly Source in the Light of the Historical Study of Biblical Hebrew a Century After Wellhausen," *ZAW* 100 (1988): 88–100. Hurvitz has been criticized by J. Becker, review of *A Linguistic Study of the Relationship Between the Priestly Source and the Book of Ezekiel: A New Approach to an Old Problem*, by Avi Hurvitz, *Bib* 64 (1983): 583–86; and Joseph Blenkinsopp, "An Assessment of the Alleged Pre-Exilic Date of the Priestly Material of the Pentateuch," *ZAW* 108 (1996): 495–518. But see Avi Hurvitz, "Once Again: The Linguistic Profile of the Priestly Material in the Pentateuch and Its Historical Age: A Response to J. Blenkinsopp," *ZAW* 112, no. 2 (2000): 180–91; and Jacob Milgrom's statement: "Ezekiel had all of H . . . before him, the language and ideas of which he refashioned. Thus, nearly all of H is preexilic; all the more so P" (Jacob Milgrom, "The Antiquity of the Priestly Source: A Reply to Joseph Blenkinsopp," *ZAW* 111, no. 1 [1999]: 10–22, esp. 13–14).

36. While it could be argued that a pro-Zion Second Temple priest-scribe would excise Jerusalem references from some of Ezekiel's oracles of curse (e.g., examples III and IV above), that still would not explain the excision of Jerusalem references from oracles of blessing (examples I and II above).

to its final form (1) before Zion theology had attained dominance, or else (2) within circles in which Zion theology was rejected. Recently, Jean Louis Ska has advanced this latter option, arguing that postexilic Judaism gave up on Zion theology.[37] However, Ska does not engage the evidence of the biblical and non-biblical postexilic or Second Temple literature, as well as the ongoing Second Temple redaction of earlier biblical documents. It is possible to demonstrate that Zion theology is well represented in Second Temple literature as a whole, and that the biblical texts that were being redacted during the postexilic or Second Temple period—the prophets, the psalms, the historical books, and so forth—continue to show interest and even confidence in Zion theology and God's ultimate fulfillment of his promises to the holy city. There is no evidence of a significant circle or subculture of postexilic Judeans who lost their theological commitment to Zion—at least not one that could plausibly have produced a document like the Pentateuch and then persuaded the other Jewish sects who were committed to Zion, as well as the Samaritans, to accept this new document as their most ancient and foundational religious text. For this reason, the latter option—that is, the origin of Pentateuch in postexilic Judean circles that rejected Zion—cannot be regarded as viable. Therefore, we must begin seriously to investigate the former option: an origin for the Pentateuch as a substantially completed document much earlier in the history of Israel. The combined evidence of Ezekiel's literary reuse of the Pentateuch and the Samaritan's acceptance of it as sacred Scripture suggests that the document arose in preexilic Israel, prior to the time when Zion theology became pervasive in Judean religious thought, and the relationship between northern Israel and southern Judah and their respective religious traditions became embittered and antagonistic.

---

37. Jean Louis Ska, "Why Does the Pentateuch Speak So Much of Torah and So Little of Jerusalem?" in *The Fall of Jerusalem and the Rise of Torah*, ed. Peter Dubovský, Dominik Markl, and Jean-Pierre Sonnet, FAT 107 (Tübingen: Mohr Siebeck, 2016), 113–28.

Bibliography

Abba, Raymond. "Priests and Levites in Deuteronomy." *VT* 27 (1977): 257–67.

Abegg, Martin, Jr., Peter Flint, and Eugene Ulrich. *The Dead Sea Scrolls Bible: The Oldest Known Bible Translated for the First Time into English.* New York: Harper-SanFrancisco, 1999.

Achenbach, Reinhard. "Zur Systematik der Speisegebote in Leviticus 11 und in Deuteronomium 14." *BZABR* 17 (2011): 161–209.

Ackerman, Susan. "Who Is Sacrificing at Shiloh? The Priesthoods of Ancient Israel's Regional Sanctuaries." In Leuchter and Hutton, *Levites and Priests*, 23–43.

Albright, William F. *From the Stone Age to Christianity.* Baltimore: Johns Hopkins University Press, 1940.

Alexander, T. Desmond, and David W. Baker, eds. *Dictionary of the Old Testament: Pentateuch.* Downers Grove, IL: InterVarsity, 2003.

Allen, James P. *The Ancient Egyptian Language: An Historical Study.* Cambridge: Cambridge University Press, 2013.

———. *Middle Egyptian: An Introduction to the Language and Culture of Hieroglyphs.* Cambridge: Cambridge University Press, 2006.

Allis, Oswald T. *The Five Books of Moses.* Phillipsburg, NJ: Presbyterian & Reformed, 1943. Reprint, Eugene, OR: Wipf & Stock, 2001.

Allison, Dale C., Jr., *The New Moses: A Matthean Typology.* Minneapolis: Fortress, 1993.

Alt, Albrecht. "The God of the Fathers." In *Essays on Old Testament History and Religion,* edited by Albrecht Alt, translated by R. A. Wilson, 1–77. Sheffield: Sheffield Academic, 1989.

Alter, Robert. *The Art of Biblical Narrative.* New York: Basic Books, 1981.

Altman, Amnon. *The Historical Prologue of the Hittite Vassal Treaties: An Inquiry into the Concepts of Hittite Interstate Law.* Bar-Ilan Studies in Near Eastern Languages and Culture. Ramat-Gan: Bar-Ilan University Press, 2004.

———. "The Kingdom of Amurru and the Land of Amurru, 1500–1200 BCE." PhD diss., Bar-Ilan University, 1973.

———. "'The Role of the 'Historical Prologue' in the Hittite Vassal Treaties: An Early Experiment Securing Treaty Compliance." *JHIL* 6, no. 1 (2004): 43–63.

———. "The Submission of Sharrupshi of Nuhasse to Suppiluliuma I (CTH 53 A obv. 2–11)." *UF* 33 (2002): 27–48.

Bibliography

———. *Tracing the Earliest Recorded Concepts of International Law: The Ancient Near East (2500–330 BCE)*. Legal History Library 8. Studies in the History of International Law 4. Leiden: Martinus Nijhoff, 2012.

Anbar, Moshe, and Nadav Na'aman. "An Account Tablet of Sheep from Ancient Hebron." *Tel Aviv* 13–14 (1986–87): 3–12.

Archer, Gleason. *A Survey of Old Testament Introduction*. Rev. ed. Chicago: Moody, 2007.

Arnold, Bill T. *1 & 2 Samuel*. NIV Application Commentary. Grand Rapids: Zondervan, 2003.

———. "The Genesis Narratives." In *Ancient Israel's History: An Introduction to Issues and Sources*, edited by Bill T. Arnold and Richard S. Hess, 23–45. Grand Rapids: Baker Academic, 2014.

Arrais, Tiago. "A Study on the Influence of Philosophical Presuppositions Relating to the Notion of the God–Human Relation upon the Interpretation of Exodus." PhD diss., Andrews University, 2015.

Assmann, Jan. *Stein und Zeit: Mensch und Gesellschaft im Alten Ägypten*. Munich: Wilhelm Fink, 1991.

Ausloos, Hans. "The 'Proto-Deuteronomist': Fifty Years Later." *OTE* 26 (2013): 531–58.

Averbeck, Richard E. "The Cult in Deuteronomy and Its Relationship to the Book of the Covenant and the Holiness Code." In Block and Schultz, *Sepher Torath Mosheh*, 232–60.

———. "The Egyptian Sojourn and Deliverance from Slavery in the Framing and Shaping of the Mosaic Law." In Hoffmeier, Millard, and Rendsburg, *"Did I Not Bring Israel Out of Egypt?"* 143–76.

———. "Factors in Reading the Patriarchal Narratives: Literary, Historical, and Theological Dimensions." In *Giving the Sense: Understanding and Using Old Testament Historical Texts (Essays in Honor of Eugene H. Merrill)*, edited by David M. Howard Jr. and Michael A. Grisanti, 115–37. Grand Rapids: Kregel, 2003.

———. "Law." In *Cracking Old Testament Codes: A Guide to Interpreting Old Testament Literary Form*, edited by D. Brent Sandy and Ronald L. Giese Jr., 113–38. Nashville: Broadman & Holman, 1995.

———. "Pentateuchal Criticism and the Priestly Torah." In Hoffmeier and Magary, *Do Historical Matters Matter to Faith?*, 151–80.

———. Review of *A Prophet Like Moses: Prophecy, Law, and Israelite Religion*, by Jeffrey Stackert. *Themelios* 42, no. 3 (2017): 520–22.

———. Review of *The Promise to the Patriarchs*, by Joel S. Baden. *Themelios* 38, no. 3 (2013): 432–34.

Avruch, Kevin. "Reciprocity, Equality, and Status-Anxiety in the Amarna Letters." In Cohen and Westbroook, *Amarna Diplomacy*, 154–64.

Baden, Joel S. *The Composition of the Pentateuch: Renewing the Documentary Hypothesis*. AYBRL. New Haven: Yale University Press, 2012.

———. *J, E, and the Redaction of the Pentateuch*. FAT 68. Tübingen: Mohr Siebeck, 2009.

———. "On Exodus 33,1–11." *ZAW* 124, no. 3 (2012): 336–39.

———. *The Promise to the Patriarchs*. Oxford: Oxford University Press, 2013.

Bailey, Randall C. *Exodus*. College Press NIV Commentary. Joplin, MO: College Press, 2007.

Baltzer, Klaus. *The Covenant Formulary: In Old Testament, Jewish and Early Christian Writings.* Translated by David E. Green. Philadelphia: Fortress, 1971.

Bäntsch, Bruno. *Exodus-Leviticus-Numeri.* Göttingen: Vandenhoeck & Ruprecht, 1903.

Barré, Michael. "'My Strength and My Song' in Exodus 15:2." *CBQ* 54 (1992): 623–37.

Barrett, David, and John Currid. *Crossway ESV Bible Atlas.* Wheaton, IL: Crossway, 2010.

Barthes, Roland. "The Death of the Author." Ubu Web Papers. http://www.ubu.com /aspen/aspen5and6/threeEssays.html#barthes.

Barton, John. "Biblical Scholarship on the European Continent, in the UK, and Ireland." In *Hebrew Bible, Old Testament: The History of Interpretation,* edited by Magne Soebø, 322–24. Göttingen: Vandenhoeck & Ruprecht, 2015.

Beale, G. K. *The Temple and the Church's Mission: A Biblical Theology of the Dwelling Place of God, New Studies in Biblical Theology.* Downers Grove, IL: IVP Academic, 2004.

Becker, J. Review of *A Linguistic Study of the Relationship Between the Priestly Source and the Book of Ezekiel: A New Approach to an Old Problem,* by Avi Hurvitz. *Bib* 64 (1983): 583–86.

Becker, Uwe. *Exegese des Alten Testaments.* UTB 2664. Tübingen: Mohr Siebeck, 2005.

Beiser, Frederick C. *The German Historicist Tradition.* New York: Oxford University Press, 2012.

Bergland, Kenneth. *Reading as a Disclosure of the Thoughts of the Heart: Proto-Halakhic Reuse and Appropriation Between Torah and the Prophets.* BZABR 23. Wiesbaden: Harrassowitz, 2019.

Bergsma, John Sietze. "The Biblical Manumission Laws: Has the Literary Dependence of H on D Been Demonstrated?" In *A Teacher for All Generations: Essays in Honor of James C. VanderKam,* edited by E. F. Mason et al., 2 vols., 1:65–89. Leiden: Brill Academic, 2012.

———. *The Jubilee from Leviticus to Qumran: A History of Interpretation.* VTSup 115. Leiden: Brill, 2007.

———. Review of *Rewriting the Torah: Literary Revision in Deuteronomy and the Holiness Legislation,* by Jeffrey Stackert. *Bib* 92 (2011): 123–27.

Berman, Joshua A. *Created Equal: How the Bible Broke with Ancient Political Thought.* Oxford: Oxford University Press, 2008.

———. "Empirical Models of Textual Growth: A Challenge for the Historical Critical Tradition." *JHebS* 16 (2016): 1–25.

———. "Historicism and Its Limits: A Response to Bernard M. Levinson and Jeffrey Stackert." *JAJ* 4 (2013): 297–309.

———. "Histories Twice Told: Deuteronomy 1–3 and the Hittite Treaty Prologue Tradition." *JBL* 132, no. 2 (2013): 229–50.

———. *Inconsistency in the Torah: Ancient Literary Convention and the Limits of Source Criticism.* Oxford: Oxford University Press, 2017.

———. "The Kadesh Inscriptions of Ramesses II and the Exodus Sea Account (Exodus 13:17—15:19)." In Hoffmeier, Millard, and Rendsburg, *"Did I Not Bring Israel Out of Egypt?"* 93–112.

———. "Supersessionist or Complementary? Reassessing the Nature of Legal Revision in the Pentateuchal Law Collections." *JBL* 135 (2016): 201–22.

248   *Bibliography*

Bernstein, Richard L. *Beyond Objectivism and Relativism: Science, Hermeneutics, and Praxis.* Philadelphia: University of Pennsylvania Press, 1983.

Bickerman, E. "Coupe une alliance." *Archives d'Historie du Droit Oriental* 5 (1950–51): 133–56.

Biddle, Mark E. *Deuteronomy.* SHBC. Macon, Ga.: Smyth & Helwys, 2003.

Blackburn, Ross W. *The God Who Makes Himself Known: The Missionary Heart of the Book of Exodus.* Downers Grove, IL: Apollos, 2012.

Blenkinsopp, Joseph. "An Assessment of the Alleged Pre-Exilic Date of the Priestly Material in the Pentateuch." *ZAW* 108 (1996): 495–518.

———. *Creation, Un-creation, Re-creation: A Discursive Commentary on Genesis 1–11.* New York: T&T Clark, 2011.

———. *Sage, Priest, Prophet: Religious and Intellectual Leadership in Ancient Israel.* LAI. Louisville: Westminster John Knox, 1995.

Bloch, Yigal. "The Prefixed Perfective and the Dating of Early Hebrew Poetry—A Re-evaluation." *VT* 59 (2009): 34–70.

Block, Daniel I. *Beyond the River Chebar: Studies in the Kingship and Eschatology in the Book of Ezekiel.* Eugene, OR: Cascade, 2013.

———. *Deuteronomy.* NIVAC. Grand Rapids: Zondervan, 2012.

———. *For the Glory of God: Recovering a Biblical Theology of Worship.* Grand Rapids: Baker Academic, 2014.

———. *The Gospel According to Moses.* Eugene, OR: Wipf & Stock, 2012.

———. "The Grace of Torah: The Mosaic Prescription for Life (Deut 4:1–8; 6:20–25)." In *How I Love Your Torah, O* LORD*! Studies in the Book of Deuteronomy*, 15–17. Eugene, OR: Cascade, 2011.

———. "Recovering the Voice of Moses: The Genesis of Deuteronomy." *JETS* 44 (2001): 385–408. Repr. in Block, *Gospel According to Moses*, 21–51.

———. "The Theology of Land in Deuteronomy." In *Lexham Geographic Commentary on the Pentateuch*, edited by Barry J. Beitzel. Bellingham, WA: Lexham, forthcoming.

———. "Transformation of Royal Ideology in Ezekiel." In Tooman and Lyons, *Transforming Visions*, 208–46.

———. *The Triumph of Grace: Literary and Theological Studies in Deuteronomy and Deuteronomic Themes.* Eugene, OR: Wipf & Stock, 2017.

———. "What Do These Stones Mean? The Riddle of Deuteronomy 27." *JETS* 56 (2013): 17–41.

Block, Daniel I., and Richard L. Schultz, eds. *Sepher Torath Mosheh: Studies in the Composition and Interpretation of Deuteronomy.* Peabody, NJ: Hendrickson, 2017.

Blum, Erhard. *Die Komposition der Vätergeschichte.* WMANT 57. Neukirchen: Neukirchener Verlag, 1984.

———. "The Literary Connection Between the Books of Genesis and Exodus and the End of the Book of Joshua." In Dozeman and Schmid, *Farewell to the Yahwist?*, 89–106.

———. "Pentateuch-Hexateuch-Enneateuch? Or: How Can One Recognize a Literary Work in the Bible?" In Dozeman, Römer, and Schmid, *Pentateuch, Hexateuch, or Enneateuch?*, 43–72.

Boadt, Lawrence. "Do Jeremiah and Ezekiel Share a Common View of the Exile?" Paper presented at the annual meeting of the SBL, Atlanta, November 2003.

Boyle, Brian. "'The Figure of the *Nasi* in Ezekiel's Vision of the New Temple (Ezekiel 40–48)." *ABR* 58 (2010): 1–16.

Braulik, Georg. "Die dekalogische Redaktion der deuteronomischen Gesetze: Ihre Abhängigkeit von Levitikus 19 am Beispiel von Deuteronomium 22,1–12; 24,10–22; 25,13–16." In *Bundesdokument und Gesetz: Studien zum Deuteronomium*, edited by Georg Braulik, 1–25. HBS 4. Freibuktedarg: Herder, 1995.

———. *Die deuteronomischen Gesetze und der Dekalog: Studien zum Aufbau von Deuteronomium 12–26*. SBS 145. Stuttgart: Katholisches Bibelwerk, 1991.

———. "Weitere Beobachtungen zur Beziehung zwischen dem Heiligkeitsgesetz und Deuteronomium 19–25." In Veijola, *Das Deuteronomium und seine Querbeziehungen*, 23–55.

———. "Were Women, Too, Allowed to Offer Sacrifices in Israel? Observations on the Meaning and Festive Form of Sacrifice in Deuteronomy." *HvTSt* 55 (1999): 909–42.

Bredenkamp, C. J. "The Covenant and the Early Prophets." *Old Testament Student* 4, no. 3 (1884): 123–27.

Brekelmans, Chris H. W. "Die sogenannten deuteronomischen Elemente in Gen.-Num: Ein Beitrag zur Vorgeschichte des Deuteronomiums." In *Volume du Congrés Genève 1965*, 90–96. VTSup 15. Leiden: Brill, 1966.

Brettler, Marc. "The Composition of 1 Samuel 1–2." *JBL* 116 (1997): 609–12.

Briggs, C. A. *General Introduction to the Study of Holy Scripture*. New York: Scribner, 1899.

Bruckner, James K. *Exodus*. Understanding the Bible Commentary Series 2. Peabody, MA: Hendrickson, 2008.

Bryce, Trevor. *Life and Society in the Hittite World*. Oxford: Oxford University Press, 2002.

Butts, A. M. "A Note on *ne'darî* in Ex 15:6." *VT* 60 (2010): 170.

Campbell, A. F. "An Historical Prologue in a Seventh-Century Treaty." *Bib* 50 (1969): 534–35.

Carasik, Michael. *Theologies of the Mind in Biblical Israel*. StBibLit 85. New York: Peter Lang, 2005.

Carmichael, Calum M. *Law and Narrative in the Bible: The Evidence of the Deuteronomic Laws and the Decalogue*. Ithaca: Cornell University Press, 1985.

———. *The Laws of Deuteronomy*. Ithaca: Cornell University Press, 1974.

———. "The Three Laws on the Release of Slaves." *ZAW* 112, no. 4 (2000): 515–18.

Carr, David McLain. *The Formation of the Hebrew Bible: A New Reconstruction*. New York: Oxford University Press, 2011.

———. "Genesis." In *The Oxford Encyclopedia of the Books of the Bible*, edited by Michael D. Coogan, 1:316–34. Oxford: Oxford University Press, 2011.

———. "Method in Determination of Direction of Dependence: An Empirical Test of Criteria Applied to Exodus 34, 11–26 and Its Parallels." In *Gottes Volk am Sinai: Untersuchungen zu Ex 32–34 and Dtn 9–10*, edited by M. Köckert and E. Blum, 107–40. Gütersloh: Gütersloh, 2001.

———. *Reading the Fractures of Genesis: Historical and Literary Approaches*. Louisville: Westminster John Knox, 1996.

———. "Unified Until Proven Disunified? Assumptions and Standards in Assessing the Literary Complexity of Ancient Biblical Texts." *JBL* 133, no. 3 (2014): 677–81.

250 Bibliography

———. "What Is Required to Identify the Pre-Priestly Narrative Connections Between Genesis and Exodus? Some General Reflections and Specific Cases." In Dozeman and Schmid, *Farewell to the Yahwist?*, 159–80.

———. *Writing on the Tablet of the Heart: Origins of Scripture and Literature.* Oxford: Oxford University Press, 2005.

Cassirer, Ernst. *The Philosophy of the Enlightenment.* Princeton: Princeton University Press, 1951.

Cassuto, Umberto. *A Commentary on the Book of Exodus.* Translated by Israel Abrahams. Jerusalem: Magnes, 1997.

———. *The Documentary Hypothesis and the Composition of the Pentateuch: Eight Lectures.* Jerusalem: Shalem, 2006.

Charlesworth, James H. ed. *The Old Testament Pseudepigrapha.* 2 vols. Peabody, MA: Hendrickson, 1983.

Charpin, Dominique. "The History of Ancient Mesopotamia: An Overview." In *Civilizations of the Ancient Near East*, edited by Jack M. Sasson, 4 vols., 2:807–30. New York: Charles Scribner's Sons, 1995.

Chavalas, Mark W., ed. *Historical Sources in Translation: The Ancient Near East.* Oxford: Blackwell, 2006.

Chavel, Simeon. "The Literary Development of Deuteronomy 12: Between Religious Ideal and Social Reality." In Dozeman, Schmid, and Schwartz, *Pentateuch*, 303–26.

Childs, Brevard S. *The Book of Exodus: A Critical, Theological Commentary.* OTL. Louisville: Westminster John Knox, 1974.

———. *Introduction to the Old Testament as Scripture.* Philadelphia: Fortress, 1979.

Chirichigno, Gregory C. *Debt-Slavery in Israel and the Ancient Near East.* JSOTSup 141. Sheffield: Sheffield Academic Press, 1993.

Cholewiński, Alfred. *Heiligkeitsgesetz und Deuteronomium.* AB 66. Rome: Biblical Institute, 1969.

Clifford, R. J. "Exodus." In *The New Jerome Biblical Commentary*, edited by R. E. Brown, Joseph A. Fitzmyer, and Roland E. Murphy, 44–60. Englewood Cliffs, NJ: Prentice-Hall, 1990.

Clines, David J. A. "Response to Rolf Rendtorff's 'What Happened to the Yahwist? Reflections After Thirty Years.'" SBL Forum Archive. http://www.sbl-site.org /publications/article.aspx?ArticleId=551.

Cody, Aalred. *A History of Old Testament Priesthood.* AB 35. Rome: Pontifical Biblical Institute, 1969.

Cogan, M. *Imperialism Religion: Assyria, Judah, and Israel in the Eighth and Seventh Centuries B.C.E.* Missoula, MT: Scholars Press, 1974.

Cohen, Chaim. "Was the P Document Secret?" *JANESCU* I (1969): 39–44.

Cohen, Chaim, Victor Avigdor Hurowitz, Avi M. Hurvitz, Yochanan Muffs, Baruch J. Schwartz, and Jeffrey H. Tigay, eds. *Birkat Shalom: Studies in the Bible, Ancient Near Eastern Literature, and Post-biblical Judaism Presented to Shalom M. Paul on the Occasion of His Seventieth Birthday.* 2 vols. 1:31–44. Winona Lake, IN: Eisenbrauns, 2008.

Cohen, Mark E. *The Cultic Calendars of the Ancient Near East.* Bethesda, MD: CDL, 1993.

Cohen, Raymond. "Intelligence in the Amarna Letters." In Cohen and Westbrook, *Amarna Diplomacy*, 85–98.

Cohen, Raymond, and Raymond Westbrook, eds. *Amarna Diplomacy: The Beginnings of International Relations*. Baltimore: Johns Hopkins University Press, 2000.

Cole, R. Alan. *Exodus: An Introduction and Commentary*. Tyndale Old Testament Commentaries. Downers Grove, IL: InterVarsity, 1973.

Colenso, John W. *The Pentateuch and the Book of Joshua Critically Examined, Part III*. 2nd ed. London: Longman, 1879.

Collins, Billie Jean. *The Hittites and Their World*. Atlanta: SBL, 2004.

Cook, Stephen L. *The Social Roots of Biblical Yahwism*. Atlanta: SBL, 2004.

Craigie, Peter C. *The Book of Deuteronomy*. NICOT. Grand Rapids: Eerdmans, 1976.

————. "The Poetry of Ugarit and Israel." *Tyndale Bulletin* 22 (1970): 3–31.

Cross, F. M. *Canaanite Myth and Hebrew Epic*. Cambridge, MA: Harvard University Press, 1973.

Crüsemann, Frank. *The Torah: Theology and Social History of Old Testament Law*. Translated by Allan Mahnke. Minneapolis: Fortress, 1992.

Currid, John D. *A Study Commentary on Exodus*. 2 vols. Auburn, MA: Evangelical Press, 2000.

Davidson, Richard M. "The Divine Covenant Lawsuit Motif in Canonical Perspective." *JATS* 21, nos. 1–2 (2010): 45–84.

————. "Earth's First Sanctuary: Genesis 1–3 and Parallel Creation Accounts." *Andrews University Seminary Studies* 53 (2015): 65–89.

————. "Gracia ardiente: La misericordia de Dios en el pacto Sinaítico." In *"La palabra que Yo te diga, esa hablarás": Estudios selectos en el Pentateuco*, edited by Merling Alomía, 85–110. Investigaciones bíblico teológicas upeuenses 2. Lima, Peru: Ediciones Theologika—Peruvian Union University, 2018.

————. "Literary Structure in the Book of Exodus: A Case Study in the Aesthetic Nature and Theological Function of Scripture." Paper presented at the annual meeting of the Adventist Theological Society/Evangelical Theological Society, Baltimore, November 19, 2013.

————. *Typology in Scripture: A Study of Hermeneutical Τύπος Structures*. AUSDS 2. Berrien Springs, MI: Andrews University Press, 1981.

Deller, K., and S. Parpola, "Ein Vertrag Assurbanipals mit dem arabischen Stamm Qedar," *Orientalia* 37 (1968): 464–66.

Dershowitz, Idan, Navot Akiva, Moshe Koppel, and Nachum Dershowitz. "Computerized Source Criticism of Biblical Texts." *JBL* 134 (2015): 253–71.

Dever, William G. *What Did the Biblical Writers Know and When Did They Know It? What Archaeology Can Tell Us about the Reality of Ancient Israel?* Grand Rapids: Eerdmans, 2001.

Dickens, Charles. *A Tale of Two Cities*. Waiheke Island: Floating Press, 1859.

Dillman, August. *Die Bücher Exodus und Leviticus*. Leipzig: S. Hirzel, 1880.

Dolansky, Shawna. "Deuteronomy 34: The Death of Moses, Not of Source Criticism." *JBL* 133, no. 3 (2014): 669–76.

Dorsey, David A. *The Literary Structure of the Old Testament: A Commentary on Genesis–Malachi*. Grand Rapids: Baker Academic, 1999.

Dozeman, Thomas B. "The Authorship of the Pentateuch." *Dialogue* 32, no. 4 (1999): 87–112.

————. "The Commission of Moses and the Book of Genesis." In Dozeman and Schmid, *Farewell to the Yahwist?*, 107–29.

————. *Exodus*. ECC. Grand Rapids: Eerdmans, 2009.

252   *Bibliography*

———. *God at War: Power in the Exodus Tradition*. Oxford: Oxford University Press, 1996.

Dozeman, Thomas B., Thomas Römer, and Konrad Schmid, eds. *Pentateuch, Hexateuch, or Enneateuch? Identifying Literary Works in Genesis Through Kings*, 43–72. AIL 8. Leiden: Brill, 2012.

Dozeman, Thomas B., and Konrad Schmid, eds. *A Farewell to the Yahwist? The Composition of the Pentateuch in Recent European Interpretation*. SBLSS 34. Atlanta: SBL, 2006.

Dozeman, Thomas B., Konrad Schmid, and Baruch J. Schwartz, eds. *The Pentateuch: International Perspectives on Current Research*. FAT 78. Tübingen: Mohr Siebeck, 2011.

Driver, Samuel R. *A Critical and Exegetical Commentary on Deuteronomy*. 2nd ed. ICC. Edinburgh: T&T Clark, 1896. 3rd ed. Edinburgh: T&T Clark, 1902.

Droysen, Johann Gustav. *Historik: Historisch-kritische Ausgabe*. Edited by Peter Leyh and Horst Walter Blanke. Stuttgart-Bad Cannstatt: Frommann-Holzboog, 1977.

Duke, Rodney K. "The Portion of the Levite: Another Reading of Deuteronomy 18:6–8." *JBL* 106 (1987): 193–201.

Durham, John I. *Exodus*. WBC 3. Waco: Word, 1987.

Elias, Norbert. *Time: An Essay*. Oxford: Blackwell, 1992.

Elwolde, John. "'Inner-Biblical Exegesis' and Bible Translation: Reflections on Bernard Levinson's Legal Revision and Religious Renewal in Ancient Israel." *Review of Rabbinic Judaism* 14 (2011): 223–34.

Enns, Peter. *Exodus*. NIV Application Commentary. Grand Rapids: Zondervan, 2000.

Even-Shoshan, Abraham. *A New Concordance of the Hebrew Bible*. Jerusalem: "Kiryat Sefer," 1989.

Eyre, Christopher. *The Use of Documents in Pharaonic Egypt*. Oxford: Oxford University Press, 2013.

Feest, Uljana, ed. *Historical Perspectives on Erklären and Verstehen*. Berlin: Springer, 2010.

Feldman, Marian H. "Mesopotamian Art." In Snell, *Companion to the Ancient Near East*, 281–301.

Firmage, Edwin B., Bernard G. Weiss, and John W. Welch, eds. *Religion and Law: Biblical-Judaic and Islamic Perspectives*. Winona Lake, IN: Eisenbrauns, 1990.

Fischer-Elfert, Hans-Werner. *Die satirische Streitschrift des Papyrus Anastasi I: Übersetzung und Kommentar*. Wiesbaden: Harrassowitz, 1986.

Fleming, Daniel E., "Genesis in History and Tradition: The Syrian Background of Israel's Ancestors, Reprise." In *The Future of Biblical Archaeology: Reassessing Methodologies and Assumptions*, edited by James K. Hoffmeier and Aland Millard, 192–232. Grand Rapids: Eerdmans, 2004.

Fleming, David Marron. "The Divine Council as Type Scene in the Hebrew Bible." PhD diss., Southern Baptist Theological Seminary, 1989.

Fokkelman, J. P. "Exodus." In *The Literary Guide to the Bible*, edited by Robert Alter and Frank Kermode, 57–58. Cambridge, MA: Belknap, 1987.

Foster, Benjamin R. "Transmission of Knowledge." In Snell, *Companion to the Ancient Near East*, 245–52.

Fox, Michael V. *Proverbs 1–9: A New Translation with Introduction and Commentary*. Anchor Yale Bible Commentaries 18. New Haven: Yale University Press, 2008.

François, Mark Steven. "Something Old, Something Borrowed, or Something New? The Relationship Between the Succession Treaty of Esarhaddon and the Curses of Deuteronomy 28." PhD diss., University of St. Michael's College, 2017.

Frankena, Rintje. "The Vassal-Treaties of Esarhaddon and the Dating of Deuteronomy." *OtSt* 14 (1965): 122–54.

Freedman, David Noel, Gary A. Herion, David F. Graf, John David Pleins, and Astrid B. Beck, eds. *The Anchor Bible Dictionary*. 6 vols. New Haven: Yale University Press, 1992–2008.

Fretheim, Terence E. *Exodus*. Interpretation: A Bible Commentary for Preaching and Teaching. Louisville: John Knox, 1991.

———. "The Priestly Document: Anti-Temple?" *VT* 18 (1968): 313–29.

Frey, Mathilde. "Sabbath in Egypt? An Examination of Exodus 5." *JSOT* 39 (2015): 249–63.

Friedman, Richard E. *The Bible with Sources Revealed: A New View into the Five Books of Moses*. New York: HarperCollins, 2003.

———. "Three Major Redactors of the Torah." In Cohen et al., *Birkat Shalom*, 1:31–44.

———. *Who Wrote the Bible?* New York: HarperOne, 1987. Reprint, New York: Summit, 1997.

Frisch, Amos. "The Exodus Motif in 1 Kings 1–14." *JSOT* 87 (2000): 6.

Frolov, Serge. "The Death of Moses and the Fate of Source Criticism." *JBL* 133, no. 3 (2014): 648–60.

Gane, Roy E. "Didactic Logic and the Authorship of Leviticus." In *Current Issues in Priestly and Related Literature: The Legacy of Jacob Milgrom and Beyond*, edited by Roy E. Gane and Ada Taggar-Cohen, 197–221. RBS 82. Atlanta: SBL, 2015.

———. *Ritual Dynamic Structure*. GD 14, R2. Piscataway, NJ: Gorgias, 2004.

Ganzel, Tova. "Transformation of Pentateuchal Descriptions of Idolatry." In Tooman and Lyons, *Transforming Visions*, 33–49.

Gardiner, Alan H. *Egypt of the Pharaohs*. Oxford: Oxford University Press, 1978.

———. "The Mansion of Life and the Master of the King's Largess." *JEA* 24, no. 1 (1938): 83–91.

Garrett, Duane A. *A Commentary on Exodus*. Kregel Exegetical Library. Grand Rapids: Kregel Academic, 2014.

———. *Rethinking Genesis: The Source and Authorship of the First Book of the Pentateuch*. Grand Rapids: Baker, 2001.

Garsiel, Moshe. "The Book of Samuel: Its Composition, Structure and Significance as a Historiographical Source." *JHebS* 10, no. 5 (2010): 1–42. http://www.jhsonline .org/Articles/article_133.pdf.

Gates, Marie-Henriette. "Archaeology and the Ancient Near East: Methods and Limits." In Snell, *Companion to the Ancient Near East*, 65–78.

Gemser, B. "The Rîb- or Controversy-Pattern in Hebrew Mentality." In *Wisdom in Israel and in the Ancient Near East*, edited by Martin Noth and D. Winton Thomas, 120–37. Leiden: Brill, 1960.

George, Andrew. *The Babylonian Gilgamesh Epic: Introduction, Critical Edition, and Cuneiform Texts*. 2 vols. Oxford: Oxford University Press, 2003.

Gerhards, Meik. "Hethitische und biblische Historiographie." *BN*, n.s., 156 (2013): 107–30.

Gertz, Jan Christian. "The Transition Between the Books of Genesis and Exodus." In Dozeman and Schmid, *Farewell to the Yahwist?*, 73–88.

254 Bibliography

Gertz, Jan Christian, Bernard M. Levinson, Dalit Rom-Shiloni, and Konrad Schmid, eds. *The Formation of the Pentateuch: Bridging the Academic Cultures of Europe, Israel, and North America.* FAT 111. Tübingen: Mohr Siebeck, 2016.

Gile, Jason. "Deuteronomic Influence on the Book of Ezekiel." PhD diss, Wheaton College, 2013.

Gispen, Willem H. *Exodus.* Grand Rapids: Zondervan, 1982.

Goody, Jack, ed. *Literacy in Traditional Societies.* Cambridge: Cambridge University Press, 1968.

Greenberg, Moshe. *Ezekiel 1–20.* AB 22. Garden City, NY: Doubleday, 1983.

———. "Some Postulates of Biblical Criminal Law." In *Yehezkel Kaufman Jubilee Volume: Studies in Bible and Jewish Religion Dedicated to Yehezkel Kaufmann on the Occasion of His Seventieth Birthday,* edited by Menahem Haran, 11–13. Jerusalem: Magnes, 1960.

———. "Three Conceptions of the Torah in Hebrew Scriptures [1990]." In *Studies in the Bible and Jewish Thought,* 14–15. JPS Scholar Distinction Series. Jerusalem: Jewish Publication Society, 1995.

Grisanti, Michael A. "Deuteronomy." In *Numbers–Ruth,* 459–61. EBC, rev. ed., 2. Grand Rapids: Zondervan, 2012.

———. "Josiah and the Composition of Deuteronomy." In Block and Schultz, *Sepher Torath Mosheh,* 110–38.

———. "Old Testament Poetry as a Vehicle for Historiography." *BSac* 181 (2004): 163–78.

Gromova, Daria. "Hittite Role in Political History of Syria in the Amarna Age Reconsidered." *UF* 39 (2007): 277–309.

———. "Idanda Archive and the Syrian Campaigns of Suppiluliuma I: New Pieces for the Puzzle." *Babel und Bibel* 6 (2012): 473–79.

Gunkel, Hermann. *The Legends of Genesis.* Translated by W. H. Carruth. New York: Schocken, 1901.

Gunkel, Hermann, Leopold Zscharnack, Alfred Bertholet, Hermann Faber, Horst Stephan, Friedrich Michael Schiele, and Oskar Rühle, eds. *Die Religion in geschichte und gegenwart: Handwoerterbuch fuer theologie und religionswissenschaft Registerband.* 2 vols. Tübingen: Mohr Siebeck, 1927–32.

Gunneweg, Antonius H. J. *Leviten und Priester: Hauptlinen der Traditionsbildung und Geschichte des israelitisch-jüdischen Kultpersonals.* FRLANT 89. Göttingen: Vandenhoeck & Ruprecht, 1965.

Gurney, O. R. *The Hittites: A Summary of the Art, Achievements, and Social Organization of a Great People of Asia Minor During the Second Millennium B.C. as discovered by Modern Excavations.* Harmondsworth: Penguin, 1962.

Hagedorn, Anselm C. "Taking the Pentateuch to the Twenty-First century." *Expository Times* 119, no. 2 (2007): 53–58.

Hallo, William W., ed. *Canonical Compositions from the Biblical World.* Vol. 1 of Hallo and Younger, *Context of Scripture.*

———. "Slave Release in the Biblical World in Light of a New Text." In *Solving Riddles and Untying Knots: Biblical, Epigraphic, and Semitic Studies in Honor of Jonas C. Greenfield,* edited by Ziony Zevit, Seymour Gitin, and Michael Sokoloff, 88–93. Winona Lake, IN: Eisenbrauns, 1995.

Hallo, William W., and K. Lawson Younger, eds. *The Context of Scripture.* 3 vols. Leiden: E. J. Brill, 1997–2002.

―――. *Monumental Inscriptions from the Biblical World*. Vol. 2 of Hallo and Younger, *Context of Scripture*.

Hamilton, Victor P. *Exodus: An Exegetical Commentary*. Grand Rapids: Baker Academic, 2011.

Haran, Menahem. "Ezekiel, P, and the Priestly School." *VT* 58, no. 2 (2008): 211–18.

―――. *Temples and Temple-Service in Ancient Israel: An Inquiry into Biblical Cult Phenomena and the Historical Setting of the Priestly School*. Winona Lake, IN: Eisenbrauns, 1985.

Hayes, Christine. *What's Divine About Divine Law? Early Perspectives*. Princeton: Princeton University Press, 2015.

Hayes, John H., ed. *Dictionary of Biblical Interpretation*. 2 vols. Nashville: Abingdon, 1999.

Hayward, C. T. R. "Sirach and Wisdom's Dwelling Place." In *Where Shall Wisdom Be Found? Wisdom in the Bible, the Church, and the Contemporary World*, edited by Stephen C. Barton, 31–46. Edinburgh: T&T Clark, 1999.

Heiser, Michael S. "The Divine Council in Late Canonical and Non-Canonical Second Temple Jewish Literature." PhD diss., University of Wisconsin–Madison, 2004.

Helck, Wolfgang, Eberhard Otto, and Wolfhart Westendorf, eds. *Lexikon der Ägyptologie*. 7 vols. Wiesbaden: Harrassowitz, 1972–92.

Hendel, Ronald. "The Exodus as Cultural Memory: Egyptian Bondage and the Song of the Sea." In *Israel's Exodus in Transdisciplinary Perspective: Text, Archaeology, Culture, and Geoscience*, edited by Thomas E. Levy, Thomas Schneider, and William H. C. Propp, 65–77. QMHSS. Cham, Switzerland: Springer, 2015.

―――. "Farewell to SBL: Faith and Reason in Biblical Studies." *BAR* 36, no. 4 (2010): 28, 74.

―――. *Remembering Abraham: Culture, Memory, and History in the Hebrew Bible*. New York: Oxford University Press, 2005.

―――. "Sacrifice as a Cultural System: The Ritual Symbolism of Exodus 24:3–8." *ZAW* 101, no. 3 (1989): 366–90.

Hess, Richard S. "Alalakh Studies in the Bible: Obstacle or Contribution?" In *Scripture and Other Artifacts: Essays on the Bible and Archaeology in Honor of Philip J. King*, edited by Michael D. Coogan, J. Cheryl Exum, and Lawrence E. Stager, 199–215. Louisville: Westminster John Knox, 1994.

―――. *Israelite Religions: An Archaeological and Biblical Survey*. Grand Rapids: Baker Academic, 2007.

―――. "Literacy in Iron Age Israel." In *Windows into Old Testament History: Evidence, Argument, and the Crisis of "Biblical Israel*," edited by V. P. Long, D. W. Baker, and G. J. Wenham, 82–102. Grand Rapids: Eerdmans, 2002.

―――. "Oral Tradition and the OT." In *Dictionary for Theological Interpretation of the Bible*. edited by C. G. Bartholomew, D. J. Treer, and N. T. Wright, 551–53. Grand Rapids: Baker Academic, 2005.

―――. "Personal Names in Cuneiform Texts from Middle Bronze Age Palestine." In *"He Unfurrowed His Brow and Laughed": Essays in Honour of Nicolas Wyatt*, edited by W. G. E. Watson, 153–61. AOAT 299. Münster: Ugarit-Verlag, 2007.

―――. "Questions of Reading and Writing in Ancient Israel." *BBR* 19 (2009): 1–9.

―――. Review of "Protective Strategies . . ." and 'Maximizing Literacy as a Protective Strategy," by Stephen L. Young. *Denver Journal* 18 (2015).

256 *Bibliography*

———. Review of *Writing and Literacy in the World of Ancient Israel: Epitraphic Evidence from the Bronze Age*, by Christopher A. Rollston. *BBR* 21 (2011): 394–96.

———. "Rhetorical Forms in EA 162." *UF* 22 (1990): 137–48.

———. "Rhetorical Forms in the Amarna Correspondence from Jerusalem." *Maarav* 10 (2003): 221–44.

———. "Smitten Ant Bites Back: Rhetorical Forms in the Amarna Correspondence from Shechem." In *Verse in Ancient Near Eastern Prose*, edited by J. C. de Moor and W. G. E. Watson, 95–111. AOAT 42. Kevelaer: Butzon & Bercker; Neukirchen-Vluyn: Neukirchener Verlag, 1993.

———. "Some Views on Literacy." The Bible and Interpretation. http://www.bibleinterp.com/opeds/views357905.shtml.

———. "Writing About Writing: Abecedaries and Evidence for Literacy in Ancient Israel." *VT* 56 (2006): 342–46.

Hill, Andrew E., and John H. Walton. *A Survey of the Old Testament*. 2nd ed. Grand Rapids: Zondervan, 2000.

Hillers, Delbert R. *Covenant: The History of a Biblical Idea*. Baltimore: Johns Hopkins University Press, 1969.

———. *Treaty Curses and the Old Testament Prophets*. BibOr 16. Rome: Pontifical Biblical Institute, 1964.

Hoffmeier, James K. *Ancient Israel in Sinai*. New York: Oxford University Press, 2011.

———. "The Arm of God Versus the Arm of Pharaoh in the Exodus Narratives." *Bibl* 67 (1986): 378–87.

Hoffmeier, James K., and Dennis R. Magary, eds. *Do Historical Matters Matter to Faith? A Critical Appraisal of Modern and Postmodern Approaches to the Bible*. Wheaton, IL: Crossway, 2012.

Hoffmeier, James K., Alan Millard, and Gary Rendsburg, eds. *"Did I Not Bring Israel Out of Egypt?" Biblical, Archaeological, and Egyptological Perspectives on the Exodus Narratives*. BBRSup 13. Winona Lake, IN: Eisenbrauns, 2016.

Holloway, Steven W. "What Ship Goes There: The Flood Narratives in the Gilgamesh Epic and Genesis Considered in Light of Ancient Near Eastern Temple Ideology." *ZAW* 103, no. 3 (1991): 328–54.

Holtz, Shalom E. "The Prophet as Summoner." In *A Common Cultural Heritage: Studies on Mesopotamia and the Biblical World in Honor of Barry L. Eichler*, edited by Grant Frame, 19–34. Bethesda, MD: CDL, 2011.

Hopkins, David. *The Highlands of Canaan: Agricultural Life in the Early Iron Age*. SWBA 3. Decatur, GA: Almond, 1985.

Horowitz, Wayne, and Takayoshi Oshima. *Cuneiform in Canaan: Cuneiform Sources from the Land of Israel in Ancient Times*. Jerusalem: Israel Exploration Society and the Hebrew University of Jerusalem, 2006.

House, Paul R. *Old Testament Theology*. Downers Grove, IL: InterVarsity, 1998.

Houston, Walter. *Purity and Monotheism: Clean and Unclean Animals in Biblical Law*. JSOTSup 140. Sheffield: Sheffield Academic Press, 1993.

Howard, Thomas Albert. *Religion and the Rise of Historicism: W. M. L. de Wette, Jacob Burckhardt, and the Theological Origins of Nineteenth-Century Historical Consciousness*. Cambridge: Cambridge University Press, 2006.

Huddleston, Jonathan. "Recent Scholarship on the Pentateuch: Historical, Literary, and Theological Reflections." *ResQ* 55, no. 4 (2013): 193–211.

Huddleston, Neal A. "Deuteronomy as *Mischgattung*: A Comparative and Contrastive Discourse Analysis of Deuteronomy and Ancient Near Eastern Traditions." PhD diss., Trinity Evangelical Divinity School, 2015.

Huffmon, Herbert B. "Covenant Lawsuit in Prophets." *JBL* 78 (1959): 295.

Hughes, Jeremy. *Secrets of the Times: Myth and History in Biblical Chronology.* LHBOTS 66. Sheffield: Sheffield Academic Press, 2009.

Humboldt, Wilhelm von. "On the Historian's Task." *HistTh* 6 (1967): 57–71.

Hurowitz, Victor. *I Have Built You an Exalted House: Temple Building in the Bible in Light of Mesopotamian and North-West Semitic Writings.* JSOTSup 115. Sheffield: Sheffield Academic Press, 1992.

———. *Inu Anum Sirum: Literary Structures in the Non-juridical Sections of Codex Hammurabi.* Philadelphia: University of Pennsylvania Museum of Archaeology and Anthropology, 1994.

———. "The Priestly Account of Building the Tabernacle." *JAOS* 105 (1985): 21–30.

Hurvitz, Avi. "Can Biblical Texts Be Dated Linguistically? Chronological Perspectives in the Historical Study of Biblical Hebrew." In *Congress Volume Oslo*, edited by A. Lemaire and M. Saebo, 123–42. VTSup 80. Leiden: Brill, 2000.

———. "Dating the Priestly Source in the Light of the Historical Study of Biblical Hebrew a Century After Wellhausen." *ZAW* 100 (1988): 88–100.

———. "Evidence of Language in Dating the Priestly Code: A Linguistic Study in Technical Idioms and Terminology." *RB* 81 (1974): 24–56.

———. "Linguistic Observations on the Priestly Term 'Edah and the Language of P." *Imm* 1 (1972): 21–23.

———. *A Linguistic Study of the Relationship Between the Priestly Source and the Book of Ezekiel: A New Approach to an Old Problem.* CahRB. Paris: Gabalda, 1982.

———. "Once Again: The Linguistic Profile of the Priestly Material in the Pentateuch and Its Historical Age: A Response to J. Blenkinsopp." *ZAW* 112, no. 2 (2000): 180–91.

Hwang, Jerry. *The Rhetoric of Remembrance: An Investigation of the "Fathers" in Deuteronomy.* Siphrut 8. Winona Lake, IN: Eisenbrauns, 2012.

Iggers, Georg G. "Historicism: The History and Meaning of the Term." *JHI* 56 (1995): 129–52.

Ishida, Tomoo. "The Structure and Historical Implications of the Lists of Pre-Israelite Nations." *Bib* 60 (1979): 461–90.

Jackson, Bernard S. *Studies in the Semiotics of Biblical Law.* JSOTSup 314. Sheffield: Sheffield Academic Press, 2000.

Jacob, Benno. *The Second Book of the Bible: Exodus.* Hoboken, NJ: Ktav, 1992.

Janzen, Gerald J. *Exodus, Westminster Bible Companion.* Louisville: Westminster John Knox, 1997.

———. "Song of Moses, Song of Miriam: Who Is Seconding Whom?" *CBQ* 54 (1992): 211–20.

Japhet, Sara. "The Relationship Between the Legal Corpora in the Pentateuch in Light of Manumission Laws." In *Studies in Bible, 1986*, edited by Sara Japhet, 63–89. ScrHier 31. Jerusalem: Magnes VIII, 1986.

Jenni, Ernst, and Claus Westermann, eds. *Theological Lexicon of the Old Testament.* Translated by Mark E. Biddle. Peabody, MA: Hendrickson, 1997.

Jindo, Job Y. "The Divine Courtroom Motif in the Hebrew Bible: A Holistic Approach." In Mermelstein and Holtz, *Divine Courtroom*, 76–93.

258   Bibliography

Johnston, Gordon. "What Biblicists Need to Know About Hittite Treaties." Paper presented at the Old Testament Backgrounds and Ancient Near East Study Group of the National Meeting of the Evangelical Theological Society, San Antonio, TX, November 16, 2016.

Johnstone, William. *Exodus*. 2 vols. SHBC. Macon, GA: Smyth & Helwys, 2014.

———. Review of *A Farewell to the Yahwist? The Composition of the Pentateuch in Recent European Interpretation*, ed. Thomas B. Dozeman and Konrad Schmid. *JSS* 54, no. 1 (2009): 276–77.

Jönsson, Christer. "Diplomatic Signaling in the Amarna Letters." In Cohen and Westbrook, *Amarna Diplomacy*, 191–205.

Joosten, Jan. "Diachronic Linguistics and the Date of the Pentateuch." In Gertz et al., *Formation of the Pentateuch*, 327–44.

———. *People and Land in the Holiness Code: An Exegetical Study of the Ideational Framework of the Law in Leviticus 17–26*. VTSup 67. Leiden: Brill, 1996.

———. *The Verbal System of Biblical Hebrew: A New Synthesis Elaborated on the Basis of Classical Prose*. JBS 10. Jerusalem: Simor, 2012.

Joyce, Paul. "Temple and Worship in Ezekiel 40–48." In *Temple and Worship in Biblical Israel*, edited by John Day, 145–63. New York: T&T Clark, 2005.

Junior, Nyasha, and Jeremy Schipper. "Mosaic Disability and Identity in Exodus 4:10; 6:12, 30." *BibInt* 16 (2008): 428–41.

Kaiser, Walter C., Jr. "Exodus." In *Genesis–Leviticus*, 344–46. EBC, rev. ed., 1. Grand Rapids: Zondervan, 2006.

———. *Toward Old Testament Ethics*. Grand Rapids: Zondervan, 1983.

Kaufman, Stephen A. "The Structure of the Deuteronomic Law." *Maarav* 1, no. 2 (1979): 105–58.

———. "The Temple Scroll and Higher Criticism." *HUCA* 53 (1982): 29–43.

Kaufmann, Yehezkel. *From the Babylonian Captivity to the End of Prophecy*. Vol. 4 of *History of the Religion of Israel*. New York: Ktav, 1977.

———. *The Religion of Israel: From Its Beginnings to the Babylonian Exile*. Translated and abridged by Moshe Greenberg. Chicago: University of Chicago Press, 1960.

Keener, Craig S. *The Gospel of John: A Commentary*. 2 vols. Grand Rapids: Baker Academic, 2003.

Keil, Carl F., and Franz Delitzsch, *Biblical Commentary on the Old Testament: The Pentateuch*. Translated by James Martin. 6 vols. Edinburgh: T&T Clark, 1864.

Kestemont, Guy. *Diplomatique et droit international en Asie occidentale (1600–1200 av. J.C.)*. PIOL 9. Louvain: Peeters, 1974.

Kikawada, Isaac M., and Arthur Quinn. *Before Abraham Was: The Unity of Genesis 1–11*. Nashville: Abingdon, 1985.

Kilchör, Benjamin. "The Direction of Dependence Between the Laws of the Pentateuch: The Priority of a Literary Approach." *ETL* 89 (2013): 1–14.

———. "Frei aber arm? Soziale Sicherheit als Schlüssel zum Verhältnis der Sklavenfreilassungsgesetze im Pentateuch." *VT* 62 (2012): 381–97.

———. "Levirate Marriage in Deuteronomy 25:5–10 and Its Precursors in Leviticus and Numbers: A Test Case for the Relationship Between P/H and D." *CBQ* 77 (2015): 429–40.

———. *Mosetora und Jahwetora: Das Verhältnis von Deuteronomium 12–16 zu Exodus, Levitikus und Numeri*. BZABR 21. Wiesbaden: Harrassowitz, 2015.

Kitchen, Kenneth A. *Ancient Orient and Old Testament.* Downers Grove, IL: InterVarsity, 1966.

———. *The Bible in Its World: The Bible and Archaeology Today.* Downers Grove, IL: InterVarsity, 1977.

———. *On the Reliability of the Old Testament.* Grand Rapids: Eerdmans, 2003.

Kitchen, Kenneth A., and Paul J. N. Lawrence. *Treaty, Law and Covenant in the Ancient Near East.* 3 vols. Wiesbaden: Harrassowitz, 2012.

Klein, Anja. "Hymn and History in Ex 15: Observations on the Relationship Between Temple Theology and Exodus Narrative in the Song of the Sea." *ZAW* 124, no. 4 (2012): 516–27.

Kleinknecht, Hermann, and Walter Gutbrod. *Law.* Translated by Dorothea Barton. London: Black, 1962.

Kline, Meredith G. *Kingdom Prologue.* South Hamilton: Gordon-Conwell Theological Seminary, 1989.

———. *The Structure of Biblical Authority.* Eugene, OR: Wipf & Stock, 1997.

———. *Treaty of the Great King.* Grand Rapids: Eerdmans, 1963.

Knight, Douglas. *Rediscovering the Traditions of Israel.* 2nd ed. Atlanta: Scholars Press, 1975.

Knohl, Israel. "Nimrod, Son of Cush, King of Mesopotamia, and the Dates of P and J." In Cohen et al., *Birkat Shalom*, 1:45–52.

———. *The Sanctuary of Silence: The Priestly Torah and the Holiness School.* Minneapolis: Fortress, 1995.

Knoppers, Gary N. "The Historical Study of the Monarchy: Developments and Detours." In *The Face of Old Testament Studies: A Survey of Contemporary Approaches*, edited by David W. Baker and Bill T. Arnold, 213–14. Grand Rapids: Baker Academic, 1999.

———. *Jews and Samaritans: The Origins and History of their Early Relations.* New York: Oxford University Press, 2013.

Konkel, Michael. "Ezekiel 40–48 and P: Questions and Perspectives." Paper presented at the annual meeting of the Society of Biblical Literature, San Diego, CA, November 22, 2014.

Korošec, Viktor. *Hethitische Staatsverträge: Ein Beitrag zu ihrer juristischen Wertung.* Leipziger rechtswissenschaftliche Studien 60. Leipzig: T. Weicher, 1931.

Kuhrt, Amélie. *The Ancient Near East, c. 3000–330 BC.* Routledge History of the Ancient World. London: Routledge, 1995.

Lackenbacher, Sylvie. *Textes akkadiens d'Ugarit: Textes provenant des vingt-cinq premières campagnes.* LAPO. Paris: Les Éditions du Cerf, 2002.

Lambert, W. G., A. R. Millard, and Miguel Civil, eds. *Atra-hasis: The Babylonian Story of the Flood.* Winona Lake, IN: Eisnebrauns, 1999.

Laroche, Emmanuel. *Catalogue des textes Hittites.* Paris: Klincksieck, 1971.

Larsson, Gerhard. "The Chronology of the Pentateuch: A Comparison of the MT and LXX." *JBL* 102 (1983): 401–9.

Larsson, Göran. *Bound for Freedom: The Book of Exodus in Jewish and Christian Traditions.* Peabody, MA: Hendrickson, 1999.

Lawrence, Paul. *The Book of Moses Revisited.* Eugene, OR: Wipf & Stock, 2011.

Lefebvre, Jean-François. *Le jubilé biblique: Lv 25—exégèse et théologie.* OBO 194. Fribourg: Editions Universitaires Fribourg; Göttingen: Vandenhoeck & Ruprecht, 2003.

LeFebvre, Michael. *Collections, Codes, and Torah: The Re-characterization of Israel's Written Law*. LHBOTS 451. New York: T&T Clark, 2006.

Leuchter, Mark. "Eisodus as Exodus: The Song of the Sea (Exod 15) Reconsidered." *Bib* 92 (2011): 321–46.

———. "The Manumission Laws in Leviticus and Deuteronomy: The Jeremiah Connection." *JBL* 127 (2008): 635–37, 651–53.

Leuchter, Mark, and Jeremy M. Hutton, eds. *Levites and Priests in Biblical History and Tradition*. AIL 9. Atlanta: SBL, 2011.

Levenson, Jon D. *Inheriting Abraham: The Legacy of the Patriarch in Judaism, Christianity, and Islam*. Princeton: Princeton University Press, 2012.

———. *The Love of God: Divine Gift, Human Gratitude, and Mutual Faithfulness in Judaism*. Princeton: Princeton University Press, 2016.

———. *Sinai and Zion: An Entry into the Jewish Bible*. San Francisco: HarperOne, 1985.

———. *Theology of the Program of Restoration of Ezekiel 40–48*. HSM 10. Missoula, MT: Scholars Press, 1976.

Levin, Christoph. *The Old Testament: A Brief Introduction*. Princeton: Princeton University Press, 2005.

———, ed. *Re-reading the Scriptures: Essays on the Literary History of the Old Testament*. FAT 87. Tübingen: Mohr Siebeck, 2013.

———. "Righteousness in the Joseph Story." In Dozeman, Schmid, and Schwartz, *Pentateuch*, 227–79.

———. "The Yahwist: The Earliest Editor in the Pentateuch." *JBL* 126, no. 2 (2007): 209–30.

Levine, Étan. "*Neofiti* 1: A Study of Exodus 15." *Bib* 34 (1973): 301–30.

Levinson, Bernard M. "The Birth of a Lemma: The Restrictive Reinterpretation of the Covenant Code's Manumission Law by the Holiness Code (Leviticus 25:44–46)." *JBL* 124 (2005): 617–39.

———. *Deuteronomy and the Hermeneutics of Legal Innovation*. New York: Oxford University Press, 1997.

———. *Legal Revision and Religious Renewal in Ancient Israel*. Cambridge: Cambridge University Press, 2008.

———. "The Manumission of Hermeneutics: The Slave Laws of the Pentateuch as a Challenge to Contemporary Pentateuchal Theory." In *Congress Volume Leiden 2004*, edited by André Lemaire, 281–324. VTSup 109. Leiden: Brill, 2006.

———. "Revisiting the 'and' in Law and Covenant in the Hebrew Bible." Paper presented at the Professor George E. Mendenhall Symposium: Law, Society and Religion, Ann Arbor, MI, October 7, 2016.

Levitt Kohn, Risa. *A New Heart and a New Soul: Ezekiel, the Exile, and the Torah*. LHOTS 358. Sheffield: Sheffield Academic, 2002.

———. "A Prophet Like Moses? Rethinking Ezekiel's Relationship to the Torah." *ZAW* 114 (2002): 236–54.

Lichtheim, Miriam. *Ancient Egyptian Literature*. 2 vols. Berkeley: University of California Press, 1976.

Lohfink, Norbert. "Fortschreibung? Zur Technik von Rechtsrevisionen im Deuteronomischen Bereich, Erörtert an Deuteronomium 12, Ex 21,2–11 und Dtn 15,12–18." In Veijola, *Das Deuteronomium und Seine Querbeziehungen*, 127–71.

―――. "The Priestly Narrative and History." In *Theology of the Pentateuch: Themes of the Priestly Narrative and Deuteronomy*, 136–72. Edinburgh: T&T Clark, 1994.

―――. "Prolegomena zu einer Rechtshermeneutik des Pentateuch." In *Das Deuteronomium*, edited by Georg Braulik, 11–55. ÖBS 23. Frankfurt am Main: Peter Lang, 2003.

―――. "Die These vom 'deuteronomischen' Dekalog-anfang: Ein fragwürdiges Ergebnis atomistischer Sprachstatistik." In *Student zum Pentateuch: Walter Kornfeld zum 60. Geburtstag*, edited by Georg Braulik, 99–109. Vienna: Herder, 1963.

Longman, Tremper, III. *Fictional Akkadian Autobiography: A Generic and Comparative Study*. Winona Lake, IN: Eisenbrauns, 1991.

―――. *How to Read Exodus*. Downers Grove, IL: IVP Academic, 2009.

Lopez, René. "Israelite Covenants in the Light of Ancient Near Eastern Covenants: Part 1 of 2." *CTS Journal* 9 (2003): 92–111.

―――. "Israelite Covenants in the Light of Ancient Near Eastern Covenants: Part 2 of 2." *CTS Journal* 10 (2004): 72–106.

Lundbom, Jack R. *Deuteronomy*. Grand Rapids: Eerdmans, 2013.

Luther, Martin. *Prefaces to the Books of the Bible*. Translated by C. M. Jacobs. In *Works of Martin Luther*, 6:363–491. Philadelphia: Castle, 1932.

―――. *Vorreden zur Heiligen Schrift*. Edited by Wilhelm Heinsius. Munich: Chr. Kaiser, 1934.

Lyons, Michael A. *From Law to Prophecy: Ezekiel's Use of the Holiness Code*. Edited by Claudia V. Camp and Andrew Mein. LHOTS 507. London: T&T Clark, 2009.

MacCarty, Skip. *In Granite or Ingrained? What the Old and New Covenants Reveal About the Gospel, the Law, and the Sabbath*. Berrien Springs, MI: Andrews University Press, 2007.

Machinist, Peter. "The Road Not Taken: Wellhausen and Assyriology." In *Homeland and Exile: Biblical and Ancient Near Eastern Studies in Honour of Bustenay Oded*, edited by Gershon Galil, Mark Geller, and Alan Millard, 469–532. Leiden: Brill, 2009.

Mann, T. W. *The Book of the Law*. Atlanta: John Knox, 1988.

Marchand, Suzanne. *German Orientalism in the Age of Empire: Religion, Race, and Scholarship*. Cambridge: Cambridge University Press, 2009..

Mayes, Andrew D. H. *The Story of Israel Between Settlement and Exile: A Redactional Study of the Deuteronomistic History*. London: SCM, 1983.

McCarter, P. Kyle, Jr. *I Samuel: A New Translation with Introduction and Commentary*. AB 8. Garden City, NY: Doubleday, 1980.

McCarthy, Dennis J. *Old Testament Covenant: A Survey of Current Opinions*. Atlanta: John Knox, 1972.

―――. *Treaty and Covenant*. 2nd ed. AnBib 21. Rome: Pontifical Biblical Institute, 1978.

McConville, J. G. *Deuteronomy*. ApOTC 5. Downers Grove, IL: InterVarsity, 2002.

―――. *Law and Theology in Deuteronomy*. JSOTSup 33. Sheffield: JSOT Press, 1984.

McKenzie, Steven L. *Covenant*. St. Louis: Chalice, 2000.

Mendenhall, George E. "Ancient Orient and Biblical Law." *BA 17* (1954): 26–46.

―――. "Covenant Forms in Israelite Tradition." *BA* 17 (1954): 49–76.

―――. "The Suzerainty Treaty Structure: Thirty Years Later." In Firmage, Weiss, and Welch, *Religion and Law*, 85–100.

Bibliography

Mermelstein, Ari, and Shalom E. Holtz, eds. *The Divine Courtroom in Comparative Perspective*. BibInt 132. Leiden: Brill, 2015.

Merrill, Eugene H. *Deuteronomy: An Exegetical and Theological Exposition of the Holy Scripture NIV Text*. NAC 5. Nashville: Broadman & Holman, 1994.

Meshel, Naphtali. "Pure, Impure, Permitted, Prohibited: A Study of Classification Systems in P." In *Perspectives on Purity and Purification in the Bible*, edited by Baruch J. Schwartz, Naphtali S. Meshel, Jeffrey Stackert, and David P. Wright, 32–42. New York: T&T Clark, 2008.

Meyer, Sias. "Leviticus 11, Deuteronomy 14 and Directionality." *Journal for Semitics* 23 (2014): 71–72.

Meyers, Carol. *Exodus*. NCBC. Cambridge: Cambridge University Press, 2005.

Milgrom, Jacob. "Alleged Demythologization and Secularization in Deuteronomy." *IEJ* 23 (1973): 156–61.

———. "The Antiquity of the Priestly Source: A Reply to Joseph Blenkinsopp." *ZAW* 111, no. 1 (1999): 10–22.

———. *Leviticus 1–16: A New Translation with Introduction and Commentary*. AB 3. New York: Doubleday, 1991.

———. *Leviticus 17–22: A New Translation with Introduction and Commentary*. AB 3A. New Haven: Yale University Press, 2000.

———. *Leviticus 23–27: A New Translation with Introduction and Commentary*. AB 3B. New York: Doubleday, 2001.

———. *Numbers: The Traditional Hebrew Text with the New JPS Translation*. JPS Torah Commentary. Philadelphia: Jewish Publication Society, 1990.

Milgrom, Jacob, and Daniel I. Block. *Ezekiel's Hope: A Commentary on Ezekiel 38–48*. Eugene, OR: Cascade, 2012.

Millard, A. R., James K. Hoffmeier, and David W. Baker, eds. *Faith, Tradition, and History: Old Testament Historiography in Its Near Eastern Context*. Winona Lake, IN: Eisenbrauns, 1994.

Millard, A. R., and D. J. Wiseman, eds. *Essays on the Patriarchal Narratives*. Leicester: Inter-Varsity, 1980.

Miller, Patrick D., Jr. "The Divine Council and the Prophetic Call to War." *VT* 18 (1968): 100–107.

Motyer, J. Alec. *The Message of Exodus: The Days of Our Pilgrimage*. The Bible Speaks Today. Downers Grove, IL: InterVarsity, 2005.

Muffs, Yochanan. *Love and Joy: Law, Language and Religion in Israel*. New York: Jewish Theological Seminary of America, 1992.

Mullen, E. Theodore, Jr. *The Assembly of the Gods: The Divine Council in Canaanite and Early Hebrew Literature*. HSM 24. Atlanta: Scholars Press, 1980.

Na'aman, Nadav. *Canaan in the Second Millennium B.C.E.: Collected Essays*. Vol. 2. Winona Lake, IN: Eisenbrauns, 2005.

———. "The Hurrians and the End of the Middle Bronze Age in Palestine." *Levant* 26 (1994): 175–87.

Nelson, Richard D. *Raising Up a Faithful Priest: Community and Priesthood in Biblical Theology*. Louisville: Westminster John Knox, 1993.

Nicholson, Ernest W. *God and His People: Covenant and Theology in the Old Testament*. Oxford: Clarendon, 2002.

Niditch, Susan. *Oral World and Written Word: Ancient Israelite Literature*. Louisville: Westminster John Knox, 1996.

Nielsen, Eduard. *Oral Tradition: A Modern Problem in Old Testament Introduction.* London: SCM, 1954.

Nihan, Christophe. *From Priestly Torah to Pentateuch: A Study in the Composition of the Book of Leviticus.* FAT, 2nd ser., no. 25. Tübingen: Mohr Siebeck, 2007.

———. "The Laws About Clean and Unclean Animals in Leviticus and Deuteronomy and Their Place in the Formation of the Pentateuch." In Dozeman, Schmid, and Schwartz, *Pentateuch*, 401–33.

Noonan, Benjamin J. "Egyptian Loanwords as Evidence for the Authenticity of the Exodus and Wilderness Traditions." In Hoffmeier, Millard, and Rendsburg, *"Did I Not Bring Israel Out of Egypt?"* 49–67.

Notarius, Tania. "The Active Predicative Participle in Archaic and Classical Biblical Poetry: A Typological and Historical Investigation." *ANES* 47 (2010): 241–69.

———. "The Archaic System of Verbal Tenses in 'Archaic' Biblical Poetry." In *Diachrony in Biblical Hebrew*, edited by Cynthia Miller-Naudé and Ziony Zevit, 193–207. Winona Lake, IN: Eisenbrauns, 2012.

Noth, Martin. *The Deuteronomistic History.* 2nd ed. JSOTSup 15. Sheffield: JSOT Press, 1991.

———. *Exodus: A Commentary.* OTL. Philadelphia: Westminster, 1962.

Nougayrol, Jean. *Le palais royal d'Ugarit.* Vol. 4 of *Publications de la Mission Archéologique Française.* Edited by Claude F. A. Schaeffer. Paris: Imprimerie Nationale, 1956.

O'Brien, Mark A. "The Story of Abraham and the Debate over the Source Hypothesis." *ABR* 38 (1990): 1–17.

O'Brien, Mark A., and Antony F. Campbell. *Rethinking the Pentateuch: Prolegomena to the Theology of Ancient Israel.* Louisville: Westminster John Knox, 2005.

Oden, Robert A. "The Place of Covenant in the Religion of Israel." In *Ancient Israelite Religion: Essays in Honor of Frank Moore Cross*, edited by Patrick D. Miller, Paul D. Hanson, and S. Dean McBride, 429–47. Philadelphia: Fortress, 1987.

Oeming, Manfred. *Contemporary Biblical Hermeneutics: An Introduction.* Surrey: Ashgate, 2006.

Olson, Denis T. *Deuteronomy and the Death of Moses: A Theological Reading.* Minneapolis: Fortress, 1994.

Oswalt, John N. "Exodus." In *Genesis–Exodus*, 259–560. Cornerstone Biblical Commentary 1. Carol Stream, IL: Tyndale, 2008.

Otto, Eckart. *Das Deuteronomium: Politische Theologie und Rechtsreform in Juda und Assyrien.* BZAW 284. New York: De Gruyter, 1999.

———. "Innerbiblische Exegese im Heiligkeitsgesetz Levitikus 17–26." In *Levitikus als Buch*, edited by Heinz-Josef Fabry and Hans-Winfried Jüngling, 125–96. BBB 119. Berlin: Philo, 1999.

———. *Die Tora Studien zum Pentateuch: Gesammelte Schriften.* BZABR 9. Wiesbaden: Harrassowitz, 2009.

Pakkala, Juha. "The Date of the Oldest Edition of Deuteronomy." *ZAW* 121, no. 3 (2009): 394–95.

———. *God's Word Omitted: Omissions in the Transmission of the Hebrew Bible.* FRLANT 251. Göttingen: Vandenhoeck & Ruprecht, 2013.

Park, Sejin. *Pentecost and Sinai: The Festival of Weeks as a Celebration of the Sinai Event.* LHBOTS 342. New York: T&T Clark, 2008.

Parker, Simon B. "Exodus XV 2 Again." *VT* 21 (1971): 373–79.

264   *Bibliography*

Patterson, Richard D. "Victory at Sea: Prose and Poetry in Exodus 14–15." *BSac* 181 (2004): 42–54.

Paul, Shalom M. *Studies in the Book of the Covenant in the Light of Cuneiform and Biblical Law*. Eugene, OR: Wipf & Stock. 2006.

Person, Raymond F. *From Conversation to Oral Tradition: A Simplest Systematics for Oral Tradition.* New York: Routledge, 2016.

Person, Raymond F., Jr. and Robert Rezetko. "Introduction: The Importance of Empirical Models to Assess the Efficacy of Source and Redaction Criticism." In *Empirical Models Challenging Biblical Criticism*, edited by Raymond F. Person Jr. and Robert Rezetko, 1–23. Atlanta: SBL, 2016.

Phillips, Denise. "Epistemological Distinctions and Cultural Politics: Educational Reform and the *Naturwissenschaft/Geisteswissenschaft* Distinction in Nineteenth-Century Germany." In Feest, *Historical Perspectives on Erklären and Verstehen*, 15–35.

Plato. *Phaedrus*. In *Complete Works*, edited by John M. Cooper. Indianapolis: Hackett, 1997.

Plaut, W. Gunther. *The Torah: A Modern Commentary*. New York: Union of American Hebrew Congregations, 1981.

Polak, Frank H. "Book, Scribe, and Bard: Oral Discourse and Written Text in Recent Biblical Scholarship." *Prooftexts* 31 (2011): 118–40.

———. "The Oral and the Written: Syntax, Stylistics and the Development of Biblical Prose Narrative." *JANES* 26 (1998): 59–105.

Popper, Karl R. *Conjectures and Refutations: The Growth of Scientific Knowledge*. London: Routledge, 2002.

———. *The Logic of Scientific Discovery*. New York: Harper Torchbooks, 1968.

Porter, Daniel. "God Among the Gods: An Analysis of the Function of Yahweh in the Divine Council of Deuteronomy 32 and Psalm 82." PhD diss., Liberty Baptist Theological Seminary, 2010.

Pritchard, James B., ed. *Ancient Near Eastern Texts Relating to the Old Testament.* 3rd ed. Princeton: Princeton University Press, 1969.

———, ed. "The Myth of Zu." In Pritchard, *Ancient Near Eastern Texts*, 111–13.

———, ed. "Temple Program for the New Year's Festival at Babylon." In Pritchard, *Ancient Near Eastern Texts*, 331–33.

Propp, William H. C. *Exodus 1–18: A New Translation with Introduction and Commentary*. AB 2. New York: Doubleday, 1999.

———. *Exodus 19–40*. AB. New York: Doubleday, 2006.

Provan, Iain. "Knowing and Believing: Faith in the Past." In *"Behind" the Text: History and Biblical Interpretation*, edited by Craig G. Bartholomew, C. Stephen Evans, Mary Healy, and Murray Rae, 229–66. SHS 4. Grand Rapids: Zondervan, 2003.

Quirke, Stephen. *Egyptian Literature, 1800 BC: Questions and Readings*. London: Golden House, 2004.

Rabin, Chaim. "Linguistic Aspects." In Radday and Shore, *Genesis*, 218–24.

Rad, Gerhard von. *Deuteronomy: A Commentary*. OTL. Philadelphia: Westminster, 1966.

Radday, Yehuda T., and Haim Shore, eds. *Genesis: An Authorship Study*. AnBib 103. Rome: Pontifical Institute Press, 1985.

Rainey, Anson F. "Taanach Letters." *Eretz-Israel* 26 (1999): 153*–62* (Hebrew).

Reill, Peter Hanns. "Science and the Construction of the Cultural Sciences in Late Enlightenment Germany: The Case of Wilhelm von Humboldt." *HistTh* 33, no. 3 (1994): 345–66.

Rendsburg, Gary. "A New Look at Pentateuchal HW'." *Bib* 63 (1982): 351–69.

———. "Some False Leads in the Identification of Late Biblical Hebrew Texts: The Cases of Genesis 24 and 1 Samuel 2:27–36." *JBL* 121 (2002): 35–45.

Rendtorff, Rolf. *The Old Testament: An Introduction*. Minneapolis: Fortress, 1991.

———. *The Problem of the Process of Transmission in the Pentateuch*. Translated by John J. Scullion. JSOTSup 89. Sheffield: JSOT Press, 1990.

Renz, Thomas. "The Use of the Zion Tradition in the Book of Ezekiel." In *Zion, City of Our God*, edited by Richard S. Hess and Gordon J. Wenham, 77–103. Grand Rapids: Eerdmans, 1999.

Richter, Thomas. *Bibliographisches Glossar des Hurritischen*. Wiesbaden: Harrassowitz, 2012.

Roaf, Michael. *Cultural Atlas of Mesopotamia and the Ancient Near East*. New York: Facts on File, 1990.

Roberts, Alexander, and James Donaldson, eds. *The Ante-Nicene Fathers*. 10 vols. 1885–87. Reprint, Peabody, MA: Hendrickson, 1994.

Robertson, D. A. *Linguistic Evidence in Dating Early Hebrew Poetry*. SBLDS 3. Missoula, MT: SBL, 1972.

Robertson, Palmer O. *The Christ of the Covenant*. Phillipsburg, NJ: Presbyterian & Reformed, 1980.

Rochberg-Halton, Francesca. "Calendars, Ancient Near East." In *ABD* 1:810–14.

Rofé, Alexander. "The Organization of the Judiciary in Deuteronomy (Deut. 16.18–20; 17.8–13; 19.15; 21.22–23; 24.16; 25.1–3)." In *The World of the Aramaeans: Biblical Studies in Honour of Paul-Eugène Dion*, edited by P. M. Michèle Daviau, John W. Wevers, and Michael Weigl, 1:92–112. JSOTSup 324. Sheffield: Sheffield Academic Press, 2001.

Rogerson, John. *Old Testament Criticism in the Nineteenth Century: England and Germany*. Philadelphia: Fortress, 1985.

Rollston, Christopher A. "The Phoenician Script of the Tel Zayit Abecedary and Putative Evidence for Israelite Literacy." In *Literature Culture and Tenth-Century Canaan: The Tel Zayit Abecedary in Context*, edited by Ron E. Tappy and P. Kyle McCarter, 61–96. Winona Lake, IN: Eisenbrauns, 2008.

———. "Scribal Education in Ancient Israel: The Old Hebrew Epigraphic Evidence." *BASOR* 344 (2006): 47–74.

———. *Writing and Literacy in the World of Ancient Israel: Epigraphic Evidence from the Iron Age*. ABS 8. Atlanta: SBL, 2010.

Römer, Thomas. "How Many Books (Teuchs): Pentateuch, Hexateuch, Deuteronomistic History, or Enneateuch?" In Dozeman, Römer, and Schmid, *Pentateuch, Hexateuch, or Enneateuch?*, 25–42.

———. *The So-Called Deuteronomistic History: A Sociological, Historical and Literary Introduction*. London: T&T Clark, 2007.

Sailhamer, John H. *Introduction to Old Testament Theology: A Canonical Approach*. Grand Rapids: Zondervan, 1999.

———. *The Pentateuch as Narrative: A Biblical-Theological Commentary*. Grand Rapids: Zondervan, 1992.

266   *Bibliography*

Samuel, Harald. *Von Priestern zum Patriarchen: Levi und die Leviten im Alten Testament*, BZAW 448. Berlin: De Gruyter, 2014.

Sanders, Seth L. "Can Empirical Models Explain What Is Different About the Pentateuch?" In *Contextualizing Israel's Sacred Writing*, edited by Brian B. Schmidt, 281–304. Atlanta: SBL, 2015.

Sarna, Nahum M. *Exodus: The Traditional Hebrew Text with the New JPS Translation.* JPS Torah Commentary. Philadelphia: Jewish Publication Society, 1991.

Schenkel, Eduardo C. "Indicios literarios y narratológicos para estructurar e interpretar el libro de Éxodo: Una propuesta." *DavarLogos* 11, no. 2 (2012): 137–56.

Schenker, Adrian. "The Biblical Legislation on the Release of Slaves: The Road from Exodus to Leviticus." *JSOT* 78 (1998): 23–41.

Schmid, Hans H. *Der sogenannte Jahwist: Beobachtungen und Fragen zur Pentateuchforschung.* Zürich: Theologischer Verlag, 1976.

Schmid, Konrad. *Genesis and the Moses Story: Israel's Dual Origins in the Hebrew Bible.* Translated by James Nogalski. Siphrut 3. Winona Lake, IN: Eisenbrauns, 2010.

Schniedewind, William M. *How the Bible Became a Book: The Textualization of Ancient Israel.* Cambridge: Cambridge University Press, 2004.

———. "Orality and Literacy in Ancient Israel." *RSR* 26 (2000): 327–32.

Schultz, Friedrich W. *Das Deuteronomium.* Berlin: G. Sklawitz, 1859.

Schwartz, Baruch J. "The Pentateuch as Scripture and the Challenge of Biblical Criticism: Responses Among Modern Jewish Thinkers and Scholars." In *Jewish Concepts of Scripture: A Comparative Approach*, edited by Benjamin D. Sommer, 203–29. New York: NYU Press, 2012.

Searle, J. R. *Speech Acts: An Essay in the Philosophy of Language*. Cambridge: Cambridge University Press, 1969.

Sharon, D. M. "A Biblical Parallel to a Sumerian Temple Hymn? Ezekiel 40–48 and Gudea." *JANES* 24 (1996): 103–5.

Shea, William H. "The Structure of the Genesis Flood Narrative and Its Implications." *Origins* 6, no. 1 (1979): 8–29.

Shreckhise, Robert. "The Problem of Finite Verb Translation in Exodus 15.1–18." *JSOT* 32 (2008): 287–310.

Simon, Richard. *A Critical History of the Old Testament.* London: Walter Davis, 1682.

Simon, Zsolt. "Die angenommenen hethitisch-biblischen kulturellen Parallelen: Das Problem der Vermittlung." *BN*, n.s., 156 (2013): 17–38.

Singer, Itamar. "A Political History of Ugarit." In *Handbook of Ugaritic Studies*, edited by Wilfred G. E. Watson and Nicolas Wyatt, 603–733. HdO 1, Nahe und der Mittlere Osten 39. Leiden: Brill, 1999.

Ska, Jean-Louis. *Introduction to Reading the Pentateuch.* Translated by Pascale Dominique. Winona Lake, IN: Eisenbrauns, 2006.

———. "Why Does the Pentateuch Speak So Much of Torah and So Little of Jerusalem?" In *The Fall of Jerusalem and the Rise of Torah*, edited by Peter Dubovský, Dominik Markl, and Jean-Pierre Sonnet, 113–28. FAT 107. Tübingen: Mohr Siebeck, 2016.

Skweres, Dieter E. *Die Rückverweise im Buch Deuteronomium.* AB 79. Rome: Biblical Institute Press, 1979.

Smith, Mark S. *Exodus.* New Collegeville Bible Commentary 3. Collegeville, MN: Liturgical Press, 2010.

———. *God in Translation: Cross-Cultural Recognition of Deities in the Biblical World.* Grand Rapids: Eerdmans, 2010.

———. "The Literary Arrangement of the Priestly Redaction of Exodus: A Preliminary Investigation." *CBQ* 58, no. 1 (1996): 25–50.

———. *The Pilgrimage Pattern in Exodus.* JSOTSup 239. Sheffield: Sheffield Academic Press, 1997.

Snell, Daniel C., ed. *A Companion to the Ancient Near East.* Blackwell Companions to the Ancient World. Malden, MA: Blackwell, 2005.

Sonnet, Jean-Pierre. *The Book Within the Book: Writing in Deuteronomy.* Edited by R. Alan Culpepper and Rolf Rendtorff. BibInt. Leiden: Brill, 1997.

Sparks, Kenton L. *Ancient Texts for the Study of the Hebrew Bible: A Guide to the Background Literature.* Peabody, MA: Hendrickson, 2005.

Spinoza, Baruch. *Theological-Political Treatise.* 2nd ed. Translated by Samuel Shirley. Indianapolis: Hackett, 1991.

———. *See also* Spinoza, Benedict de.

Spinoza, Benedict de. *Theological-Political Treatise.* Edited by Jonathan Israel. Translated by Michael Silverthorne and Jonathan Israel. Cambridge Texts in the History of Philosophy. Cambridge: Cambridge University Press, 2012.

———. *See also* Spinoza, Baruch.

Sprinkle, Joe M. *"The Book of the Covenant": A Literary Approach.* JSOTSup 174. Sheffield University Press, 1994.

Stackert, Jeffrey. *A Prophet Like Moses: Prophecy, Law, and Israelite Religion.* Oxford: Oxford University Press, 2014.

———. *Rewriting the Torah: Literary Revision in Deuteronomy and the Holiness Legislation.* FAT 52. Tübingen: Mohr Siebeck, 2007.

Stager, Lawrence E. "Jerusalem and the Garden of Eden." In *Eretz-Israel: Archeological, Historical and Geographical Studies; Frank More Cross Festschrift,* 183–94. Vol. 26 of *Eretz-Israel: Archeological, Historical and Geographical Studies.* Jerusalem: Israel Exploration Society / Hebrew Union College, 1999.

Stahl, Nanette. *Law and Liminality in the Bible.* JSOTSup 202. Sheffield: Sheffield Academic Press, 1995.

Stern, Sacha. *Time and Process in Ancient Judaism.* Oxford: Littman Library of Jewish Civilization, 2007.

Sternberg, Meir. *The Poetics of Biblical Narrative: Ideological Literature and the Drama of Reading.* Bloomington: Indiana University Press, 1985.

Stuart, Douglas K. *Exodus: An Exegetical and Theological Exposition of Holy Scripture.* NAC 2. Nashville: Broadman & Holman, 2006.

Sweeney, Marvin. "Dating Prophetic Texts." *HS* 48 (2007): 55–69.

Taggar-Cohen, Ada. "Covenant Priesthood: Cross-Cultural Legal and Religious Aspects of Biblical and Hittite Priesthood." In Leuchter and Hutton, *Levites and Priests,* 11–24.

———. *Hittite Priesthood.* THeth 26. Heidelberg: Universitätsverlag Winter, 2006.

Taracha, Piotr. "Zum Festritual des Gottes Telipinu in Ḫanḫana und in Kašḫa." *AoF* 13 (1986): 180–83.

Thompson, Thomas L. *The Historicity of the Patriarchal Narratives: The Quest for the Historical Israel.* BZAW 133. Berlin: De Gruyter, 1974.

268   *Bibliography*

———. "On Myths and Their Contexts: An Issue of Contemporary Theology? A Response to Jeffrey Morrow." The Bible and Interpretation. http://www.bibleinterp .com/articles/2017/01/tho418030.shtml.

Tigay, Jeffrey H. *Empirical Models for Biblical Criticism.* Philadelphia: University of Pennsylvania Press, 1985.

———. "'Heavy of Mouth' and 'Heavy of Tongue': On Moses' Speech Difficulty." *BASOR* 231 (1978): 57–67.

Tooman, William A. *Gog of Magog: Reuse of Scripture and Compositional Technique in Ezekiel 38–39.* Tübingen: Mohr Siebeck, 2011.

Tooman, William A., and Michael A. Lyons, eds. *Transforming Visions: Transformations of Text, Tradition, and Theology in Ezekiel.* PTMS 127. Eugene, OR: Pickwick, 2010

Tov, Emanuel. *Textual Criticism of the Hebrew Bible.* 3rd ed. Minneapolis: Fortress, 2012.

Tugendhaft, Aaron. "How to Become a Brother in the Bronze Age: An Inquiry into the Representation of Politics in Ugaritic Myth." *Fragments* 2, no. 1 (2012): 89–104. http://hdl.handle.net/2027/spo.9772151.0002.008.

Utzschneider, Helmut, and Wolfgang Oswald. *Exodus 1–15.* IECOT. Stuttgart: W. Kohlhammer, 2015.

VanderKam, James C. "Covenant and Pentecost." *CTJ* 37 (2002): 239–54.

Van der Toorn, Karel. "Cuneiform Documents from Syria-Palestine: Texts, Scribes, and Schools." *ZDPV* 116 (2000): 97–113.

———. *Scribal Culture and the Making of the Hebrew Bible.* Cambridge, MA: Harvard University Press, 2007.

Vang, Carsten. "When a Prophet Quotes Moses: On the Relationship Between the Book of Hosea and Deuteronomy." In Block and Schultz, *Sepher Torath Mosheh,* 277–303.

Van Goudoever, Jan. *Biblical Calendars.* Leiden: Brill, 1961.

———. "The Liturgical Significance of the Date in Dt 1,3." In *Das Deuteronomium: Entstehung, Gestalt und Botschaft,* edited by N. Lohfink, 145–48. BETL 68. Leuven: Leuven University Press, 1985.

Van Seters, John. *Abraham in History and Tradition.* New Haven: Yale University Press, 1975.

———. *The Edited Bible: The Curious History of the "Editor" in Biblical Criticism.* Winona Lake, IN: Eisenbrauns, 2006.

———. *In Search of History: Historiography in the Ancient World and the Origins of Biblical History.* New Haven: Yale University Press, 1983.

———. "An Ironic Circle: Wellhausen and the Rise of Redaction Criticism." *ZAW* 115, no. 4 (2003): 487–500.

———. *A Law Book for the Diaspora: Revision in the Study of the Covenant Code.* Oxford: Oxford University Press, 2003.

———. *The Yahwist: A Historian of Israelite Origins.* Winona Lake, IN: Eisenbrauns, 2013.

Van Wolde, Ellen. *Reframing Biblical Studies: When Language and Text Meet Culture, Cognition, and Context.* Winona Lake, IN: Eisenbrauns, 2009.

Veijola, Timo, ed. *Das Deuteronomium und seine Querbeziehungen.* SFEG 62. Helsinki: Finnische Exegetische Gesellschaft, 1996.

Veit-Brause, Irmline. "Science and the Cultural Politics of Academic Disciplines in Late 19th-Century Germany: Emil Du Bois-Reymond and the Controversy over the Role of the Cultural Sciences." *History of the Human Sciences* 14, no. 4 (2001): 31–56.

Versteegh, Kees, Mushira Eid, Alaa Elgibali, Manfred Woidich, and Andrzej Zaborski, eds. *Encyclopedia of Arabic Language and Linguistics.* 5 vols. Leiden: Brill, 2006–9.

Vogel, Christian. "The Structure of Exodus." The Word: A Personal Journey. https://fascinatedbytheword.wordpress.com/2013/04/14/the-structure-of-exodus/.

Vogt, Peter T. "'These Are the Words Moses Spoke': Implied Audience and a Case for Pre-Monarchic Dating of Deuteronomy." In *For Our Good Always: Studies on the Message and Influence of Deuteronomy in Honor of Daniel I. Block,* edited by Jason S. DeRouchie, Jason Gile, and Kenneth J. Turner, 61–80. Winona Lake, IN: Eisenbrauns, 2013.

Waltke, Bruce K., and Charles Yu. *An Old Testament Theology.* Grand Rapids: Zondervan, 2007.

Walton, John H. *Ancient Israelite Literature in Its Cultural Context: A Survey of Parallels Between Biblical and Ancient Near Eastern Texts.* Grand Rapids: Zondervan, 1989.

———. *Ancient Near Eastern Thought and the Old Testament: Introducing the Conceptual World of the Hebrew Bible.* Grand Rapids: Baker Academic, 2006.

———. *Covenant: God's Purpose, God's Plan.* Grand Rapids: Zondervan, 1994.

Watts, James W. *Reading Law: The Rhetorical Shaping of the Pentateuch.* BibSem 9. Sheffield: Sheffield Academic Press, 1999.

———. *Ritual and Rhetoric in Leviticus: From Sacrifice to Scripture.* Cambridge: Cambridge University Press, 2007.

———. "Ritual Rhetoric in Ancient Near Eastern Texts." In *Ancient Non-Greek Rhetorics,* edited by Carol Lipson and Roberta Binckley, 39–66. West Lafayette, IN: Parlor, 2009.

———. "Song and the Ancient Reader." *PRSt* 22, no. 2 (1995): 135–47.

———. "Story–List–Sanction: A Cross-Cultural Strategy of Ancient Persuasion." In *Rhetoric Before and Beyond the Greeks,* edited by Carol S. Lipson and Roberta A. Binkley, 197–212. Albany: State University of New York Press, 2004.

———. "The Torah as the Rhetoric of Priesthood." In *The Pentateuch as Torah: New Models for Understanding Its Promulgation and Acceptance,* edited by Gary N. Knoppers and Bernard M. Levinson, 319–31. Winona Lake, IN: Eisenbrauns, 2007.

Weeks, Noel. *Admonition and Curse: The Ancient Near Eastern Treaty/Covenant Form as a Problem in Inter-cultural Relationships.* JSOTSup 407. London: T&T Clark, 2004.

Weinfeld, Moshe. "Covenant Making in Anatolia and Mesopotamia." *JANESCU* 22 (1993): 135–39.

———. "Covenant Terminology in the Ancient Near East and its Influence on the West." *JAOS* 90 (1970): 190.

———. "The Decalogue: Its Significance, Uniqueness, and Place in Israel's Tradition." In Firmage, Weiss, and Welch, *Religion and Law,* 12–15.

———. *Deuteronomy and the Deuteronomic School.* Oxford: Clarendon, 1972. Reprint, Winona Lake, IN: Eisenbrauns, 1992.

———. *Deuteronomy 1–11.* AB 5. New York: Doubleday, 1991.

270   Bibliography

———. "The Uniqueness of the Decalogue and Its Place in Jewish Tradition." In *The Ten Commandments in History and Tradition*, edited by Ben-Tsiyon Segal, translated by Gershon Levi, 21–27. Jerusalem: Hebrew University, 1987.

Weingreen, J. *From Bible to Mishna: The Continuity of Tradition*. New York: Holmes and Meier, 1976.

Wellhausen, Julius. *Die Komposition des Hexateuchs und der historischen Bücher des Alten Testaments*. 3rd ed. Berlin: G. Reimer, 1899.

———. *Prolegomena to the History of Israel*. Translated by J. S. Black and A. Menzies. Edinburgh: Black, 1885. Reprint, Atlanta: Scholars Press, 1994.

———. "Ueber den bisherigen Gang und den gegenwärtigen Stand zer Keilentzifferung." *Rheinisches Museum für Philologie* 31 (1876): 153–75.

Wells, Bruce. "Law and Covenant in the Neo-Babylonian Period." Paper presented at the Professor George E. Mendenhall Symposium: Law, Society and Religion. Ann Arbor, MI, October 7, 2016.

Wenham, Gordon J. *The Book of Leviticus*. NICOT 3. Grand Rapids: Eerdmans, 1979.

———. *Exploring the Old Testament: The Pentateuch*. London: SPCK, 2003.

———. *Genesis 1–15*. WBC 1. Waco: Word, 1987.

———. "The Structure and Date of Deuteronomy: A Consideration of Aspects of the History of Deuteronomy Criticism and Re-examination of the Question of Structure and Date in the Light of That History and of the Near Eastern Treaties." PhD diss., University of London, 1969.

Westbrook, Raymond. "The Character of Ancient Near Eastern Law." In *A History of Ancient Near Eastern Law*, edited by Raymond Westbrook and Gary M. Beckman, 1–90. Leiden: Koninklijke Brill, 2003.

———. "Cuneiform Law Codes and the Origins of Legislation." In *The Shared Tradition*, 73–95. Vol. 1 of Westbrook, *Law from the Tigris to the Tiber*.

———. "The Female Slave." In *Cuneiform and Biblical Sources*, 149–74. Vol. 2 of Westbroook, *Law from the Tigris to the Tiber*. Originally published in *Gender and Law in the Bible and the Ancient Near East*, edited by V. H. Matthews, Bernard M Levinson, and Tikva Simone Frymer-Kensky, 214–38. JSOTSup 262. Sheffield: Sheffield Academic Press, 1998.

———. "International Law in the Amarna Age." In Cohen and Westbrook, *Amarna Diplomacy*, 28–41.

———. *Law from the Tigris to the Tiber: The Writings of Raymond Westbrook*. Edited by Bruce Wells and Rachel Magdalene. Winona Lake, IN: Eisenbrauns, 2009.

Westermann, Claus, and Robert Henry Boyd. *Genesis 12–36: A Commentary*. Translated by John J. Scullion. Minneapolis: Augsburg, 1985.

———. *Handbook to the Old Testament*. Minneapolis: Augsburg, 1967.

Weyde, Karl William. *The Appointed Festivals of* YHWH: *The Festival Calendar in Leviticus 23 and the Sukkot Festival in Other Biblical Texts*. FAT, 2nd ser. no. 4. Tübingen: Mohr Siebeck, 2004.

Whybray, Roger N. *The Making of the Pentateuch: A Methodological Study*. JSOTSup 53. Sheffield: JSOT Press, 1987.

Wilamowitz-Moellendorff, Ulrich von. *Erinnerungen 1848–1914*. Leipzig: K. F. Koehler, 1928.

Wilson, James V. K. *Studia Etanaica: New Texts and Discussions*. Münster: Ugarit-Verlag, 2007.

Wise, Michael Owen. *A Critical Study of the Temple Scroll from Qumran Cave 11.* SAOC 49. Chicago: Oriental Institute of the University of Chicago, 1990.

Wiseman, Donald J. "Abraham in History and Tradition, Part 1: Abraham the Hebrew." *BSac* 134 (1977): 126.

———. "Abraham Reassessed." In *Essays on the Patriarchal Narratives,* edited by A. R. Millard and D. J. Wiseman, 147–55. Leicester: Inter-Varsity, 1980.

Wittgenstein, Ludwig. *Philosophical Investigations.* Translated by G. E. M. Anscombe. Oxford: Blackwell, 1968.

Wold, Donald J. "The Meaning of the Biblical Penalty Kareth." PhD diss., University of California, Berkeley, 1978.

Wolters, Al. "Not Rescue but Destruction: Rereading Exodus 15:8." *CBQ* 52 (1990): 223–40.

Woods, Edward J. *Deuteronomy.* Tyndale Old Testament Commentaries. Downers Grove, IL: IVP Academics, 2011.

Wright, Christopher J. H. *God's People in God's Land: Family, Land, and Property in the Old Testament.* Grand Rapids: Eerdmans, 1990.

Wright, David P. "Deuteronomy 21:1–9 as a Rite of Elimination." *CBQ* 49 (1987): 387–403.

———. *Inventing God's Law: How the Covenant Code of the Bible Used and Revised the Laws of Hammurabi.* Oxford: Oxford University Press, 2009.

Wright, G. Ernest. "The Levites in Deuteronomy." *VT* 4 (1954): 325–30.

Wright, Paul A. "Exodus 1–24 (A Canonical Study)." PhD diss., University of Vienna, 1993.

Yoo, Philip Y. "The Four Moses Death Accounts." *JBL* 131 (2012): 423–41.

———. "The Place of Deuteronomy 34 and Source Criticism: A Response to Serge Frolov." *JBL* 133, no. 3 (2014): 661-68.

Young, Edward J. *An Introduction to the Old Testament.* Rev. ed. Grand Rapids: Eerdmans, 1989.

Young, Ian M., ed. *Biblical Hebrew: Studies in Chronology and Typology.* London: T&T Clark International, 2003.

———. "Israelite Literacy and Inscriptions: A Response to Richard Hess." *VT* 55 (2005): 565–67.

———. "Israelite Literacy: Interpreting the Evidence, Part I." *VT* 48 (1998): 239–53.

———. "Israelite Literacy: Interpreting the Evidence, Part II." *VT* 48 (1998): 408–22.

Young, Ian, and Robert Rezetko. *Linguistic Dating of Biblical Texts.* Vol. 1, *An Introduction to Approaches and Problems.* London: Equinox, 2008.

Young, Ian, Robert Rezetko, and Martin Ehrensvärd. *Linguistic Dating of Biblical Texts.* Vol. 2, *A Survey of Scholarship, a New Synthesis, and a Comprehensive Bibliography.* London: Equinox, 2008.

Young, Stephen L. "Maximizing Literacy as a Protective Strategy: Redescribing Evangelical Inerrantist Scholarship on Israelite Literacy." *BibInt* 23 (2015): 145–73.

Younger, K. Lawson Jr. "Heads! Tails! Or the Whole Coin?! Contextual Method and Intertextual Analysis: Judges 4 and 5." In *The Biblical Canon in Comparative Perspective,* edited by K. Lawson Younger Jr., William W. Hallo, and Bernard F. Batto, 110–16. Lewiston, NY: Edwin Mellen, 1991.

Zadok, Ran. "A Prosopography and Ethno-Linguistic Characterization of Southern Canaan in the Second Millennium BCE." *Michmanim* 9 (1996): 97–145.

Bibliography

Zahn, Molly. "Reexamining Empirical Models: The Case of Exodus 13." In *Das Deuteronomium zwischen Pentateuch und deuteronomistischem Geschichtswerk*, edited by Eckart Otto and Reinhart Achenbach, 33–56. Göttingen: Vandenhoeck & Ruprecht, 2004.

Zammito, John H. "Historicism." In *The Oxford Handbook of German Philosophy in the Nineteenth Century*, edited by Michael N. Forster and Kristin Gjesdal, 779–805. Oxford: Oxford University Press, 2015.

Zevit, Ziony. "Deuteronomy and the Temple: An Exercise in Historical Imagining." In *Mishneh Todah: Studies in Deuteronomy and Its Cultural Environment in Honor of Jeffrey H. Tigay*, edited by Jeffrey H. Tigay, Nili Sacher Fox, David A. Glatt-Gilad, and Michael James Williams, 201–18. Winona Lake, IN: Eisenbrauns, 2009.

Zimmerli, Walther. *Ezechiel 25–48*. BKAT, vol. 13, no. 2. Neukirchen-Vluyn: Neukirchener Verlag, 1969.

ANCIENT SOURCE INDEX

Hebrew Bible
Genesis
1 135
1–2 190
1–11 83
1:1–2:4 136, 192
1:14 117
2:13 237
2:4 122, 154
4:30 146
5:1 31, 154
5:9 147
6–9 120, 129
6:9 154
7:11 114, 124, 126, 127
8:4 114, 123, 124
8:5 114, 124
8:13 114,117, 119
8:13–14 124
8:14 114, 126, 127
8:19 147
8:20 123
9:15 144, 148
9:16 144
9:23 146
10:1 154
11:10 154
11:16 147
11:27 154
11:27–25:11 137
11:27–35:29 137

11:28 141
11:30 139
12–37 67, 68, 69, 70, 71
12–50 83
12:1 141
12:1–3 29, 156
12:2 145, 146
12:3 145
12:5 141
12:6 141, 240
12:7 140
12:10 140
12:10–20 150
12:13 140
13:7 141
13:10 142
13:14–17 140
13:16 144
13:17 145
13:18 70
14:1 71
14:2 137, 142
14:5 142, 143
14:6 142
14:8 71, 142
14:10 71
14:18 71
14:18–20 198
14:19–20 146
14:20 138
14:21 71

14:22 71
15 66
15:1 145
15:1–7 29
15:1–21 143
15:6 146, 147, 148, 151, 152
15:7 143
15:7–21 140
15:9 70
16:10 134
16:11 140
15:13 145
15:13–14 150
15:13–21 154
15:14 150
15:16 142
15:18 140, 142, 144
15:19–21 143
16:2–19:22 148
17 135, 136
17:1 141, 146, 151, 152, 155
17:3 147
17:7 144, 156
17:7–8 144, 155
17:8 144
17:9–10 148
17:10–14 152
17:14 148
17:16 146

273

274 Ancient Source Index

Genesis (cont'd)
17:19 144, 156
17:20 139, 145, 146
17:21 144
17:23 152
18:2 147
18:10 148
18:14 139
18:15–22 139
18:16–33 152
18:17–19 134
18:18 145
18:19 145, 147, 151, 152, 171
18:22 146
18:23 148
18:25 147, 148
18:28 139
19:1 147
19:2 142
19:8 137
19:13–14 139
19:19 140
19:20 137
19:21 138
19:22 142
19:23 142
19:25 137, 138
19:29 138
19:30 142
20:1–18 141
20:2 71, 142
20:5 137
20:5–6 141
20:7 139
20:9 166
20:11 146
20:11–13 142
20:13 140
21:8 145
21:10–13 150
21:22 145
21:22–33 104
21:23 140
21:23–24 146
21:27 144
21:32 144
22:1 148, 151, 169

22:2 138
22:5 147, 151
22:7–8 70
22:12 146, 151, 152
22:16–18 134
22:17 139, 144, 145, 146
22:18 145, 146, 151
23 135, 136
23:2 70
23:3–9 142
23:7 147
23:10 142
23:12 147
23:17–18 140
23:18 142
23:19 70
24 146
24:1 146
24:3 141, 146, 148, 151
24:4 141
24:6 149
24:7 141, 145
24:12 140, 146
24:14 140, 146
24:20 151
24:27 146
24:31 146
24:35 146
24:37 141
24:40 146
24:48 147, 151
24:49 140, 146
24:60 145, 146
24:67 138
25:11 146
25:12 154
25:19 154
25:19–35:29 137
25:20 142
25:20–21 155
25:23–34 145
25:28 138
26:1 71
26:3 137, 145, 146
26:4 137, 139, 140, 144, 145
26:4–5 134
26:5 134, 146, 149, 152

26:7 137
26:8 71
26:10 147
26:12 146
26:22 140
26:24 134, 139, 144, 145
26:26–31 104
26:28 144
26:28–29 145
26:29 146
26:34–35 148
26:44–54 104
27:4 138
27:4–28:6 146
27:9 138
27:14 138
27:27 146
27:28 139, 140
27:29 145, 147
27:37 139, 145
27:39 140
27:46 148
27:46–28:9 136
28:1 148, 151
28:3 139, 146
28:5 142
28:13 140, 144, 145
28:14 144, 145
28:15 134
28:20–22 138
29:18 138
29:25 147
29:30 138
29:30–32 138
29:32 138
30:17 147
30:30 145
30:33 148
31:3 141
31:13 141
31:20 142
31:24 142, 149
31:42 145
31:44 139, 144
31:48 139
31:52 139
31:54 201
32:1 146

32:4 145
32:10 141, 146
32:11 140
32:12 144
32:13 146
32:26 146
32:27 146
32:29 146
32:31 170
33:3 147
33:6 147
33:7 147
33:18 142, 240
33:18–20 141
33:20 141
34 143
34:2 142
34:2–26 240
34:3 138
34:8 138
34:9–10 148, 151
34:10 139
34:16 148
34:16–17 148
34:18 141
34:20 142
34:21 148
34:30 139, 141, 142
35:1–4 134
35:2 139
35:2–4 153
35:4 139, 240
35:5 145
35:9 146
35:9–15 136
35:11 145
35:12 140
35:22 143
35:27 70
36:1 154
36:9 154
36:12 143
36:16 143
36:20 142
36:21 142
36:29 142
36:30 142
36:31–39 31

36:43 140
37–50 150, 155
37:2 154
37:3 138
37:4 138
37:7 147
37:9 147
37:10 147
37:14 70
37:27 240
38:12–30 240
38:25 137
38:26 147, 148
40:10 137
40:14 140
41:46 146
42:6 147
42:18 146
43:15 146
43:26 147
43:28 147
43:32 138, 139
44:16 148
44:20 138
45:20 139
46:1–7 150
46:3 145
46:6–7 144
46:27 150
46:34 138
47:7 146
47:9–28 156
47:29 140
47:31 147
48:1–22 240
48:3–7 136
48:12 147
49:3–4 143
49:5–7 143
49:8 147
50:11 141
50:24 145

Exodus
1 178
1–2 178
1–11:10 176
1–13 189

1–14 177
1–15 174, 175
1–17 175
1–18 155, 175, 176, 177
1–19 174
1–24 176
1:1–7 181, 189
1:1–22 186
1:1–2:10 178, 189
1:1–2:25 177
1:1–6:1 177
1:1–6:27 177, 178, 181
1:1–12:30 83
1:1–12:36 186
1:1–13:16 176, 177
1:1–14:31 176
1:1–15:21 175, 176
1:5 186
1:7 150
1:8–22 181, 189
1:9–14 186
1:10 186
1:11 186, 190
1:14 42, 43, 44
1:15–22 186
1:16 137
1:17 146
1:21 146
2 178
2:1–10 181, 186, 189
2:11–12 189
2:11–15 187
2:11–25 181, 186, 189
2:11–7:7 178
2:13–15 189
2:14 186
2:16 189
2:18 189
2:16–20 189
2:17 186
2:18–22 187
2:20 186, 189
2:21 189
2:22 189
2:23–25 189
2:24 99, 144, 154
2:28 150
3–4 163, 178, 187

Ancient Source Index

Exodus (cont'd)
3–6 177
3:1 162, 190
3:1–4:17 178
3:1–6:27 190, 192
3:1–7:7 177, 178
3:1–12 181
3:1–13 187
3:2–12 190
3:4 162
3:6 144, 162
3:7 140
3:8 143
3:9 154
3:9–15 162
3:11 166
3:12 155
3:13 144
3:13–15 181, 185, 187,
    190, 192
3:15–16 144
3:16–4:17 181, 190
3:17 143
3:20 139
3:21–22 162, 191
4 63
4:1 146
4:5 144, 146
4:8 146
4:9 146
4:10 63
4:10–13 63
4:12 64
4:17–18 162
4:18–6:30 178
4:18–31 181, 190
4:20 162
4:22–23 191
4:24–26 190
4:27 64
4:29–31 187
4:30 64
4:31 146
5 178
5–11 187
5:1–4 181
5:1–15:21 178
5:4 190, 192

5:4–21 190
5:5 190, 192
5:5–6:13 181
5:6–6:1 187
6 178
6:1–8 190
6:2 104
6:2–15:21 177
6:4 144
6:4–5 99
6:4–7 156
6:5 144
6:6–8 104, 154
6:7 144
6:12 63
6:14–27 181
6:20 158
6:28 192
6:28–7:7 182
6:28–7:13 190
6:28–11:10 182, 190
6:28–13:16 178
6:28–15:21 177
6:29 104
6:30 63
7:1 139
7:1–12:30 178
7:3 190
7:5 104
7:8–11:10 177, 178
7:8–13 182
7:8–15:21 178
7:11 178
7:14–8:19 182
7:14–11:10 190
7:14–12:32 192
7:17 104
8:2 187
8:9 64
8:18 104
8:19 190
8:20–23 182, 185
8:22 138, 190
8:24–10:29 182
9:27 148
10:1–2 190
10:2 104
11:1–8 182

11:9–10 182
11:10 192
12 113, 118
12–13 120, 182
12–16 120
12–18 176
12:1–2 121
12:1–28 182, 187, 190,
    193
12:1–13:16 177, 178
12:1–15:21 178
12:2 114, 117, 120, 187
12:3 114, 117, 119
12:3–12 121
12:3–13 120
12:6 114, 115, 118, 119
12:12 104, 190, 193
12:13 139, 186, 187
12:14 190
12:14–20 119, 120, 121
12:18 114, 187
12:21–23 121
12:23 190, 193
12:24–27 121
12:25–27 120
12:26–27 187
12:27 187, 190, 191
12:28–41 121
12:29 118, 191
12:29–30 182
12:29–35 191
12:29–36 187
12:29–13:16 191, 192
12:30–18:27 83
12:31 187
12:31–42 182
12:31–14:31 178
12:36 191
12:37 186
12:37–41 191, 193
12:37–13:22 186
12:37–40:38 186
12:38 186
12:40–41 191
12:41 156
12:42–49 121
12:43–50 182
12:43–51 186

Ancient Source Index 277

12:43–13:10 191
12:50 187
12:50–13:1 121
12:51 182, 185
13 139
13:1–2 182
13:3–4 114, 120
13:3–10 182
13:3–16 121
13:5 143, 145
13:6 190
13:8–10 120
13:10 149
13:11–16 182, 191
13:17–22 182, 191, 193
13:17–15:21 178
13:17–18:27 176
13:17–19:2 177
13:17–19:25 177
13:17–24:11 176
13:20 191
13:20–22 180
13:21–22 191, 193
13:22 191
14 50, 52, 53, 54, 55, 59, 64, 65
14:1–2 183, 189
14:1–15:21 186
14:1–15:22 183
14:1–15:27 189
14:2–29 183
14:3–10 189
14:4 104
14:11–15:21 189
14:18 104
14:30–31 180, 183, 185, 186, 189, 193
14–40 189
15 49, 50, 51, 52, 53, 54, 55, 64, 65
15–18 177
15:1 59
15:1–18 50, 54
15:1–21 176, 179, 183
15:2 51, 144
15:5 51
15:6 50
15:7 51

15:8 51
15:9 51
15:10 51
15:12 51
15:13 51, 52
15:15 51
15:16 51, 145
15:17 51, 52
15:19–20 59
15:22 183
15:22–23 189
15:22–27 59
15:22–17:15 179
15:22–18:27 175, 176, 177, 178, 183, 186
15:22–19:25 178
15:22–40:38 175
15:23–24 183
15:24 186, 189
15:25 148, 186, 189
15:25–27 183
15:26 104, 134
15:27–18:27 189
16 186
16:1 114, 126, 183
16:1–36 127
16:2–3 183, 189
16:4 148
16:4–36 183, 185
16:10–12 189
16:12 104
16:28 149, 151
16:35 119
16–40 174, 175
17:1 183, 189
17:1–7 186
17:2 148
17:2–3 183, 189
17:3 186
17:4 31
17:4–7 183, 189
17:7 148
17:8–16 183
17:14 86, 154
18 179, 187
18:1 189
18:1–23:33 102
18:1–27 162, 183

18:2 189
18:3–4 189
18:4 144
18:12 189
18:13–27 100, 187
18:20 102, 109
18:21 99, 100
18–24 175
19–20 178
19–24 163, 176, 177, 178, 179, 187, 190, 192
19–31 176
19–40 175
19:1 114, 118, 122, 123
19:1–2 190
19:1–25 183
19:1–20:26 178
19:1–24:11 183, 187
19:1–24:18 176, 177
19:1–31:18 177
19:1–40:38 175, 176
19:2–9 162
19:3–25 190
19:3–20:14 177
19:5 99
19:5–6 156
19:8 183
19:9 146
19:13 183
19:16 118
19:16–17 162
19:18 162
19:19 162
19:20 118
20 40
20–23 187
20–40 174
20:1 102
20:1–17 183
20:1–23:19 190, 192
20:1–23:33 162
20:1–24:11 178
20:1–31:18 177
20:2 144
20:2–17 153
20:3 139
20:6 138, 140
20:8–11 192

278   *Ancient Source Index*

Exodus (cont'd)
20:11 39
20:12 140
20:18–24 183
20:20 148
20:21 118
20:22–23:19 154
20:22–24:11 177
20:24 184, 185
20:24–26 38
20:25–26 184
20:27–24:18 178
21 32, 33, 34, 35, 36, 37,
   39, 40, 41, 42, 44, 45,
   46, 47
21–23 178, 184
21:2 34, 42, 45
21:2–3 46
21:2–6 37, 40
21:2–11 26, 32, 34, 37,
   39, 40, 41, 47, 95
21:3–5 40, 46
21:4–5 34
21:5 138
21:5–6 34, 41, 42
21:6 38, 42, 43, 44
21:7 37
21:7–11 34, 36, 37, 40
21:8 35, 36
21:8–10 40
21:9 36
22:17 144
22:20 145
22:30 103
23:1–8 99, 100
23:7–8 148
23:9 145
23:10–17 115
23:11 45
23:12 192
23:13 139
23:20–31 154
23:20–33 190
23:23 143
23:26 139
23:27 145
23:32 99, 144
24 178

24:1 184, 190
24:1–11 184, 187
24:3–8 162, 190
24:4 31, 86, 154
24:4–8 190
24:6 212
24:7 31, 184
24:7–8 99
24:8 144
24:9 184
24:9–11 190
24:12 149
24:12–15 162
24:12–18 184
24:12–31:18 178
24:12–34:28 177
24:12–39:43 187
24:12–40:38 176, 184
24:13 87
24:15 118
24:16 190
24:18 162
25–27 237
25–31 176, 177, 178,
   179, 190, 192
25–40 175, 176, 207
25:1–9 190
25:1–31:11 184
25:1–31:18 177, 178, 192
25:1–40:38 176
25:2 187
25:8 190
25:8–9 207
25:9 187
25:10–31:18 190
25:40 187, 207
26 237
28–29 199
28:1 207
29 222
29–30 216
29:33 188
29:36 188
29:37 188
29:46 104, 144
30:10 188
30:11–16 118
31:12–18 184, 190, 192

31:13 104, 190
30:15 188
31:16 99, 188
31:18 153
31:18–32:14 162
32 178
32–33 179
32–34 176, 177, 178
32–40 176, 178
32:1–29 184
32:1–35 118
32:1–34:10 190, 193
32:1–34:28 178
32:1–34:35 177
32:1–40:38 177
32:4 144
32:5 190
32:6 190
32:10 145
32:11–13 212
32:13 144, 145
32:15–25 162
32:19 190
32:20–28 190
32:25 190
32:28 118
32:30 188
32:30–35 162
32:30–33:11 184
32:31 118
32:35 118, 187
33 163, 222
33–34 178
33:1 145
33:1–6 168
33:1–11 169
33:2 143
33:4–6 118
33:6 162, 168, 169
33:6–7 163
33:6–11 162, 163, 168,
   169
33:7 169
33:11 170
33:12 171
33:12–34:7 184
33:13–34:9 185
33:17 171

Ancient Source Index 279

33:19 190, 193
33:21 118
33:23 193
34 179, 227
34:1 162
34:2 118
34:4 162
34:5 162
34:6–7 190, 193
34:8 191
34:8–9 184
34:10 99, 139, 144
34:10–13 191
34:10–35 184
34:10–40:33 191, 192
34:11 143
34:12 99, 144
34:14 139
34:14–28 191
34:15 99, 144
34:15–16 148
34:18 191
34:18–24 115
34:19–20 191
34:21 190
34:24 140
34:25 191
34:27 144
34:27–28 86, 99
34:28 118
34:28–29 153, 162
34:29–40:38 177, 178
34:38 119
35–40 163, 176, 177, 178
35:1–3 184, 190, 192
35:1–36:7 191
35:1–40:33 179, 192
35:1–40:38 177
35:4–29 118
35:4–40:8 184
35:30–36:1 118
36:8–19 192
36:18–39:31 191
36:20–38 192
37:1–9 192
37:10–16 192
37:17–24 192
37:25–29 192

38:1–7 192
38:8 192
38:9–20 192
39:1–31 192
39:32 191
39:43 191
40:1 114, 117, 124 187
40:1–16 187
40:2 191
40:3–15 187
40:9–38 184
40:16 187
40:17 117, 191
40:17–38 187
40:18 114, 124
40:33–38 187
40:34–38 179, 181, 193
40:36–38 191
40:38 191

Leviticus
1 216
1–7 216, 218
1–16 195, 196, 197, 200,
    204, 207, 209, 211,
    212, 224
1–17 199
1:1–27:34 102
1:2 209
2:3 199
2:10 199
2:13 99
3 201, 202, 216, 217
3:5 204
3:11 204
3:16 204
3:16–17 205
3:17 217
4–5 103, 218
4:1–5:13 203
4:2 209
4:23 218
4:27–35 218
4:28 218
5:1 218
5:3 218
5:4 218
5:6 218

5:11 137
5:14–16 205
5:14–26 203
5:15 203
5:17 218
5:18 218
6:9 196
6:9–11 199
6:11 196
6:19 196, 199
6:22 196, 199
6:24 216
7:1 216
7:1–7 203
7:6–10 196, 199
7:11–36 201
7:15–21 204
7:16–18 198
7:18 232
7:22–25 205
7:23 209, 222
7:25 205
7:28–34 204
7:28–36 205
7:29 209
7:29–36 202
7:31–34 199
7:31–36 196, 199
7:32 216
7:34 199
8 199, 212
8–9 196
8–10 219
8:5 102
8:35 149
8:36 102
9 199
9:5–6 196
9:6 102
9:22–24 196
10–11 196
10:1–2 196
10:3 196
10:7 102
10:11 209
10:17–18 196
11 220, 221, 222
11:1–20 221

Ancient Source Index

Leviticus (cont'd)
11:2 215
11:2–23 220
11:39 137
11:44–45 104
11:45 144
12 222, 224
12–15 222
12:2 215
13–14 214, 215, 222
13:1 215
13:1–14:32 215
13:2 215
13:3 215
13:6 137
13:10 137
13:21 137
13:46 223
14:1 215
14:2 215
14:3 215
15:16 223
15:31 196
16 223, 224
16:1–2 196
16:16 196
16:31 137
17 217, 222, 223
17:1 154
17:2 102, 223
17:3 222
17–26 39, 226
17–27 154
17:13 217, 218
17:13–14 217, 218
17:15 222
18–20 223
18:1 154
18:2 104
18:4 149, 234
18:4–6 104
18:5 149
18:21 104
18:22–30 138
18:26 149
18:27 137
18:30 104, 149
19 148

19:1 154
19:2–4 104
19:4 145
19:6–8 198
19:7 232
19:10 104
19:12 104, 146
19:14 104, 146
19:15 148
19:15–16 99, 100
19:16 100, 104
19:18 104, 138
19:19 149
19:25 104
19:28 104
19:30–32 104
19:32 146
19:34 104, 138
19:36 144, 148
19:36–37 104
19:37 149
20:1 154
20:3 230
20:7–8 104
20:8 149
20:13 138
20:17 137
20:18 137
20:22 149
20:23 234
20:24 104
20:26 103, 104
21–22 223
21:1–24:9 199
21:6 230
21:8 104
21:9 137
21:12 104
21:15 104
21:16 154
21:23 104
22:1 154
22:2 230
22:2–3 104
22:8 232
22:8–9 104
22:9 149
22:16 104

22:17 154
22:18–25 223
22:19–20 223
22:21 139
22:26 154
22:27 222
22:30–33 104
22:31–32 223
22:32 230
22:33 144
23–27 117, 223
23:1 154
23:4–43 115
23:9 154
23:11 116, 129
23:14 129
23:15 123
23:22 104
23:23 154
23:26 154
23:33 154
23:39–43 123
23:43 104
24:1 154
24:8 99
24:10–23 100, 103
24:13 154
24:22 104
25 32, 33, 39, 40, 41, 44,
    45, 46, 47
25:1 154
25:15 146
25:17 104
25:36 146
25:38 44, 104, 144
25:39 42, 44
25:39–41 45
25:39–43 26, 32, 46, 47
25:39–46 42, 95
25:39–55 41, 103
25:40 41
25:42 144
25:43 44, 146
25:44–46 33, 44
25:46 41, 42, 43, 44
25:47–53 41
25:53 44
25:54 41

25:54–55 41	5:1–4 223	15:1–41 102
25:55 144	5:1–6:27 102	15:3 139
25:55–26:2 104	5:3 223	15:8 139
26 103, 235	5:13 137	15:27 218
26:3 231, 238	5:14 137	15:31 102
26:3–4 229	6:2 139	15:32–36 100, 103
26:9 99, 144	6:19 201	15:41 104, 144
26:12 144	7:1 117	16 199
26:13 104, 144	8:26 149	16:5 169
26:15 99, 148	9 113	17–18 219
26:22 235	9:1–3 114, 120	18 199, 216, 219, 220
26:25 99, 235	9:1–14 100, 103	18:1–3 196
26:26 233, 235, 236	9:6–13 208	18:3 149
26:30 139	9:11 114, 120, 208	18:4 149
26:31 231	9:15 117	18:4–5 196
26:39 233	9:19 149	18:5 149
26:42 99, 144	9:23 149	18:9 216
26:43 234	10:10 104	18:12 140
26:44 148	10:11 114, 126, 128	18:17 222
26:44–45 99, 104	10:11–21:35 83	18:19 99
26:45 144, 231	10:33 99	18:20 199
26:46 154, 156	11 162, 163	18:21–28 138
27 199, 203	11:11–12 162, 163, 168	18:23–24 199
27:1 154	11:14–17 162	19 218
27:2 139	11:16–17 163	19:1–22 102
27:10 203	11:24–30 162	20:1 114, 117
27:30–32 138	11:25 164, 165	20:12 146, 231
27:34 156	11:26–29 165	20:22–29 125
	11:28 87	20:29 125
Numbers	11:29 139, 165, 166	20:39 118
1:1 114, 122, 124	12 168, 215	21:1–3 125
1:17 114	12:1 162, 167	21:4 125
1:18 124	12:2 167	21:4–9 125
1:18–19 125	12:2–8 167	21:14 31
1:46 125	12:2–15 162	21:16–20 125
1:53 149	12:6 139, 168	21:21–26 125
3 219, 220	12:6–8 167	21:31–35 125
3:1 154	12:8 168	22:1–24:25 125
3:7 149	12:14–15 223	25:1–18 125
3:8 149	13:16 158	25:12–13 99
3:13 104	13:29 143	26:1–65 125
3:28 149	14:11 146	26:62 199
3:32 149	14:12 145	27:1–11 100, 103, 125
3:38 149	14:13–19 212	27:1–30:17 102
3:39 125	14:16 145	27:12–23 125
3:41 104	14:22 148	27:14 231
3:45 104	14:35 104	27:18–23 87
4:23 43	14:44 99	28:1–29:40 125

282 Ancient Source Index

Numbers (cont'd)
28:18–29:40 115
30:1–16 125
30:2–3 102
31:1–36:13 125
31:30 149
31:47 149
33:2 86, 154
33:3 114, 118, 120
33:38 114, 124, 125, 126
33:50–36:11 102
33:50–36:13 102
33:52 139
34–35 237
35:33–34 218
35:34 104
36:6 102

Deuteronomy
1–3 82, 83
1–30 130
1:1–43 109
1:1–5 87
1:1–6 88
1:3 114, 124, 125, 156
1:5 85, 149
1:6–18 88, 91
1:6–4:43 83, 87, 88, 91
1:8 145
1:10 144
1:16 148
1:16–17 99, 100
1:17 100, 142
1:19–45 88, 91
1:23 140
1:27 139
1:32 146, 151
1:38 87
2:1–23 88, 91
2:10–11 142
2:10–12 86
2:11 143
2:12 30, 139, 140, 142
2:20 143
2:20–21 143
2:20–23 86
2:21 139
2:22 139, 142

2:23 139
2:24–37 88, 91
2:25 145
3:1–11 89, 91
3:9 86
3:11 86, 143
3:12–20 89
3:12–29 91
3:13 143
3:13–14 86
3:21–29 89
4:1 144
4:1–8 152
4:1–40 89
4:1–28:69 102
4:2 92, 102
4:3 139
4:6–8 145
4:7–8 145
4:8 85, 149
4:9 149
4:9–31 156
4:10 102, 146, 151
4:12–13 102
4:13 99, 109, 153
4:20 91
4:23 99, 144, 149
4:26 139
4:27 231
4:30 151
4:31 99, 144, 145
4:32–34 91
4:35–38 91
4:36 101
4:37 138, 145, 151
4:40 140, 146
4:41–43 89
4:41–5:1 86
4:42 137
4:43–28:68 83, 87, 91
4:44 149
4:44–5:30 89
4:44–11:32 89, 93, 156
4:44–26:19 88, 89, 91, 109
4:44–28:68 89
5–11 88, 93
5:1 101, 109

5:1–6 93
5:2 144
5:2–3 99
5:3 144
5:5 102
5:6 143, 149
5:6–22 153
5:7 139
5:9 151
5:10 138, 140
5:12 40
5:14–15 39
5:15 91, 149
5:16 40, 140, 146
5:22 102, 109
5:29 140, 146
5:31 101
5:33 147, 151
6 110
6:1 101
6:1–25 89
6:2 146, 149, 151
6:3 140, 144, 146
6:4–5 85
6:5 138
6:6 102, 110
6:6–9 110, 111
6:7 110
6:8 110
6:9 109, 110, 148
6:10 93, 145
6:12 39, 149
6:13 146, 151
6:14 139
6:15 139
6:16 148
6:18 140, 145, 146
6:20–25 39, 111, 152
6:21 149
6:21–23 91
6:23 145
6:24 146, 234
6:25 147, 148, 151, 153
7:1 143, 148
7:1–26 89
7:2 99
7:2–4 148, 151
7:3–5 153

7:4 139
7:6–7 145, 151
7:7 138
7:7–8 85
7:7–11 93
7:8 39, 91, 138, 145, 149
7:9 99, 138, 140, 146, 148
7:12 99, 140, 145
7:13 138, 139, 145
7:14 139
7:16 139, 148
7:18 39, 93
7:18–19 91
7:21 145
7:22 137
7:23 139
7:24 139
7:25 138
7:26 138
8:1 145
8:1–20 89
8:2 148, 151
8:3 93
8:6 146, 147, 151
8:7 233
8:7–10 233
8:8 233
8:9 233
8:11 149
8:14 39, 149
8:16 140, 146, 148, 151
8:18 99, 144, 145
8:19 139
8:20 146
9:1–10:11 89
9:3 139
9:4–5 148
9:4–6 148
9:5 145
9:8 139
9:8–21 139
9:9 99, 144
9:10 102
9:11 99
9:12 39
9:14 139
9:15 99

9:19 139
9:20 139
9:23 146, 151
9:25 139
9:25–29 39, 139
10:1–5 109, 153
10:2 102
10:4 102
10:6–9 86
10:8 99, 146, 151
10:9 199
10:12 138, 146, 147
10:12–22 89
10:13 149
10:15 138, 145, 151
10:17 146
10:18 138
10:19 39, 138, 145, 150
10:20 146, 151
10:22 144, 150
11 110
11:1 138, 149, 151
11:1–32 89
11:2 101
11:9 145
11:13 138
11:14 127, 139
11:16 139, 149
11:18 102, 110
11:18–21 110, 111
11:19 110
11:20 109, 110
11:21 145
11:22 138, 147, 149
11:24 142, 145
11:25 145
11:28 139
11:29 238, 240
11:30 141
12 38, 217, 218, 222
12–26 89, 93
12:1 144, 217
12:1–4 89
12:1–31 89
12:1–26:19 156
12:4–7 217
12:4–12 217
12:5–6 230, 238

12:5–14 89
12:6 138, 216
12:7 146
12:8–12 217
12:10 234
12:11 138, 216
12:12 199
12:13 149, 216
12:13–18 217
12:13–19 217
12:14 216
12:15 218
12:15–25 38
12:15–27 216
12:15–28 89
12:16 217, 218
12:17 138, 139, 216
12:19 149
12:20 140
12:20–28 217
12:21 40
12:25 140, 146
12:26 230
12:27 216
12:28 102, 140, 146
12:29–31 89
12:30 139, 149
13:1 102
13:1–8 89
13:1–14:29 89
13:2–6 139
13:3 139, 151
13:4 138, 148
13:5 146, 149, 151
13:6 143, 147, 149
13:7 139, 234
13:9 139
13:11 39, 149
13:14 139
13:16 150
13:19 146, 149
14 221, 222
14:1 223
14:1–20 221
14:1–21 89
14:2 103, 145, 151
14:3–20 220
14:4–5 222

284   *Ancient Source Index*

Deuteronomy (cont'd)
14:21 222
14:22 138
14:22–29 89, 219
14:23 138, 139, 146
14:24 146
14:27 199
14:28 138
14:29 146, 199
15 32, 33, 34, 35, 36, 37, 38, 39, 40, 41, 42, 44, 45, 46, 47
15:1–11 45, 47
15:1–18 90
15:1–16:17 89
15:2 102
15:3 35
15:4 146
15:5 146
15:6 146
15:8 35
15:9 149
15:10 146
15:12 34, 35, 37, 38, 41, 45
15:12–17 36
15:12–18 26, 32, 34, 37, 39, 40, 41, 46, 47, 95
15:13–15 38, 39
15:14 146
15:15 102, 149
15:16 138
15:16–17 34, 41
15:17 37, 38, 43, 44
15:18 37, 146
15:19 43
15:19–23 219, 223
15:19–16:17 90
16:1–3 39
16:1–17 115
16:6 39
16:10 146
16:12 39, 149
16:15 146
16:18 148
16:18–20 100, 219
16:18–17:20 90
16:18–18:22 90, 219

16:19–20 99, 100
16:20 147, 148, 151, 152
17:1 223
17:2 99
17:3 139
17:8 139
17:8–13 100
17:11 149
17:14 234
17:14–20 210, 219
17:18 85, 109, 149
17:19 102, 146, 149, 151
18 218
18:1 216, 219, 220
18:1–2 199, 220
18:1–8 216, 219, 220
18:1–22 90
18:2 40
18:3 199, 204, 206, 216
18:3–5 220
18:4 139
18:5 146, 151, 220
18:6–8 220
18:7 220
18:9–14 219
18:15–18 219
18:20 139
18:23–28 148
19:1–14 90
19:1–22:8 90
19:4 102
19:8 140
19:9 138, 147, 149
19:11 137
19:13 139
19:15 100
19:15–21 90
19:21 139
20:1 39, 144
20:1–20 90
20:3–4 145
20:4 148
20:14 225
20:17 143
21:1–9 90, 218
21:5 218
21:8 218
21:10–22:8 90

21:11 138
21:15–16 138
21:16 139
21:18 146
21:19 142, 218
21:20 146
21:22–23 100
22:7 140, 146
22:9–12 90
22:9–23:18 90
22:13–29 90
22:15 142
22:16–17 150
22:19 139
22:24 142
22:25 142
22:29 139
23 215
23:1–18 90
23:4–7 150
23:6 138
23:7 145
23:8 145, 150
23:8–9 150
23:11 222, 223
23:11–12 223
23:13 222, 223
23:15 223
23:19–26 90
23:19–24:7 90
23:21 146
24–26 155
24:1–7 90
24:4 139
24:8 40, 214, 215, 222, 225
24:8–9 215, 221
24:8–16 90
24:8–25:4 90
24:9 215
24:11 149
24:12 146
24:13 148
24:16 100, 148
24:17–22 39
24:17–25:4 90
24:18 102, 149
24:22 102, 149

Ancient Source Index   285

25:1 99, 100, 147, 148, 151
25:1–3 100
25:5–19 90
25:5–26:15 90
25:12 139
25:15 148
25:17 39
25:18 146
26:1–15 90
26:2 230
26:3 145
26:4 150
26:5 140, 142, 144, 145
26:5–10 39
26:7 140, 144
26:10 151, 230
26:12 138, 139
26:14 146
26:15 146
26:16–19 90
26:17 146, 147, 149, 151
26:17–19 144
26:18 149
26:19 145
27:1 86, 149
27:1–4 109
27:1–28:69 90
27:1–29:1 109
27:1–30:20 88, 91
27:3 85, 102, 144, 149
27:4 238, 240
27:8 102, 149
27:8–10 109
27:9 86
27:9–10 144
27:10 146
27:11 86
27:12–13 240
27:13 238
27:26 102, 149
28 103
28:1 145
28:1–2 146, 151
28:1–24 146
28:1–69 156
28:9 147, 149
28:10 145

28:11 145
28:13 145
28:14 102, 139, 150
28:15 146, 149
28:20 139
28:24 139
28:36 139
28:45 139, 146, 149
28:48 139
28:51 139
28:58 86, 102, 109, 146, 149
28:59 139
28:61 109, 139, 149
28:62 144, 146
28:63 139, 140, 146
28:64 139, 231
28:66–67 145
28:68 91
28:69 99, 102, 144
28:69–29:1 86
29–30 83, 87, 91
29:1–2 86
29:1–28 90
29:1–30:20 90
29:2–31:13 109
29:5 104, 119
29:8 99, 148
29:9 148, 151
29:11 99, 142, 144
29:13 99
29:19–20 109
29:20 99, 149
29:20–21 86
29:22 138
29:24 99, 144
29:25 139
29:26 109
29:27 86
29:28 149
30:1 232
30:1–10 85, 91
30:1–20 90
30:2 146
30:3 229, 231
30:4 231
30:6 138
30:8 146

30:10 86, 109, 146, 149
30:10–14 110
30:11 139
30:15 146
30:16 138, 139, 146, 147, 149
30:17 139
30:19 88, 90, 91
30:20 138, 145, 146
31 86
31–33 90
31:1–2 86
31:1–8 91
31:3 139
31:4 139
31:6 145
31:7 86, 145
31:7–8 87
31:8 145
31:9 31, 85, 87, 99, 149
31:9–10 86
31:9–13 86, 88, 91, 91, 101, 109, 130, 133, 154
31:10–12 155
31:11 149
31:12 86, 146, 149, 151
31:13 86, 146, 151
31:14 86
31:14–16 86
31:14–22 91
31:14–32:47 109
31:16 99, 139, 144, 148
31:18 139
31:19 31, 86, 88, 90, 91, 109, 154
31:20 99, 148
31:21 139, 145
31:22 31, 86, 87, 109, 154
31:22–23 86
31:23 87, 91
31:24 87, 149
31:24–25 86
31:24–26 86, 109
31:24–30 91
31:25–26 99
31:26 90, 139, 149
31:28 90

286   *Ancient Source Index*

Deuteronomy (cont'd)
31:30 31, 86, 109
32 51, 91, 155, 235
32:1–43 31
32:4 148
32:12 139, 150
32:23–24 235
32:32 142
32:42 235
32:43 218
32:44–46 86
32:46 149
32:48 86, 126
32:48–34:12 109
33 91
33:1–2 86
33:2 102
33:4 149
33:6 143
33:7 240
33:8 148
33:9 99, 148, 151
33:10 149
33:11 146
33:13 140, 146
33:13–17 240
33:19 148
33:21 147, 148
33:24 146
33:27 139
33:28 139, 140
34 30, 87, 161
34:1–3 142
34:1–4 86, 91
34:1–8 91
34:4 145
34:5–8 91
34:5–12 86
34:7 156
34:8 118, 126
34:9 87
34:9–12 91
34:10 170, 171, 212
34:10–11 170
34:10–12 162, 170
44:3 210
45:16–17 210
45:22 210

46:2 210
46:4 210
46:12 210

Joshua
1:1 87
3:10 143
3:15 127
4:19 129
5 113
5:10 129
6:23 222
8:30–33 240
8:30–35 210
9:1 143
11:3 143
11:14–15 210
12:8 143
13:14 210, 216
13:33 210
13–19 237
15:20–63 240
16–17 240
21:21 240
24:1 238, 240
24:11 143
24:14 153
24:23 153
24:25 238, 240
24:32 139, 238, 240

Judges
2:1 148
2:12 234
3:5 143
4 50
5 50, 51
6:11–12 158
6:22 170
7:1 141
9:8–15 164
9:28 166
9:29 166
10:16 139, 153

1 Samuel
1:3 201, 202
1:3–4 202

1:21 202
1:25 202
2 200, 202, 204, 205
2:12–17 201, 202
2:13 202
2:13–14 201, 202
2:13–16 199
2:13–17 201
2:15–16 201, 202
2:16 202, 205
2:27–28 201
2:27–30 206
2:27–36 200, 202, 206
2:28 216
3:10–18 206
3:2 169
3:3 202
4:3–4 202
7:3 139, 153
10:5–11 165
10:11 165
12:2 169
12:17–18 128
14:3 201, 202
18:10 165
22:9 201
22:11 201
22:20 201
27:11 201

2 Samuel
3:29 233
6:20 167
8:15 147
21:10 127

1 Kings
1:33 237
1:38 237
1:45 237
2:2–4 156
2:3 210
5–9 207
6–7 237
6–8 237
6:1 123
6:16–20 237
8 203

Ancient Source Index 287

8:3–4 203
8:6 203
8:9 210
8:10–11 203
9:1 138
9:19 138
10:19 147
18:29 165
22:8 165
23:3–16 156

2 Kings
12 203
12:5 203
12:6 203
12:17 203
14:6 210
17:8 234
17:15 234
18:6 210
18:12 210
21:8 210
22:4 203
22:8 208
22:10–11 208
23:2–3 208
23:4 203
23:21 208
23:22 208
23:23 208
23:24 208
23:25 211
25:18 203

Isaiah
2:2 229
9:4 122
10:32 229, 236
11–12 51
11:9 170, 230
15:5 142
21:4 138
22:1 166
22:16 166
28:7 206, 212
31:4 229, 236
33:19 63
38:17 138

41 53
41:1–5 53
41:8 151
48:14 151
51:14 233
56:7 230
57:13 230
58 104
61:11 170, 230
65:4 232
65:25 230
66:20 230, 236

Jeremiah
1:5 171
2:8 206
5:31 206
6:13 206
8:23 166
9:1 166
14:14 165
22:13 42, 43
23:11 206
25:4 127
25:14 42, 43
27:7 43
29:14 232
29:18 232
30:8 43
31:31–34 111
31:33 111
33:17–18 203
33:20–21 203
34 32
34:8–22 104
34:9 37, 38
34:9–11 43
34:9–16 41
36:22–23 208
43:5 232
43:7 91
46:28 232
48:34 142
49:36 232

Ezekiel
3:5–6 63
4:13 232

4:13–14 232
4:13–17 232, 233, 236
4:14 232
4:16 236
4:16–17 233
4:17 233
5 235
5:5 234, 236
5:5–7 234, 236
5:5–17 234, 235, 236
5:8 231
5:8–15 236
5:16–17 235, 236
8 228
11:17 231
16 228
17:23 230
20 228
20:9 231
20:14 231
20:22 231
20:34 231
20:35 170
20:39 230
20:39–40 230
20:39–41 230, 231, 236
20:40 230, 238
20:41 229, 231
22:26 206
24:23 233
28:25 231
29:13 231
30:9 122
34:24 237
34:26 231, 238
34:26–27 229, 235
34:27 43
36:23 231
37:10 165
37:24–26 237
37:25 237
38:16 231
39:27 231
40–43 236, 237, 238
40–48 207, 236, 237
40:38–43 216
41:2 237
41:4 237

288   *Ancient Source Index*

Ezekiel (cont'd)
42:13 216
44–46 236, 237, 238
44:3 237
45:7–9 237
45:16–17 237
45:22 237
46:1 122
46:2 237
46:4 237
46:8 237
46:10 237
46:12 237
46:16–18 237
46:24 201
46:26 201
47–48 237, 238
47:1–12 236, 237
47:13–48:35 236, 237
48:21–22 238
48:22 238

Joel
2:1 230, 236
2:23–24 127
2:28 165
3:17 230
4:17 236

Amos
3:2 171
4:6 233

Obadiah
16 230

Micah
3:11 206
4:1 229

Habakkuk
2:2 86

Zephaniah
3:4 206
3:11 230, 236

Haggai
2:11 129

Malachi
1:6–2:9 206
2:6 129

Psalms
2:6 230, 236
2:6–10 236
3:5 230
8:5 166
15:1 230
20:1 122
24:3 230
26:6 141
42:2 170
43:3 230
44 53
46:4 237
48:1 230, 236
48:1–2 230
48:2 236
55:7 166
68:16–17 230
68:19 230
73:13 141
74 51
77 51
78 51
78:68–69 230
87:1 236
87:1–6 236
91:14 138
98:2 231
99:9 230, 236
105 51
106 51
114 51
137:7 122

Proverbs
12:3 168
12:9 233
26:1 128

Job
38:12 169

Daniel
9:16 230, 236
9:20 230, 236

Nehemiah
8:1–18 156

1 Chronicles
1:43–50 31
24:1 201
24:3 201
28:11–19 207

2 Chronicles
8:6 138
15:10–15 122
20:7 151
26:18 204
29 204
30:15 208
30:18 208
30:26 208
33:15 139, 153
35:18 208

New Testament
Luke
24:44 158

Acts
2:1–4 122
7:22 63

Other Ancient Jewish and Christian Sources
1 Maccabees
1:56 158n129

Baruch
3:36b–4:4 153

Genesis Apocryphon
21:29 143n58

Josephus, *Antiquities*
11:7, §2 239
11:8, §2–4 239
12:4, §1 239

Ancient Source Index

Letter of Aristeas 158n129

Origen, *Against Celsus*
1.49 226

Sirach
44:19–20 153
44:20 152n109

Temple Scroll 7

Other
Ancient Near Eastern
Sources
Ancient Near Eastern
Texts Relating to the Old
Testament (ANET)
111–13 81n34
331 210n55
334 210n57

Atrahasis Epic 7

Annals of Hattusilis 81n33

Archives royales de Mari
(ARM)
26 24:10–13 81n31

Catalogue des textes
hittites (CTH)
46 78, 78n21
47 78, 78n21
52.1 80–81n29
70 81n34
71 81n34
106 81n32
106.2 81n30
264 210n55

Code of Lipit-Ishtar 87n50

The Context of Scripture
(*COS*)
1.46:114 108
1.77:199 207n43
1.83:217 210n55
1.111:402 107
1.113:416 107n50
1.143:474 107
2.155:417 207n39
2.155:417–33 207n40
2.155:419 207n41
2.155:423–24 207n41

El-Amarna Tablets (EA)
74 81n31

Enuma Elish
Tablet VII 107

Etana Epic 7

Gilgamesh Epic 7

Hittite Diplomatic Texts
(*HDT*)
4:30–31 78, 78n21
6B:47–48 80n29–81
28A:151–52 78, 78n21

Horus and Seth
1.1 92n60
1.55A:377 92n60
1.56A:397 80–81n29
1.60:463 92n60
1.61:459–64 78, 78n21
1.73:625 81
1.74:641 81n32, 92n60

Keilschrifttexte aus
Boghazköy (KBo)
IV 8 81n34

Keilschrifturkunden aus
Boghazköy (KUB)
XIV$_4$ 81n34

Laws of
Hammurabi 84n39, 87n50

Merenptah Stele 61

Le palais royal d'Ugarit
(*PRU*)
4:XLVIII–XLIX 78n21
4:XXIV–XXV 78n21

Piye Stele 61

Ras Shamra (RS)
17.227 78n21
17.340 78n21

Die satirische Streitschrift
des Papyrus
Anastasi I 108

Tale of Horus and Seth 61

Treaty, Law and Covenant
in the Ancient Near East
(*TLC*)
1.1 92n60
1.55A:377 92n60
1.56A:397 80–81n29
1.60:463 92n60
1.61:459–64 78, 78n21
1.73:625 81
1.74:641 81n32, 92n60

SUBJECT INDEX

Aaronide Priesthood
  abuses, 200–2, 201n23
  accountability, 206, 212
  authority, 196–97, 206, 206n38, 212
  control, preexilic, 197, 200–4, 212
  Hophni and Phinehas, 201, 204–5,
    205n35
  and King Jehoash, 203
  limits of, 199–200
  monopoly, 195, 197–200, 202, 204, 206,
    211–12
  origin of, 199
  responsibilities, 196
  writing skills, 209n51
Abraham
  characterization of, 150–53
  familial narratives of, 67, 69, 71, 137
Akkadian flood story, 17
Akkadian peoples cf. Hebrew, 35, 35n23
Alalakh, 67, 69
aliens, treatment of, 85n45
allegory, political, 162, 164
Altman, Amnon, 80, 81, 83
Amarna letters, 69, 77n17, 82
Amorite, 68
ancient Near East
  data, 17
  epigraphic evidence, 7, 16–19
  law, 39–40, 97–99, 101–3
  literary compositional patterns, 30
  literature 25, 84n40
  priesthood, 198–99, 198n10
  religion and culture, 80

scribal practices, 30, 32
scribes and revered texts, 107
treaties, 73–94, 92–93n61
ANE, see ancient Near East
archaism in Exodus, 50n5, 50–51
assembly of gods, see council, divine
Assurbanipal's hymn for Shamash, 107

Babylonian New Year festival, 210
Baden, Joel, 161, 163, 168, 169, 172
Berman, Joshua, 79, 82, 83
Bible
  as history, 14, 26, 28
  as literature, 26
  as theological text, 26
Bible festivals and dates
  Feast of Booths, 116, 123
  Feast of Trumpets, 116, 117n8
  Feast of Weeks, 116, 122–23
  New Moon, 123–26
  New Year's Day, 117–19
  Passover and Unleavened Bread,
    119–21
  timing of, 115–17
Bible narratives, dated
  exodus, 120, 129
  flood, 123, 124, 126–28, 129
Bible second-month dates
  flood begins, 126
  flood recedes, 126
  journey from Sinai, 126
Book of the Covenant, 163–64

Subject Index

calendar, lunar, 116, 117
Canaan, southern, 69–71
Canaanite righteousness, 141–42
Cartesian anxiety, 23
Catalog of dates, 114
causation, narratives of, 13
Codes
  Covenant, 32, 34, 37, 42
  Deuteronomic, 32–34
  historical order in, 33n16
  Holiness, 32–34, 46, 95
commandment keeping, 147
compositional
  history, 10, 18
  theory, 22–23, 24
  theory and Hebrew Bible, 11
consistency within sources, 21, 25
council, divine, 77, 80–83
covenant, biblical
  and ANE, 73–75, 74n5
  breach of, 83, 103
  changes in, 92, 92n60
  development, 74–75n9
  language, 84, 93
  renewal, 85, 85n46
  structure, 87
Covenant, Book of, 154
Covenant Code and Deuteronomy, 213
covenant curses, 103, 232, 235, 236
covenant formula, 143–46
covenants, Pentateuchal, 93n62
critical method, 21
culture, West Semitic, 68, 70, 71
cuneiform law, 97

data, verifiable vs. theoretical, 27–30, 40,
  48
Decalogue, 86, 88, 89, 93, 134, 153, 155,
  163, 178, 183, 184
Deuteronomic law
  clean vs. unclean, 220–22
  and common people, 214–15, 218n17,
  221–23
  God's dwelling, 217
  Holiness Code, 213, 223, 224
  Leviticus 1–7, 216–18
  murder, 218
  Priestly Torah, 224

sacrifice vs. slaughter, 217–18
  uncleanness, 223
  use of blood, 217, 218
Deuteronomy
  appointment of offices, 219
  authorship, 76, 82, 86, 86n49, 87
  hermeneutical key, 214–15
  historiography, 83
  law in, 86
  as legal statement, 94
  literary structure, 87–91
  Moses's benediction, 109
  oral speech, 109
  origins, 74, 75, 85
  patriarchal narrative, 85n46
  Persian revision, 221
  priest vs. Levites, 220
  priestly legislation, 214
  song and poetry, 84
  synchronic reading, 76, 84n41, 86
  target audience, 214, 223, 224
  and Tetrateuch, 136
  textual integrity, 75
  unified literary document, 94
  vocabulary, 87–88n53
Deuteronomy and Patriarchal Narrative
  links
  ancestral promises/covenant, 143–46
  characteristics of, 136–37
  ethnicons, 137, 142–43
  faith and obedience, 137
  morphological links, 137–38
  shared lexemes, 137, 138–39
  shared phrases/idioms, 137, 139–40
  toponymic links, 137, 140–42
devices, rhetorical
  chiastic structures, 69
  formulas, 68, 69, 71
  parallelisms, 69
  repetitions, 69, 71
diachronic perspective, 31, 47
diachronic study, 8, 9, 10, 16, 21, 24–25,
  48, 174
diplomatic signaling, 82
Documentary Hypothesis, 159–62, 159n2,
  173, 173n2, 195, 206
documentation of tradition, 154–55

Egypt, portrayal of, 149–50
Egyptian history periods
New Kingdom, 59, 64
Ptolemaic, 56, 59, 60
Third intermediate, 56, 59
Egyptian language
Coptic, 55, 56, 60, 62
Demotic, 55, 56, 58, 59, 60
Middle Egyptian, 55–62
New/Late Egyptian, 55–62
Old Egyptian, 55, 57, 60, 62
practice, 55–59
stages, 55, 56, 57, 57n48, 59–65, 64n78, 64n79
Egyptian script
coptic, 56
demotic, 56, 58, 60
hieratic, 56, 60
hieroglyphic, 55, 56, 58, 60
Eninnu temple, 207
Enūma Elish, 107
epigraphic record, 7, 16–19
evidence
empirical, 18, 24
internal, 15–16, 18–19, 25
Exod 14 and 15 connections, 50–55
Exod 15 linguistic elements, 50–53
Exod 21 vs. Deut 15, 34–40, 36n27
Exodus
artistry and symmetry, 179, 193, 194
composition: block parallelism, 179, 185, 193; chiasm, 177, 179–80, 181–84, 185, 193; macrostructure, 174, 179–80, 192–94; microstructure, 179–80, 181–85; parallel panel, 180, 180n42, 185, 186–87, 189–91
diachronic analysis, 174
geographical markers, 174–77, 179
history of interpretation, 173
nonlinear structural schemes, 179
structure: bifid, 174–75, 174n8; five-part, 176–77; four-part, 176; multi-part, 178–79; seven-part, 177–78; six-part, 177; tripartite, 175–76
synchronic arrangement, 174
theological organization, 174, 175, 176, 177, 178, 179

exodus
influence of, 103
month of, 117n9
Ezekiel
conflationary activity, 229
conflationary text, 227, 229
as forerunner of R, 227
fusion of Deuteronomic language, 228
and Holiness Code, 226, 228, 229, 238, 241
literary dependence, 242
macrostructural fusion, 236–38
microstructural fusion, 229–36
and Pentateuch, 226–29, 227n4
Pentateuchal sources, 230, 231, 232–36, 241–43
receptor of P/H, 242
Zion theology, 228, 229, 236, 237, 238, 242, 243
Zion tradition reflected, 237

foundationalists, 23
fronting, 62

Genesis, oral traditions, 66–69, 71–72
German, nineteenth century
biblicists, internal and external sources, 17
historicism, 11, 12, 13, 16
historicism and experimental method, 19–23
historicist tradition, 11–12
scholarship, 9–16, 18, 22
Greek language, 58, 59, 60
Goudoever, Jan van, 113, 114, 115, 118, 125, 128, 130
Gudea, 207, 208

ḫābiru, 35
Hazor, 69
Hebrew, biblical
archaic, 50, 51, 52
classical, 50
Hebrew Bible
compositional history, 8, 10, 18
compositional theory, 11, 22, 23
irregularities of text, 7, 14, 15, 18, 21
Israelite context, 15

294   *Subject Index*

Hebrew Bible (cont'd)
  Near Eastern context, 15
  skepticism of historical–critical analysis, 9–11
Hebrew language
  conjugation, 53
  history of, 49–50
  stages, 49–65
Hebrew poetry, 49–54, 51n10, 53n26, 59, 64–65
Hebrew Scriptures, *see* Hebrew Bible
Hebrew text, novel interpretations, 170, 171
Hebron tablet, 69–72
hereditary appointment of priests, 219
historical-critical
  approach, 26–27, 30, 47, 195
  study of Hebrew Bible, 8, 9–11, 22
historicism
  agenda of, 11
  era, dawn of, 19
  and primary sources, 13–14
history
  history as science, 11, 13, 19–20
  nineteenth century, age of, 11
history, Pentateuchal, 83–84
Hittite
  deities, 81n33, 81n34
  historical prologues, 73–94
Horus and Seth, 61
human sciences, 20
Hyksos, Second Intermediate Period, 57
Hypothesis, Neo-Documentary, 28

Iliad and the Odyssey, 66
individuation, 12
Instruction of Any, 108
intermarriage with Canaanites, 148
intuition, role of, 9, 13, 19–21, 22, 23
Israel
  ancient, literary output, 18
  history of study of, 73n4

JEDP Hypothesis, 87n51
Jubilee, 32, 41, 44–47

Late Bronze Age, 54, 209
law, biblical, 97, 99

law, debt slave
  females, 35–40, 43, 47
  law collections in Pentateuch, 32–34
  manumission, 32, 32–33n15
  marriage, 36, 36n25
law, legislative vs academic, 98
law in Torah, 39n35
laws, Levitical
  attributed to Moses, 211
  and cult of YHWH, 197
  and cultic norms, 205
  derivation of authority, 196–97
  for shared sacrifice, 204
  purpose of, 196, 197
Levinson, Bernard, 28, 32, 37–46
Leviticus
  authorship, 206, 207
  classical Hebrew, 210
  didactic strategies, 195–97, 199, 211
  speech introductions, 215
literacy, ancient Israel, 68–69, 71, 110n64, 154
literature, Canaanite, 51
liturgical calendar, 115
Lundbom, Jack, 37, 39, 40

Marduk, 107
Mari, 67, 68, 69
Melchizedek, 141, 198
Merenptah Stele, 61
methodological control in scholar's work, 7, 9
Middle Babylonian history, 91
Middle Bronze Age, 68, 70
millennium
  first, 67
  second, 67, 69–72
models, empirical, 7–9, 12, 16–17, 18–19, 22–24
Mosaic Festival Calendar, 116
Moses
  as author, 206–12
  burdened by leadership, 163, 164, 168
  death of, 161
  desideratum of, 165–66
  direct communication with YHWH, 168, 170–71
  exodus from Egypt and sin, 180

Subject Index   295

foreshadows Israel, 188
historicity of, 206–8, 211, 212
instructor of law 100, 102
last true prophet, 162–64
service to Pharaoh vs. service to God,
  188
"slow of speech", 63–64, 63n75,
  63n76, 63n77
Song of, 183
and sons of Korah, 169
speaker and writer, 86, 87
superior prophet, 162, 164, 168, 170
motifs, shared theological, 149–53
MT syntax, 169
Mukish, 78
mythology
  Caananite, 54
  Egyptian, 54

narratives
  ancestral, 134, 143, 154
  biblical, 25
  exodus, 154
  patriarchal, 134, 136–37
Neo-Assyrian treaties, 74
Neo-Documentarian approach, 161, 162,
  172
New Year's Day events, 117–119
Ningirsu, 207
Niqmaddu II, 77–79, 79n23, 92n60
Nuhashshi, 78, 79
Nuzi, 67

oral tradition, 154–55
Origen, 226

Passover
  alternate Passover, 114, 127, 127n24
  in liturgical calendar, 115
  instruction, 121
  original Passover, 128–29
paterfamilias, 45–47
Pentateuch
  authorship of, 133–36
  compilation era, 240
  composition, 26–48, 153–58
  copies neglected, 208–9
  dates, liturgical function, 113–30

Deuteronomic elements, 133–36,
  136n22, 153–56
growth of, 138
Moses, author of, 133, 158
Non-Zion theology, 242–43
order of constitutional documents, 153
and poetry, 66
post-Mosaic features, 30–31
Sinai/Horeb experience, 157
single author, 135, 155
sources, 16, 17
studies, 17
uniqueness, 59, 64
work of redactors, 134–36
perspectives, historiographical, 87, 91
Piye Stele, 61
Priestly Document, 226
priestly writers, 171–72
Prolegomena, 14, 15, 17, 18, 28
propaganda theory, 77, 79, 80, 83
prophecy vs. written law, 162
prophets, genuine, 163, 164, 165, 168
  Eldad and Medad, 165
  Miriam and Aaron, 167
  Saul, 165
  seventy elders, 165–67
prose and oral tradition in Bible, 66–69,
  71
protasis-apodosis construction, 169

received text, 7, 10, 14, 18, 19
record, epigraphic, 7, 16, 17, 18, 19
redaction of documents, 159, 161
Redactor(s)
  D, 134, 137–41, 143, 146–49, 152–54, 156
  Document E, 161, 162–64, 167, 170, 171
  Document J, 159, 160, 161
  E, 134, 135
  E, D, and P, 162, 171
  J, E, and P, 135, 193
  J, E, D, and P, 134, 134n8, 138, 159, 161
  P and D, 214–15, 220, 221–22, 224–25,
    227
  PN, 137–41, 148–50, 155–56
  R, 228
redactors, post-priestly, 215
Reuben, curse/benediction, 143

296   *Subject Index*

revelation, divine, as textual authority, 105n42
Rosetta Stone, 58

Samaria
  and cultic claims, 239
  Mt. Gerizim, 239, 240
  vs. Jerusalem, 239–40
  and Yahwism, 239
scribes, 67, 69, 71, 72, 107–8
Second Ramses's battle at Kadesh, 61
Second Temple period, 195, 200, 210, 211
Semitic language, 49, 55, 57, 59, 65
  Hamito-Semitic, 55
  loan words, 57
  Proto-Semitic, 55
servanthood, indentured, 42n45, 45
Shamash, 107
Shattiwaza of Mitanni, 80
shemittah, 45
Simon, Richard, 10–11, 24
Sinai, arriving at, 122
slavery
  deliverance theme, 103–4
  perpetual, 42–44
  and sin, 188
slaves, foreign, 35, 42, 44
Song of the Sea, 50, 50n5
song, victory, *see* Song of the Sea
source analysis, 15
source critical documentary approach, 28
source criticism, 14, 15, 18, 161
source documents, post-exilic, 160
source text, 159–61, 164, 172
source-critical theories, 106
sources, primary, 13–14
Spinoza, Benedict de, 9–11, 24
Stackert, Jeffrey, 28, 29, 39, 41, 46, 162–72
Suppiluliuma I, 77, 78, 79, 92n60
synchronic perspective, 31, 47, 75–76, 84, 86, 174

tabernacle construction, 118–19
Telipinu, 198
Tell er-Rumeideh, 70
Tent of Meeting, 163

text
  ancient, cultural role, 110n63
  canonical, 205, 210, 212
  cuneiform, 54, 66, 68, 70, 71
  early written, 68–69
  preexilic, 200
textual development, *see* textual growth
textual growth
  ancient Near East, 7, 8, 16
  Hebrew Bible, 7–9, 12, 16, 17, 19, 23, 24, 25
  models, 8, 12, 16–17, 23–24
  Pentateuch, 8
Thoth, 211n58
Tiberias Project, The, 136
time, in biblical world, 115n6
Torah
  authors, different, 95–96
  comparison to ANE legal texts, 102n27, 103
  concepts, anachronistic, 96
  diversity of perspectives, 27
  embodied in Jesus, 110n65
  influence on judiciary, 100n19
  instruction: covenantal, 96–106; embodied, 100n19, 107, 110, 111, 112; how to live, 102, 102–3n29, 103, 105; normative covenantal, 96, 98–99, 104
  legal corpora, 95n3
  legislative concept, 96–99, 101, 103, 104, 106
  memorization of, 107, 110, 111, 112
  oral speech in, 109–11
  Passover story, 130
  Reuse: exact, 96, 104, 105, 106, 106n46, 107, 112; fluid, 96, 98, 99, 101, 111; legal, 95–112; literary, 96, 99, 105; memorized, 96, 97, 106, 107, 109, 111, 112
  variation in legal instructions, 106n46
  wisdom in, 100n17
  YHWH as final legal authority, 100, 100n18, 101, 104, 105
transmission, oral, 52
treaties, Mesopotamian, 76, 76n15, 76n16
treaty, Akkadian, 78
Tudhaliya IV, 80–81

Ugarit, 78–79
Ugaritic Baal cycle, 66
Ulmi-Teshub (Kurunta), 81, 92n60

Watts, James W., 195–97, 200, 204, 211–12
Wellhausen, Julius, 9, 14–15, 18, 27–28, 30

Yahweh
  and covenant, 183–84, 190
  delivers from Egypt, 183, 185, 189
  instructions, 182
  provides, 183
  revealed, 181, 184, 185
  and sanctuary, 184, 190
  signs and wonders, 170, 182
Yahwist, 160
YHWH
  covenantal relationship, 105, 106
  responses to, 146–49
  revealed will, 163, 164, 167–68
  song of, 109, 155

BULLETIN FOR BIBLICAL RESEARCH SUPPLEMENTS

1. *Bridging the Gap: Ritual and Ritual Texts in the Bible*, by Gerald A. Klingbeil
2. *War in the Bible and Terrorism in the Twenty-First Century*, edited by Richard S. Hess and Elmer A. Martens
3. *Critical Issues in Early Israelite History*, edited by Richard S. Hess, Gerald A. Klingbeil, and Paul J. Ray Jr.
4. *Poetic Imagination in Proverbs: Variant Repetitions and the Nature of Poetry*, by Knut Martin Heim
5. *Divine Sabbath Work*, by Michael H. Burer
6. *The Iron Age I Structure on Mt. Ebal: Excavation and Interpretation*, by Ralph K. Hawkins
7. *Toward a Poetics of Genesis 1–11: Reading Genesis 4:17–22 in Its Near Eastern Context*, by Daniel DeWitt Lowery
8. *Melchizedek's Alternative Priestly Order: A Compositional Analysis of Genesis 14:18–20 and Its Echoes throughout the Tanak*, by Joshua G. Mathews
9. *Sacred Ritual: A Study of the West Semitic Ritual Calendars in Leviticus 23 and the Akkadian Text Emar 446*, by Bryan C. Babcock
10. *Wrestling with the Violence of God: Soundings in the Old Testament*, edited by M. Daniel Carroll R. and J. Blair Wilgus
11. *Wealth in Ancient Ephesus and the First Letter to Timothy: Fresh Insights from Ephesiaca*, by Xenophon of Ephesus, by Gary G. Hoag
12. *Paul and His Mortality: Imitating Christ in the Face of Death*, by R. Gregory Jenks
13. *"Did I Not Bring Israel Out of Egypt?" Biblical, Archaeological, and Egyptological Perspectives on the Exodus Narratives*, edited by James K. Hoffmeier, Alan R. Millard, and Gary A. Rendsburg
14. *Honor, Shame, and Guilt: Social Scientific Approaches to the Book of Ezekiel*, by Daniel Y. Wu
15. *Hostility in the House of God: An Investigation of the Opponents in 1 and 2 Timothy*, by Dillon T. Thornton
16. *Hope for a Tender Sprig: Jehoiachin in Biblical Theology*, by Matthew H. Patton
17. *Making Sense of the Divine Name in Exodus: From Etymology to Literary Onomastics*, by Austin Surls

18. *Trees and Kings: A Comparative Analysis of Tree Imagery in Israel's Prophetic Tradition and the Ancient Near East*, by William R. Osborne

19. *Bearing Yhwh's Name at Sinai: A Reexamination of the Name Command of the Decalogue*, by Carmen Joy Imes

20. *Poor and Rich in James: A Relevance Theory Approach to James's Use of the Old Testament*, by Nelson R. Morales

21. *"I Will Walk Among You": The Rhetorical Function of Allusion to Genesis 1–3 in the Book of Leviticus*, by G. Geoffrey Harper

22. *Signs of Continuity*: The Function of Miracles in Jesus and Paul, by Greg Rhodea

23. *Atonement in the Priestly Torah: The Meaning of kipper and the Purpose of the Israelite Sanctuary*, by James A. Greenberg

24. *The Law's Universal Condemning and Enslaving Power: Reading Paul, the Old Testament*, and Second Temple Jewish Literature, by Bryan Blazosky

25. *You Shall Know that I Am Yahweh: An Inner-Biblical Interpretation of Ezekiel's Recognition Formula*, by John F. Evans

26. *Death and Divine Judgment in Ecclesiastes*, by Kumiko Takeuchi

27. *Exploring the Composition of the Pentateuch*, edited by L. S. Baker Jr., Kenneth Bergland, Felipe A. Masotti, and A. Rahel Schafer Wells

CPSIA information can be obtained
at www.ICGtesting.com
Printed in the USA
BVHW032050171120
593305BV00002B/2